AF902442

Technology for Efficient Learner Support Services in Distance Education

Anjana
Editor

Technology for Efficient Learner Support Services in Distance Education

Experiences from Developing Countries

Springer

Editor
Anjana
Indira Gandhi National Open University
Regional Centre
Noida, Uttar Pradesh, India

ISBN 978-981-13-2299-0 ISBN 978-981-13-2300-3 (eBook)
https://doi.org/10.1007/978-981-13-2300-3

Library of Congress Control Number: 2018952600

© Springer Nature Singapore Pte Ltd. 2018
This work is subject to copyright. All rights are reserved by the Publisher, whether the whole or part of the material is concerned, specifically the rights of translation, reprinting, reuse of illustrations, recitation, broadcasting, reproduction on microfilms or in any other physical way, and transmission or information storage and retrieval, electronic adaptation, computer software, or by similar or dissimilar methodology now known or hereafter developed.
The use of general descriptive names, registered names, trademarks, service marks, etc. in this publication does not imply, even in the absence of a specific statement, that such names are exempt from the relevant protective laws and regulations and therefore free for general use.
The publisher, the authors and the editors are safe to assume that the advice and information in this book are believed to be true and accurate at the date of publication. Neither the publisher nor the authors or the editors give a warranty, express or implied, with respect to the material contained herein or for any errors or omissions that may have been made. The publisher remains neutral with regard to jurisdictional claims in published maps and institutional affiliations.

This Springer imprint is published by the registered company Springer Nature Singapore Pte Ltd.
The registered company address is: 152 Beach Road, #21-01/04 Gateway East, Singapore 189721, Singapore

Dedicated to my parents

Preface

One of the main challenges for open and distance learning providers is to ensure an effective learner support system to help learners make the paradigm shift from traditional teacher-centred delivery mode to mediated distance learning. It is important for the distance educators to take into consideration the expectations of the learners in ODL systems in order to cater to the needs, aspirations and individual differences of the target groups. With the global advancements in information and communication technology in open and distance learning system, the scope for providing effective learner support services to the learners around the world has increased to a great extent and the technology is being used by the open universities in many ways.

This book aims at understanding the ways in which technology is being used by the open universities of the developing countries in extending learner support services to the distance learners. The main emphasis of the book is to share the best practices that are being followed by different open universities so that the same may be replicated by other universities for extending better support services to their learners.

Chapter "Open and Distance Education System and Learner Support Services: An Introduction" by Dr. Santosh Kumari presents an introductory account of the open and distance education system and the important role of learner support services in this system. This chapter traces the evolution of open and distance education at the global level over a period of time and makes a comparative assessment of the advancements made in this field by the developed world and the developing countries. Further, the role of information and communication technology in the evolution of distance education has been discussed. Chapter "Tools of ICT in Open and Distance Learning for Inclusive Education in Developing World" by Dr. Manminder Kaur contains a comprehensive picture of major technologies used in open and distance learning and their benefits for students with diverse educational needs and how these tools of information and communication technology can be used in inclusion. Chapter "Helping the Distance Education Learners in Getting Effective and Efficient Delivery of Learner Support Services in Developing Countries Through Use of Technology" by Prof. Rajendra Vinayak

Vadnere discusses various issues in implementing the technology in an appropriate manner so that the decision-makers do not blindly follow the technology bandwagon but assess the situations at their locations and take wise decisions. Various innovative technological interventions have been discussed with a view to the scenario of appropriateness in the context of its application. Chapter "Need for Integration of ICT for Extending Learner Support Services to the Distance Learners in ODL System in Developing World" by Dr. H. U. W. Ratnayake presents various initiatives taken up by the Open University of Sri Lanka in order to extend learner support services to distance learners by integrating ICT into courses it offers. It focuses upon the need for integration of ICT for extending learner support services to the distance learners in ODL system in the developing world.

Chapter "E-Learning as a Medium for Facilitating Learners' Support Services Under Open and Distance Learning: An Evaluative Study" by Dr. Trisha Dowerah Baruah presents an evaluative study on the usage of e-learning as a medium for facilitating learners' support services under open and distance learning by Krishna Kanta Handiqui State Open University. Chapter "Use of Technology for Learner Support Services: A Case Study of IGNOU" by Dr. V. Venkata Subrahmanyam highlights the contribution of Indira Gandhi National Open University to higher education in the country, effective use of technology for internal processes, digital initiatives in providing learner's support, challenges faced in implementation of technology and best practices being followed by the university. Chapter "Technology-Mediated Learning Support Services at Wawasan Open University, Malaysia" by Dr. Ramesh Chander Sharma discusses the applications of ICT as adopted at Wawasan Open University, Malaysia, for designing and developing learning resources, instructional delivery, feedback, assessment, quality assurance and training.

Chapter "Technology Affordances at the Open University of Mauritius" by Perienen Appavoo and associates provides a discourse of the different technological tools implemented at the Open University of Mauritius, the benefits that they bring to the learning environment and the frequent challenges that have to be dealt with. Chapter "Use of Technology at the Open University of Cyprus (OUC) to Support Adult Distance Learners: To What Extent Is Being Informed by the Learner-Centred Education (LCE) Paradigm?" by Dr. Maria N. Gravani discusses the extent to which technology is used at the Open University of Cyprus to support adult teaching and learning and promote learner autonomy. Chapter "Information and Communication Technologies (ICTs)-Based Learner Support in Distance Education in Pakistan" by Dr. Irshad Hussain presents the usage of modern information and communication technologies for instructional as well as learners' support services by Allama Iqbal Open University. Chapter "Role of Technology in Dissemination of Science Education" by Dr. Anuradha Dubey emphasizes the role of technology in the dissemination of science education, extending academic and non-academic support to the learners and the best technological practices followed by Vardhman Mahaveer Open University. Chapter "An Introspection of the Responses of the Ruralites and the Elderly to Information and Communication Technology in Open Distance Learning" by Dr. Kajal De and Dr. Sampurna Goswami discusses the use of ICT in open and distance learning in India and inquires into the rate of success of ICT-enabled learner's support system and to what extent the elderly and the rural students are able to gain from such arrangements with reference to Netaji Subhas Open University. Chapter "Tackling Challenges for Higher Education: Learner Support Services for Distance Learning for Sustainable Collaborative Learning Communities" by Suma Parahakaran presets a model that can help distance learning in a sustainable way by helping the learners to sustain their education without dropping out and at the same time gain skills for employment.

The concluding Chapter "ICT for Learner Support Services in ODL System in Developing Countries: Challenges and the Road Ahead" by Dr. Moumita Das and Prof. Prabir Kumar Biswas discusses the current use of ICT in higher education in the developing countries and the advantages of the ICT tools and also explores the learner readiness in these countries to use ICT for learning purposes. It touches upon several challenges being faced by the developing countries in terms of infrastructure, skills, resources and policies for extending learner support services. It also attempts to provide suggestions to help improve the quality of the learner support services through policies, infrastructure, planning and innovation.

I express my deep sense of gratitude to all the contributors for taking their valuable time for writing the chapters. I would also like to acknowledge the support that I have received from Ms. Suvira Srivastava and her associates for execution of this project.

Noida, Uttar Pradesh, India Anjana

Contents

About the Editor

Dr. Anjana is currently working as Assistant Regional Director at Indira Gandhi National Open University (IGNOU) Regional Centre, Noida. Her research interests include application of information and communication technology for efficient delivery of learner support services in open and distance learning system, massive open online courses and technology-enabled learning. She has a number of research papers, review articles and chapters to her credit and has participated in various national and international conferences, symposia and webinars.

Open and Distance Education System and Learner Support Services: An Introduction

Santosh Kumari

Introduction

Open and distance learning system has shown a tremendous growth during the last few decades. It is, however, observed that the demand of this ODL is increasing due to various reasons; for example, it is due to the associated potentials for new innovations and use of information and communication technologies (ICTs) in providing the learner support services to the distant learners. It is felt that for the success of any distance education programme, the learner support system is very important. It is recognized as an integral and important component in distance education. It is therefore imperative that while providing distance education to the learners, it is to be ensured that good quality of learning support should be provided to them. It is, therefore, imperative for facilitation of interaction and communication between students and academic staff in distance education that more emphasis has to be given for the provision of education support to the learners. (Kember and Dekkers 1987a, b; Sewart 1992a, b; Hillman et al. 1994a, b).

At the global level, the system of distance education has gained its popularity due to various reasons, stated below:

There are many advantages of distance education which have been stated as below (Kaya 2002):

- Provision of various education options.
- Facilitation of mass education.
- Provision of information from the first source.
- Responsibility is provided to the individuals for their learning.
- Facilitate the individuals for an independent learning.

S. Kumari (✉)
Regional Centre, Indira Gandhi National Open University (IGNOU), I.T.I. Building, Bulepur, Khanna District, Ludhiana 141401 Punjab, India
e-mail: santoshk@ignou.ac.in

© Springer Nature Singapore Pte Ltd. 2018

Anjana (ed.), *Technology for Efficient Learner Support Services in Distance Education*, https://doi.org/10.1007/978-981-13-2300-3_1

- The students are provided an environment where maximum learning is possible.
- Provision of cost-effective education.
- Raising a standard in education programme.
- Minimizing the inequality of opportunity.

Keeping into view, all the advantages of distance education, first of all we have to be familiar ourselves with the history of distance education system.

Distance Education and its History at the Global Level

Distance education is a structured learning in which the teacher and the taught are separated by time and place. Nowadays, distance education system is the fastest growing form of domestic and international education. Now, this system is becoming one of the integral parts of mainstream of education. Earlier, it was considered a unique form of education using non-traditional delivery systems.

The Emergence of Distance Education System at the Initial Stage

The concept of distance education has emerged in very early years. It was in the late 1800s, the first pioneer correspondence programme in the USA was established at the University of Chicago, in which the student and the teacher were at different locations. Even before this time, specifically in pre-industrial Europe, the accessibility to higher education was available to males only and this category of male population belongs to the higher strata of society. During those days, the most effective form of providing education to the students was that all the learners are asked to get together at one place and at one time where the instructions were used to be provided by one of the masters. Even today, that traditional form of providing education is still going on. When in 1890, the educators like William Rainey Harper made their efforts to try to bring alternatives to this method, and the people during those days did not like it. Correspondence study which was designed to provide education opportunities, to those learners who do not belong to the highest strata of living or those who do not belong to rich class of society and this type of education was provided to those people who could not afford full-time residence at an educational institution, and this kind of education was considered as inferior type of education. Even, many of the educators considered correspondence courses as simply used for monetary benefits only. The people belonging to the elitist category were offended by the correspondence system of education, and this system was considered by them as extremely undemocratic system of education (Pittman 1991). However, it is always the part of our democratic ideals that equal opportunities of education are to be provided to all. In this way, correspondence education system took a new turn.

With the development of radio during the First World War and later on with the use of television in the 1950s, the traditional classroom instruction through which the education was provided to the learners, they had found suddenly a new delivery system of instructions in the classroom. However, there are many precepts, whereby in the schools the distance education instructions were provided at a distance to the learners by making the use of radio and television.

In the 1920s, it was the early effort of Wisconsin's School of the Air where it was thought that the boundaries of the school were the boundaries of the state. Even the use of audio and computer teleconferencing has influenced the delivery of educational instructions in public schools, higher education, the military, business and industry. Even, with the establishment of the Open University in England in 1969 and Charles Wedemeyer's innovative uses of media in 1986 at the University of Wisconsin, new technology was began to use the system of correspondence studies. In this way, by using this technology distance education was begun to be provided to the learners more effectively.

While tracing the history of distance education, we can notice that there was a development during the second part of the nineteenth century from the first singular attempts in antiquity to the unexpected and astonishing spread of this form of teaching and learning all over the world. During the last 25 years, this development has become quite dramatic with the coming of Open Universities, and at present, it is taking place with very fast speed with the establishment of virtual universities. If we visualize the future, we might predict that this development will continue in future also. It will be strengthened further. Ultimately, it will be expanded more and more in the long run and become an integral part of all higher education in most of the universities all over the world. Especially, in developing countries, its relative cost-effectiveness alone will be critical in this process. The first experiments in distance education were singular and isolated ones. However, it was felt that they were very important for those persons involved because the subject matter was religion and religious controversy, and during that time, it was taken very seriously. It can be referred here to the Apostle Paul for the purpose of teaching Christian communities in Asia, Minor. Whereby, he wants to teach them how to lead a life as Christians, in an adverse environment, he wrote his famous epistles. For the purpose of doing his missionary work without being compelled to travel, he made use of technology of writing and transportation. Vividly, this was, we can say, already a substitution of face-to-face teaching and preaching by mediated and asynchronous teaching and preaching. It was a pre-industrial approach, which was totally a technology-based. All over the world, in the twentieth century, during that time, nobody could think or imagine the outstanding importance which was attached to this very approach. Even, we can say, it seems even more so in the twenty-first century. In the middle of the nineteenth century, correspondence education the first general approach to distance education can be identified; wherever, industrialization had transformed the technological, vocational and social conditions of life.

Shifting from Correspondence Study to Distance Education

International Council for Correspondence Education changed its name to the International Council for Distance Education in the year 1982 for reflecting the developments in the field. With the passage of time and due to technological advancement, there is an evolution of systems for delivering information to its population. The main focus of distance education is to provide equality of access of education. Due to this, today, there are distance education courses which are being offered by a number of public and private organizations and institutions as well as schools, colleges, universities, the military and a large number of corporations.

Desmond Keegan (Keegan 1980) has identified various prospects and promises of distance education which have been given below.

- There is always a distance between the teacher and the learner.
- There is an influence of an educational organization.
- Electronic media is used for linking teacher and the student.
- For establishing a relationship between student and teacher.
- Two-way communication is possible by exchanging the views between teacher and learner.
- Consideration of learners as individuals rather than grouped.
- Educators are considered as an industrialized form.

Traditionally, it has been observed that educational instructions through distance education were provided through print or electronic communication media. It has been provided to persons who are involved in planned learning in a place or time which is different from that of the instructor or instructors.

Due to technological advancement, the traditional definition of distance education is vanishing from its sight because new technological developments challenge educators to reconceptualize the idea of schooling and lifelong learning. With the development of new communication technology, interest in the unlimited number of possibilities of individualized distance education is growing day by day. Although, it has been accepted by all, educational technologists, that it is, only due to the systematic design of instruction that can bring development of distance education. It is due to the rapid development of computer related technologies that has captured the attention of the public. There are countries like USA which has seen rapid growth in the use of technology for distance education, but maximum pioneering work has been done in abroad.

It was in the 1840s that the first distance course in the modern sense was provided by Sir Isaac Pitman. He started to teach a system of shorthand to the students by mailing the texts transcribed into shorthand on postcards, and afterwards, he was receiving transcriptions from his students in return for correction. This factor of student feedback of Pitman's system was a crucial innovation one (Alan Tait). It was in 1840 (IAP) this scheme was made possible by the introduction of uniform postage rates all over England.

However, this early beginning proved itself very successful. It was 3 years later that the phonographic correspondence society was founded to establish these courses on a more formal basis. In this way, the society laid a stone for later formation of Sir Isaac Pitman Colleges across the country (Moore and Kearsley et al. 2005).

In the USA, the first correspondence school was the Society to Encourage Studies at Home, founded in 1873.

Distance Education and the Developed World

While assessing the distance education scenario in the developed world, it presents a very bright and prospective picture for the twenty-first century. The Open University in UK, that is UK Open University, plays an important role in the country, and it has also become the country's largest university which plays a very prominent role in the credit transfer and award validation mechanisms that knit British higher education and training together (John Daniel1995). This university played a model for various other countries. For example, many developing countries had adapted the distance learning system of UK Open University in their countries. If we assess the European Distance Education Network, it shows that the European countries have accepted the strength of the distance and open learning system as part of their educational enterprise. There are countries like Australia, Japan and North America that have developed their own distance teaching and learning systems in various forms which are flexible enough to cater to the varied needs of their different learner clientele (Sewart and David 1995).

It is due to the advancement in communication technology in the developed countries which has been incorporated in distance and open learning institutions making the individualized teaching and learning very effective. It is due to well-established academic traditions and wider provision of basic primary and secondary education which has created a strong foundation for providing higher vocational and unconventional educational programmes to those adult people who have very limited or no access to campus-based face-to-face education in the different areas at the tertiary level.

When we assess the characteristics and prominent features of distance and open learning system of advanced countries, then we would be able to understand the complete situations of those countries. For example, the various developed countries like Canada, USA, UK, Germany, France, Japan, Australia where the system of distance and open learning is functioning very effectively due to various reasons can be stated like this:

- Adult learners in developed countries have an appreciable degree of basic, primary and secondary education.
- The medium of instruction in these countries for providing distance education is through the mother tongue of the learners.

- There are maximum facilities of latest technology and communication provided to the learners.
- There are well-equipped and advanced institutions for which the learners have easy accessibility of these facilities.
- Availability of sufficient resource mobilization.
- There is very expertise, committed academic leadership.
- The curriculum is very flexible and need-based.
- Very qualified, committed and trained staff.
- Educational programmes are well planned and implemented effectively.
- The student support services are provided adequately and efficiently.
- Provision of continuous evaluation and monitoring.
- Provision of review and evaluation.
- There is a political support to back up the projects and institutions.

It can be revealed while going through the history that the advanced countries in the West and also a country like Japan had developed a very good network of communication systems. In the nineteenth century, in Europe, the process of transportation and communication was speeded up due to the development of locomotives, road transport, steam navigation, telegraphs and telephones. The nations were able to improve their transportation to carry out their economic, trading, commercial and military activities successfully due to industrial revolution. As a result of all these advanced technological developments, the efforts were still going on to find out new ways of teaching and learning; though the pace of it was slow, it was going on. Humanistic education was struggling against the blind faith and centuries-old sectarian and religious dogmas in the nineteenth century when the most dominant mode of teaching was the campus-based classroom teaching. It was with the efforts of Sir Isaac Pitman, who planted the seed of the modern correspondence education. In the year 1840, Sir Isaac Pitman started offering postal tuition on shorthand in Britain. At that time, he would have imagined that his small educational venture would take the form of a significant system of education which will spread over the globe after a century, i.e. in late nineteenth and early twentieth centuries. MDE-411, Block-5, pp-71–72.

Distance Learning and the UK

The using of technology was started when British Open University was established in the year 1969. In this way, it has supplemented well-designed courses by providing print-based material to the learners. This learning material was provided to maximum number of learners, especially in three programmes, for example, at the level of under graduation, post-graduation and to the associate students. The course material which was provided to these learners was in the form of print material only but the students were supported by using various kinds of technologies for enhancing the comprehension of the subject matter. For taking the admission in the

British Open University, it was not compulsory that one should have attained any kind of formal educational qualification. Before delivery of the courses, these were closely monitored. After rigorous monitoring of these courses, then only these were delivered successfully to more than 100,000 learners. The Open University model was adopted by many countries not only by developing countries, even the developed countries have adopted it due to the outcome of direct results of its success (Keegan 1986). The researchers in the UK has played the role of leaders for the identification of problems and further proposing the solutions for the practitioners in the field (Harry et al. 1993). In the British University, there was a centre, known as the International Centre for Distance Learning. The role was to maintain the complete holdings of the literature which contains both research and practice of international distance learning. All the material concerning distance education was available through online or quarterly accessions lists. This available material contains various forms, for example, course modules, books, research studies, journal articles, evaluation reports and other ephemeral material.

The System of Distance Education and the United States

The introduction of distance education in the marketplace in the USA was very slow. But when this education was entered, it was felt that this distance education was unique to its needs evolved. There may be some of the countries which may not have the economic problems or there may have some illiteracy problems with the developing nations, but it was found that the USA had never faced the problems of economy of delivery. Even, there were other problems like the shortages of teachers in various areas, like math, science and foreign languages combined to it with state mandates to rural schools which produced a climate. It was the period of late 1980, when it was felt that this period was very conducive for the growth of the commercial courses which were offered via satellite in Texas at Oklahoma State University by the TI-IN Network, and it was in the year 1989 that all the states have taken the steps to start distance learning programmes, whereas in the year 1987, there were less than ten states which had taken the initiation to start distance learning. But it was only after one year, the number was increased to two-thirds of the states. It was in the report, given by the (Office of Technology Assessment, in the year 1989), which has been considered one of the important political documents and this report describes the state of distance learning and also describes the role of teachers and reports of local, state and federal projects. This report also describes the use of technology in the schools of USA. There are two projects which serve the example of operating video networks which are functioning efficiently and cost-effectively, and these projects are named as the Iowa Educational Telecommunications Network and the Panhandle Shared Video Network.

Presence of Distance Education as a Movement at the Global Level

Due to the progress of distance education in Europe and Western countries, now it has emerged at global level. It had been written in a recent report that a European Open University to begin in 1992 which was proposed by 12 members of the European Association of Distance Teaching Universities. It was the outcome of the direct response to the European Parliament, the Council of Europe and the European Community (Bates 1990). It was written in the report by describing the articles from authors in nine European countries describe the use of media and technology in higher Education in Europe and further it has emphasized upon the need for providing unified educational access in the form of a European Open University to a culturally diverse segment of population. With the use of technology, it has linked the people at the global level. It is also the telecommunication network which circles the globe and the borders of our global community continuing to shrink. Due to this, we are making our continuous efforts to search for new methods and ways to improve communication by providing maximum access to information on an international level. There are two most cost-effective ways which can provide the solutions to the problems of sharing information and promoting global understanding among these people: these are emerging communication technologies and telecommunications. Due to the advancement in technology, it has been felt that the extent to which the information is being provided to the masses will increase year by year. For easily accessing to the information, economic and political power plays an important role. Many educators like Takeshi Utsumi, President of Global Systems Analysis and Simulation (GLOSAS) have worked to develop such kinds of models of the Global University and the Global Lecture Hall which are contributing to provide such kinds of resources which are allowing to less-affluent countries so that they may keep up their pace to bring advancement in global research and education by making their unstinted efforts (Utsumi et al. 1990).

Distance Education and the Developing Countries

There are millions of people around the world who wish to access higher education but are not able to do so. The reason for this is that there are massive problems in the world due to which they are unable to get the educational opportunities for themselves as well as for their children. These problems are, for example, poverty, illiteracy and various kinds of diseases. There is only one solution to all these problems, that is, online learning. Online learning is one way of distance learning which can provide an opportunity to the distant learners and which can bridge the gap of disparities to access higher education across the developing countries. It is only through this system where the governments or other private organizations do not have to spend a lot of investment in the establishment and expansion of traditional universities. In most of the developing countries, for example, like Bangladesh, distance education gives an opportunity to its population by which the information can be provided, through which new ideas, attitudes and an understanding can be cultivated through the layers of the disadvantaged surrounding and environments (Shah 1989). The various developing countries like India, Pakistan and China and these countries have adapted the model of the British Open University. These countries with the combination of the modern methods of teaching and emerging technology have provided low-cost instruction for basic literacy and for providing professional skills as well as job and vocational training. Turkey has recently joined those nations which are involved in large-scale distance learning. It is only twelve years old that their distance education programme which has enroled almost one million learners and is the sixth largest distance education programme in the world (Demiray and Mclsaac 1993).

The system of distance and open learning has shown a tremendous growth during the last few decades. It has been noticed that the demand of this open and distance learning has been increased due to various reasons. The most important reason of its demand is due to the weightage given to use of information and communication technologies and for the associated potentials for new innovations in providing learner support services to the distant learners.

Different scholars have defined the meaning of distance education in different ways. In the views of Sherry (1996), the definition comprises a few components: there is a distance between teacher and the learner in terms of space and time, a learning process; the communication between the teacher and taught is possible through the use of print media and information and communication technology. The learning in this system is under the control of the learner rather than that of the teacher. In this way, this definition demands that distance learning is to be supported effectively, and therefore, the learners have to depend on both paper and pencil and use of information and communication technologies. They have to collaborate with themselves and take care to develop their study skills (UNESCO 2002). It is due to lack of or limited use of information communication technologies because of power problems, shortage of ICT equipment and inability to use them; the main method of the students residing in rural areas has remained to use paper and pencil, especially in developing countries (Braimoh and Osiki 2008).

International Agencies and its Role

There are many international agencies which can play an important role in the promotion of globalization of distance education. To name a few of these agencies are: Asian Development Bank, COL, UNESCO, World Bank, etc. The competencies of distance education institutions can be strengthened by these international agencies in the developing countries for the cooperation and collaboration with institutions in the developed countries on equal terms. In this direction, commonwealth of learning is making its efforts by building data bank on reliable and comprehensive information on distance education, Commonwealth Credit Bank for transfer of programmer and credits, etc. (Dhanarajan et al. 1996). For the purpose of ensuring the elimination of unfair competitive practices, the other international agencies should develop norms and guidelines for global distance education programmes.

After knowing the history of the system and its functioning in the developed and developing countries, it is imperative to know to what extent it is catering the educational needs of the learners through learner support system.

The System of Students Support in Distance Education

In the system of distance education, the aim of this system is to provide the educational facilities to the learners as they are located at a distance from a university, college or a school. In the views of Simpson (2000), the learner's support system in distance education mode can be defined to provide all the activities and facilities beyond the production of course material and further the delivery of the same which assist in the progress of the studies of the learners. These can be in the form of all types of facilities, provision of supplementary reading materials and references, administrative assistance, human interaction like interaction between teacher and learner, peer group interaction, advice and even moral support.

The learner support can be divided into two areas:

- Academic support services
- Non-academic support/administrative support.

Academic Support Services

In the system of distance education, the provision of distance education support is provided to the learners in various ways. Generally, a mechanism is evolved by which support is provided to the learners at various stages, for example, pre-entry stage, during studies and post-study stage. In conventional education system, the learner gets maximum opportunities to interact with their teachers and friends, but in distance education mode, the distance between the student and teacher can be bridged by making the interaction through learner support centres and by making use of electronic and communication media.

This academic support is provided through teachers, counsellors, tutors and distance education facilitators who facilitate the learners to enable them to solve their academic problems. According to Simpson (2000), distance education deals with supporting the students to solve their problems or issues related to cognitive, intellectual domain which can be the outcome of pursuing their course or courses of studies. These issues or problems might be related to the development of learning skills, knowledge and literacy.

With the technological advancement, comprehensive support is provided to the learners, besides the traditional technologies such as print material, broadcast television and radio. In this way, new technology enhances the comprehension of the subject matter and also brings the qualitative teaching and learning support. In this way, these facilities include various interactive multimedia, computer-based learning packages, use of audio and video tapes, audio and video teleconferencing and video on demand. Due to the advancement of the information and communication technology, it provides the opportunity to the learners for facilitating the interaction and possibility increases to easily access instructional resources provided by computer communication network, which is popularly referred as Internet, the World Wide Web (WWW) or the Information Super Highway (Taylor 1997).

While studying the learners may face various problems, e.g.

- How to write the assignments and how to proceed with studies through reading the materials and how to use the multimedia inputs while undergoing the process of learning.
- Whether it will be helpful for the learners if they go through the print material available with them.
- How the learners will be helped when they feel that the language of the study material is incomprehensible.
- How the learners will cope up with his family engagements, office work, social engagements, etc.
- How the learners can organize the study schedule systematically.

Some of these types of questions come under the purview of academic support. This academic support is further classified under two heads.

Tutorial and Counselling Support

Tutorial Support

The academic counsellors provide different kinds of academic support at the initial stage of studies, during the course of studies when the learners are pursuing the different programmes and also when they have completed their studies. This type of help is provided to the learners in the learner support centres as well as in the laboratories/workshops, the Sunday/holiday classes, extended contact programmes, summer/winter schools, etc. Tutorials are also organized with the help of local area networking through ICT.

Counselling Support

The support which is provided to the learners includes advising and helping the learners when they face any type of problems while studying. This support has the following objectives:

- To make use of available information about a student to solve his problems.
- Mutual understanding is developed between the counsellors and the learners.
- Learners are helped to work out a plan for solving their difficulties.
- The learners are helped so that they may know their interests, abilities, aptitudes and opportunities.
- The learners are encouraged to develop special abilities and positive attitude among themselves.
- The learners are also assisted in planning for educational and vocational fields.

The learners are also helped to sustain their motivation in continuation of their study.

Non-academic Support/Administrative Support

In distance education system, the second category of student support system is non-academic support, and it means other than the academic support. This student support deals in terms of the organizational aspects of their studies (Simpson 2000). There are various examples given by which we can understand the type of support given to the learners; these are counselling services, course registration, orientation programmes, news bulletin and the student's association. The learner support system is an important service in distance education because through this support which is provided to the learners by educational institution because of the characteristics of distance learners, as these learners are isolated from their teachers as well as peer groups and also come from diverse backgrounds, for example, economic, social educational and occupational. The provision of such an educational support to the learners ensures to facilitate easy communication between the teacher and the taught as well as academic and other supporting staff like administrators which cater the administrative needs of the students (Kember and Dekkers 1987a, b; Sewart 1992a, b; Hillman et al. 1994a, b).

In an open and distance education learning system, the learners are to be provided all possible educational support because it is the essential component of the system. For running any system smoothly, it is essential that all the educational facilities are to be given to the learners because they are the most important stakeholders in any educational system. Therefore, distance education providers have to provide a quality learner support services possible to all of them as without their presence, a distance education programme will not succeed effectively (Ravisankar and Murthy 2000).

It is accepted by all the educators that the responsibility of learning is in the hands of the learners. The support which is provided to the learners should be learner-centred and meets the learners' expectations and needs. For achieving the educational and personal goals, the learners themselves are well aware or are in the best position to know what kinds of support systems are important. It is pertinent to mention here that distance education learners are adults and they are in the best position to determine quality according to their individual needs (Mellroy and Walker 1993).

Non-academic or administrative support is to be provided to the learners as per the details given below:

- The learners are to be made aware of the programmes available through distance mode.
- Availability of application forms for the learners or registration of various programmes through online mode.
- Information about credit transfer scheme.
- Distribution of study materials by post, at learner support centres or online.
- Conduct of entrance tests or Term End Examinations.
- Distribution of counselling schedule or made it available on the website.
- Making arrangement for practical classes or Term End Practical Examinations or other course-based activities.
- Organization of the evaluation or assessment of papers. Two-way communication with the learners of the progress made by them from time to time.
- Recording and resolving the grievances of the learners by adopting a proper mechanism.
- Maintain the database of the prospective learners as per the enrolment in various programmes year-wise and session-wise.
- Dealing with the queries of the fresh enroled learners and all those learners who have got re-registration in various programmes.
- Other support is provided to the learners who want to change their learner support centres due to transfer of their parents, spouse, etc.
- The learners are also helped if they want to change course, medium of study or if they face any problem.
- Arrangements are also made for conduct of viva voce as per the requirement of various programmes.

Administrative support can be provided by making the use of technology like emails, sending SMSes to the learners or uploading the information on websites or passing it through newsletters, newspapers, radio, television, mobile, teleconferencing or through regional centres or learner support centres. MDE-413, Block-1, pp.15–17.

Evaluation of the Learner Support Services

Although student support services may differ from one educational institution to another institution, the motive of all is one only that is to overcome the isolation of the students and have a feel of belonging. Through the provision of quality support services, the students have the full faith in the system that they are not being left on their own in the academic journey while pursuing the programme of study. Crosby (1979) defines quality as conformance to fulfil the customer needs. Juran (1989) has also emphasized upon the importance of satisfying client needs. Quality is considered as fitness for use which includes to identify the customer needs and further attempts are made to meet these needs. Thus, when it is to be translated into educational terms, it can be equated with the learner-centred approach (McIlroy and Walker 1993). A prominent concept in current approaches to manage quality is keeping the students on the forefront (Nunan and Calvert 1991; Mills and Paul 1993; Robinson 1994) and further designing procedures and courses which match the students' needs as minutely or as closely as possible.

To assess the quality in distance education, it is primarily based on performance indicators of input and outcome measures and little attention has been paid to customer satisfaction as a measure of quality or through a fitness for purpose or use definition. For this, there is one reason; that is, both concepts are used synonymously (Abrami 1989; D'Apollonia and Cohen 1990). For bringing the quality in student support system, attention should be paid to know about what quality means to the distance education learners. It is mandatory that the distance education providers should take care of the needs and expectations of the learners. It is generally found that adult learners demand quality in the products and services offered by the distance education providers and value for their money. Therefore, in the system of distance education, adult learners are in the best position to assess the quality of the learners' support that is provided to them.

In distance education system for maintaining the quality of programmes, the learners are provided the feedback in various ways so that they may be benefitted from the student support services which are provided to them at the learner support centres; for example, for the assessment of assignments, the learners are provided the feedback so that they may improve their performance during Term End Examination. This is a major function of academic counsellors. Academic support is provided to the learners, and they have given the guidance on how to attend to different kinds of assignments incorporated as course requirements. The counsellors assess the learners' assignments to ensure learner performance in studies. They give comments to make learners aware of their progress in studies.

Importance of Learner Support Services

The learner support services play an important role in imparting quality education to distance learners, but their management is probably the toughest task. When a learner takes admission afresh in distance education system for the first time, he finds himself in an unfamiliar situation, because he has the experience of conventional education system where he receives the full-time support of the teacher in classroom. But in distance education system the course is completed by himself in the absence of a teacher. Another important factor is that the learners in this system are mostly adults and are basically part-time learners who are not sure of their capacities and capabilities. The learning experience for them may be unpleasant experience as they have lost touch with their studies. In the system of distance education, the main purpose of the learner support services is to promote self-study or independent study, particularly in the absence of regular face-to-face contact. However, the process of learning through the mode of distance education system requires the interaction of the learners, both with the materials and with the teacher. The quality of the support system affects learning, and this is the basic rationale for the purpose of learner support services in the system of distance education.

Learner-Specific Requirements

The position of the learner is very important in any system of education because the entire process of teaching and learning revolves around the learners. Therefore, in the system of the distance education it is assumed that he is a mature adult learner and wishes to learn at his own pace. For this reason, he feels sometimes isolation from his peer groups and teachers concerned. Because of the physical and psychological isolation, he needs academic and emotional support from the distance teaching teachers and the distance education institutions.

Course-Specific Requirements

For the purpose of providing course-specific assistance to the distant learners, it is felt that learner support services play an important role in the system of distance education. It starts with the pre-admission counselling and continues till the students complete the programme. The most of the learners get this support during the counselling sessions and for writing the assignments. For making the learners self-reliant, self-confident and independent, the print course material is to be provided to the learners. While evaluating the assignments which are submitted to the counsellors, they write the constructive comments on the assignments which work as two-way didactic communication among the learners and counsellors. During counselling, the students are helped to solve their problems related to their study.

Learners Are Helped to Sustain Their Motivation

In the field of teaching and learning process, motivation is one of the most important factors. As the distance learners are generally the adult learners and they are simultaneously engaged in various social and other economic activities while pursuing their studies. It is very difficult for them to sustain motivation for completion of their studies. But with lots of efforts and proper counselling, the motivation level of these learners can be restored.

A learner in the beginning, when he joins a programme through the system of distance mode, he is motivated to some extent. Without motivation, nobody would like to spend their money and time to be successful in their studies. It is only the motivation by which the learners develop their interest to complete the programme. Motivation from distance teachers, tutors and counsellors at various stages helps the learners overcome their difficulties and give up the idea of dropping out from the programme.

Supply of Information at the Entry Stage is Very Helpful for the Learners

Accuracy and timely supply of information about the course and programme at the initial stage would help the learners decide about their strategies of learning. Timely admission, timely dispatch of study material, dispatch of counselling schedule and assignments submission schedule instil confidence in the learners and inspire them to study hard. If these services are not properly monitored, the students face difficulty and their performance level gets affected.

Timely Supply of Feedback on Evaluation of Assignments

The assignment responses submitted by the learners must be assessed, evaluated and commented upon and returned in time. The purpose of assignments is to teach the learners effectively by giving them timely feedback on their strengths and their weaknesses. This feedback is helpful to the learners in tracking their own progress. The very aim of distance education is defeated if in time feedback on the evaluation of assignments is not provided to the learners.

Need of Face-to-Face Counselling for Distant Learners

Counselling is very much necessary in distance education system. The isolated distance learners always need the opportunity of face-to-face meeting with their peer groups and teachers. Counselling sessions are one of the best channels through which the learners interact freely with the counsellors and peers and solve majority of their problems. It is, therefore, imperative on the part of distance education institutions to see that counselling classes are organized systematically and good counsellors are entrusted with this noble cause. This will bring motivation to a great extent and help to satisfy the very purpose of distance education.

Preparation of the Distant Learners for Examination

The preparation for the Term End Examination is a great challenge for the distance education learners. Timely conduct of examinations and timely declaration of results give tremendous amount of satisfaction to the distance education learners, and this motivates the learners to continue and complete the learning activities on time.

Student Support Services and Use of Communication Technology

As it has already been discussed due to isolation of the distant learners from their teachers and peer groups, the distinct learners are provided various student support services during the pre-entry of their programme, during their study and till they complete it. With the provision of print course material, audio–video cassettes and use of other electronic media, use of educational technology plays an important role in the present days for providing direct communication to the distant learners.

ICT plays an important role for the purpose of delivery of student support services effectively and efficiently. It has become inevitable for the distance learners that they may be benefitted by this technology. We can also notice the shift from mass produced generic resources to tailored personalized support and communications. This is prevalent in the context of globalization of the economy and the changing expectations of students as consumers.

Importance of Information and Communication Technology for Distance Learners

It has globally been felt that earlier distance and open education was relied mainly on giving the print material to the learners, use of audio–video cassettes, radio and TV broadcasting. But now these gazettes have been replaced by new online tools and technologies which have the power to transform the learning environment.

Reasons for Using Technology in the Institutions of Distance Education

To improve the quality of teaching and learning by adding suitable technology that increases the amount of interaction between the learner and a teacher and between learner and learner.

- To provide learners with suitable technology literacy for work and life.
- For the purpose of improving the access to quality education and training using online and mobile learning platforms.
- For reducing the cost of education.
- For the purpose of improvement of cost-effectiveness of education.
- To meet the technological imperative.

Benefits of Technological Developments

Here are the details given of technological developments which bring to the distance learners.

- Teachers and students can avail the benefits by making use of Internet and World Wide Web facility because this is the source of information and knowledge that provides an opportunity to the learners and teachers for self-development, and this facility can be incorporated into the classroom teaching environment also.
- By using email and other Internet-related feedback mechanisms, students can get opportunity to reduce isolation and time delay associated with distance education.
- Teaching and learning with enhanced graphics, animation, interaction and visualization can be enriched through the use of extraordinary pace of software development.
- For getting the greater opportunity for basic accessibility, video conferencing, online interactive learning and live interaction with the central place of a

distance education programme are possible due to lowering telecommunications bandwidth costs and emergence of enhanced cable, wireless and satellite systems.
- The people who belong to the lower income group and those who are residing in rural areas can make use of the benefits of distance education through community access schemes.

For Internet-based resources, a powerful distribution mechanism is very small aperture terminal (VSAT) satellite systems, which can be used with ready access to interactive learning tools and email. It can be further linked or packaged with key educational website sources, servers and services. Many of the bandwidth and delivery speed limitation of terrestrial systems can be overcome with the use of very small aperture terminal (VSAT), particularly in developing countries.

Use of information and communication technology depends on the following factors.

Depends on the Geographical Size of the Country

Large countries with diversified population and communities have an additional benefits and motivation to use the facility of communication to deliver the educational services cost-effectively.

Due to Change of Policy on Telecommunications

Because of the use of Internet, information technology and education, privatization and liberalization of telecommunication services and the Internet are improving its quality, lowering costs and this has been accelerating the innovation around the world.

Size of Market and Population

If the size of the market is small, it attracts fewer investors and less competition. It also offers fewer economies of scale which would lead to price reduction, whereas the regional schemes can overcome that aggregate market size and achieve scale economies.

Depends on Per Capita Means

To address start-up investment challenges and the market affordability which can attract the commercial players to ease the way to change and growth.

For Fulfilling Educational and Developmental Needs

It can be related to challenges which can be faced while delivering educational services. These challenges can be arisen due to geographic or cultural isolation. These challenges can be further reduced by adapting to the demands of the information economy which can only be seriously addressed with information and communication technologies.

Conclusion

It is felt that distance education is more cost effective than the conventional education system, due to which distance mode of education is gaining a momentum and becoming more popular than the traditional mode of education all over the world. One of the biggest advantages of distance education is that the learner can study according to his own convenience and can complete the course at his own pace and place. Therefore, in the system of distance education the learner has been given more flexibility than that of the conventional education system as they can earn while they learn. The popularity of distance education has been increased even in developed countries, and the learners prefer distance learning than that of the conventional education system. Due to the use of modern technology, mass education is attained through distance learning, where the world is becoming boundary-less. It is because of the technological developments which have brought revolution for the development of distance education among the masses. After depicting and going through the history of distance education system, it has been analysed that this system has become more effective and learner-centred due to the use of educational technology.

References

Abrami, P. C. (1989). How should we use student ratings to evaluate teaching? *Research in Higher Education, 30*(2), 221–227.

Alan, T. 2003. Reflections on student support in open and distance learning. *The International Review of Research in Open and Distance Learning*.

Bates, 1990. Media and technology in European distance education. Milton Keynes, UK: Open University.
Braimoh, D., & Osiki, J. O. (2008). The impact of technology on accessibility and pedagogy: the right to education in Sub-Saharan Africa.
Crosby, P. B. (1979). *Quality is free*. New York: McGraw-Hill.
Daniel, John S. (1995). *"Preface", in open and distance learning* (Today ed.). Routledge, London and New York: Fred Lockwood.
D'Apollonia, S., & Cohen, P. (1990). Validity of student ratings of instruction: what we know and what we do not? *Journal of Educational Psychology, 82,* 219–231.
Demiray, U., & McIsaac, M. S. (1993). Ten years of distance education in Turkey. In B. Scriven, R. Lundin, & Y. Ryan (Eds.), *Distance education for the twenty-first century* (pp. 403–406). Oslo, Norway: International Council for Distance Education.
Dhanarajan, G. (1996). Response to tony pritchard. *Open Praxis, 1*.
Harry, Keegan, D., & Magnus, J. (Eds.). (1993). *Distance education: New perspectives*, London: Routledge.
Hillman, D. C. A., Willis, D. J., & Gunawardena, C. N. (1994). Learner-interface interaction in distance education: an extension of contemporary models and strategies for practitioners. *American Journal of Distance Education, 8*(2), 30–34.
IAP. distance learning. *A Magazine for Leaders*, 2(6), 18. ISBN 9787774554229.
IGNOU SIM of MDE-411: Growth and Philosophy of Distance Education, Block No. 05, page No. 71–72.
IGNOU SIM of MDE-413: Learner Support Systems and Services, Block No. 01, Page No. 10–12, 15-17.
Juran, J. M. (1989). *Juran on leadership for quality: an executive handbook*. New York: The Free Press.
Kaya, Z. (2002). Uzaktan Eğitim [Distance Education]. (1. Baskı). Ankara: Pegema Yayıncılık.
Keegan, (1986). The foundations of distance education (2nd ed.) London: Routledge.
Keegan, D. (1980). On defining distance education. *Distance Education, 1*(1), 13–36.
Kember, D., & Dekkers, J. (1987a). The role of study centres for academic support in distance education. *Distance Education, 8*(2), 30–42.
Kember, D., & Dekkers, J. (1987b). The role of study centres for academic support in distance education. *Distance Education, 8*(1), 4–17.
McIlroy, A., & Walker, R. (1993). Total quality management: some implications for the management of distance education. *Distance Education, 14*(1), 40–54.
Mills, R., & Paul, R. (1993). Putting the student first: management for quality in distance education. In T. Evans & D. Nation (Eds.), *Reforming open and distance education critical reflections form Pacific*. London: Kogan Page.
Moore, M. G., Kearsley, G. (2005). *Distance education: A systems view* (2nd ed.). Belmont, CA: Wadsworth. ISBN 0-534-50688-7.
Nunan, T. & Calvert, J. (1991). Investigating quality and standards in distance education—An interpretation of issues. Paper presented at the 10th Biennial Forum, Australian and South Pacific External Studies Association, NSW, Australia, 15–19 July 1991.
Office of Technology Assessment. (1989). *Linking for learning*. Washington, DC: United States Government Printing Office.
Open and distance learning in developing countries: the past, the present and the future (pdf download available). Retrieved January 17 2018 from https://www.researchgate.net/publication/242113800_open_and_distance_learning_in_developing_countries_the_past_the_present_and_the_future.
Pedagogy: The right to education in Sub-Saharan Africa. *Asian Journal of Distance Education*.
Pittman, V. (1991). Rivalry for respectability: Collegiate and proprietary correspondence programs. In *Second American Symposium on Research in Distance Education*, .University Park, PA: Pennsylvania State University.
Ravisankar, K., & Murthy, C. R. K. (2000). Student participation circles: an approach to learner participation in quality improvement. *Indian Journal of Open Learning, 9*(1), 73–85.

Robinson, B. (1994). Ensuring quality in the planning and development of distance learning courses. Paper presented at the 20th Anniversary International Conference on Distance Learning, Colombia, 20–22 September 1994.

Sewart, D. (1992). Student support systems in distance education. Paper presented at the 16th Conference of the International Council for Distance Education, Thailand, 8–13 November 1992.

Sewart, D. (1992b). Student support systems in distance education. In B. Serven, et al. (Eds.), *Distance education for the twenty-first century* (pp. 120–129). Australia: ICDE & Queensland University of Technology.

Sewart, D (Ed.). (1995). One world many voices: quality in open and distance learning. In: 17th World Conference for Distance Education, Birmingham. 26–30 June 1995.

Shah, G. (1989). A distance education strategy for Bangladesh. *International Council for Distance Education Bulletin, 19,* 9–14.

Sherry, L. (1996). Issues in distance learning. *International Journal of Educational Telecommunications, 1*(4), 337–365.

Simpson, O. (2000). *Supporting students in open and distance learning*. London: Kogan Page.

Taylor, J. C. (1997). Flexible learning systems: opportunities and strategies for staff development in industry. In P. C. Chew (Ed.). Quality Assurance in Distance and Open Learning. Conference Proceedings of the 11th Annual Conference and Exhibition (Vol. 1). Asian Association of Open Universities, Kuala Lumpur, Malaysia, 11–14 November 1997.

The Handbook of research for Educational and communications technology AECT.

UNESCO. (2002). *Open and distance learning: trends, policy and strategy consideration*. Paris: UNESCO.

Utsumi, T., Rossman, P., & Rosen, S. (1990). The global electronic university. In M. G. Moore (Ed.), *Contemporary issues in American distance education* (pp. 96–110). New York: Pergamon Press.

Tools of ICT in Open and Distance Learning for Inclusive Education in Developing World

Manminder Kaur

In the year 2000, most of the world's administrations embraced the Education for All (EFA) objectives and the Millennium Development Goals (MDGs), the two most essential systems in the arena of instruction. As a basic human right and an empowering power for feasible advancement, education assumes a key part in helping nations meet their universal improvement plans and has noticeably included in all worldwide historic point summits sorted out from that point forward.

Evolution of Distance Education

The idea of open learning and distance education framework centers around open access to training and preparing to make the students free from the imperatives of time and place and offering adaptable learning chances to group of learners and individuals. Open and distance learning is a standout among the most quickly developing arenas of education these days, and it has considerable effect on delivery system of all types of instruction.

Garrison and Nipper were among the first to utilize this term to portray three eras of distance education which are connected truly to the advancement of creation, circulation, and correspondence advances (Nipper 1989, p. 63).

In the ***first era,*** the medium for the communication was in the form of composed and printed material. The development of radio in the 1920s permitted the start of radio-drove courses comprising of a progression of talks; sometimes, a set book or other pieces of literature and nearby examination bunches were included. It was in the 1950s that TV-drove courses have been widely utilized, regularly with print and nearby gatherings, sporadically appraisal of the learners.

M. Kaur (✉)
BCM College of Education, Ludhiana, Punjab, India
e-mail: me.manminder@gmail.com

© Springer Nature Singapore Pte Ltd. 2018

Anjana (ed.), *Technology for Efficient Learner Support Services in Distance Education*, https://doi.org/10.1007/978-981-13-2300-3_2

In 1969, the start of the **second era** was set apart by the Open University of the UK. This was for the first run through when a purposely coordinated different media approach was utilized for open and distance instruction, despite the fact that the print remained the overwhelming medium. The Open University grew substantial amounts of high caliber, extraordinarily composed distance learning resources. The print material coordinated with broadcasts was the one-way correspondence that was used from university to students as later on audio tapes were also included. Correspondence coaching, personal contact programs, and short residential schools were the main means of two-way communication between teachers and taught.

The information and communication technologies became the basis for the ***third era*** of distance education, offering a variety of forms, i.e., text, graphics, audios, moving pictures, either synchronous, for example videoconferencing and sound illustrations, or asynchronous, for example electronic mail, the Internet, and PC conferencing as two-way communication in distance education. Third era of distance education was emphasizing on communication and learning as a social process also known as interactive, multimedia distance education through adding up of interactive media such as audio graphics, videoconferencing or computer-assisted communications.

The ***fourth era*** or 'Flexible Learning Model' is designated as the blend of interactive multimedia with access to WWW resources and asynchronous computer conferencing. This Flexible Learning Model combines the high-quality interactive multimedia benefits with access to gradually broad range of teaching–learning material and improves interaction through computer-assisted communication by connecting to the Internet. This fourth generation of distance education is based on the use of information and communication technologies for creating an inclusive setup for the developing world.

Main Steps Toward Inclusive Education

In the process of inclusion learners with diverse needs enroll themselves in the general schools with the normal average children. They are formally incorporated into the general instruction program and are appraised by a distinctive training instructor and reinforced by a specialized curriculum educator. Inclusive education implies that all learners whether they are negative or positively skewed from the normal average children in terms of qualities or shortcomings in any zone became the part of school social group. They are incorporated into the sentiment having a place among different learners, educators, and care staff.

The consideration of learners with diverse needs in regular schools is a part of global movement to safeguard the human rights. Learners from the various backgrounds and areas have a privilege of learning, paying little respect to their individual qualities or troubles. In the course of the most recent couple of decades, the model of inclusion has turned out to be vital to universal instruction arrangement and has constrained the significant changes in national enactment in numerous nations. Beginning in the 1980s, inclusive education has intended to advance scholastic learning, social capability and value inculcation, skill enhancement and attitude change as well as positive associate relations in comprehensive settings for understudies with exceptional needs.

Digital Inclusion Creating Equal Opportunities for All

Rapid technological advancement brings opportunities and threats to the people with diverse needs. It has made them aware about their rights to have the same standard of living as every other member of the society had. For this, they need to overcome further obstacles before they enjoy services presented by the ICTs to the fullest. For example, the blind people need appropriate hardware and software to be developed to substitute images to the text and then the text can further be translated into an audible system through screen reading devices specially designed for this purpose. It can also be made accessible by printed Braille text. On the other side, large format text and effective color contrast can be used by the people with low vision. People with learning disabilities, cognitive impairments, sensory impaired may also be benefitted by using simpler language or alternative text formats. As in today's era of technological advancement, information has become a social necessity and a fundamental human right that demands to include all learners from any group to be included in it. Thus, it becomes essential to find out the means to include these types of persons into the era of modern information and technological advancements.

The Role of ICTs in Inclusive Education

ICT is frequently utilized as an equivalent term for IT yet is normally a more broad term that emphasizes the part of communication to be added in the recent information technology. ICT comprises every single specialized means used to deal with data provided and support correspondence among the learners, including PC with updated required hardware and software. The instructive needs of individuals with differing needs are boundlessly various. Firstly, they should, as their peers, get knowledge and skills required in the society in which they live. Secondly, they have other needs caused by practical constraints which influence students' capacity to get to standard instructive strategies for guideline, in this way, avoiding their instructive advancement. In this unique situation, ICT application is critical as it assumes a fundamental part in giving great instruction to students with diverse needs. ICTs have been brought into the educating learning process with a specific end goal to enhance quality, bolster curricular changes and new learning encounters. Along these lines, it is likely to meet the particular adapting needs of various student gatherings, incorporating the students with diverse needs. In spite of the fact that particular uses of ICTs are amazingly assorted and shifted, they might be categorized as the following uses:

- ICT for compensation uses;
- ICT for didactic uses;
- ICT for communication uses.

Compensation Uses of ICT

ICT for compensation uses is the utilization of new advancements as a specialized help that enables understudies with extraordinary necessities to take dynamic part in the process of interaction and communication: Difficulties with reading in pupils with dyslexia include mainly text editing, use of different fonts, special educational software, improving teaching process, use of multimedia, and technical assistance may be provided to write in motor disability or to read with the Braille if a person is having visual impairment. In this way, ICTs help in developing the students' ability to make adjustments with the environment, develop problem-solving ability, and give access to data and content material, and along these lines improve correspondence with others both locally and globally. It can be concluded that assistive technology and technological advancement can recover or substitute the absence of regular capacities of persons with disabilities.

Didactic Uses of ICT

Information technologies utilized as a learning device have incited another measurement of training and propelled the change of the instructive methodologies. ICT application brings an assortment of new instructing and appraisal procedures for understudies with various instructive needs. ICTs have prompted new dimensions of education and revolutionized various educational approaches. Here, we should take note of that data innovations as a didactical device is appropriate for executing the comprehensive instruction. Keeping in mind the end goal to improve self-improvement, instructive activities inside the comprehensive educational programs must go for addressing special needs, contrasts, and capacities of an individual; henceforth, they should be completely upheld to accomplish these objectives at a suitable pace. Technological advancement consequently will turn into a significant asset for successful inclusion.

Communication Uses of ICT

Innovations can facilitate correspondence with individuals having inabilities. Assistive gadgets and programming to address the issues of learners with diverse needs correspondence challenges are particular to each inability. We discuss the PC as an asset that facilitates and makes the correspondence conceivable, enabling a man with open issue to display his/her capacities in a more helpful manner, or individuals with engine and informative issue to begin correspondence, demonstrate the requirements and make the requests. Besides, where instructors are hard to find especially in the case of a specialized curriculum distance instructive strategies can help give exceptional facilities between scattered learners and educators.

ICT for Successful Inclusion in Distance Learning

For enhancing the learning opportunities, whether formal or non-formal ICT is a potentially influential instrument. ICTs are not only meant for the learners, it additionally encourages access to specialists, researchers in the field of education, mentors and resource persons, experts, coaches, business pioneer, and associates everywhere throughout the world for enhancing the application and quality education. These innovations incorporate PCs, the Web, broadcasting devices like radio and TV, phones, mobiles, and other communication devices.

This may incorporate a wide range of learning advances, for example, print, sound, video, and the personal computers as well. The utilization of computers has made the distance learner self-sufficient and also has given new academic methodologies for effective learning. The advanced innovations utilized as a part of open and distance learning are teleconferencing, mobile learning, sound designs, videoconferencing, PC conferencing drill and training, fiber optics, teletext, and videotext, mixed media and hypermedia, computer-assisted instruction, e-books, www, online database, online discourse, satellite, and so on. The instructors' expert in the respective fields must have mastery over these devices to effectively communicate with their diverse learners. With the advent of various eras of distance education, a dire need has been felt for a potent framework for the development of knowledge-based economy. In the idea of introducing new innovations, distance learning offers media-based training content matter to the learners using standard information system administration, conventions, and framework. The basic significance of utilizing advances in open and distance learning is low in cost, freedom of time and place, quality access to the education that results in the huge creation of the subject matter, educating a considerable number of learners all together and helpful in finding a great deal of instructive assets.

ICT-based open and distance learning helps the persons with diverse needs by:

- Facilitating interactive correspondence among instructor and instructed;
- Supplying educational sources;

- Giving access to learning assets.

Due to physical or scholarly inabilities of certain group of individuals, they cannot approach to formal education. ICT gives different helpful intends for such target gathering of individuals to accomplish their objectives and enhance their capacities and abilities.

The most important aspect in the teaching–learning process of persons with diverse needs is the access to the relevant information, as these data resources must be customized to the diverse needs of various learners. There is an assortment of techniques to address the issues of open and distance learning students. For instance, route apparatuses assist people with low vision, upgrade the span of visual data on the screen, and increment text dimension of the content; if understudies cannot read print of any size, the screen reader programming may be valuable to make the content on the screen available by using Braille or through addressing the learners. In the same way, to have an access to computer persons having impairment in mobility can utilize progressive gadgets like different keyboards, voice recognition tools. Indeed, assistive technology advances in distance education are progressively offering instructive openings to differently abled persons.

Tools of ICT to Achieve Benefits of Open and Distance Learning for Inclusive Education

There are various types of ICT innovations utilized as a part of open and distance learning for inclusive education. Every form of ICT used in inclusive setup is characterized by how a teacher and a student convey and get instructive guidelines and resources. In this way, the methods and media utilized in this procedure assume a vital part. For realizing the objectives, vision and mission of its instructive plan the distance education program ought to subsequently choose proper innovations presented by the recognized organization.

Individuals accountable for offering open and distance education to differently abled children should undoubtedly comprehend the fundamental standards of a dynamic program and a model of classifying the procedures utilized in this procedure. Johansen et al. in 1991 have suggested a model of 'The 4-Square Map of Groupware Options' for information system by classifying the various technologies into both individual and collaborative uses. The present model suggests that all communications can be at:

- Same time/different place: two-way video, screen sharing;
- Different time/different place: computer conferencing, voice mail;
- Same time/same place: PC projectors, workstation networks;
- Different time/same place: team rooms, stations for shiftwork.

However, nowadays the most popular way of describing the Distance Education technology to support materials' delivery and interaction is to divide it into two main types: synchronous and asynchronous. The asynchronous and synchronous teaching/learning processes can be accomplished in a place-dependent or in a place-independent manner. The detailed list of possible technologies that might fall in each category is presented below.

These above said four groups are utilized to represent the technological advancements which are presently bolstering the distance education. Though these days the most prevalent method for depicting the technological advancements in open and distance learning to make provision of a accessing content information and communication is to classify it into two key forms, i.e., synchronous and asynchronous. The synchronous and asynchronous procedures of teaching and learning can be made proficient by time and place dependent as well as independent of a particular time and place. The probable technologies that constitute these two forms are as follows.

(I) Synchronous Communication and Collaboration Tools

Synchronous communication implies in which communication between participants is immediate. The process of teaching and learning is represented as 'synchronous' when the instructor of the course and the learner meets up in the meantime. Synchronous learning is the inverse of asynchronous learning, where student connects with instructors and/or learners online in the meantime from the diverse places. Inside the synchronous condition, a teacher presents data, answers inquiries, and observes deliberations; learners progressively collaborate with each other and related instructors.

As a result, everything is like conventional classrooms. Like traditions personal contact program or videoconferencing, a few advances can visualize the members so the participants could spot their identity making discussions with, and can respond to their reactions, and resolve misapprehensions. Notwithstanding, the synchronous method of connection requires verbal mastery and quick responses. The learners must have the capacity to express their considerations immediately, which is not generally appropriate for learners with unique adapting needs, as their debilitations or individual learning style obstruct speedy correspondence. Besides, the two, the learners and educators, need to buy distinctive kinds of varying media hardware which might be modestly or exceptionally costly, contingent upon the nature of a gadget. What is more, the members must sit before the PC/TV or other gadget at an assigned availability. Few examples of synchronous distance learning advances are depicted beneath.

Instant Messaging

Service of instant messaging is an online framework that empowers the educators to effortlessly observe whether a particular student is linked with the Internet that enables him to interchange instant messages with them. With the help of instant messaging service, new techniques are opened up for unconstrained correspondence for the individuals with hearing and speech impairment. This service is considered by numerous as an intense method to permit equal opportunities to interact, without the assistive technology or administrations intended for learners with loss of hearing. MSN Messenger, ICQ, and so on services offer the chance to recognize individuals who are online in the meantime and interchange content actually. For effective communication and reflections, some messaging services are so advanced that they incorporate voice chat, document exchange, and other different applications which can be fundamental for successful inclusion.

Chat Room

Online chat alludes to a two-way communication on the Internet. At least, two or more than two individuals at remote PCs associate with a similar chat room and type text in a chat mode to communicate with each other. All these typed messages and content are seen by all the participants on a screen shared by them. The interaction through online chatting is considered as a 'real-time' interaction. For instance, numerous teachers will build up virtual available time, during which they will be accessible to talk with any of the learners who may have queries to some related content and course. Since the talk happens on the Internet, there are no telephone charges to stress over!

The utilization of chat room in open and distance learning has turned into a significant purpose for Web-based learning. Chat rooms being synchronous specialized apparatuses enable the learners to have an interaction with other related members by means of composed content progressively without being at a similar place. For an effective online chatting, the members must write their remarks and enquiries in the chat rooms. Chat rooms are a part in each significant course administration framework and are accessible for nothing on numerous sites, where the educators can make their own particular classroom region. Not exclusively does it enable understudies to impart progressively to examine the subjects of the course, yet it enables less demanding access to the instructor with a specific end goal to convey and clear up main themes of discussion. The benefits of collaborative online chatting are that the correspondences are synchronous and the immediate feedback can be provided to the learners and their queries are satisfied and doubts are clarified.

Whiteboards

The term whiteboard is additionally used to allude to interactive whiteboards. Whiteboards are referred to certain features of computer programming applications that recreate whiteboards. Such 'virtual whiteboards' enable one or more than one individuals to draw pictures or write on a simulated canvas. This is a typical component of numerous virtual gathering, coordinated effort, and instant texting applications. These whiteboards as graphical talk instruments enable learners to write, draw, paint, and opportunity to offer existing graphical documents continuously with an assistance of a mouse or uncommonly composed pen, which has turned into noteworthy in addition to for the diverse learners who cannot operate mouse properly or see the learning content.

Audio Conferencing

A video chat is the live conversation and mass delivery of data among a few people, and machines remote from each other yet connected by a broadcast communications framework. Sound conferencing, phone conferencing, and telephone conferencing are some terms used likewise in some cases to denote to video chatting. The broadcast communications framework may bolster the video chat by giving at least one of the accompanying: sound, video, and information benefits by at least one means, for example, phone, PC, telex, teletypewriter, radio, and TV. Telephones or the Internet are the means through which audio conferencing can be possible.

This way of interaction includes two or conferencing more members working together by means of oral discourse progressively. Phone-based sound meetings are the most established and least difficult type of communication in open and distance learning. Through audio conferencing, a student can get to the openings of open and distance learning, communicate with specialists, get updated information, and in addition can share thoughts with different applicants. Mobile phone invention has expanded the approachable locations; for example, for videoconferencing phone may assist as a potent factor in distance learning as an audio tool. At the point when utilized alone, audio technology presents basic verbal data only, and it misses the visual part of interaction which results in lack of observing the gestures, responses, and facial expressions that can enable speakers to make a few focuses or enhance understanding of the audience.

Videoconferencing

Videoconferencing enables at least two clients to communicate continuously by means of video and sound conferencing broadcasts. Developments in video innovations have drastically extended its utilization and access to open and distance learning. New levels of association are accomplished whenever students and instructors see each other. With the use of videoconferencing, a wide range of intuitive instructing and learning is improved. Consequently, the distance education in view of present-day innovation utilize rehearses fundamental to all up close and personal class associations—brainstorming, collaborative learning, demonstrating skills, etc. Open and separation learning oriented with video innovations falls into two general classifications: one-way communicative video and two-way collaborative video. One-way communicative video implies that video signals are transmitted one way: from educator to students. Components of broadcast system incorporate to deliver programs and a site for students to see the projects on a standard TV.

Two-way collaborative video accommodates video and sound interaction among students and educators. It might incorporate two-way video and sound or one-way video/two-way sound broadcast. Presently, there exists an assortment of videoconferencing innovations: Integrated Services Digital Network satellite and link communicate, and Instructional Television Fixed Service. For open and distance learning, it is essential to know about video relay services and telecommunication relay service which bolster media transmission between hearing impaired and hearing individuals. Two-way translation can be possible through telecommunication relay services between the text and speech. The learners with hearing power interact orally, and on the other hand, the hearing impaired learners interact with the help of typing. Videoconferencing disengaged students can be empowered with the help of videoconferencing to share their learning with the other learners residing in the remote areas to decrease etymological seclusion by enabling same first dialect students to examine and convey remotely.

Multi-user Domain Object-Oriented Environments (MOOs)

Numerous operators can be associated at the same time in a content-based online virtual reality framework called MOO (MUD, object-oriented). The term MOO is utilized as a part of two distinctive, however related, faculties. One is to refer to those projects plunged from the unique MOO server, and the other is to refer to any MUD that utilizes object-oriented strategies to compose its database of articles, especially on the off-chance that it does as such in a comparable manner to the original MOO or its subsidiaries. MOOs are virtual online situations intended for critical thinking, live communications, and collaborative effort. A MOO is a synchronous content-based device which gives the client a control over ‘symbols’ passing through the virtual world, cooperating and imparting by means of discourse produced by client-composed guidelines. The instrument provides assistance in involving the learners in basic reasoning, role playing, and critical thinking exercises. With a specific end goal to be available, a content depiction of the virtual world and a constant content transcript are required. Some of the time programming for synchronous correspondence can posture planning challenges for understudies whose information way is moderate. Consequently, understudies with constrained hand limit who can enter data gradually or understudies with particular learning weaknesses for whom to form an idea requires some time might be partly incorporated in the conversation. For this situation, other methods for involvement for such learners must be utilized; for example, email is the best suited asynchronous tool for communication to meet the children with diverse needs.

(II). Asynchronous Communication and Collaboration Tools

Asynchronous communication implies that type of communication where the groups do not have the interaction at the same time. Asynchronous learning takes place when the user is potentially utilizing a Web-based learning stage from various time and places according to his convenience, for example, using one's emails and discussion forum for the effective learning. The process of learning is called asynchronous at the point when training is unfixed in time. Naturally, along these lines of correspondence is less troublesome than synchronous sorts, as learners are allowed to make up their own particular timetable. With asynchronous provision of instruction, an understudy can audit the online substance a few times and appreciate extra time to thoroughly consider the learning material and respond to it accordingly.

It is of great importance to the learners with diverse needs, because input/output of information, thinking and conceptualization can take longer time because of their impedances. Also, educators are accessible through email as well as phone, if an understudy has inquiries or apprehensions related to any course. A general ease and time adaptability are the benefits of such type of communication. However, the extensive volume of composing and interchanging the data can introduce a few issues. The following are the few examples of asynchronous communication tools used in open and distance learning.

Email

The most typical and modest means for learners to interact with their counselors or teachers is sending email messages. Sometimes, emails are utilized as the main strategy for the correspondence of a whole distance education program. In some cases, email might be utilized to supplement sound or video technological advancements. Electronic programming is currently so advanced and easy to understand that even new operators require email next to no preparation to begin. It is a quick and simple method for sending messages starting with one individual then onto the next or to a gathering either by utilizing numerous beneficiaries or through an email conveyance list. In these two cases, a user may choose application for particular customer programming relying upon his/her needs and similarity with the favored assistant technology programming and equipment. Users access their messages online or download them into their own computers and reply to messages or send messages to other users by transmitting to the central computer, which then assigns the messages to the appropriate mailbox. The extensive utilization of email makes it a typical initial step for teachers wandering in the realm of online correspondence with their learners. The benefits of email interchanges incorporate adaptability and accommodation. Workstations and local area networks can be connected via the public telephone system to other networks or sites. For instance, regional offices may be connected to the headquarters for local registration of students or for entering grades for assignments or even for examinations done locally. Since data can be sent through telephone lines or even by satellites, it is possible to use emails for international connections, at very low cost, i.e., much cheaper and faster than sending a letter and cheaper than fax.

Notwithstanding sending straight content, most email frameworks presently enable learners to attach documents with them. That implies that they can send PowerPoint presentations, spreadsheets, or some other sort of record to each other from distance. The importance of email is that it can be retrieved to wherever and whenever of the day or night timings. Most importantly, students can access an email for a less amount or practically at no cost at all.

Mailing List

The mailing list can be defined as an accumulation of names and addresses utilized by an individual or an association to send material to various beneficiaries. The term is frequently stretched out to incorporate the general population bought into such a rundown, so the gathering of endorsers is alluded to as 'the mailing list', or in simple words the list only. A mailing list is a programmed mailing framework, which enables the gathering to impart without sending singular messages to everybody in the gathering. It reports to the whole class, so when somebody sends emails to the mailing list, a replica is transmitted to all endorsers. Like some other email messages, these messages to and from mailing records are sent and got in the same and convenient way. In any case, mailing records do not give a component sorting out the messages by subject. These messages are generally shown up in the email box in an unarranged manner. This is the reason that most of the teachers incline toward forum than mailing lists.

Forum

Forums are also one of the other types of asynchronous correspondence. The bulletin boards or message boards are the other words used for forum. The principle consecutive distinction between forum and mailing records is that messages created by the mailing records are consequently sent to followers' email inboxes, whereas the users of bulletin board must visit a particular zone on the Web to peruse and post messages. Yet, some bulletin boards currently give the alternative of accepting photocopies of posts by means of email. Another vital contrast is that in bulletin boards and forum, messages about a specific subject are assembled together so that it can be easily discussed. Learners can answer and attach their message with a particular one officially posted.

Various online diaries and bulletin boards have been made for open and distance learning, for example, DEOS-L, sorted out by the American Center for Open and Distance Learning at University of Penn State and accessible on the Web. Therefore, any communication or article posted is acquired automatically by the individuals who have joined a specific package for this purpose. These types of diaries and bulletin boards can only be read by the subscriber, and it can permit them to include their own particular messages.

Web Repositories

Web sources have become one of the extensively used media for transferring subject matter in open and distance learning. The most remarkable benefit of the Web technologies is their talent to offer audiovisual aids and the hypertext. The hypertext links permit the consumer to move from one information source to another straight linked with the previous source of learning. Physically connected data can be put away on another remotely found PC. Multimedia used to indicate vibrant changes of an object after some time and graphically introduced printed data can upgrade learning of the learners in open and distance learning. A moderately minimal effort of conveyance, simplicity of asset advancement, and wide accessibility of understudy's entrance make it a perfect instructional supply source. Learning assets are put away in the Internet such that an understudy can get to them whenever and from wherever he wished. With the Internet-based open and distance education understudies effortlessly pick up advice and directions for acquisition from the teacher in synchronous and non-concurrent approaches.

Video Transmission Pre-recorded

Video transmission includes the rebroadcast of a course portion which has been recorded and incorporates no ongoing connection between an understudy and an educator (pre-recorded). Asynchronous video devices, e.g., videotapes, can pass on add-on data to students or record talks of resource persons for later review. The content matter that is pre-recorded might be communicated on a nearby TV channel. The type of visual and sound data utilized as a part of video broadcast can represent certain availability troubles for the learners with diverse educational needs.

Videotapes and DVDs

Tapes and DVDs offer famous, simple-to-utilize groups for teaching–learning materials. All learners mostly have an easy approach to a tape or DVD player in the homes, and these are basic at schools also. Tapes and DVDs have a few favorable circumstances for providing the instructional material to the learners from open and distance learning. Notwithstanding simple access to the equipment, the disks and videotapes are very modest. Video is moderately simple to record with the help of video recorder. Pre-recorded demonstrations and presentations by the faculty can be sent to students who can tune in or watch it whenever they feel comfortable. Content from television can be recorded on and replayed from electro-attractive tape. Videotapes can be duplicated and disseminated through the mail. Videotape machine can record and playback, empowering both 'time move' recording and playback from TV programs, and furthermore replay of pre-recorded instructive projects. Videocassettes store images in a linear, analog form.

Audio Files and Compact Disks

Sound documents and CDs are modest, effortlessly copied, and exceptionally adaptable. These can be utilized in lecture method, group discussions, or guidelines for the open and distance learning students. Audio files are particularly helpful in courses that require the subtleties of affectation, for example, foreign dialects, or those that are intended for those who are not able to read. Sound records have an important place in the open and distance modes of learning. Sound documents are likewise very simple to make, can be easily copied and very convenient to utilize. Drawbacks of sound documents incorporate the way that they are not intelligent, and they do not give the visual components that learners with diverse needs want to enhance their abilities and capabilities.

The World Wide Web

World Wide Web (www) is a graphical hypertext-based Internet device that gives access to persons folios, organizations, and associations. There is presently little hesitation to say that the World Wide Web is the best instructive device to have showed up in quite a while. It consolidates and coordinates content, sound and video with communication among members. It can be utilized on a worldwide scale and is stage autonomous. While to a great extent an asynchronous medium, it can likewise be utilized for synchronous occasions. It is not astounding in this way that mentors, instructors, distance education suppliers, and showing organizations at all levels are progressively utilizing the World Wide Web as a medium for course arrangement.

Supportive Inclusive Instruction Through ICT Application

Comprehensive training presents a chance for learners with diverse needs to go to conventional classrooms with their peers of same age. To understand this, we have to accommodate the applicable situations of beating the hindrances to the learning procedure. Especially, these conditions are achieved through the help of ICT framework for inclusive education, incorporation of ICTs into comprehensive training educational programs and preparing of ICT professionals in inclusive education. Advancing ICT foundation for learners special need-based education is important with a specific end goal to accommodate the fitting states of educating and learning in the inclusive setting. The circumstances in each kind of inclusive setup zone cannot be effectively made without the application of suitable ICT apparatuses. Assistive devices must be utilized to enable learners with special educational needs to take an interest in the educational procedure in light of extraordinary approaches and devices.

For few learners, a mechanical arrangement will be the best way to guarantee that they can make their requirements, assessments, and perspectives known. For them, access to ICT-based arrangements is a lifesaver to the inclusion model. ICT assistance in inclusion is imperative since it covers issues that apply to a range of prospective educational needs of these learners. The key manners by which ICTs can support educational openings for individuals with diverse educational needs are as per the following:

- By identifying the initial level of self-improvement in terms of various skills or in other words the beginning stage of learning skills and attitudes;
- By helping in self-improvement by molding new abilities or refreshing existing ones;
- By refining the access to data;
- By overpowering topographical or social segregation by means of correspondence provision and systems;
- Enhancing the picture/view of a territory by enlightening inspiration and attentiveness with respect to the ICT aids in diverse educational needs.

It is additionally imperative to perceive that with ICTs alone we cannot take care of all issues. The second step requires the eagerness of instructors to create imaginative showing strategies or to change and embrace the current ways to deal with suitable new ideas of uncommon needs training and present-day innovations. On the off-chance that a student cannot deal with a specific movement (because of physical or tangible hindrances), elective exercises must be outlined or adjusted, so he/she gets an opportunity to get the required data and exhibit the outcomes. To execute this goal, ICTs must be completely coordinated in SNE educational program. Educational modules change is not about its rearrangements for a few understudies or settling for what is most convenient option. The adjusted educational modules must save the abilities or information required for a specific course and appropriates learning and preparing assets in a more innovative manner and on a more equivalent premise.

In the new thousand years, online conveyance has turned into the most pervasive method for introducing the up and coming data to understudies in the speediest, most adaptable, and inventive ways that could be available. Instructive courses can use an assortment of innovations to encourage learning and connection between members: non-concurrent and synchronous correspondence and joint effort devices (email, announcement sheets, whiteboards, talk rooms, videoconferencing, and remotely coordinating), intuitive components (recreations, immersive situations, and amusements), different testing and assessment techniques (self-appraisal, various decision testing, and so on). Instructive substance can be exhibited in different media: message on a site, sight and sound, for example, advanced sound, computerized video, energized pictures, and virtual reality conditions. This substance can be made in an assortment of ways, using an assortment of writing instruments. Therefore, ICTs change instructive flow by giving option, definitive wellsprings of data, which expects instructors to end up facilitators and, at times, go-betweens between particular data sources and a student. In the meantime, ICTs can break educator's segregation, furnishing them with prospects to convey past the customary school administration pecking order.

It is additionally critical to perceive that with ICTs alone we cannot take care of all the issues. The other action requires the readiness of instructors to create inventive techniques or to change and embrace the current ways to deal with oblige new ideas of extraordinary needs training and present-day innovations. In the event that a student cannot deal with a specific action (because of physical or tactile obstructions), another technique must be planned or adjusted, so he/she gets an opportunity to get the required data and exhibit the outcomes by the maximum realization of capabilities of diverse learners. To actualize this aim, information and communication technologies must be completely incorporated in educational modules for the education of persons with disabilities. Educational modules alteration is not about its rearrangements for a few understudies or settling for what is most convenient option. The changed educational programs must protect the aptitudes or learning required for a specific course and conveys information and preparing assets in a more imaginative manner and on a more equivalent premise.

In this modern age of technological advancement, online delivery has turned into the most common method for exhibiting the latest data to understudies in the speedy, most adaptable, and creative ways that are available. Instructive courses can use a range of technological advancements to encourage learning and cooperation between members: email, whiteboards, bulletin boards, teleconferencing, chat rooms, and videoconferencing, collaborative components including conducive environment, mockups, and various gaming techniques, different testing and assessment techniques like self-evaluation, MCQs.

Instructive subject matter can be introduced in different modes: message on a site, mixed media, for example, computerized sound, advanced video, vibrant pictures, and simulated reality situations. This type of content can be made available through various ways, using an assortment of writing instruments. Therefore,

ICTs change instructive flow by giving option, definitive bases of data, which expects educators to wind up facilitators and, at times, delegates between particular data sources and a student. In the meantime, ICTs can break educator's inaccessibility, giving them prospects to impart past the traditional school administration pecking order.

Benefits of Information and Communication Technology-Based Distance Education for Learners with Diverse Educational Needs

ICT-based learning situations for students with diverse needs with incapacities have turned into an essential need, as new innovation with its progressive openness highlights and intelligent attributes are equipped for making up for the absence of common capacities, hence adding to proper learning situations to be made for these types of students. Though, the ICT actualized is no panacea to all inconveniences of a specialized curriculum. Through significantly enhancing the admittance to information and supportive devices, they can turn into an intense key—instructive and correspondence implies—which, thusly, would lay the reason for real advance in self-improvement permitting the interest of individuals with different needs in group life. ICT-based open and distance learning has specific focus points for differently abled learners with various significant needs as:

- **It removes hindrances of place**—Physical classrooms end up unnecessarily in the conventional sense, and learners can attend classes from their selected position. This might be viewed as verifiable preferred standpoint, especially for 'homebound' differently abled learners.
- **It evacuates time obstacles**—One part of learning style inclination is obliging, as learners seek after learning with a more adaptable calendar; non-concurrent exchange of ideas with the help of chat room empowers them to join that class at individually suitable intervals.
- **It hinders reliance on a recommended data source** (for the most part reading material)—Assets might be taken from numerous areas, in changing configurations, with the potential preferred standpoint of getting to additional current and important data.
- **It reduces the help**, for instance, that of library and other staff.
- **It expands the chance of dynamic commitment in the learning procedure**—This can happen through simplicity of acquiring data, more prominent decision of accessible materials and commitment to brain storming in this virtual reality.
- **It affords individuals with a scope of frailties a simpler access to learning assets**—For example, learners having low vision, hearing impaired, speech disorders, learning disabilities, and orthopedically handicapped have the chance to speak with their associates utilizing both better outlined standard technological advancements accessible to normal average learners and the suitable

assistive devices meeting their specific needs. Indeed, even the individuals who want to interact with others in the natural condition at home may discover electronic access a useful option.

Along these lines, ICT-based open and distance learning infers an awesome potential for individuals with assorted instructive needs, as it conquers customary hindrances while moving long distances and gets information in an equivalent way, thinking about the necessities of diverse individuals. These various tools of ICT are playing an important role in productive and relevant open and distance learning for inclusive education in this developing world. This type of delivery of technology-assisted open and distance learning continues to grow and evolve. The success and rapid growth of distance education as a viable alternative have been, to a great extent, due to development and utilization of information technology. The development in the field of information technology has not only made the learning and the delivery system increasingly learner-centered but has also directly influenced the way the students and the teacher interact. ICT has not only promoted individualized—learning and collaborative—learning among learners but also ushered in a silent revolution in educational planning, management, and administration. It is, therefore, natural that when one thinks of flexible and open distance education one has to think in terms of ICT-enabled education.

References

Alavi, M., Yoo, Y., & Vogel, D. R. (1997). Using information technology to add value to management education. *Academy of Management Journal, 40*(5), 1310–1333.

Babbitt, B. C. (2003). Features of effective graduate degree training in assistive technology at a distance. In *Proceedings of the 18th Annual International Conference Technology and Persons with Disabilities*. Los Angeles, Online: http://www.csun.edu/cod/conf/2003/proceedings/142.htm.

Barden, R. A. (1996). The case for linear instructional design and development: a commentary on models, challenges and myths. *Educational Technology, 2,* 5–23.

Christina, S. (2001). *The use of information technology for the management of education in Singapore*. London, United Kingdom: Commonwealth Secretariat.

Erickson, T., & Kellogg, W. A. (2000). Social translucence: An approach to designing systems that support social processes. *ACM Transactions on Computer-Human Interaction, 7*(1), 59–83.

Foley, A. R. (2003). Distance, disability, and the commodification of education: web accessibility and the construction of knowledge. *Current Issues in Comparative Education.* (6), 1. http://www.tc.columbia.edu/cice/articles/af161.pdf.

Garrison, D. R. (1985). Three generations of technological innovations in open and distance learning. *Open and Distance Learning, 6*(2), 235–241.

Haddad, W., & Drexler, A. A. (2002). *Technologies for education: Potentials, parameters, and prospect*. AED, Paris UNESCO: Washington D.C.

Johansen, R., Martin, A., Mittman, R., & Saffo, P. (1991). *Leading business teams: How teams can use technology and group process tools to enhance performance*. Reading, MA: Addison-Wesley Publishing Company.

Kim-Rupnow, W. S., Dowrick, P. W., & Burke, L. S. (2001). Implications for improving access and outcomes for individuals with disabilities in post-secondary open and distance learning. *The American Journal of Open and Distance learning., 15*(1), 25–40.
Millbank, G. (1994). *Writing multimedia training with integrated simulation.* Paper presented at the Writers' Retreat on Interactive Technology and Equipment. Vancouver, BC: The University of British Columbia Continuing Studies. http://www.nwlink.com/~donclark/hrd/elearning/proscons.html.
Moore, M. G., & Kearsley, G. (1996). *Distance education: A systematic approach.* Belmont: CA, Wadsworth.
Navarro, P., & Shoemaker, J. (2000). Performance and perceptions of distance learners in cyberspace. *The American Journal of Open and Distance learning, 14*(2), 15–35.
Nipper, S. (1989). *Third generation distance learning and computer conferencing.* In Mason, R., & Kaye, A. (Eds.). *Mindweave: Communications, computer, and distance education* (63–73). Oxford: Pergamon Press.
OFSTED. (2000). *Evaluating educational inclusion: Guidance for inspectors and schools.* London: TheOfficeforStandardsinEducation. http://www.ofsted.gov.uk/publications/index.cfm?fuseaction=pubs.displayfile&id=459&type=pdf.
Pelton, J. N. (1991). Technology and education: Friend or foe? *Research in Distance Education, 3* (2), 2–9.
Sankaran, S., & Bui, T. (2001). Impact of learning strategies and motivation on performance: A study in web based instruction. *Journal of Instructional Psychology, 28*(3), 191.
Schutte, J.G. (1996). *Virtual teaching in higher education: The new intellectual superhighway or just another traffic jam?* http://www.csun.edu/sociology/virexp.htm.
Sherry, L. (1996). Issues in distance learning. *International Journal of Educational Telecommunications, 1*(4), 337–365.
Taylor, J. C. (1992). Distance education and technology in Australia: A conceptual framework. *International Council of Distance Education Bulletin, 28,* 22–30.
Taylor, J. C. (1995). Distance education technologies: The fourth generation. *Australian Journal Educational technology, 11*(2), 1–7.
Victoria, L. Tino. (2002). *ICT in education.* Kuala- Lumpur: UNDP-ADIP.

Helping the Distance Education Learners in Getting Effective and Efficient Delivery of Learner Support Services in Developing Countries Through Use of Technology

Rajendra Vinayak Vadnere

Education as a Developmental Need of Developing Nations

Concept of 'Developing Nations' in the Backdrop of an Ideal 'World Government'

An ideal situation for the planet earth could be that in which all territories are governed by a single political entity with all humanity as its citizen with equal right of social, political, and spiritual nature. This concept of 'world government' has been espoused by a number of thinkers, politicians, philosophers, and thought leaders. Such a world government can come to existence by violent means of military domination or through peaceful means of reconciliation.

Examples of such advocacy of world government may be found in Immanuel Kant (World Government 2017 'Immanuel Kant' para #1).

Immanuel Kant published an essay in 1795, on finding everlasting peace through what he called a philosophical sketch. Through this publication, he proposed three fundamental necessary conditions for structuring interactions among societies and nations so that any wars in present as well as in future could be completely done away with. This, he thought, would help in founding an age of perpetual harmony all across the globe. For this, he prescribed two steps in his proposed peace plan.

Accordingly, the first step would be in the form of 'preliminary articles' which would have to be taken immediately with fastest possible speed through deliberate steps. These *preliminary articles* should ensure that:

R. V. Vadnere (✉)
School of Continuing Education, Yashwantrao Chavan Maharashtra Open University, Nashik 422222, India
e-mail: dir_cnt@ycmou.digitaluniversity.ac

© Springer Nature Singapore Pte Ltd. 2018

Anjana (ed.), *Technology for Efficient Learner Support Services in Distance Education*, https://doi.org/10.1007/978-981-13-2300-3_3

- States do not enter into any secrete peace process which incorporate in it any seeds for a future war. Such treaties would not be accepted as valid by international communities.
- States (irrespective of their size in terms of population or area) are not be subjected to a dominion status to another state as a consequence of donation, inheritance, exchange, or purchase.
- States abolish all their standing armies in a timely manner.
- States do not indulge in such practices as hiring of assassins or poisoners, incitement of treason or breach of capitulation in the opposing states during wars as these steps would make the subsequent peace impossible.
- States do not interfere with the constitution or governance of other states.
- States do not indulge in practice of contracting national debts to other state with a view to cause external friction among states.

Once these have been established, the second step may be taken up. As a second step, he suggested three definitive articles to be institutionalized.

1. Each and every one of the states should have a republican constitution as principle of their civil laws.
2. The constitutions of such states should be based on a principle of union of free constituent states.
3. The conditions of universal hospitality would form the basis for the law of 'World Citizenship.'

These conditions should ensure not only stopping of enmity but also building lasting peace among states.

These principles had been loosely used as guiding principles when League of Nations (LoN) was established after the First World War (World Government 2017 'League of Nation' para #1).

The LoN was formally established as an intergovernmental organization subsequent to the Treaty of Versailles in 1919–1920. At its peak (September 28, 1934, to Feb 23, 1935), the membership stood at 58 states. The objectives of the LoN included upholding what was called 'Rights of Man' (including ladies, soldiers, and people other than white,) as well as averting wars by means of collective securities; disarmament; resolution of conflicts among nations using diplomacy and negotiations; and improving quality of life of all persons on the planet.

However, the LoN lacked many elements which were required to maintain lasting peace. The league had appointed 'Great Powers' the tasks of implementing its resolutions or enforcing economic embargoes against an earring state. This was because it did not have its own army. The Great Powers were reluctant to provide armies to the league when required, and thus the LoN was unable to prevent the Second World War. As Hitler wanted to take over the power of Europe, he made Germany withdraw from LoN. The other nations of the Axis Power soon followed him, and the league collapsed having failed in its primary objectives.

The League was made up of the three organs called the General Assembly, the Council, and the Secretariat. There were a number of constituent organs under these. The representatives of the states used to discuss the matters in the Assembly. Each of the member states was allowed three delegates and one vote in the Assembly.

After the Second World War, the United Nations (UN) was established. The UN is very close to the concept of world government. However, its role is more of advisory in nature and not so much of executive, military, or judicial type.

Destruction unparalleled in the history of humankind was witnesses during the Second World War (1939–1945) with more than 60 million dead. Most of these were non-fighting citizens. The war also witnessed weapons of mass destructions being applied in scales unprecedented in the history. The heinous acts committed during the war of such magnitude that they were considered to be the act of crimes against humanity itself. This caused a great shock in the minds of sensitive thought leaders who called for a solution to permanent elimination of deadly international conflicts. At such a juncture, the UN was founded in 1945. It adopted 'Universal Declaration of Human Rights' immediately in 1948. The thought leaders like Albert Einstein, M. K. Gandhi, Bertrand Russel, and Winston Churchill voiced their concern and called upon governments to ensure that UN does not remain a forum for discussion and coordination but gradually becomes an effective and efficient federal world government.

The main role of the UN is to develop international law, means to ensure global safety, economies of the states, ensure human right, social progress, and ultimately global harmony where wars would be impossible. The major strength of UN is in its repetitiveness: Of 196 nations on earth, 193 are the members of UN. Almost all the nations are in UN. The UN meets regularly to resolve major problems. There are six official languages recognized by UN for its business: Arabic, Chinese, French, English, Russian, and Spanish. The finance to UN comes from some of the wealthiest countries. The flag of UN shows the map of the earth with all the populated continents (World Government 2017 'United Nation' para #1).

In the absence of such an ideal world government, with jurisdiction extended over the entire planet which holds the 'right of man' (including women and transgender) as supreme principle, we have differential systems of governances and inequalities, wars, and unfair trade practices among the states and nations. Some of the nations are socially, technically, and militarily more powerful than others. The idea of developing and developed nations and various ways to balance the divide are the subject matter of various debates at the global level.

Developing Nations

A developing nation or country is a nation or a sovereign state which has a comparatively less developed 'industrial base' and a low 'Human Development Index (HDI)' relative to other countries (O'Sullivan et al. 2003). It is debatable as to which countries fit into these two categories as also about what really should be the criteria for quantifying 'development' (United Nations 2017a, b). However, the per capita GDP is often taken as a measure of 'quality of life.' It may be noted that the less general term 'less developed country' may cause some confusion as to mean the specific least developed country. The term 'developing' connotes that the country is not 'sufficiently developed' and does not necessarily mean that it has the 'tendency' of movement toward 'development.' Thus, a country in which the per capita GDP is showing retardation is also called a 'developing' country. Since the late 1990s, developing countries tended to demonstrate higher growth rates than the developed ones (Dr Gilbert Ahmar, Korotayev and Zinkina 2014).

The use of terms 'developing' and 'developed' countries has been objected to by various countries on various grounds. One such point of objection is that it connotes inferiority or backwardness on part of a country labeled as 'developing country' or 'undeveloped country' in comparison with another labeled as 'developed country.' This is not acceptable to many countries. Second dimension of disagreement shown by many critics is on criteria of industrialization or that of material development being given undue weight. Some countries like Bhutan and Cuba observe that there is traditional Western model of economic development taken as paradigm of development which may not be correct for many other contexts (Karma Ura 2017). Alternative measures of 'development' like that of a parameter called 'Gross National Happiness' have been suggested. There are some countries which are on the border between 'developed' and 'developing.' These are often termed as newly industrialized countries (Paweł Bożyk 2006; Waugh 2000; Mankiw 2007) or LMICs which is abbreviation for "Low and Middle Income Countries".

Thinkers like Walt Whitman Rostow Walt (Rostow 1971) put it this way that developing nations are in transition from conventional ways of life to the modern (industrial) lifestyle which is a hallmark of the Industrial Revolution in the eighteenth and nineteenth centuries.

The World Bank has taken a decision, which is implemented in the 2016 edition of the World Development Indicator published by it, according to which it does not differentiate between 'developed' and 'developing' nations (World Bank 2016).

A nation which may not be called as a 'developed' country is alternatively called as 'less economically developed nation' or 'less developed nation' and in the exceptional cases 'least developed nation' or 'least economically developed nation.'

If we see it from such perspective, the criteria for calling a nation 'non-developed' nation may be derived by using the opposite of the criteria for calling a country 'developed' one. Thus, a nation which cannot be termed as a developed one would have:

- Citizen has shorter life reflected in lower life expectancy.
- Citizen has academically inferior status reflected in low literacy rate and inferior quality of education.
- Citizens have lesser financial resources as reflected in less money (income).
- Women are subject to more pregnancy experiences as reflected in higher fertility rate and pregnancy.

A measure of the 'developmental stage of a nation' has thus been developed and called Human Development Index (HDI) ('Human Development Index' (n.d.).). This index is a single number which is dependent on other indicators like life expectancy, per capita income, education, and literacy. This index is applied in ranking nations into four types of human development. Thus, nations with higher scores of HDI are those for whom the citizens have higher life spans, higher academic accomplishments and have financially sound status. Amartya Sen, eminent Indian economist, and Mahbub Al Haq, another economist of great eminence from Pakistan, played pivotal role in the development of theoretical background which was adopted by UNDP in devising HDI (UNDP 2010).

A country may score very high on the basis of a very small part of population which is extremely well placed in terms of life expectancy, education, and income. Such country where high score coexists with extremely biased distribution of wealth, education, and health parameters should not be seen as an ideal society. This leads to adjustments against 'inequality.' The Human Development Report published in 2010 incorporated these aspects when it formulated a parameter called 'Inequality-adjusted Human Development Index' (IHDI). Even though the plain HDI is still a relevant statistic, experts now believe that the IHDI denotes a *corrected* level of development of the citizenry (after adjusting for inequality). Alternatively, the HDI can be seen as an indicator of 'potential' human development as it is the maximum IHDI that could be achieved if there were no inequality.

The HDI has in its foundation the 'human development approach,' proposed by Mahbub Ul Haq, and is further reinforced with the work of Amatrya Sen in the area of human capabilities. It asks philosophical questions terms of whether members of a society are able to 'do' pleasing things in their life at the same time as they are reaping the benefits of development. These theories focus on 'beings' (characterizing the status of the members of society) and 'doing' (indicating the actions the members engage into). In a society with desirable human development having been achieved, the members have the status of being well-fed, sheltered, healthy, and they carry such activities as practicing their occupations, voting their governments, participating in community experiences. The theory further recognizes the importance of freedom of choice. In a country where citizen chooses to be hungry (for health or religious reasons) cannot be compared with another where citizens are forced to be hungry due to unavailability of food (UNDP 2017). The Fig. 1 shows the world map with territories of the various countries color coded according to the values of their HDI ranking.

In this connection, we may invoke former Secretary General of the United Nations Kofi Annan. He described a developed nation as a nation that permits all its people to enjoy a liberal and healthy life in a secure surrounding. It may, however, be noted that United Nations Statistics Division does not distinguish between developing or developed nations. 'There is no established convention for the designation of "developed" and "developing" countries or areas in the United Nations system' (United Nations 2017a, b).

It further states that the designations 'developed' and 'developing' are used for statistical convenience and as such do not necessarily denote a judgment about the status reached by a particular nation or territory in the process of development (United Nations 2017a, b).

The UN also notes that it is a common practice to treat nations like Japan, Canada, the USA, Australia, and New Zealand and nations in the Western Europe as 'developed' nations or regions. Another source of information comes from international trade statistics. According to it, Israel is considered to be a 'developed' nation and the Southern African Customs Union is considered as a 'developed region' The nations which came into being due to disintegration of erstwhile Yugoslavia are commonly labeled as 'developing nations,' and countries of Central Europe and of the Commonwealth of Independent States in Europe are not considered under either 'developing' or 'developed' (United Nations 2017a, b).

Let us now see how International Monetary Fund (IMF) classifies the countries. The situation before April 2004 was like this: Nations of Central and Eastern Europe (together with central European countries that still belong to the 'Eastern Europe Group' in the UN organs) and the countries which resulted due to disintegration of erstwhile Soviet Union (USSR) in the central Asia (like Kazakhstan, Turkmenistan, Uzbekistan, Tajikistan, and Kyrgyzstan) and Mongolia were considered as 'nations in transition,' thus avoiding being labeled either as "developing' or 'developed' regions. This is despite the fact that they are otherwise generally regarded (as per various international reports) as 'developing' nations or regions.

The IMF utilizes a system of classification, which is flexible. It takes into account (1) per capita income level as a measure of richness of citizens, (2) diversification of export as a measure of soundness of nation's economy, and (3) how much does the nation participate in international trade. This ensures that oil-exporting regions which have high per capita GDP would not be labeled as the 'advanced' because around 70% of its exports are oil and thus fail the criteria of diversification (International Monetary Fund 2011).

Let us now see how the World Bank considers this aspect. It categorizes nations into four income groups (World Bank 2016). These are set each year on July 1. Economies were sorted according to 2016 GNI (Gross National Income) per capita with the following ranges of income:

- Low-income nations were those which had GNI per capita of US$1,025 or less.
- Lower middle nations were those which had per capita GNI in the range US $1,026 to US$4,035.
- Upper middle-income nations were those which had per capita GNI in the range of US$4,036 to US$12,236.
- High-income nations are those which have per capita GNI more than US $12,237.

After 2016, the World Bank has given away practice of categorizing countries into categories of 'developing' and 'developed' criteria as it treats such terminology and concepts as being outdated.

The World Bank puts the following indicators in the form of 17 Sustainable Development Goals (SDGs) (World Bank 2016).

SDG 1	Elimination of poverty.
SDG 2	Eradication of hunger (people may be hungry by choice but not due to compulsion).
SDG 3	Citizens are physically, mentally, emotionally, and spiritually healthy and maintain general wellness.
SDG 4	Proliferation and ubiquity of high-quality education.
SDG 5	Citizens are treated fairly irrespective of their gender.
SDG 6	Proliferation and easy availability of clean water and sanitation.
SDG 7	Clean energy is available at affordable price and abundantly.
SDG 8	Citizens are productively employed and contribute to economic growth.
SDG 9	Nations have ample infrastructure to pump its industry and trade, and they use innovative techniques to overcome their challenges.
SDG 10	Reduction in inequality among its members.
SDG 11	Cities and communities progress in a sustainable manner.
SDG 12	Nations harness the natural resources and produce value in the process in a responsible manner.
SDG 13	Nations take actions on maintaining climate and ecology.
SDG 14	Life below water is sustained at a healthy level.
SDG 15	Life on land survives to minimize number of endangered species.
SDG 16	There is an overall ambience of peace; justice is done and seen to be done, and strong institutions flourish to ensure continuity of goodness.
SDG 17	Nations work for partnership for global development

In addition to the present status of achievement, nations may be categorized in terms of how significantly a SDG indicator has improved during a pre-decided period of time (UNCTAD 2012). It may be represented in terms of absolute numbers or country rankings.

Needs of Developing Nations

In order to make 'progress' to achieve the Sustainable Development Goals (SDGs) as advocated by the World Bank, the developing nations face a number of challenges, which may be summarized under various heads as given below:

Challenges associated with health hazards in developing countries

- Problems of getting safe water to citizens,
- Problems of avoiding indoor smoke,
- Challenges regarding tropical and infectious diseases,
- How to tackle air pollution,
- Unpredictability due to climate change,

- How to minimize road traffic accidents,
- Challenges of unintentional poisoning (World Health Organization 2016).

Trends and issues in forthcoming periods

- How to manage increasing population (in some poor countries).
- Rapid development may be leading to environmental and health disasters.
- Development without meticulous planning may lead to traffic fatalities and air pollution.
- Rapid urbanization may lead to unmanageable spread of communicable diseases.
- Rise in neo-rich may lead a lifestyle of physical inactivity leading to obesity and health issues.
- Countries are indulging into blind industrialization and intensified agricultural production without consideration to the environmental issues like air, water, and soil pollution.
- Unplanned industrialization may lead to unsustainable use of energy resources.
- Countries may take dangerously bold steps to enrich their economy through industrial growth and implement techniques for increasing agricultural production, which may endanger the delicate ecosystem and disturb the biodiversity, thereby creating climate changes and health hazards.
- In some countries, the dependence on natural resources for basic livelihood may lead to exploitation of the nature and deplete the resources beyond repairs.
- High degree of industrialization may lead to decrease in access to clean water.

Factors stimulating growth

- Nations and societies which recognize the citizens as their asset, including their habits, knowledge, social and personal attributes (Human Capital (Schultz 1961)) grow much better than those which do not.
- Open and fair trade policies stimulate growth in comparison with restrictive and unfair trade policies (Harrison 1996).
- Nations which have citizens who invest and have good sense of use of their economic resources tend to have a positive effect on growth (Edwards 1991).
- Societies where the strata of its members have minimal knowledge gap (Edwards 1991) tend to have a positive outcome in terms of growth.

Growth may be hindered due to factors like

- Diseases like tuberculosis, malaria, AIDS lead to decreased productivity in labor force, and nation's resources get diverted to management and control of epidemic, thereby impairing attention to trade and industry (Russel 2004).

- The developmental potential of more than 200 million children in the 'developing' countries is not achieved due to malnutrition or underdevelopment of the body and brain (Grantham-McGregor and Sally 2007).
- Knowledge gap (Edwards 1991) (which may be due to unequal distribution of 'knowledge' in various strata of the society) among the sections of society leads to impairment of process of growth.
- Political instability (Edwards 1991) leads to fear of investment in the foreign investors, and the uncertainty leads to policy paralysis affecting growth decisively.
- Political corruption (Williams 2007) leads to a servile and inert citizenry which further deteriorates the growth of the nation.
- Child marriage tends to have negative impact on growth of countries.

Role of Education in Addressing the Challenges Faced by the Developing Nations

It may be easily seen from the list of the challenges faced by the developing nations that institutionalization of quality education system would form a backbone of solutions to sort out most of the challenges faced by the developing nations.

We listed in under the heading 'health risks,' the factors like non-availability of safe water; proliferation of fume and smoke inside the households, management of epidemics of infectious diseases; pollution of air, soil, and water; changes in climate; problems of traffic mishaps on road and issues of curbing food poisoning which may happen unintentionally due to ignorance. A quality education system would help develop the developing nation a qualified workforce in medicine and management of hygiene. A course which may be common to all the streams of knowledge and disciplines on environmental awareness may help the citizens to understand the importance of water pollution, indoor smoke, infectious diseases, air and soil pollution, ecological changes, and accidental poisoning. The general courses on value education would help people to understand important precautions to undertake in order to avoid road accidents.

The general courses also help spread awareness to curb various superstitions, irrelevant traditions and practices which lead to growth of population in poor countries. For example, in many societies it is believed that children are gifts from gods which must not be refused. Introduction to advancements of science makes the citizens to be aware of scientific understanding of process of conception, birth control, and family planning.

Similarly, the awareness of importance of clean water may help the communities to undertake conservation activities leading to optimum utilization of the drinkable water.

The developing nations also face challenges covered under the 'factors stimulating growth' heading in the preceding section. The importance of 'human capital' needs to be properly appreciated by the representatives of the people and people involved in public planning. Education can play an important role in assuring such appreciation. Human capital is a term popularized by Gary Becker, an economist from the University of Chicago, and Jacob Mincer that refers to the stock of knowledge, habits, social and personality attributes, including creativity, embodied in the ability to perform labor so as to produce economic value (Human Capital 2017). Similar problems and issues emerge in study and practice of macroeconomics and in business administration.

The implementation of appropriate educational intervention also helps in bridging the 'knowledge gap.' The hypothesis of 'knowledge gap' states that knowledge is a type or form of wealth. Hence, similar to other types of wealth, knowledge is many times distributed across the social strata in a differential manner. The theory further notes that as a consequence of availability of mass media technologies the percolation of information into a social system has increased. The inequality in the purchasing power of the various socioeconomic strata of the society leads to situation where the section of society with higher socioeconomic status tends to access and consume this information more effectively and efficiently in comparison with their lower status counterparts. Thus, the gulf or gap in knowledge as an asset between these sections has a tendency of widening rather than narrowing. The knowledge gap hypothesis was first proposed in 1970 by three University of Minnesota researchers (Phillip J. Tichenor, who was then Associate Professor of Journalism and Mass Communication along with George A. Donohue, Professor of Sociology, and Clarice N. Olien, Instructor).

Importance of Distance Education for Developing Nations

Distance Education Defined

Distance education (DE) can be defined as

> Institution-based, formal education where the learning group is separated, and where interactive telecommunications systems are used to connect learners, resources, and instructors (AECT 2017).

This definition envisages four main ingredients, namely institution-based, separation of teacher and pupil in space and time, interactive telecommunications, and sharing of learning experiences.

First ingredient of distance education requires it to be institutionally based. This factor is required in order to make a distinction between distance education and self-study. Even though the term 'institution' may generally mean the educational institutions like school or university, we are having non-traditional institutions like business organizations, companies corporations offering distance education programs. There is a trend of favorable outlook for distance education programs and institutions which offer credible, good-quality education rather than acting as diploma-churning machines.

The second ingredient of the definition of distance education is the requirement of a distance or separation of the teacher and the pupil in space and/or time. Generally, separation is considered in geographic terms (physical distance): That is, teacher and learner are in different locations (as against that in a classroom).

There is a provision of separation of teachers and students in time also in the definition of distance education. For example, the teacher teaching through a recorded video means that teacher and pupil are engaged in learning at different instances. 'Asynchronous mode of distance education' is a term coined to represent situation where the instructions offered to the learners are accessed by the learners at the time of their convenience, with the time of generation of instruction not coinciding with that of access or retrieval of instruction. The concept of asymmetry in the intellectual level of the teacher and the taught is also important. The teacher is expected to have the expertise, cognitive skills, and a deeper level of understanding of the domain knowledge in comparison with the learners. With this in mind, the minimization of 'intellectual distance or gap' becomes one of the goals of the distance education system.

The third component in the definition is the application of interactive telecommunications. Here, the interaction can be synchronous or asynchronous. That is, the interaction may happen instantly (the time gap between information of instruction or feedback from the sender and reception of information by receiver is negligible) or at a significant time gap.

Interaction plays a very important role in distance education. However, care should be taken that it does not affect the delivery of content. It is important that the students should interact among themselves and exchange ideas, thoughts, doubts, difficulties, suggestions, solutions, and visions with their peers. Such exchange may also take place between pupil and instructional material like e-resources. The learners should also be able to interact with their teacher. Even though ability to interaction may not be the primary characteristic of instruction, it should be available, ubiquitous, and relevant.

Even though the words 'telecommunications systems' are generally used in the context of electronic media, such as the Internet, telephone, and television, non-electronic media may also serve the purpose. We may define 'telecommunications' as 'communicating at a distance.' Then, the term 'telecommunication' will also include communication using the post (as correspondence study and other non-electronic methods of communication of older era used to practice). Of course, the electronic telecommunications systems are improving and become more cost-effective, commonplace, and pervasive; they will be the principal modes of communication for future distance education systems. The older methods, however, may continue to exist for various reasons.

The final concept is that of sharing or connecting learners, resources, and instructors. Thus, the learners share their learning experiences with the world including the fellow learners, teachers, and society at large. Similarly, the teacher not only may share his instructions with learners but also may assign such tasks which need learners to complete, construct, and cooperate with system or society. Resources should undergo instructional design processes, so that they are well organized and facilitate learning experiences which should enhance learning and should include such tools in them which can be observed (like video), felt (like samples of texture of fabric), heard (like audio), or may be completed (e.g., an assignment).

Thus, these four components define 'distance education.' If any one or more of such components are missing, what you will have is not the same (though it may be similar to DE) as distance education. When we talk about distance education, we are also talking about distance learning and distance teaching. Distance teaching incorporates planning, designing, developing, managing, and evaluation of systematic learning plans leading to pupil achieving specific learning objectives (Seels and Richey 1994). Distance learning means to use these resources in the learning experiences to accomplish learning. It may be noted that by virtue of the very definition of distance education, distance learning is not possible if distance teaching does not take place.

We have presented an analysis of a definition and explain what is required for an education system to be termed as 'distance education' system. However, it may be noted that this definition is not acceptable to all and there are many more interpretations of what constitutes distance education and accordingly a large number of 'definitions' have been offered based on different perspectives and paradigms. To give an example, Rudolf Manfred Delling (1987) defined DE as a planned and systematic activity comprising of the choice, instructional preparation including presenting the instructional media and supervision and support of a learner's learning experience. We can say that the instruction ensures that the physical and psychological gap is bridged. This is expected to happen through use of appropriate instructional and communication media.

Another attempt to define DE goes to Perraton (1988) who pointed out that DE is a process of education where somebody who is separated in physical space and time does the major job of teaching. This description is close to one of the requirements of the definition of DE discussed (from AECT) in detail by us earlier in the beginning of this section.

For the Office of Educational Research and Improvement, under US Department of Education, DE is the use of ICT devices to enable learners to get instructions which emanates from a distance location and a possibility of interaction with program and instructor directly on periodic basis. Again, this definition is a subset of our earlier AECT definition, incorporating criteria of 'distance' 'use of telecommunication technology' and 'sharing of learning experience' to a certain extent.

Another definition due to Rumble (1989) envisages four components for DE process, namely a teacher, one or more students, a curriculum (which the teacher would teach and learners would try to learn), and a contract (which may be formal or informal) between student and teaching institution (or teacher) which recognizes the roles of teacher and learner. He further mentions that DE is a methodology of instruction in which there is a separation in physical sense between learner and teacher or the teaching institution. The DE methodology may be used as a stand-alone strategy for instruction or may be clubbed with other methods like face-to-face interaction. The teaching contract should incorporate the teaching, assessment, guidance, preparation for examinations which may or may not be conducted by the teaching institution. There should be a two-way communication to achieve these tasks. The learning may be in a group or in isolation from no instructor physically present.

Keegan (1986) combined the following four approaches in order to get an essence of the concept of DE:

1. First, the paradigm of the French government may be considered to identify the concept of DE. They had, through a law enacted in 1971, identified DE as a form of education where the teacher is physically present for only a select type of task or not physically present at all.
2. The second approach due to Börje Holmberg has been selected by Desmond Keegan. In it, distance education encompasses a number of methods of study at various such that continuous and immediate type of supervision by instructors on the learning experiences is not required. There is, nevertheless, provision of a supporting organization for planning, teaching, and guidance.
3. The third paradigm proposed by Otto Peters has been identified by Keegan for inclusion in the definition of DE. It emphasizes the role of technology and says that distance teaching/education (Fernunterricht) is a way of developing knowledge, skills, and attitudes such that this development benefits from the application of principles of 'division of labor' and managerial principles as well as by the widespread use of automation and technology in the form of instructional and learning management software. This leverages in multi-copying of high-quality teaching material (employing principle of economy of scale) making possible teaching of a large number of learners (batch processing) simultaneously at their respective places of residence or work. This paradigm draws parallel with the business industry and recognizes DE as an industrial form of instruction.
4. Keegan further collected work of Michael Moore in an attempt to identify the defining ingredients of DE. In this approach, the related concept of 'distance teaching' is seen as family of instructional technology such that teaching tasks are carried out independently of the learning tasks, in contrast to the traditional method in which 'teaching' and 'learning' take place simultaneously and at the same place and cannot be independent of one another. This independence of 'teaching' and 'learning' in DE requires use of such technologies and methods as communication through print (self-instructional books), electronic (Web-based learning, interactive TV, etc.), and other media.

Keegan (1986) collected and recognized five main elements from these four approaches and used them to arrive at a comprehensive definition of DE. The five major elements are:

1. 'Distance.' It is a quasi-permanent separation of instructor and pupil during the learning activity (this criterion is essential to distinguish DE from traditional mode of learning).
2. 'Institution.' An educational organization is required for designing, planning, and development of educational resources (this criterion is essential to distinguish between DE and DIY Teach Yourself courses).
3. 'Technology.' As the physical presence of the teacher is missing, instruction needs to be carried out using technical media—print, audio, video, or computer.
4. 'Communication.' A two-way communication between teacher and learner and also among the peer enables initialization of a dialog for clarification of difficulties in learning and to generate self-validating feedback (this distinguishes it from other uses of technology in education).
5. The quasi-permanent absence of the learning group throughout the length of the learning process so that people are usually taught as individuals and not in groups. Included is the possibility of occasional meetings for both didactic and socialization purposes.

Garrison and Shale (1987) point out that Keegan's definition is not adoptive enough to account for advancement in technology and does not foresee future developments. For example, the possibility of peer interaction using social media technology may make a sea change in the way DE is delivered which would be in contrast to the element (at serial number 5) recognized by Keegan as a defining attribute. Even though they do not give a definition of DE, they prescribe the following three criteria as essential for characterizing the DE process:

1. Distance education implies that the majority of educational communication between (among) teacher and student(s) occurs non-contiguously.
2. Distance education must involve two-way communication between (among) teacher and student(s) for the purpose of facilitating and supporting the educational process.
3. Distance education uses technology to mediate the necessary two-way communication.

What are central to all the definitions of distance education are the concepts of 'distance' and 'education.' The broadest definition would include these concepts and leave corrections to the 'description' of DE to the practitioners as per the technical advancements. Accordingly, one may talk about different 'generations' of DE: from correspondence courses to satellite-mediated massive online open courses (MOOCs) accounting for the technological evolution witnessed by mankind.

Relevance of Distance Education in Solutions to the Problems of Developing Nations

We have seen in section 'Needs of Developing Nations' how education plays pivotal role in attaining the Sustainable Development Goals and challenges faced by developing nations.

As we saw in the preceding section, distance education has four principal ingredients, namely institution-based, separation of teacher and pupil in space and time, interactive telecommunications, and sharing of learning experiences. Proper integration of these components makes learning through distance education mode not only highly effective and appropriate to the learning situation but also most cost-effective.

The advancements in the technologies particularly that of information and communication technology (ICT) are making unit cost of distance education to go down at a remarkable pace. Thus, the cost of maintaining a student in the distance education mode is becoming more affordable than ever.

The activities in the distance education mode, at most of the universities, include program design and development, enrollment of learners, collection of registration fees, providing learning experiences through classroom-like didactic or through scenario-based learning, administration of assignments for formative evaluation purposes, collection of learner evaluation fees, administration of end examination (summative evaluation), maintain question banks, setting evaluation question papers, maintaining record of students performance, analysis of performance of learners, program evaluation and revision of program design and curricula.

It can be easily seen that the processes for almost all these activities can be re-engineered to make them Web-based or Web-enabled. The use of Internet provides such advantages as communication almost at the speed of light, extremely low cost, ability to reach multiple users simultaneously, redundancy of information (so that if information is deleted by accident at one place, it can be recovered through another source), availability across the planet (and even in the space like International Space Station). With such process re-engineering, the unit cost of teaching the courses to the distant learner becomes highly affordable particularly the resource-starved population of the developing nations.

Such application of modern technology was hindered by the lack of technological backbone in the developing nations. As the satellite-launching expertise of developing nations like India became particularly refined, agencies like Indian Space Research Organization (ISRO) are helping other developing nations in their communication needs. India has evolved as a major space player achieving objectives for its space missions in an extremely cost-effective and time-efficient manner. The developing nations regard India as a dependable agent to harness the benefits from space technology. The scope of international cooperation has become wider and diverse, as ISRO has made tremendous progress in recent time (ISRO 2017a, b).

Prasad (1997) has discussed various other issues about applicability of distance education in developing nations.

He discusses the problems and issues which the developing countries have to encounter about the policy decisions they have to take regarding implementation of distance education. He discusses at length about globalization and neocolonialism.

The trade-off between 'invasion' and 'access' needs to be understood adequately by the policy makers in charge of distance education in developing countries and decided in the best interest of the community. In order to provide access to education to the larger and larger segment of population, the countries have to import technology from the developed countries. This poses the danger of 'invasion' by the corporate world from the developed countries, reminding of the era of colonization by the European counties of the rest of the world from Columbian era (fifteenth century) to twentieth century. This sentiment was echoed by Terry Evans too when he says that globalization makes nations face a dilemma: They access the world but the world invades them (Terry Evans 1995). The unevenness of development results in some countries dominating the scenario of education in the resource-depleted countries.

Another issue of relevance is that solutions to provide access are also driven by market demands, which may or may not be in line with the priorities and needs of the receiving countries but may depend on priorities and needs of the technology donors, who play the deciding role. When we couple this with the dynamics of market forces in the developing countries, we note that the access to the global programs which is supported by the costly technology offered by the technology donors would be restricted only to the affluent segments of society (who can afford the cost) in the developing countries. Thus, the knowledge gap among the sections of society would be widened and not narrowed down. The affluent sections of the society would continue to become richer in financial terms as well as in respect of knowledge, information, and managerial skills. Thus, the economic and educational inequalities within and among the countries become enhanced rather than mitigated.

There are some developed countries which use globalization only as a means for liberal access to the markets of developing countries. The phenomenon of 'big fish swallowing the small fish' may be observed in this context. The unequal competition among the technology providers could result in the survival of the fittest player. This 'fittest player' may not be providing solutions and contents in education which are in the long-term interests of the 'buying' nation but may be only catering to the commercial and existentialist goals of the player. While it is exciting to note the technological advancements leading to development of information superhighways, one should also note the limitations of use of such superhighways. The flow of 'satisfaction of interest' is such that donors of technology get satisfaction of their economic objectives fulfilled, while the receivers of the technology may not have addressed to fulfillment of many of its national priorities. The donor of the educational content and technology from the developed counties sells the readily available software, which the receiver may not need so urgently. On the other hand, the educational content and technology required to address the problems and issues in the developing (receiving) counties may be requiring efforts and resources which the donor (developed) agency may not be willing to spend. Thus, the receiving society ends up feeding the technology provider without meeting its own objectives. Further, the institutions may lose their identities and initiatives.

Prasad concludes that the developing countries must build capacities to resolve their challenges on their own terms and not merely become vehicles of educations to serve someone else's interests. He cites Mahatma Gandhi's dictum that we should let all the windows open and let the wind blow from all directions but keep out feet rooted firmly in the ground. The developing countries should take assistance from all the quarters but keep the vision of development in their own perspective and peculiar circumstances in place.

The developing nations should thus not remain aloof from the technological development but have a systematic plan of developing their capacities. They would then have no need to fear 'invasion' from the foreign technology donors. There is also a need for a developing nation to understand the hidden agenda of the donor developed nation which may derail the very process of developmental needs of the receiving developing nation.

Various Specific Tools Used in Learner Support Services

Let us now discuss various tools used in automation of the distance education processes.

Learning Management System

A Learning Management System (LMS) (Learning Management System 2017) is a software solution which helps us in managing, tracking, reporting, archiving, and delivering the various aspects of the academic programs including training programs (Ellis 2009). These are used to assist the teachers in instruction; taking tests; maintaining records of attendance and academic progress; analyzing the learning curves; identifying issues faced by the learners and/or the class and finding solutions to the challenges; maintaining record of certifications; and similar other activities. LMS is developed keeping in mind the online learning method of delivery. They may, however, support other delivery methods also like blended learning, flipped classrooms. LMSs also keep record of students' profiles and achievements which may be subjected to various methods of analysis. These analyses may be used to identify the various issues and challenges in learning and also find solutions to the various challenges. For example, analyses of the assignments may point out that the learning curve for a student has reached a plateau even though the level of achievement is still not satisfactory. The instructor may go through a one-on-one session with the learner to find issues of academic, motivation, fatigues, or other origins and suggest remedies to overcome the same.

Purpose

An LMS may be an integrated package to help the institution in process of student registration including a payment gateway; online learning administration; assessment and end examination delivery and evaluation and reporting modules (Gilhooly 2001). Some LMSs may also manage progress toward the learning outcomes achieved. The LMSs may be commercially available or custom made by institutions for their internal requirements. The LMSs may be open source (e.g., Moodle, Canvas, ATutor, Chamilo), SAAS/cloud-based (e.g., Google Classroom, DoceboLMS, Cornerstone OnDemand Inc., CallidusCloud, EthosCE, WizIQ), and propriety (e.g., CERTPOINT Systems Inc., Blackboard Learning System, Desire2Learn, EduNxt, Engrade, JoomlaLMS, Kannu, and WizIQ).

The student registration module may incorporate the archiving of student's profile, his or her contact details, a formal contract between the learner and institution including details of course work, evaluation methodology, and responsibilities of institution and learners. This module may be supplemented by a payment receiving mechanism like integration with a payment gateway or Point of Sale (POS) hardware/software. The registration module may also be designed to work as 'alumni management software' for the learners who pass out, maintaining record of the placement service provided by the institution.

The delivery mechanism used by the LMS may include adaptive presentation of the learning units. The software keeps track of units or even part of the unit completed by the user. There are tests embedded in the learning units which serve to break monotony of instructions as well as reinforcing of content learned in addition to be used as evaluating tools. Serious evaluation of the content learned in the unit is, however, presented as 'End Question' at the end of units. Some training modules working on principle of 'programmed learning' require that a learner completes at least 80% of the end questions to around 80% of satisfactory levels to migrate to next unit.

The LMSs usually also keep track of the assignments completed within the stipulated time frame. The LMS does the management of assignments at both the learner's end and the tutor's end. The LMS may depict the progress made by a learner toward the learning objectives. Some LMS may also have performance management systems, which may include performance appraisal by employer. It may also include competency management in which the employer (or user) may set a learning objective to inculcate a specific skill set and chart progress in achieving the stated goals toward development of competencies in that skill set. LMSs may also perform skill gap analysis, indicating the difference between present and desired levels of a skill. They may also include succession planning and multi-rater assessments in the form of 360° reviews.

An alternative set of terms is used to describe various digital aids and techniques for education. Examples include course management system, virtual classrooms, managed learning platforms, computer-based learning environment. However, the term LMS has gained more currency and a widespread use.

Application to Distance Education

As the audio video communication got started being used for distance learning, the concept of 'e-learning' started to develop in the first part of twentieth century ('The History of LMS Software' (n.d.)). Thus in 1909, E.M. Forster authored story 'The Machine Stops' which narrated the benefits of audio communication in delivering lectures for pupil at remote locations (Forster 1909).

The first teaching machines were developed by Sidney L. Pressey in 1920. They offered a number of practical exercises and question formats. Professor M. E. Zerte of the University of Alberta extended this concept into a problem cylinder in 1929 which was able to compare problems and solutions (David (n.d.)a). The focus of research shifted to video communication. The University of Houston decided in 1953 to arrange telecast lectures for their students with 13–15 h of such time in a week. In 1956, a very adaptive teaching system called SAKI was released for the corporate world by Robert McKinnon Wood and Gordon Pask (David (n.d.)b). The University of Illinois experts were inspired by the idea of automating the teaching operations, and they developed a product called Programmed Logic for Automated Operations (PLATO), thereby enabling users to exchange the content irrespective of their locations. The period between 1970 and 1980 saw rapid developments in educational venues as idea of computerizing the courses was being rapidly evolving and first accredited online degree was offered by Western Behavior Science Institute from California.

Distributed Classrooms

The use of satellite communication technology makes it possible to deliver a lecture by an expert which may be viewed by learners sitting in classrooms with video projection facility across a wide territory (or even globally). The learners are able to see the visuals of the teacher along with presentation slides, video clips, simulation, or practical demonstration through video motion capture and listen to the accompanying audio. The 'Learning Management System' allows the learners from classrooms to 'raise hand' if they have a question to ask. The expert teacher can choose any one of the 'classrooms' from among the 'distributed classroom' locations, the learner from the chosen classroom goes live on air, and his visuals and audios get accessible to the expert teacher and the peer classroom learners.

Such arrangements need fairly small bandwidth to the tune of 2 megabits per second (MBPS) for transmission through satellite. The number of Student Interaction Termini (SITs) is limited only by the cost of establishing the hardware setups.

Developing nations like India have been making optimal use of such distributed classroom technology. The ISRO had launched a special satellite called GSAT-3, also known as EDUSAT for educational purposes. This satellite was launched on September 20, 2004, by ISRO and was the first Indian satellite with an exclusive focus on educational services. The main intension of the satellite was to meet the perceived need for interactive distance education program using satellite communication to facilitate distributed classroom (ISRO 2017a, b).

There were five Ku band transponders which provided spot beams, while one Ku band transponder provided national beam and six transponders which operated at extended C band giving national coverage beams. The EDUSAT was decommissioned in September 2010 and was transferred to 'graveyard' orbit.

A typical setup using the satellite (like EDUSAT) for distributed classroom is shown in Fig. 2.

Such 'distributed classroom' or 'virtual classroom' setups are generalized to the concept of 'distributed learning.'

Distributed learning (2017) is a model of teaching and learning in which the teacher, the learners, and the learning resource may be situated at distinct non-centralized locations allowing the teaching and learning to take place independent of space and time. This method may be used in conjunction with the traditional mode of learning (which is also referred to as 'blended learning'), or the entire course may be delivered using distributed classrooms.

Distributed classroom method is a valuable option for various students of all age groups who wish to learn and obtain education. The salient features of this method include the following (2017):

- Provides opportunity of education to deprived section who cannot go to traditional classroom due to various reasons networking.
- Learner can choose his pace of learning.
- Learner may schedule his learning calendar avoiding overlaps with important business or vocational opportunities.

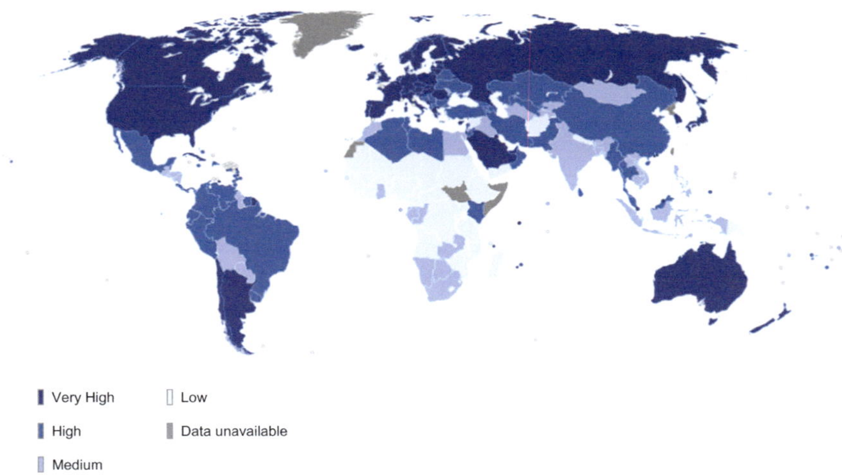

Fig. 1 United Nations Human Development Index (HDI) rankings for 2017 (*Source* Wikipedia, 'Developing Countries,' by BlankMap-World6,_compact.svg: Canuckguy et al., derivative work: Ricardomarins29 (talk), published under CC_BY_SA license)

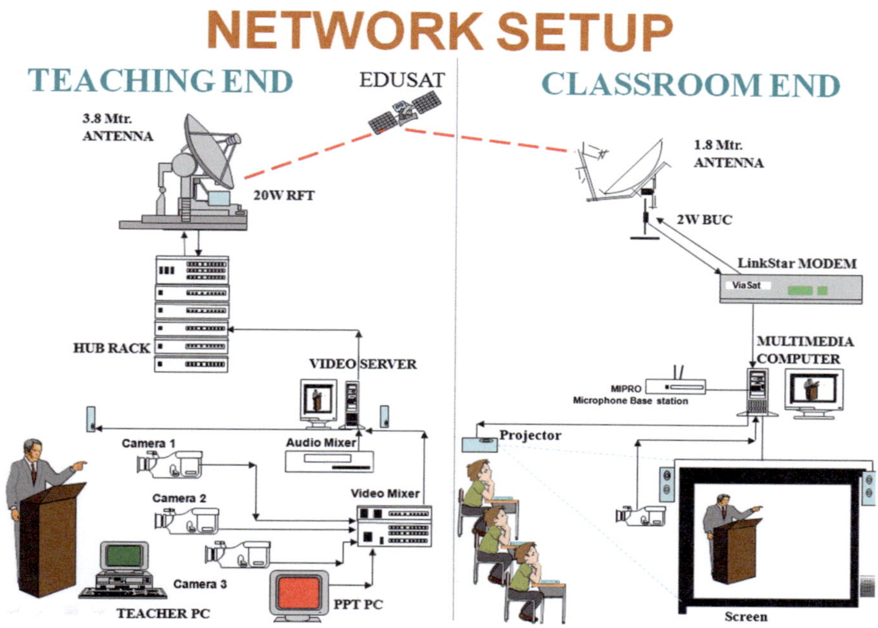

Fig. 2 Distributed classroom setup using satellites (like ISRO EDUSAT) is an example of developing nation's use of ICT

- Money of the learner may be saved as he does not have to sacrifice his business or vocational opportunities to meet learning cycles.
- Learner and teachers do not have to travel great distances to do teaching and learning.
- Since one teacher can deliver instructions to a large number of pupils, the very best of teachers may be selected for the purpose.
- The cost of satellite communication is independent of number of nodes or learning locations; hence, a larger number of learning stations may be used.
- The recording of the lecture is possible (by recording the satellite feed).
- Teaching may be very effective as the pupil may listen to recorded lectures any number of times and at any point of time stamp.
- It allows learning while working.
- It allows immense flexibility in place, place and time of learning.
- As the learning can be scaled to a very large population of pupil, the economy of scale renders this method very cost-effective.
- The method amenable to use of very advanced technology like satellite communication or Internet communication or communication at the smartphone of the learner (the method is not likely to be outdated because of advancements in technology).

- It allows the individual learner to raise his difficulty and concern through use of textual or audio or video mode.
- International networking is possible.

The policy makers of the education systems should therefore consider integrating distributed classroom and distributed learning into their system of education.

Simulation

'Simulation' is emerging as a very important and novel tool for education at various contexts.

Simulation (2017) is the imitation of the operation of a real-world process or system over time (Banks et al. 2001). In order to simulate anything, one has to first develop a model on understanding how the real-world phenomena work. For example, if a teacher is teaching how an object travels in space under the influence of gravity with effect of the viscosity of air and rotation of earth being neglected, he may invoke a model based on kinematic equations of physics to predict the position of the object at any desired time. For more complex system of an intercontinental projectile fired with known angle of fire and velocity at the time of launch, more complex mathematical model would be required which would account for variation in acceleration due to gravity, rotation of earth, viscosity of air at various altitudes, etc. Thus, the model represents the salient features of the real-world system itself and desired precision to which the behavior needs to be predicted and encompasses data as well as underlying principles of nature to predict the behavior. The simulation experience would generate an 'instance' of the behavior of real-world phenomenon, in terms of time evolution of the system. For example, a simulation experiment would predict the trajectory of the object in case of an intercontinental projectile if angle of launch is 15° and initial velocity of fire is 6 km/s. This is an instance of behavior of the system.

Simulation may be used for testing, training, education, testing the efficacy of a theory, optimization of performance, process engineering, and in developing video games. Thus, computer simulation software may be used to predict the behavior of a physical system under a controlled environment and the predicted parameters may be tested against the experimental values, thereby validating the theoretical model. The range of parameters within which the simulation values match within the acceptable tolerances gives the validity for the physical theory along with the computer algorithm in conjunction with the hardware. Such simulation may be obtained for domains of physical sciences as well as social sciences like economics (Smith 1998). Simulations can also be used in situation where it is not practical to engage the real system. For example, in training pilots to work on fighter planes, it is customary to use a trainer flight simulator rather than real planes in order to avoid risk to the life of the trainer and trainee as well as to save cost of damages to hardware. Sometimes, the simulation is used because the real system is yet to be designed or built and may simply not exist (Sokolowski and Banks 2009).

The development of simulation software includes deciding theoretical model which maps the behavior of real system to that of the theoretical concepts. Such decisions may be based on the considerations like academic level of understanding of the target group, complexity of the problem, available time and financial resources, degree of precision or accuracy required the fidelity and validity of simulation outcome. The outcome of the simulation experiment depends on the soundness of the theory, versatility of the computer algorithm and code as well as the computational hardware being deployed. The study of procedures and protocols for verification and validation of models is a subject matter of academic disciplines and is being continually refined through research and development in the field of core domains as well as in the fields of mathematics and computer science.

Simulations can be used in distance education in a variety of ways. Some simulation models are available freely as Java-enabled applets. For example, the University of Colorado at Boulder makes available a number of simulations in the domain of physics, mathematics, chemistry, biology, and earth science using HTML 5 platform (University of Colorado 2017a). These simulations may be embedded in the Web-based teaching resources. Alternately, a teacher may ask the learners to download or use the simulation through online mode. The teacher may ask the learner to observe the behavior of the simulated system and to note and observe interesting features of the nature. For example, the quantum mechanical tunneling phenomena can be 'observed' by the learner using the Java-based applet (University of Colorado 2017b).

Recorded or Live Lectures

It has been observed that the teacher in a classroom does more than 'information transfer.' The teacher communicates a great deal of stimuli through verbal and nonverbal use of intonation, body and face gestures. The very act of writing on a blackboard is a gradual process and creates 'anticipation' in the mind of the learner which creates new neural pathways, thus strengthening the learning process.

Recorded and live lectures have been popular, and recent phenomena like emergence of Ted Talks and Khan Academy 'lectures' show the continued interest of people in the chalk and talk practice.

The recorded lectures may require an elaborate setup, particularly if there is audience participation. In such cases, more than one camera with 'online' editing (vision mixing) facility may be needed. If there is a 'PowerPoint' type of presentation also involved, then there may be a need to do off-line editing in which various slides need to be meticulously synchronized so that the learners can learn effectively. Incorrect editing may result in confusion rather than lucid learning.

Considering the paucity of funds and availability of expert editors in developing nations, a single camera setup which does not require elaborate vision mixing or

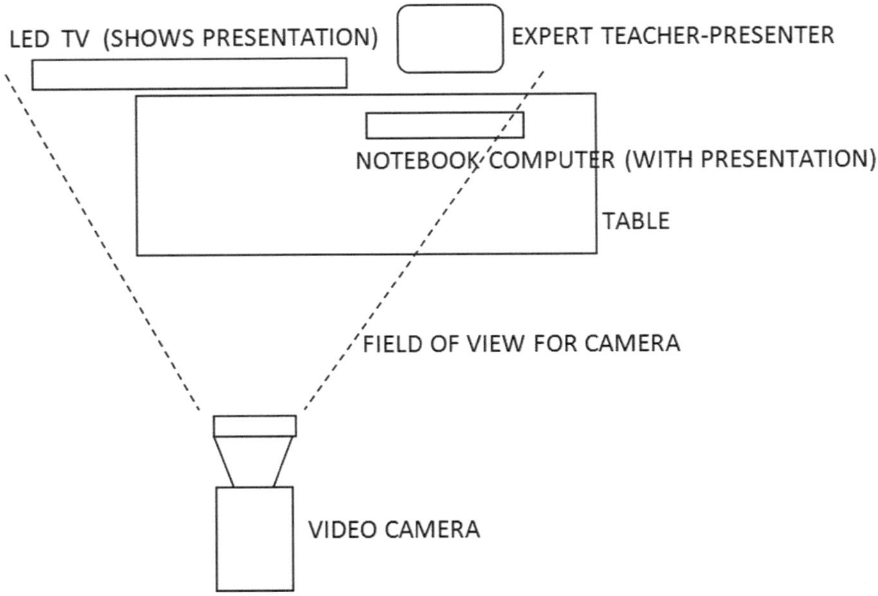

Fig. 3 A simple setup using a single camera which does not require vision mixing or video editing

video editing setup may also be devised. The block diagram of such setup is shown in Fig. 3.

A screenshot of such a video production is shown in Fig. 4. The author has used such a setup to produce a number of video lectures which are available on YouTube (Vadnere 2016).

Discussion Forum

The distance learners' community is likely to be a group of isolated individuals. As the methodology of distance learning does not envisage engagement of learners on regular basis at the study centers, the peer-to-peer interaction among the learners is likely to be very dilute. One of the important tools which makes it possible to institutionalize the learner interactions on peer-to-peer as well as on learner–tutor basis is 'discussion forum.' The discussion forums may be integrated with the 'Learning Management System.' The learners who are registered for a distance education course may become members either by default or by design. The discussion is in the form of textual string of interaction. This development has been inspired by the concepts of Internet forum and that of 'blog.'

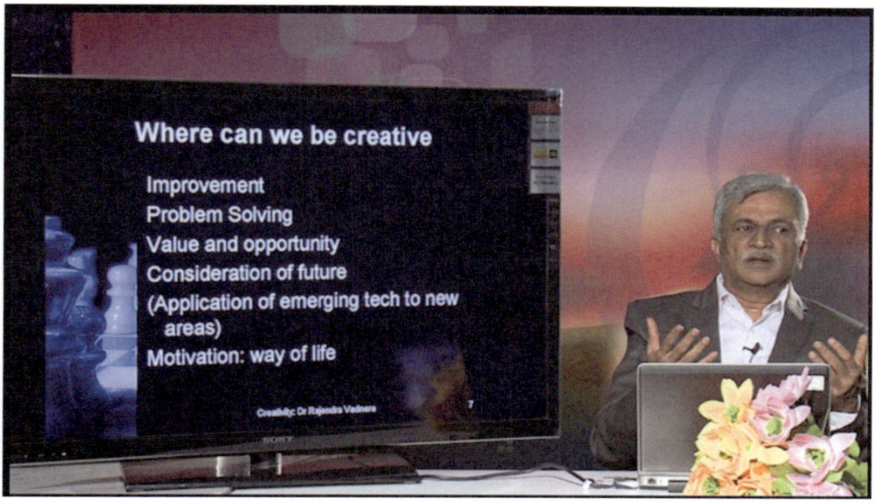

Fig. 4 A screenshot of video production using a single camera setup shown in Fig. 3

An Internet forum, (2017) or message board, is an online discussion site where people can hold conversations in the form of posted messages (Bulletin Community Forum 2001). There is a difference between chat rooms and Internet forum. The messages in Internet discussion forum are usually longer than one line messages used in chats. The messages are at least archived temporarily in forum. Many forums require that the messages are approved by the moderator before being visible to all members.

Forums have a specific terminology or jargon associated with them. For example, we call a single conversation as a ‘thread’ or ‘topic.’ A discussion forum may be treelike (hierarchical). That means that a forum may contain a number of sub-forums and each of these sub-forums may have several threads or topics. Within a forum’s ‘topic,’ whenever a new discussion started, it is called a thread. It may be replied to by any numbers of members.

Depending on the forum’s settings, users can be anonymous or have to register with the forum and then subsequently log in in order to post messages. On most forums, users do not have to log in to read existing messages.

The discussion forums offer advantages that an intelligent question or a ‘popular misconception’ about a topic in a course can be answered by the expert and such ‘question-and-answer’ session may be treasured for the future batches. They may inspire the tutor to design multiple-choice questions where he may use the ‘popular misconception’ as a ‘distracter.’

Discussion forum, however, suffers from the disadvantage that it requires the learners to be Internet savvy and well versed in use of keyboard for texting the questions and comments. These conditions may not be prevailing in many of the developing countries.

Massive Open Online Courses

According to Wikipedia (Massive Online Open Course 2017), a massive online open course (MOOC) is described as an online course which targets at large number of participating learners and provides open participation through Internet (Kaplan et al. 2016). The MOOCs may provide interactive forum for learners and tutors to facilitate learning through recorded lectures, e-books, problems sets, and interactions with peers and teachers. MOOCs made entry into the scene way back in 2006 and have become successful as promising methods of teaching–learning, thereby generating a remarkable interest in the research and development community working in distance education (Pappano 2012; Lewin 2013).

The initial MOOCs usually had open licensing of content and encouraged remixing and reuse of resources. Even though still called as ‘MOOCs’, many later variants did not use open licence but may have had ‘free’ access to student (zero cost). The word ‘free’ has two connotations: ‘free’ as zero financial burden and ‘free’ as freedom to use, alter, and distribute. Open license normally means the freedom to alter, use, and distribute (Wiley 2012; Adamopoulos 2013).

MOOCs offer following benefits (Massive Open Online Course 2017):

MOOCs improve access to higher education
MOOCs can be seen as significant devices to provide benefit of higher education (HE) for masses, thereby widening the access to HE. By educating a very large section of population particularly in the developing countries, MOOC may enhance the standard of life for them. MOOCs also serve as an agent which is transforming the scenario of HE by bringing in democratization at local as well as global scale. This is happening as MOOCs also content to be scripted by a large section of experts from various walks of life and representing diverse strata of society and also as the technology allows the content to reach the masses. The learners from the deprived sections of society are also able to enroll into various complete courses offered by institutions and universities of global repute. The availability of cost-effective technology is making MOOCs to be delivered by renowned institutions and teachers (Patru and Balaji 2016).

MOOCs can provide an inexpensive alternative to traditional system
One of the reasons for the higher education to be costly is that the institutions offering them have a tendency to offer too many services bundled with the education. The philosophy and methodology of MOOC allow some other players in public or private sector to cater to a few of the services which would have been rendered by the intuition. The operational philosophy of MOOC is aligned with having a large number of participants. These participating learners may access the content of the course at their pace and schedule from their places of convenience. These MOOCs are open to almost anyone without entry qualifications and give total course learning experience for free through online communication mode (Mulder and Jansen 2015; Patru and Balaji 2016).

MOOCs may help countries to achieve sustainable development goals
As the philosophy and methodology of MOOC have in their core the concept of mass education through use of technology which is affordable, MOOCs may play very significant role in transforming a developing country from a resource-starving to a healthy, clean, and rich knowledge society. We have seen that many of the evils of a developing country may be cured through application of appropriate education. It is also obvious that many of the SDGs can be achieved through interventions in which MOOCs can play crucial role.

India has accepted MOOC as a game changer for higher education. The MOOC model developed by India is called 'Study Webs of Active Learning for Young Aspiring Minds' (SWAYAM). The University Grants Commission has issued a Gazette Notification on July 19, 2016 (UGC 2016), which envisages MOOCs courses for learning in higher education programs. It is mandatory for the universities in India to give credit transfer to the candidates who successfully completed a MOOC under the SWAYAM platform by virtue of Sect. 6.2 of the notification. The Sect. 6.2 of notification (UGC 2016) states that "No university shall refuse any student for credit mobility for the courses earned through MOOCs."

The SWAYAM model can be summarized by the 'four-quadrant' approach elaborated in the 'Guidelines-for-online-courses-under-SWAYAM' document published by the Ministry of Human Resources Development (MHRD), Government of India (MHRD 2017).

The model of MOOC espoused by the Indian government envisages what they call as 'four-quadrant approach.' Thus, the e-learning through MOOCs is designed to have four components.

The first quadrant comprises of e-tutorial (with video and audio inputs in a well-planned format with utilization of animation, simulation, video recording showing demonstrations, virtual laboratories, and other similar inputs).

The second quadrant is called e-content and is expected to contain self-instructional e-books with ample illustrations, case studies, presentations, historical development of the subject matter, anecdotes which make subject interesting, etc. It should also make use of resources available on Internet to inculcate in the students the habit of referring to Web resources, open source content, links, and journals.

The third quadrant envisaged in the design of MOOC is the 'discussion forum.' This facilitates posing interesting problems by the tutor and/or learners in respect of the subject matter which would enable deeper understanding of the topics and also serve as a way to resolve difficulties and doubts regarding the subject matter. The course coordinator and his team are expected to resolve these issues in near real-time scale.

The fourth quadrant is regarding learner evaluation. It therefore contains assignments, problems, and their solutions. It may contain problems in the form of multiple-choice questions, matching questions, descriptive short and long answer questions, quizzes, fill-in-the-blank questions. It may also contain frequently asked questions and clarify the common misconceptions regarding a topic.

The SWAYAM MOOCs are uploaded by MHRD on a portal with URL https://swayam.gov.in. The students can register in SWAYAM MOOCs in various sectors of disciplines like:

(a) Postgraduate (PG) degree programs (excluding technology areas),
(b) Undergraduate (UG) degree programs (excluding technology areas),
(c) UG and PG degree programs in technical or engineering disciplines,
(d) Diplomas and certificates programs,
(e) Programs in school education for children in grade 9th to 12th grade,
(f) Management programs,
(g) Teacher training program (MHRD 2017).

Conclusion

In this chapter, we have seen the plight of the developing countries. We have glanced through the various challenges that the developing nations have to face to survive with grace. These include: problems of poverty, sustainable growth, health risks, population growth, making best use of human capital, trade policy, and knowledge gap. We observed that the educational interventions play pivotal role in addressing to the challenges which stare at the face of the developing nations. Distance education offers quality along with access and equity at the affordable cost of material and human resources to be invested. We have seen a number of academic tools which developing countries can deploy with the optimal resources at their disposals. The tools which we discussed included Learning Management System, distributed classrooms, simulations, recorded or live video lectures, discussion forum, and MOOCs. It is hoped that the discussion in this chapter should help the policy makers in the developing nations to take proactive steps in implementing the distance education programs with the use of various technologies available at affordable unit cost.

References

Adamopoulos, P. (2013). What makes a great MOOC? An interdisciplinary analysis of student retention in online courses. In ICIS 2013 Proceedings in AIS Electronic Library (AISeL) (pp. 1–21). Retrieved November 22, 2017, from http://aisel.aisnet.org/icis2013/proceedings/BreakthroughIdeas/13/.

AECT. (2017). Retrieved November 25, 2017, from http://www.aect.org/pdf/DistED/CH_1.pdf.

Banks, J., Carson, J., Nelson, B., & Nicol, D. (2001). *Discrete-event system simulation* (p. 3). Prentice Hall. ISBN 0-13-088702-1.

Bulletin Community Forum. (2001). Bulletin community forum—FAQ: What is a bulletin board? vBulletin.com. Retrieved September 01, 2008.

Carr, D. F. (2013). Udacity hedges on open licensing for MOOCs. *Information Week*. Retrieved August 21, 2013.

David, S (n.d.)a. A critical understanding of learning management system. Retrieved November 22, 2017, from http://www.academia.edu/3681177/A_Critical_Understanding_of_Learning_Management_System.

David, S (n.d.)b Teaching Machines. Retrieved November 22, 2017, from http://teachingmachin.es.

Delling, R. M. (1987). Towards a theory of distance education. *ICDE Bulletin, 13*, 21–25.
Distributed Learning. (2017). In Wikipedia (n.d.) retrieved on 20 Nov 2017.
Dr Gilbert Ahamer, Korotayev, A., Zinkina, J. (2014). On the structure of the present-day convergence. *Campus-Wide Information Systems 31*(2/3), 139–152.
Edwards, S. (1991). Trade orientation, distortions and growth in developing countries. *National Bureau of Economic Research.*
Ellis, R. K. (2009). Field guide to learning management. ASTD Learning Circuits.
Evans, Terry. (1995). Globalisation, post-Fordism and open and distance education. *Distance Education, 16*(2), 1995.
Forster, E. M. (1909). The machine stops. Retrieved November 22, 2017, from http://archive.ncsa.illinois.edu/prajlich/forster.html.
Garrison, D. R., & Shale, D. (1987). Mapping the boundaries of distance education: Problems in defining the field. *American Journal of Distance Education, 1*(1), 7–13.
Gilhooly, Kym. (2001). Making e-learning effective. *Computerworld, 35*(29), 52–53.
Grantham-McGregor, S. et al. (2007). Developmental potential in the first 5 years for children in developing countries. *Lancet, 369*(9555), 60–70. (PMC. Web. 28 November 2014).
Guillén, M. F. (2003). Multinationals, ideology, and organized labor. The limits of convergence. Princeton University Press. ISBN 0-691-11633-4
Harrison, A. (1996). Openness and growth: A time-series, cross-country analysis for developing countries. *Journal of Development Economics*, *48*(2), 419–447 (1996).
Human Capital. (2017). In Wikipedia (n.d.) Retrieved November 15, 2017.
Human Development Index. (n.d.). In Wikipedia. Retrieved November 15, 2017.
Internet Forum. (2017). In Wikipedia (n.d.). Retrieved November 21, 2017, from https://en.wikipedia.org/wiki/Internet_forum.
International Monetary Fund. (2011). http://www.imf.org/external/pubs/ft/weo/2011/01/weodata/weorept.aspx?pr.x=46&pr.y=4&sy=2010&ey=2010&scsm=1&ssd=1&sort=country&ds=.&br=1&c=603&s=PPPGDP&grp=1&a=1.
ISRO. (2017a). Retrieved November 15, 2017, from https://www.isro.gov.in/international-cooperation.
ISRO. (2017b). Edusat. Retrieved November 21, 2017, from https://www.isro.gov.in/category-spacecraft/edusat.
Kaplan, A. M., & Haenlein, M. (2016). Higher education and the digital revolution: About MOOCs, SPOCs, social media, and the Cookie Monster. *Business Horizons, 59*(4), 441–50. Retrieved November 22, 2017, from http://www.sciencedirect.com/science/article/pii/S000768131630009X?via%3Dihub.
Keegan, D. (1986). *Foundation of distance education*. London: Croom Helm.
League of Nation. (2017). In Wikipedia (n.d.). Retrieved 20 Nov 2017.
Learning Management System. (2017). In Wikipedia (n.d.). Retrieved November 15, 2017.
Lewin, T. (2013). Universities abroad join partnerships on the web. New York Times. Retrieved November 22, 2017, from http://www.nytimes.com/2013/02/21/education/universities-abroad-join-mooc-course-projects.html.
Mankiw, N. G. (2007). *Principles of economics* (4th ed.). ISBN 0-324-22472-9.
Massive Open Online Course. (2017). In Wikipedia (n.d.). Retrieved November 22, 2017.
MHRD. (2017). Guidelines-for-online-courses-under-SWAYAM. Retrieved November 22, 2017, from http://www.sakshat.ac.in/officeDocumentUploaded/27-06-2017/Guidelines_SWAYAM.pdf.
Mulder, F., & Jansen, D. (2015). MOOCs for opening up education and the OpenupEd initiative. In C. J. Bonk, M. M. Lee, T. C. Reeves, & T. H. Reynolds (Eds.), *MOOCs and open education around the world*. New York, NY: Routledge.
O'Sullivan, A., & Steven, M. S. (2003). *Economics: Principles in action* (p. 471). Upper Saddle River, New Jersey: Pearson Prentice Hall. ISBN 0-13-063085-3.
Pappano, L. (2012). The year of the MOOC. The New York Times. Retrieved November 1, 2017, from http://www.nytimes.com/2012/11/04/education/edlife/massive-open-online-courses-are-multiplying-at-a-rapid-pace.html?pagewanted=all&_r=0.

Patru, M., Balaji, V. (2016). Making sense of MOOCs: A guide for policy-makers in developing countries (PDF). Paris, UNESCO. (pp. 17–18, 21–22, 24). ISBN 978-92-3-100157-4. Retrieved November 22, 2017, from http://unesdoc.unesco.org/images/0024/002451/245122E.pdf.

Paweł Bożyk (2006). Newly industrialized countries. In *Globalization and the transformation of foreign economic policy*. Ashgate Publishing, Ltd. ISBN 0-7546-4638-6.

Perraton, H. (1988). A theory for distance education. In D. Sewart, D. Keegan, & Holmberg, B. (Eds.), Distance education: International perspectives (pp. 34–45). New York: Routledge.

Prasad, V. S. (1997). Distance education in developing countries: globalization and new challenges in the new learning environment: A global perspective.In *Conference papers for the 18th ICDE world conference*, Pennsylvania State University, State College, Pennsylvania, 2–6 June. http://web.worldbank.org/archive/website00236B/WEB/INN_02.HTM.

Rostow, W. (1971). *Politics and the stages of growth*. Cambridge University Press.

Rumble, G. (1989). On defining distance education. *The American Journal of Distance Education, 3*(2), 8–21.

Russel, S. (2004). The economic burden of illness for households in developing countries: A review of studies focusing on malaria, tuberculosis, and human immunodeficiency virus/acquired immunodeficiency syndrome. *The American Journal of Tropical Medicine and Hygiene*.

Schultz, T. W. (1961). Investment in human capital. *American Economic Review, 51*(1), 1–17.

Seels, B. B., & Richey, R. C. (1994). Instructional technology: The definition and domains of the field. Washington: Association for Educational Communications and Technology.

Simulation. (2017). In Wikipedia (n.d.). Retrieved November 20, 2017.

Smith, R. D. (1998). Simulation article. *Encyclopedia of Computer Science*. Retrieved November 21, 2017, from http://www.modelbenders.com/encyclopedia/encyclopedia.html.

Sokolowski, J. A., & Banks, C. M. (2009). *Principles of modeling and simulation* (p. 6). Hoboken, NJ: Wiley. ISBN 978-0-470-28943-3.

UGC. (2016). UGC (Credit Framework for Online Learning Courses through SWAYAM) Regulation, 2016. Published in Gazette of India, 19 July 2016. Retrieved November 22, 2017, from https://www.ugc.ac.in/pdfnews/0272836_moocs.pdf.

UNCTAD. (2012). Retrieved November 15, 2017, from http://unctad.org/en/PublicationsLibrary/ldc2012_en.pdf.

UNDP. (2010). The human development concept. UNDP. Retrieved July 29, 2011.

UNDP. (2017). What is human development. Retrieved October 27, 2017.

The History of LMS Software (n.d.), financesonline.com. Web 16-11-17 https://learning-management-system.financesonline.com/#history-of.

United Nations. (2017a). Retrieved November 15, 2017, from https://qz.com/685626/the-world-bank-is-eliminating-the-term-developing-country-from-its-data-vocabulary/retrieved.

United Nations. (2017b). https://unstats.un.org/unsd/methodology/m49/.

University of Colorado. (2017a). Retrieved November 21, 2017, from https://phet.colorado.edu/en/simulations/category/new.

University of Colorado. (2017b). Quantum tunneling and wave packets. Retrieved November 21, 2017, from https://phet.colorado.edu/en/simulation/legacy/quantum-tunneling.

Ura, K. (2017). The Bhutanese development story. Retrieved November 1, 2017, from http://archiv.ub.uni-heidelberg.de/savifadok/volltexte/2009/305/pdf/mono_1en_bt_dev_stry.pdf.

Vadnere, R. V. (2016). Expert talk on creativity-1 by Dr. Rajendra Vadnere. published on 06 January 2016. Retrieved November 21, 2017, from https://www.youtube.com/watch?v=xirvJPRpEdI.

Waugh, D. (2000). Manufacturing industries (chapter 19), World development (chapter 22). In *Geography, an integrated approach* (3rd ed.) (pp. 563, 576–579, 633, and 640) Nelson Thornes Ltd. ISBN 0-17-444706-X.

Wiley, D. (2012). The MOOC Misnomer. Retrieved November 22, 2017, from https://opencontent.org/blog/archives/2436.

Williams, J. (2007). Political factors that affect development. Retrieved November 15, 2017, from https://makewealthhistory.org/2007/07/01/political-factors-that-affect-development/.
World Bank. (2016). Retrieved November 15, 2017, from https://openknowledge.worldbank.org/bitstream/handle/10986/23969/9781464806834.pdf.
World Government. (2017). In Wikipedia (n.d.), Web, 15 November 2017.
World Health Organization. (2016). Environment and health in developing countries. Priority environment and health risks. World Health Organization, 8 September 2016.

Need for Integration of ICT for Extending Learner Support Services to the Distance Learners in ODL System in Developing World

H. U. W. Ratnayake

Introduction

Advancement of information and communication technology (ICT) has made a huge impact on lives of people and it continues to change the way people learn, collaborate, and advance the daily life. Communication—which used to be a simple way of *Keeping in touch*—has made a paradigm shift touching the grassroot level of people via the Internet in the form of different social media and various other types of Web resources accessible through laptops, PCs, tablets, and mobile phones. *ICT in education* is described by Belagra et al. (2012) as the use of technology to create, share, and save information for future use. It includes learning through digitized text books, multimedia and animation, and interactive online sessions. How it is done within each of these methodologies differs based on how simple or complex the technology use is. Learner support invariably includes assessments and reflective writing where integration of ICT plays an important role.

Growth of technology has increased Internet access, use of smart mobile phones, or simple availability of computers at affordable prices. This change has the same phenomenal effect in education. It is evident that ICT can be used effectively to harness the opportunity given. Especially for learners in Open and Distance mode, ICT provides an economically viable solution.

H. U. W. Ratnayake (✉)
Department of Electrical and Computer Engineering, The Open University of Sri Lanka, Nugegoda, Sri Lanka
e-mail: udithaw@ou.ac.lk

© Springer Nature Singapore Pte Ltd. 2018

Anjana (ed.), *Technology for Efficient Learner Support Services in Distance Education*, https://doi.org/10.1007/978-981-13-2300-3_4

History of ICT in Education

For more than a decade, higher educational institutes in developed countries have been using ICT to enhance the quality of learning. First, it was the use of Web as hypermedia to make learning material and general use of the Internet to find learning resources. With the expansion of the Internet, earlier developed video resources or lectures became available to a larger audience via the Internet. Even before the expansion of the Internet, educational games and animations using multimedia were being developed to assist students from primary level to undergraduate level. With the popularity of the Internet, these became accessible to more and more students worldwide. Development of infrastructure, low cost of the computer hardware, and development of open source software made it possible for developing countries also to make the use of educational software. It is the development of both information technology and communication technology that gave birth to learning management system (LMS) incorporating digitized learning materials, interactive forums, assessment options, reflective journals, and many more features.

For any teaching learning method to be successful, it has to be interactive. During the last decade, many types of interactive tools such as online discussion forums and blogs; collaborative tools such as wikis; personal response systems have been used in institutions that utilize ICT in education. Over the years, an abundance of research had been done on numerous aspects of ICT integrated education and its effectiveness. Universities and Colleges Information Systems Association (UCISA), UK, has done several surveys which were conducted during 2001–2016 with the aim of enhancing the quality of learning and teaching in the UK. They have identified that improving access for students to learn off-campus would enhance the higher education in the UK as a primary driver in meeting student expectations. In their published research, it had been identified that top three barriers to technology-enhanced learning (TEL) developments are a lack of time, remuneration, and knowledge of the academic staff.

As we all know, access for learning off-campus is the prime necessity of an institution offering courses in Open and Distance learning (ODL) mode. With the ability to reach students engaged in self-study, mostly without peer groups close by, integrating ICT to courses can play a major role in enhancing opportunities in education as well as making it effective.

There are many ways that OUSL has taken advantage of ICT to enhance teaching and learning by integrating ICT. The key player is the learning management system (LMS), while a plethora of interactive multimedia incorporated course material and a few virtual laboratories are being developed. As continuous assessment components, online assessments have been practiced during the last decade and they are becoming very popular among educators. However, these attempts being made coursewise as individual projects need to be practiced widely in order to get the full benefits.

Integration of ICT for ODL at OUSL

In the following section, various projects done in OUSL in order to integrate ICT into enhanced teaching and learning are presented and discussed.

Learning Management Systems

OUSL deployed Manhatton Virtual Class during the year 2002 and encouraged academics to use it to give additional support for students. Many academics were keen to use the opportunity and created online classes as a means of giving additional new information to enhance the effectiveness of courses offered. At that time, use of online quizzes for assessments also became popular as many educators started including quizzes for self-assessment modules and compulsory continuous assessment modules. By about the year 2007, an early version of Moodle LMS was installed in an OUSL server, and most of the courses developed in Manhatton Virtual Class were transferred to Moodle.

Moodle is the most widely used LMS in Sri Lanka due to the fact it is a free and an open source. It embeds common types of learning resources and various educational activities which can be upgraded by add-on modules and plugins. A variety of log data for student interactions are also recorded in Moodle.

The Distance education modernization project (DEMP) which was started in the year 2003 was an initiative of the Ministry of Higher Education to increase public access to tertiary education through a technology-enhanced distance mode. The project "National Online Distance Education Services (NODES)" was the key player to make this vision a reality. At the inception, NODES consisted of three main technological entities, namely the Network Operation Center (NOC), Disaster Recovery Center (DR), and 26 NODES Access Centers (NACs) spread out over the country. Most of these NACs were housed at the regional and study centers of OUSL. Each NAC was given 25 PCs with multimedia facilities and Internet access, printers, scanners etc. They also facilitated video conferencing facility.

Since the inception of Moodle courses, Center for Education Technology and Media (CETMe) of OUSL has been giving the necessary training to the academic staff and the support needed to create classes in Moodle. CETMe offered two modes of classes for academics to choose from supplementary class or blended class based on the compulsory activities conducted through the LMS. Workshops on instructional design and development for online classes were conducted many times during the time of DEMP by consultants and later by CETMe, occasionally as and when a need arises. University administration encouraged the faculties to select few courses and develop them with action plans in place to monitor progress till completion. At the end of the DEMP project, it was declared that by 2018, all courses in OUSL would be having supplementary or blended online classes in Moodle.

However, the journey was not smooth all the time and problems arose regarding the technical support given by the NODES center which involved issues with administration. Then, the Ministry of Higher Education handed over the existing resources and the administration of NODES and all NACs housed in OUSL regional and study centers to OUSL. The transition period which lasted about two years resulted in many technical non-functionalities which prompted more keen and motivated educators to host their courses in other Moodle servers and other learning management systems deployed in the cloud. By the end of 2017, the data center at OUSL was fully functional and the operations were more or less steady. It was reported by the Director of CETMe in January 2018 that by the end of the year 2017, about 300 online classes have been developed and offered in OUSL.

Out of these, about 200 courses were from faculties of science and engineering, whereas OUSL has five faculties. The other three faculties—education, health sciences, and social science and humanities—offer a less number of different courses comparatively. Majority of the online classes currently offered are in supplementary mode. It is noted that 26 courses offered by the Department of Social Sciences and 25 courses from the Department of Electrical and Computer Engineering are offered in blended online mode, which means that these courses have compulsory activities with marks being added to continuous assessment total marks.

From the inception, CETMe opened up the online class for students only after reviewing it for accepted quality standards. At the start of each new academic year, educators update the online class and request the CETMe division to review and open to students. To motivate academic staff to offer their courses in Moodle and to be creative in enhancing student interaction, an award for the best online class is being offered annually by the university.

However, as the current trend in the world, mobile phones have become more available to general public than PCs/laptops for Internet access. Smart mobile phones have become the most popular communication media among the young generation. New versions of Moodle offer a corresponding mobile app which makes it convenient for students to use Moodle via the mobile phone. At OUSL, there have been few research projects aimed at harnessing the wide availability of mobile phones to improve student accessibility to online classes.

In one such research project, Gunathilaka and Premasiri (2016) report that the mobile phone is very popular in Sri Lanka as the rest of the world, because many of "human needs are served by a single touch on the screen on a mobile device." They also state that, though such a technology with advanced capabilities is available, it is not used much to enhance the educational aspects in Sri Lanka. Therefore, they have embarked in a research to design and develop a system to deliver an interactive virtual mobile learning environment for distance learners. It will facilitate learning by embedding existing features and functionalities in popular learning management systems. Their system will keep learners in ODL mode alert on services delivered via Moodle. They have also used portability of many Moodle services and hope to deliver the most important functionalities of Moodle through an interactive mobile app which students can access using their mobile devices.

Further, they are continuing the research (Gunathilaka et al. 2017) in "individual personalization approach in virtual learning environment according to the dynamically changing learning styles and knowledge levels of the learner." Here, they are more concerned about traditional pedagogical approaches being teacher-centered rather than learner-centered and take into account individual differences of knowledge levels. Authors propose to make their mobile application to "personalize the learning material delivery among the individual students according to their own static and dynamic learning behaviors and the dynamically changing knowledge levels." Path personalization is done as a tree traversal approach in the lesson plan. Various learning styles have been analyzed through a literature-based study, and the learning behaviors have been obtained through students' login profiles in a LMS.

Authors also state that reasons for student failure in a course can be accounted for less interactivity, lack of awareness of features offered by virtual learning environments, and diminished motivation of students in actual learning. They further state that many students are attending to the coursework with the sole intention of passing the examinations. They believe that if an individual's preferred ways of learning can be offered, it will motivate them further in the education process.

Fully Online Classes

The Open University of Sri Lanka has launched many fully online short courses for professional development.

In 2015, a six-month course titled "OER for e-learning" was successfully conducted for the academic staff with the intention of promoting awareness of open educational resources (OER) and integrating them in e-learning among the academics. According to Karunanayaka et al. (2015), many objectives have been achieved by developing and conducting the course. One major objective has been to impart the knowledge on course design process. According to them, although efficient integration of OER is supported by ICT, their effective use for teaching and learning can be achieved only by proper course design. This course was designed with a set of real-life learning scenarios progressively taking the learner through a series of events which were either a part of learning process or assessment. Many reading materials have been prescribed; to reinforce the knowledge gained, completing quizzes and drawing mind maps have been encouraged, and lastly, the learners were to upload their draft answer to the assignment questions asked. Once assignment answers were uploaded and discussion forum started, learner would get feedback from their peers on the answers they provided. It was noted that discussion forums turned out to be very much alive with many discussions going and peer feedback being received (Karunanayaka et al. 2016). Only after getting peer feedback, the learners could revise their answers and upload the final answer.

Another major objective of the course was to enlighten the participants from where to find OER and how to integrate appropriate OER in the teaching learning process. Learners had hands-on experience regarding searching and integrating OER for their work presented. This course consisted of five modules, and each module consisted of two or three assignments which served as assessments. Each assessment included three sections, namely specific individual tasks, participating in the group discussion forum, and writing a self-reflection (Karunanayaka et al. 2017). Marks have been given based on the assessment rubrics prepared for each assignment.

The online learning environment was created in Moodle. At the end of this course, facilitators and participants were enlightened how peer learning can be used to build knowledge as well as the effectiveness of the discussion forums for peer learning.

Another initiative by OUSL in developing and conducting a fully online course was the cross-border professional development online course to train online tutors and mentors in 2014 (Jayatilleke et al. 2017). Thirty participants of the course have been professionals living in Sri Lanka, Pakistan, and Mauritius. It had been facilitated by OUSL academics and e-mentors from the USA.

Both courses had been used for qualitative studies based on reflections of both faculty and participants. Collected data had comprised of reflections and informal anecdotal records of the OUSL facilitators, self-reflection instruments (pre-, mid, and final) administered to participants, and participants' reflective journal entries. Findings have revealed that though there were many accomplishments in the design and delivery of the courses, there were many challenges in conducting fully online courses, especially technical issues. Since then OUSL administration had taken many steps to minimize technical aspects that hinder the delivery of online courses, but it is evident that new challenges come up every day.

Challenges

The main challenge in maintaining an online class to supplement a course is the time required to update the course every year as well as the time need to be spent on assisting students online. Many teachers have kept the online class at supplementary level in order to make updating simple as possible and to minimize required interactive time.

Web-based lesson material requires use of graphics and interactive multimedia which need to get done by professionals. Currently, CETMe at OUSL supports creation of these materials but requires comprehensive story boards to done by teachers when giving the work to graphic/multimedia designers.

For fully online classes to be functional, reliability of network connection is essential. When a deadline is given, if students cannot access the site, the deadline has to be postponed. Then the schedules overlap. Especially within the university, any technical fault in the network or in the server would take few hours or few days to be fixed depending on how many outside parties such as telecommunication services need to collaborate or value of the purchase items needed due to financial regulations. This unreliability of network availability causes undue stress for the teachers and coordinators whenever a compulsory online activity is due.

Depending on the number of concurrent users, bandwidth limitation also affects the performance. When more than 100 students login to a one-hour online quiz, login time and closing time make the system slow which results in server time-outs.

Virtual Laboratory Classes

Compared to social sciences and business studies, science and engineering education needs more hands-on, practical-based approach to learning. It is mandatory for any science or engineering curriculum to have adequate learning hours in laboratory-based practicals for students to understand the theoretical concepts. In conventional education systems, it is the norm to have practical classes in parallel with theoretical concepts being taught. This is the main challenge when delivering science and engineering courses in ODL mode. Faculty of Engineering Technology and Faculty of Science at OUSL offer many diplomas, higher diploma, and undergraduate programs in ODL mode. Those programs in science and engineering require students to participate in mandatory laboratory classes scheduled in the main campus and at many regional centers. However, it is apparent that students find it difficult to make time according to the schedule to engage in laboratory activities. It is even more difficult to change a laboratory class or request an additional class. Moreover, increase of student numbers in any course further reduces the opportunities per student to use instruments in a laboratory class. This is an area where integration of ICT is essential. As alternatives to conventional laboratory classes, virtual laboratories and interactive e-learning materials can be introduced for science and engineering courses offered in open and distance mode. For this purpose, much research and relevant projects have been carried out worldwide as well as at OUSL.

As rightly said by Premaratne (2016), "the main challenge of teaching electrical engineering at a distance is conducting practicals at a distance." Practical experiments other than field work require to be done in dedicated laboratories under proper supervision of qualified, competent persons. This in turn makes it mandatory for students to attend a laboratory at the main campus or an authorized technical institute. Though it is evident that delivery of electrical engineering courses completely in the distance mode is difficult, learners can practice pre-laboratory sessions that are delivered online. Remote workshops on laboratory sessions online have been implemented and presented by Apse-Apsitis et al. (2012) as well. They believe that this practice enables students to spend less number of hours physically present in the laboratory.

It is apparent that not only by educators in ODL there have been much research done to find alternatives to laboratory classes by institutes having full-time students also based on different e-learning architectures.

Nandana et al. (2012) and de Mel and Nandana (2015) have been involved in research projects to develop virtual laboratories for students enrolled in mechatronic engineering at OUSL. Believing that a major cause for the dropouts of engineering students in the second year is due to nonattendance of assigned laboratory class, they have designed and developed many different types of virtual laboratories.

Samaranayaka and de Mel (2017) describe use of a new low-cost remote laboratory setup to carry out the experiments through the Internet, which provides hands-on experience also. For the prototype, they have implemented an experiment that uses Arduino in mechatronics, and the students are provided with the necessary equipment to carry out the practical. The remote laboratory setup Website provides guidelines and necessary instructions to setup the laboratory at student's premises. A student can login to connect via Web, write the program, and upload to the university PC where the programs will be checked and verified. The server would display a message mentioning whether the program is correct or not. If it is correct, the program is executed in the server side Arduino board. Finally, the student can run the program in his/her PC and programs can be uploaded from his/her practical setup after making necessary circuit connections. All necessary circuit diagrams will be provided in the Website. Through the camera, the student can observe the university-side Arduino. In addition to that, the video can be recorded and can be used later.

Through this process, educators expect to develop students' programming skills as well. The camera provides visual communication between student and laboratory setup and is also used for recording purposes. Student's knowledge gain has been assessed through a questionnaire. They claim that the results show a reduction in number of dropouts and student performance is comparable to those who did the practical in the face-to-face session. However, they report that students do not recommend complete replacement of the traditional laboratory from the course. Therefore, it can be used as an additional educational tool which will enhance the learning process of students, and the option is available for employed students who prefer this method.

The researchers claim that this project was done to reduce the existing high cost in developing and installing remote laboratories based on expensive tools such as data acquisition cards (DAQs), general purpose interface bus (GBIP) modules, and field programmable gate array (FPGA) kits. Though expensive, they may not provide hands-on experience for the students either which is also given serious consideration.

de Mel (2016) describes a solar energy e-learning laboratory, which has an experimental setup via LabVIEW instruments over a network. It enables the users to access the experimental setup via the Internet in either real-time or recorded mode. According to authors, remote panels that are used in both real-time and recorded modes are exactly the same as what are used in a conventional hands-on laboratory. In real-time setup, experiments are done through LabVIEW's Web server controlled by the students via the Internet. In recorded mode, forms on HTML pages are used to generate client's requests that are sent to the server.

This experimentation setup had been done with the intention of serving the courses in solar energy offered in OUSL and partner universities in Europe.

There are few more projects done by the Department of Mechanical Engineering at OUSL to popularize ICT-enabled laboratory work online. Another experimental setup for the course microprocessor-based systems is being built by the Department of Electrical and Computer Engineering and not completed yet.

There are many different virtual laboratory softwares available in the market, but the cost makes it not feasible to use at state-funded open universities. Cao and Zhu (2010) describe how iEELab hybrid laboratory model, connect via a network, can be used for practical experiments required for courses in electrical engineering. In this setup, physical instruments are connected to a Web-based network and the users can operate them from different premises. Although this system provides a good solution for the non-availability of laboratory classes, this system can be bought. In another attempt, Valdez et al. (2014) have proposed a laboratory containing only virtual instruments based on their study on VEMA laboratories. Since this laboratory setup does not have any physical instrument, students are supposed to use the virtual instruments as they would do in a laboratory with physical instruments. The system requires online connectivity to perform the activities.

Thus, it is evident that the use of ICT can make a great contribution to laboratory-based learning in science and engineering. Due to the high cost of available products and also in order to make the laboratory setup as much as suitable for the local environment and the course offered, educators in OUSL are engaged in various research projects to develop virtual laboratories. It is important to popularize these efforts and make the benefit available to a larger number of students.

Challenges

Though there are many virtual laboratory softwares available in the market, high cost makes it unaffordable to mainly state-funded open universities like OUSL, where student fees compensate for approximately a third of the course fee. Due to this reason, there is a substantial interest among academic staff of the Faculty of Engineering to engage in relevant research and projects. However, unless the research team is adequately technically competent, these projects are not viable.

Another major factor is the time needed. Implementation and testing of such software applications are highly time-consuming.

Enabling Visualization

Certain theories are better understood by students if they were taught by enabling visualization of the concept. It is important that learners should understand how theory can be applied to the real physical systems.

With the advancement of ICT, many platforms were developed for online course delivery with smart phones and tablet computers. S.m.i.L.E technology developed in Germany (Goebel et al. 2016) enables students to use smart mobile phones and tablets to read multimedia-enriched lesson materials.

There are many instances of research and case studies carried out and published which stress the importance of visualization of science and engineering theories. One example is the research carried out by Vandewalle (2011), which shows how difficult it is to teach a course like *Electrical Circuits and Systems* using only printed material.

As expected, with the increase of online classes at OUSL, use of graphics and animation to supplement the reading materials has increased. CETMe, OUSL provides the necessary support upon request with a story board describing what need to be developed.

A novel project was done recently at OUSL which enhances learnability of printed course material. Namely as "Printed Course Material Amelioration via Smartphones (PCMAS)" incorporates quick response (QR) codes near the contents which require more explanations. Once these QR codes are scanned via a QR code reader application in a smartphone, it directs the user to a video tutorial, an e-book, a Website, or an explanatory note. Haroon and de Mel (2017) who had carried out the project said that they wanted to give the sense of "Lecturer is close at hand" feeling for students.

Challenges

Since graphic designers and multimedia application developers are not subject experts, they need to be given comprehensive storyboards which is a time-consuming task for the teacher. Even after making the storyboard, many time-consuming meetings with the application developers will be necessary to explain what is in the mind of the relevant teacher.

Interactive MultiMedia

It is accepted without doubt that for effective learning, interactivity in learning material is essential. Many case studies have been carried out in this regard, and one example is Porebska and Wantuch (2015), where they "compare the role of computer supported tools in electrical engineering education with the traditional learning environment."

There is no doubt of the effective learning experiences provided by interactive materials to students online or offline. However, it is not a simple option for educators as they require either expensive multimedia tool licenses to be bought by the university or computer programming knowledge and time to spend writing code.

There have been many instances where educators at OUSL have embarked on producing interactive multimedia to enhance the learnability of course material.

Kulasekara et al. (2011) have carried out a study to investigate learner perceptions on the instructional design features of an interactive multimedia (IMM) designed to enhance the learnability of a microbiology course at OUSL. The aim of this software package had been to explain the dynamic abstract concepts and processes of bacterial genetics that are difficult to understand by reading printed course material. They have stated that when developing this software package, "emphasis was placed on the interface design, navigational design, and instructional design." Instructional design had been based on Gagne's nine events of instructions and Mayer's cognitive theory of multimedia learning. The IMM package includes basic features such as learning outcomes, a brief introduction to each lesson, self-assessment questions, and glossary. Furthermore, animations with narrations were extensively used to explain abstract processes. The aim of these design features was to enable active learning while visualizing the dynamic abstract bacterial processes over time. Learners' knowledge gain has been tested together with immediate feedback, allowing them to achieve a meaningful learning experience. They have gathered learners' perceptions about instructional design features in the course via quantitative and qualitative research methods such as questionnaires, interviews, and direct observations. Evaluation of the collected information has revealed many positive features and a few negative features in the design of IMM. They have noted that findings of this study have revealed important aspects to consider when "designing effective learner-centered multimedia learning material."

Premaratne (2016) has presented that an open source software tool OCATAVE can be used as a numerical computing software to develop an architecture to present interactive laboratory sessions. As he has also noted, MATLAB is widely considered to be the most used numerical computing software for engineering applications and engineering education. To use MATLAB, institutions have to buy the license which is relatively expensive to afford in developing countries. OCTAVE is an open source alternative to MATLAB. Though both the software packages have similar features, both contain certain limitations as well. However, Premaratne (2016) notes that the circuit simplification techniques, control systems simulations, and graphical representation of variables of OCTAVE are quite adequate for basic electrical engineering courses.

Octave is an open source software with creative common CC-BY-SA license. According to Premaratne (2016), AC theory concepts in electro-technique course at OUSL have been offered to students using this software. The author has noted it has increased the interest of students to engage in studies and the integrated self-assessment has encouraged the students to test their newly gained knowledge and repeat the process until they are competent. The programming part involved in this maneuver had been writing mathematical functions and minimal programming, so that in-depth programming knowledge would not be required for teachers. The author is keen on developing more supportive learning scenarios for electrical engineering courses based on this e-learning architecture.

Another recent project carried out in OUSL was digitizing one session each from a course in nursing, pharmacy, and medical laboratory sciences while incorporating interactive multimedia (Jayatilleke et al. 2017). After the m-learning application (MLearn) was designed and developed, it has been given to five groups of stakeholders as they have stated "content experts to validate the content, instructional designers to check the alignment of technical and pedagogical features, novice users to check the overall effectiveness of the application, developer to check the ease of usage, and researchers to identify the impact of this innovation. These stakeholders were closely involved throughout the whole process which lasted over a period of four months." Main challenges in this process had been the time factor and the high production cost.

Interaction Among Learners in Online Learning

It is an uncontested fact that providing a platform for students to discuss online with peers and teachers is essential, especially in ODL. One recent initiative at OUSL was to create an online forum integrated with social media (W. A. S. N. Perera, B. K Werapitiya, S. Rajasingham, I. A. Premaratne). They have created online classes integrated with Facebook to make interaction very convenient. However, researchers claim that merely providing the platform did not motivate the students to actively participate. Therefore, different types of motivators have been used to improve the active participation. They have stated that "much early research have reported that enjoyment, social presence, and learning as the main intrinsic motivators while awards, creativity, and the reputation as the main extrinsic motivators. Most of these motivators are already implemented in social media such as Facebook, Twitter, LinkedIn, and Instagram which are very popular among the young generation." For the research, first two courses had been selected from the Department of Electrical and Computer Engineering at OUSL and later it had been offered to all courses in Diploma in Information Systems and Technology Programme.

The authors have measured the active participation of students in terms of number of comments, replies on comments, number of participants seen a post, and number of reactions. To motivate students to interact, facilitators have asked questions. Here smileys and stickers have been used as enjoyment factors, sharing photographs taken in the course-related activities as social presence factors, and enabling students to brainstorm based on what was taught by the teacher as learning factors. Reward given was the awarding of points to very active students.

Posting tasks allowing students to think creatively was regarded as a creativity factor, whereas promoting students to solve problems was taken as a reputation factor. They conclude that it is necessary to identify the motivational factors to include in learning activities which would increase active participation of students in online discussions.

It is evident that integrating ICT is mandatory to increase the learnability of the course material. These tools/applications must be interactive and promote collaborative learning as much as possible from the learner's perspective, and easy and quick to be developed from the teacher's perspective.

Challenges Faced by Developing Countries in Usage of ICT for Educational Purposes

Challenges faced by countries similar to Sri Lanka would broadly fit into two main categories: available infrastructure and motivation and the technical knowledge of the educators.

Infrastructure

As developing country, Sri Lanka face more challenges than specified by universities and colleges information systems association (UCISA). Rathiranee (2013) has reported in her case study that students were confused with the online learning system since they were unable to change their traditional learning system (face-to-face). This case study was done with students enrolled for Bachelor of Business Management (BBM) online degree programme at University of Jaffna, Sri Lanka. Further, problems with infrastructure as non-availability of electricity, unavailability of Internet access, and low bandwidth were highlighted regarding the students living in rural areas of Northern province. This case study is quite relevant to OUSL as well, as the OUSL clientele are dispersed all over the country. When decisions are made about compulsory course components and assessments with online access, it is essential to consider available infrastructure in rural areas.

Educating the Educators

From the perspective of educators, use of technology for educational purposes is curtailed due to many reasons. One major factor is that educator's unwillingness to take challenges due to limited time to teach a syllabus and extra time needed to create additional learning materials. Sometimes, it is the reluctance to use new technology due to non-familiarity, but at OUSL awareness sessions and workshops are regularly being conducted for anybody who is not familiar with new technology advancements.

In many case studies, it is shown that an educator's "teaching belief" affected integration of technologies into education. A teacher's familiarity with a learning management system (LMS) also affects in gaining the maximum student support to have an interactive learning process (Shieh 2012; Price and Kirkwood 2014; Rathiranee 2013). There is a very high probability that somebody who is familiar with a LMS would use it for his/her own course than somebody who has never used a LMS.

It is inevitable that quality of students learning would depend on quality of teaching/facilitating. Therefore, it is vital to improve teachers' instructional design skills and educational practices periodically.

As Dori and Belcher (2004) state, when students are used to teachers using traditional methods for teaching, they then face difficulties in accepting learner-centered education techniques (Dori and Belcher 2004) which is true in Sri Lanka for both students and teachers.

Future of ODL with Integration of ICT

While online classes which provide access to information, platforms to interact and virtual laboratory environments are being developed and used, there are more advancements in ICT that can be used for education.

One such concept is gamification, which is used in software corporations to motivate the workforce, which can similarly be used to motivate learners in ODL mode. Gamification is the use of "game dynamics" to influence the behavior of a person. It is known that everybody likes having rewards, sense of achievement, provision for competition ability for self-expression, etc. In general, people tend to go out of their way to engage with a task if they see how it will match with the above. Gamification uses proven techniques from game design to satisfy workforce and customers to motivate them to engage with whatever they are doing and motivate to do better. Same concept can be applied to teaching and learning by motivating students to engage in studies. There have been several attempts by the project students of the Department of Electrical and Computer Engineering to incorporate gamification techniques to selected courses, but only a few simple software applications have been developed.

Another important concept is collaborative learning which is an educational approach to teaching and learning where groups of learners collectively work to solve a problem or complete a task. It is founded on the concepts that knowledge can be constructed and that learning can be achieved by enabling participants to talk among themselves. Collaborative learning motivates learners and gives necessary support to peers to learn difficult sessions as well as reinforce learning. Currently, the usual practice is to form a team of students to explore a solution for a problem or to create a project where they can interact online. Another scenario is to have groups of students, share an assignment, and work together over the Internet. However, this is mostly done via traditional discussion forums or chat groups. Since there are no simple tools widely available that can monitor progress in terms of student logging, making helpful suggestions, sending alerts to participant if interaction time is low, and good collaborative platforms need to be designed and developed.

It is evident that integration of ICT for education will definitely promote usage and development of OER leading to open education practices. Usage of OER includes identifying, evaluating, adapting, and integrating OER into course material. Usage invariably promotes educators to develop their teaching material as OER giving a larger benefit to the community. If a good infrastructure is in place, ODL can vastly benefit from plethora of OER available in the form of course material as well as courses themselves in the Web. In 2016, OUSL signed a memorandum of understanding with Commonwealth of Learning to develop two course materials in ICT together with embedded videos and screen casts. It was a part of a larger project where six open universities undertook to develop two courses each which can be shared. At the completion of this project in 2017, each open university was able to make use of 12 courses in ICT as OER, together with the videos uploaded to YouTube. A team from the academic staff of the Department of Electrical and Computer Engineering developed the two courses selected by OUSL.

The importance of visualization of physical models, especially in science and engineering, cannot be undermined. Most research done in digitization is for individual courses which cannot be used the same way for another course. Open source tools for digitization would also be very beneficial to educators in ODL to develop their courses.

A fairly new concept, augmented reality (AR) is a live view of a real-world environment with computer-generated visuals. Such an environment may include many sensory modalities such as visual, auditory, olfactory, haptic (giving the sense of touch by applying forces, vibrations, etc.), and somatosensory (sensory systems giving conscious perception of touch, pressure, pain, etc.). These sensory information could be used as constructive, i.e., adding more to the natural environment or destructive, i.e., covering up or hiding a part of the natural environment. This kind of manipulated natural environment would offer a user an artificially enriched experience. Thus, AR technologies would make the user feel that the surrounding real world is interactive which makes educational activities exciting and engaging. AR is known to entrap attention of students as well as motivate them to study. Augmented reality would change the user's current perception of his/her environment unlike virtual reality which will be described in the next section. There has been only one simple project carried out in the Department of Electrical and Computer Engineering based on AR which was not continued after making a preliminary prototype.

Unlike augmented reality, virtual reality (VR) generates realistic images, sounds, and other sensory experiences that simulate a user's physical presence in an imaginary environment which is termed as "virtual". In this simulated environment, users have to wear "virtual reality headsets" or stay in specific areas where imaginary environments are projected to large screens around the place. The special headsets consist of a head-mounted display having a small screen in front of the eyes. In some situations, props like movement of the seats and moisture sprays are combined to make the users feel as if they were actually staying in the created virtual environment. When a person wearing a virtual reality headset looks around, he/she can interact with virtual elements in the surrounding. This interactive effect is obtained by the use VR headsets or the special projections to multiple large screens.

Augmented reality (AR) and virtual reality (VR) are considered to be powerful technologies that are heavily built on ICT. With their capabilities increasing and costs coming down, AR/VR technologies could play a major role in education, especially ODL in future.

Reflective writing encourages the development of metacognitive skills of students by helping them to sort out what they know and what they don't know. Here, students write down their own thoughts and ideas. It is helpful when they learn new concepts and trying to learn complex concepts, material where there are no proper right or wrong answers. Writing a reflection after a learning activity or even evaluating is very convenient if done through the reflective journal in a LMS. It is an important feature that integration of ICT brings in for courses, especially in social sciences and law, which had been practiced in education faculties. Though not widely used currently, it would be very beneficial for science and engineering courses as well, if the practice can be promoted among educators to make use of available reflective journals in Moodle.

It is envisaged that personalized education will be in demand in the future. Frameworks, applications, and tools developed based on learning behaviors of students will be in common place and not only in research. For modeling static and dynamic behaviors of learners, data such as login profiles, time spent on each activity, frequently accessed resources need to be analyzed when designing personalized systems. These innovative developments will not be possible without reliable and fast Internet access.

Innovative learning platforms, frame works, and tools are designed and developed in open universities for fostering ODL concepts to enhance the process of education would be best to publish as OER. Otherwise, similar research and similar projects will be repeatedly done in many institutions, in many countries simply due to the involved cost factor. Even OER, when used in different countries in different contexts, it is necessary to adopt them to fit into the local context. To keep innovations related to education as "open access" and adopting the "4R" concept—reuse, revise, remix, and redistribute—would be the best practice which enables a larger audience to reap the benefits.

It is very clear that more and more novel approaches and innovations are based on the assumption of readily available Internet access, adequate bandwidth, and primary facilities of infrastructure, thus making integration of ICT vital for ODL.

References

Apse-Apsitis, P., Avotins, A., Krievs, O. & Ribickis, L. (2012). Practically oriented e-learning workshop for knowledge improvement in engineering education computer control of electrical technology. In *Proceedings of the 2012 IEEE Global Engineering Education Conference (EDUCON)*.

Belagra, M., Benachaiba, C. & Guemid, B. (2012). Using ICT in higher education: Teachers of electrical engineering department at the University of Bechar: Case study. In *Proceedings of the 2012 IEEE Global Engineering Education Conference (EDUCON)*.

Cao, X. & Zhu, S. (2010). iEELab practice. A hybrid remote laboratory for distance education in electrical engineering. *IEEE Transactions on. Industrial Electronics.*

de Mel, W., & Nandana, W. (2015). Integrated laboratory experiment setup to empower the engineering education in distance mode. In *Proceedings of the 29th Annual Conference of the Asian Association of Open Universities AAOU.*

de Mel, W. (2016). Solar energy remote laboratory an e-learning experimentation setup. In *Proceedings of 30th Annual Conference of Asian Association of Open Universities AAOU.*

Dori, Y. & Belcher, J. (2004). How does technology-enabled active learning affect undergraduate students. *The Journal of the Learning Sciences.*

Gunathilaka, T. & Premasiri, L. (2016). Moodle integrated mobile learning environment for distance learning. *International Journal of Scientific and Research Publications.*

Gunathilaka, T., Fernando, M. & Pasqual, H. (2017). Identification of the learning behavior of the students for education personalization. In *2017 International Conference on I-SMAC (IoT in Social, Mobile, Analytics and Cloud) (I-SMAC).*

Goebel, H., Siemund, H. & Kracht, M. (2016). Smart education in electrical engineering with S.m. i.L.E-mobile. In *Proceedings of the 2016 IEEE Global Engineering Education Conference (EDUCON).*

Haroon, M. & de Mel, W. (2017). Development of a hybrid learning system to enhance ODL; printed course material amelioration via smartphones. In *Proceedings the 31st Annual Conference of the Asian Association of Open Universities.*

Jayatilleke, B., Ranawaka, G., Wijesekara, C. & Kumarasinha, M. (2017). Development and testing of a mobile application through design-based research. In *Proceedings the 31st Annual Conference of the Asian Association of Open Universities AAOU.*

Jayatilleke, B., Kumarasinha, M. & Gunawardena, C. (2017). Implementing the first cross-border professional development online course through international e-mentoring. *Reflections and Perspectives, Open Praxis.*

Karunanayaka, S. P., Naidu, S., Rajendra, J. C. N., & Ratnayake, H. U. W. (2017). Designing reflective practice in the context of OER-based e-learning. *Journal of Learning for Development-JL4D*, 4.

Karunanayaka, S. P., Naidu, S., Rajendra, J. C. N., & Ratnayake, H. U. W. (2015). From OER to OEP: Shifting Practitioner Perspectives and Practices with Innovative Learning Experience Design. *Open Praxis*, 7. https://doi.org/10.5944/openpraxis.7.4.252.

Karunanayaka, S. P., Rajendra, J. C. N., Ratnayake, H. U. W., & Naidu, S. (2016). Peer-facilitated discussions to enhance OER-based e-learning. *Asian Association of Open Universities Journal, 11,* 90–104. https://doi.org/10.1108/AAOUJ-07-2016-0022.

Kulasekara, G., Jayatilleke, G. & Coomaraswamy, U. (2011). Learner perceptions on instructional design of multimedia in learning abstract concepts in science at a distance. *Open Learning: The Journal of Open, Distance and e-Learning.*

Nandana, W., de Mel, W. & Priyankara, H. (2012). Online remote laboratory for open distance learning. In *First International Conference on Open and Distance e-Learning*, Philippines.

Perera, W., Werapitiya, B., Rajasingham, S. & Premaratne, I. (2017). *Intrinsic Motivation Factors to Encourage Student Discussions in Online Classrooms: Integrating Facebook* (Only abstract published).

Premaratne, I. (2016). Development of an e-learning architecture based on numerical computing software for electrical engineering education in open and distance mode. In *8th Pan Commonwealth Forum,* Malaysia, Kuala Lumpur.

Porebska, A. & Wantuch, A. (2015). The role of computer-supported tools in the education of future engineers. The case of electrical engineering laboratory. In *8th International Conference on Human System Interaction (HSI).*

Price, L. & Kirkwood, A. (2014). Using technology for teaching and learning in higher education: a critical review of the role of evidence in informing practice. *Higher Education Research & Development.*

Rathiranee, Y. (2013). Challenges in Online learning towards better learning environment : A Case study on Bachelor of Business Management (BBM) Online Degree Programme at University of Jaffna, Sri Lanka. In *12th International Tamil Internet Conference*, University of Mala.

Samaranayaka, T. & de Mel, W. (2017). Extending the boundaries of remote laboratory by providing hands on experience. In *Proceedings of the The 31st Annual Conference of the Asian Association of Open Universities AAOU.*

Shieh, R. (2012). The impact of technology-enabled active learning (TEAL) implementation on student learning and teachers' teaching in a high school context. *Computers and Education, 59*(2).

Valdez, M., Ferreira, C., Martins, M. & Barbosa, F. (2014). *Virtual labs in electrical engineering education—The VEMA environment.* IEEE.

Vandewalle, J. (2011). Challenges and opportunities for introducing basic circuits and systems in electrical engineering education. In *7th International Conference on Electrical and Electronics Engineering (ELECO).*

E-Learning as a Medium for Facilitating Learners' Support Services Under Open and Distance Learning: An Evaluative Study

Trisha Dowerah Baruah

Introduction

The buzzword in communication today is technology. It becomes even more relevant when communication takes place over long distances and across countries. Any form of education, be it traditional or distance education uses a wide array of teaching aids and learning tools so as to make the distance learning system more interactive and informative. These days, open and distance learning system is considered at par with the conventional system of education. This is mainly because of the fact that a lot of emphasis is given in developing quality self-learning materials which are the lifeline of this educational system along with ICT-based tools. Its flexible nature has garnered widespread interest in the minds of the common people, especially the students who have dropped out of the formal system of learning owing to certain personal problems.

The practice of distance education is soon catching up in with almost all the countries of the world—whether it is a developed, an underdeveloped or a developing nation. What remains to be found is whether these countries are able to tap into the resources to the best of their ability or not.

Concept of Learner Support Services

Learner support services form an integral part of open and distance learning system of education. Since the learners are not in direct face-to-face contact with the instructors/teachers except for counselling classes during the weekend in the ODL

T. D. Baruah (✉)
Bhupen Hazarika School of Mass Communication, Krishna Kanta Handiqui
State Open University, Guwahati 781017, India
e-mail: trisha.baruah@gmail.com

© Springer Nature Singapore Pte Ltd. 2018

Anjana (ed.), *Technology for Efficient Learner Support Services in Distance Education*, https://doi.org/10.1007/978-981-13-2300-3_5

system, they need to be provided with adequate support services so that they are given education at par with the face-to-face conventional system. Learner support services comprise all the assistance provided by a distance education system to the learners so that they do not feel isolated from the educational system and get adequate academic and administrative support. Initially, correspondence system was in vogue whereby the study materials were sent by post to the learners' addresses. However, with the growth and development of ICT, the services that are given to the learners changed. The study materials have been supplemented by ICT tools and technologies. The use of ICT has facilitated the delivery mechanism and has made learning more accurate and cost-effective. Although most of the distance learning institutes/universities use technology-enhanced support services, yet study materials in the form of SLMs are increasingly used to supplement learning. Instructors have integrated new media into the teaching–learning process under distance education. Group interactions, face-to-face counselling, weekend tutorial, teleconferencing, webcasts, online chat forums, etc., have opened up new vistas for learning. Such form of communication gives the opportunity of getting feedback from the learners along with clearance of doubts, evaluation of progress reports and giving appropriate counselling.

Most of the support services are well supported by information and communication technology (ICT). ICT tools not only speeds up the delivery of the support services, but also makes learning more interactive and interesting. Innovation in the media sector coupled with the use of the radio and television has accelerated the delivery of support services within the shortest possible time frame. For instance in New Zealand and Australia, Radio tutorials and Radio conferences are used on a wide scale to deliver need-based learning to the learners. Most of the developed countries of the world use a combination of traditional and technological methods of distance delivery courses and services. Cable TV, electronic blackboard, fibre optics and telephone are used in conjunction with study materials and counselling sessions. Videotape and video discs are also important forms of communication tools through which the study materials are copied in the form of diskettes and can be provided to the learners. This proves to be quite handy to the learners as they can view the video clips and also go through the study materials. Audio cassettes and videotapes are important forms of communication tools, and the basic advantage they have over the radio and TV is that it enables the learner to listen or watch the clips at their own discretion. Phonograph records, flexi disc and educational film strips are some of the tools that are considered to be a substantial part of learners' support services.

Telephone is another important tool of communicating with the learners and the teachers. Telephonic conversation lends a human touch to the interaction process. Tele-tutoring and teleconferencing are two important widely used tools of communication in distance education. With the easy availability of smartphones in the market, learners can communicate with their instructors or peers over different social media platforms. Android mobiles have facilitated mobile-based learning which is fast catching up as one of the preferred methods of imparting learning.

Whatever be the level and area of operation, the learners' support services should basically address the following issues:

(i) ***Information support***: Learners should be provided all necessary information before and during the duration of their programme so that they can make appropriate decisions about their studies and also have access to all necessary resources and support services. This is inclusive of information about various programmes, admission requirements, fee structure, study material, system of assessment and other support services offered by the institution.

(ii) ***Institutional support***: The learners must be provided with information relating to academic counselling sessions, who the counsellors are, provision of assignments, provision of practical for practical-based programmes, use of electronic media such as audio, video, teleconferencing, interactive radio counselling.

(iii) ***Learning centres***: Provision must be made at the study centres where the learners will be accessible to the counsellors, library facilities and use of electronic equipment to supplement the learning material, submission and evaluation of assignments, term-end examinations and other support.

(iv) ***Feedback***: Learners must also be given the liberty to generate feedback via assignment response sheets. Feedback can be provided on different issues—course structure, delivery mechanism, administrative and educational facility, learner support services, etc. Simply providing the learners with pages and pages of study material will not result in fruitful educational discourse. This has to be backed by the requisite needs and preferences of the learners. This is because through feedback, the authorities will be able to gauge the problems faced by the learners and accordingly offer necessary solutions. This results in a free flow of communication between the instructors/administration and the learners resulting in effective communication.

The Indian government has laid special emphasis on harnessing special technology to be used in the ODL system. There must be a judicious mix of media relevant to the needs of the learners. Special attention must be paid to plan and build up an effective infrastructure of learner support services which are essential to the distance education teaching–learning processes.

The following questions needs to be answered in order to formulate an effective learner's support service.

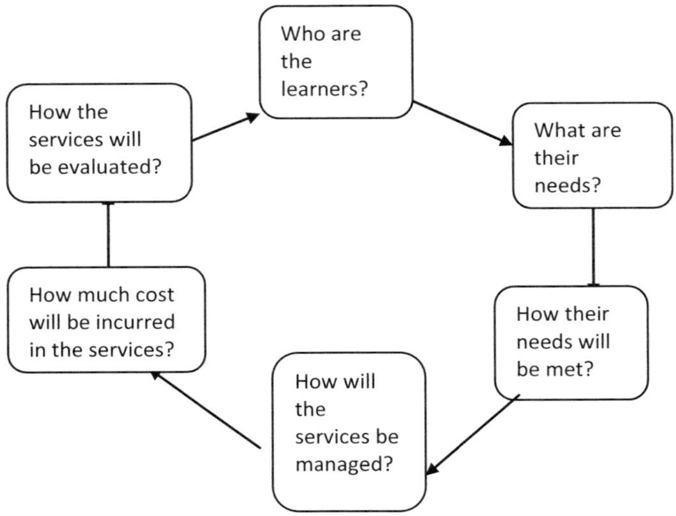

Diagram: A framework for planning and managing learners support services *Source* Husain M (2003), Distance Education: Theory and Practice, Encyclopedia of Distance Education. New Delhi: Anmol Publications

Identifying the Learners

Learners occupy the central position in any distance education system. In order to make the learner support services appropriate and effective, we need to identify background of the learners. While identifying the background, it is necessary to take into account the age, gender, educational background, language, access to information and communication tools, etc., of the learners. Accordingly, support services will have to be provided keeping in view the different categories of learners and different levels of programmes.

Identifying Learner's Needs

The second most important criteria that must be taken into consideration while providing a full-fledged learner support services is to identify what the needs of the learners are. This is necessary because only then the support services can be properly utilized by the learners.

Ways to Meet the Needs and Preferences of the Learners

Once the needs of the learners are identified, the question that pops up in the minds of the educationists is to chalk out ways to prepare the learner for a better tomorrow.

The learners are provided certain support services to aid them in their academic and personal needs. The range of services that is provided through activities are—

- Pre and post-admission counselling
- Providing tutoring classes during the weekends
- Equipping the learners with learning skills
- Providing peer group support
- Providing feedback to the learners regarding the home assessment and the subsequent progress that needs to be made
- Providing language support to the learners
- Provision of career counselling.

Media tools such as correspondence, face-to-face counselling, telephone, teleconferencing, radio, television, social media tools, web-based media, electronic communication tools (email, online chat, podcasting, etc.) provide a range of means which differ widely in their effectiveness for individuals and groups in ways that are as yet inadequately understood, and need constant monitoring if provision is not to replace service. The parent institution/university delineates the support services to be provided to the learners at some specially designated study centres. Though some major services are provided from the institution itself, yet the majority of the services are provided by the study centres. Study centres form an established part of the great majority of model ODL systems, providing the physical space for a range of activities to take place on a face-to-face basis—enquiry services, pre-study advice, application, tutoring, counselling, interactive radio and TV, telephone services, audio–visual playback facilities, library, tutor training, independent study spaces, laboratory facility, examination facilities, student peer meetings, publicity and marketing, storage and collection point for study materials and decentralized office accommodation.

Costs and Management of the Learner Support Services

This is the most important aspect of any learner support services. This is because it is easy to provide the services to the learners, but it is rather cumbersome and difficult to maintain and manage them. In terms of management, Paul (1990) identifies two principal areas specific to the management of learners' support services in ODL, namely the management of structures which are developed from the institution's headquarters and which involve centre–periphery relations and the management of part-time of campus tutors and counsellors.

Adequate, qualitative and effective learner support services have now become an important part of most of the good distance education institutes/universities. It has been well established that support services must be provided to the distant learners who most of the time remain isolated, away from the instructors and their peers. The main purpose of providing learner support services is to help the learners overcome the feeling of isolation and to facilitate learning. A good relationship between the learners and the instructors/teachers is necessary in order to support a well-balanced support service. For efficient functioning of a distance education institute, the following basic provisions must be made in order to attract learners:

(i) Basic amenities (sitting room along with washroom and clean drinking water)
(ii) High-quality self-learning materials
(iii) Responsive administration
(iv) Professionally competent and dedicated faculty
(v) Library facilities
(vi) Audio–visual learning materials
(vii) Computer laboratory, Internet facilities
(viii) Feedback
(ix) ICT-based tools, educational radio and television, web-based learning tools.

For any learner support service to prosper, the relationship between the learner and then instructor–teacher must be cordial, responsive and strong. This is because without a personal relation, the learner might feel lost and isolated. The harmonious relationship depends upon the sincerity, earnestness and cooperation between the two. Learner support services in distance education system are of prime importance because learners suffer from a host of problems like-

- Lack of physical proximity resulting in lack of confidence and thus the need of constant support and guidance from the faculty
- Lack of adequate infrastructure—books, library services, etc.
- Lack of adequate time as most of the time he/she remains busy in some occupation or the other
- Lack of guidance
- Fear of examinations, etc.

In order to reduce the problems to a certain extent, good learner–teacher relationship is a must in ensuring the success of a learner in completing the course and understanding the tenets of education.

An effective learner–teacher relationship would go a long way in:

(i) Encouraging learner participation a sine qua non for the smooth functioning of the open and distance educational system.
(ii) Supplementing the efforts of the distance education system in the conduct of its affairs.
(iii) Strengthening the values of responsibility in the minds of the learners.
(iv) Enlisting respect in the practices of distance education institute.
(v) Developing bonds of friendship and goodwill between learners and faculty and vice versa.
(vi) Avoiding social unrest, tensions, violence and other social upheavals which have become the order of the day on the campus.

Apart from better personal relations between learners and service providers, the following services are equally important:

Provision of Basic Amenities

By basic amenities, we mean that the university/institute must make provision for a reception office to deal with the queries of the internal and the eternal public, restroom, washroom and the provision of potable drinking water facility. Though these facilities are not generally counted among the support services, nevertheless such facilities can build bridges of understanding between the learners and the institute.

Responsive Administration

Distance education learners need a lot of clarification regarding their educational needs for which they write letters or come personally to meet the administrators/ instructors at the institutes/study centres. The administrative unit of the distance education institutions must address the queries of the learners promptly and efficiently. The people in charge of the administration must take their duties seriously and with devotion. The head of the institution must ensure good administrative support to the learners. In distance educational system, we need to apply total quality management (TQM) which has been designed to create learner-centred high performing organization by involving all employees in process improvement efforts.

In this way, distance education institute/organization can improve the quality of products and services, increase job satisfaction and enhance learner satisfaction. This would eventually lead to growth and development of the institutes/universities. However, for all these to succeed, transparency and accountability must be maintained in the system without which the administrative set-up would collapse. However, in practice, the administrative system is not effective resulting in dropouts, incurring expenditure by learners to visit the institutes in person and voice their grievances and problems. The head of the institution/university must take full responsibility in delineating their duties towards the learners by injecting administrative improvements and keeping a constant watch on key issues. The institute must be able to motivate the learners to pursue their academic goals and strive for excellence in whatever field they want to go.

Competent and Dedicated Faculty

Faculty members are the lifeline of any distance educational system. However, we find that the teachers are quite hesitant to venture into the open and distance educational mode of teaching than the traditional mode. This has resulted in the employment of less and less teachers leading to a downfall in quality management. So, utmost steps are necessary to encourage the teachers and give them special bonus or stipends to take extra classes. Most of the time, it has also been seen that the instructors do not come to the office or the study centres on time leading to utter chaos. Dedication enthusiasm and zeal are missing. As such, competent, dedicated and honest teachers are the need of the hour. Teachers training programmes must be conducted by the respective institutions/universities in order to impart the necessary values of head and heart in them. They must be given proper environment to work and given special amenities so that they do not feel inferior to their counterparts engaged in the conventional system of education. Leadership skills, expertise in their respective subjects and the ability to handle pressure in the face of adversity are the marks of a good teacher/instructor.

Library Facilities

Library and information technology-based library tools occupy an important place in the area of distance education. A well-equipped library with the latest technology not only helps the learners in their academic line but also provides them motivation to aim for higher studies.

Functional Study Centres

Study centres are also an important component of open and distance learning system. Every study centre should act as an information, publicity and guidance cell. The centres must be well organized with proper facilities of library, personal contact programmes and other audio–visual tools like CDs, cassettes, conferencing facilities, radio and television broadcasts, overhead projectors, and apart from functioning as a centre of learning, study centres also serve the following functions-

(i) It helps in assessing the local educational requirements which in return can help in designing new programme.
(ii) It can also serve as a meeting place for the learners where interaction takes place leading to discussion and mutual understanding.
(iii) It serves as a meeting place for interaction between the learners and the tutors which can lead to socialization.
(iv) It serves as a place for socio-psychological satisfaction.
(v) It serves to keep distance learners at ease.

Most of the open universities and DEIs have study centres of their own for the learners to take benefit of proximity and avail the facilities that are provided to them.

Networking

Networking refers to pooling of resources and sharing of benefits by distance education system. This would improve the quality of services as an individual institution cannot afford the quality required to implement distance education programmes.

Importance of Technology in ODL

Technology has come to be an important part in the teaching–learning process of distance education. Different ICT-based communication tools are used extensively to suit the needs and preferences of the learners. Gone are the days when self-learning materials used to be the main instructional material for the learners. However, these days, such conventional materials are supplemented by ICT-based tools and techniques. This form of blended learning is most appropriate for distance education system as it has opened the doors to new alternatives for providing education and training in ways not possible just a few decades back.

An effective distance learning system uses a variety of technologies to support the instruction. The important elements in any distance learning system have been provided in the following diagram.

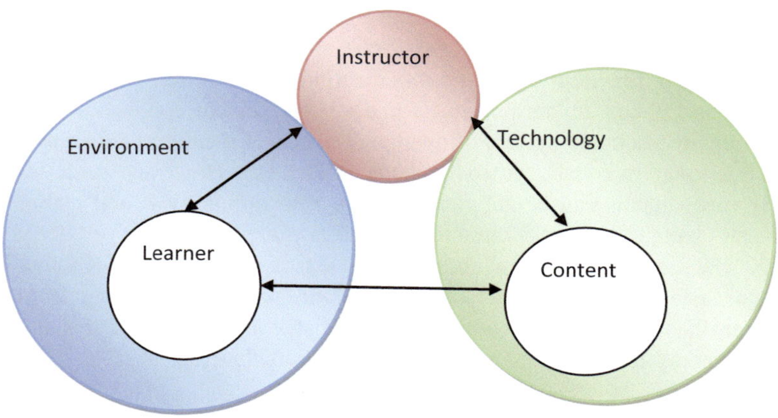

Diagram: Core elements in a distance learning environment

The learner stands at the apex of a distance educational system. This is basically due to the fact that the transfer of knowledge takes place with the learner at the centre. Learners are provided with requisite support services in the form of print and audiovisual materials. Study materials (SLMs) constitute an important aspect of learner support services as they are portable and easy to understand. The study materials are well supplemented by technology in the form of synchronous and asynchronous communication tools.

For the proper transfer of knowledge to the learners, technology comes in handy as it helps to assimilate the learning tools for the betterment of the learners. Of course, the concerned university or the distance educational institute must have the requisite infrastructural facility (for instance, high-speed broadband connection, videoconferencing facility) to support the technology-enhanced learning. Then comes the role of instructor who is responsible for coordinating the entire teaching–learning process. The instructor paves the way for the proper utilization of the technology-based learning by the learners. This is because many a time, the learner is not aware of the latest tools and technologies employed by the educational institution. If the instructor does not properly shoulder his or her responsibility, then the learners are bound to suffer academically and their grades will come down.

Hence, the instructor, learner and the instructional content must work in tandem in order to achieve the desired result.

Thus, the whole of distance educational system consists of the learner, content, technology, instructor/counsellor and environment and these components are related to one another.

Delivering Learners' Support Services Through ICT-Enabled Environment at KKHSOU

Distance education represents a paradigm shift in the world of education. Improvement in the field of telecommunications and related information technologies has opened up new vistas for open and distance education delivery. Initially, the instructional system of open and distance learning mainly consisted of self-instructional materials, video cassettes, CDs, etc. However, such forms of delivery mechanisms can be supplemented by new online tools and technologies which can change the way communication takes place.

K. K. Handiqui State Open University was established under the Krishna Kanta Handiqui State Open University, Act' 2005 and started functioning from 11th December, 2006. It is worth mentioning here that it is the first and the only State Open University in the entire north-eastern region of India.

The main aim of the university is to provide quality higher education by utilizing different educational technologies. In other words, KKHSOU aspires to be widely recognized as the first choice of-

- learners who want relevant, top quality courses/educational programmes
- researchers who want to create a local, regional and transnational sphere of research
- other players and institutional agents that want strategic partnerships.

The University offers a number of programmes including vocational, Ph.D. and M.Phil. programmes in different disciplines catering to the needs of the learners. The short-term vocational training programmes are offered through some of the selected Industrial Training Institutes and Polytechnics.

The University also has a well-defined learners' support system which is well supported by technology-enabled learning resources. The various learners' support services that are given by the university to the learners are given below-

- Self-learning materials that are provided to the learners at the time of admission.
- Counselling classes are held at different study centres for the benefit of the learners.
- Provision of library facilities both at the study centres and at the Central Library of the University.
- Availability of audio–video materials on select modules in the University's website.
- Availability of different community radio programmes in online platforms.
- Broadcast of learner-centric radio programme (Eklavya, which is also simultaneously relayed by All India Radio, Dibrugarh) and live phone-in programme by All India Radio, Guwahati. In the phone-in programme, learners can post any queries to the University officials or faculty members and interact with them on a variety of educational and administrative issues.
- Interaction by way of email, social media and online discussion forums. Learners are encouraged to keep a tab on the latest information related to academic and administrative work by contacting the respective administrative and academic officials through email, social media and online discussion forums. For the said purpose, email IDs and other relevant information are provided to the learners.
- The University has its own Android app known as 'KKHSOU' that has been specifically designed for the learners to be able to gather information pertaining to the different academic programmes, detailed list of the study centres, list of contact numbers of the concerned persons of the study centres, etc. This particular app can be downloaded from the Google Play Store and is free of cost.
- There is also the provision of Short Messaging Service (SMS) which the learners can register free of cost. The main reason behind providing such kind of service is to keep the learner updated regarding admission schedule, upcoming examination schedule, information regarding examination results, etc.

Apart from the above mentioned support services, the University also provides free education to the jail inmates of certain central district jails of the state and necessary learner support services are provided to them absolutely free of cost. The University has truly upheld its motto, 'Education Beyond Barriers', by providing free education to the jail inmates of three district jails in Guwahati, Jorhat and Abhayapuri. The differently-abled learners of the state have also not been left behind in their quest for academic excellence as special provision has been made for them by providing learning materials in Braille and audio cassettes.

Instructional Delivery Mechanism Under KKHSOU

Blended learning system is in place for delivery of learning materials. Not only are self-learning materials provided to the learners at the different study centres, but pre-recorded CDs are also distributed to the learners for academic purposes. These CDs contain academic discussions on a range of topics. Social media, emails, discussion forums are some of the online platforms with the help of which the learners interact with their peers as well as with the officials/faculty members of the University. Thus, we can summarize the instructional delivery mechanism by focusing on the following three ways.

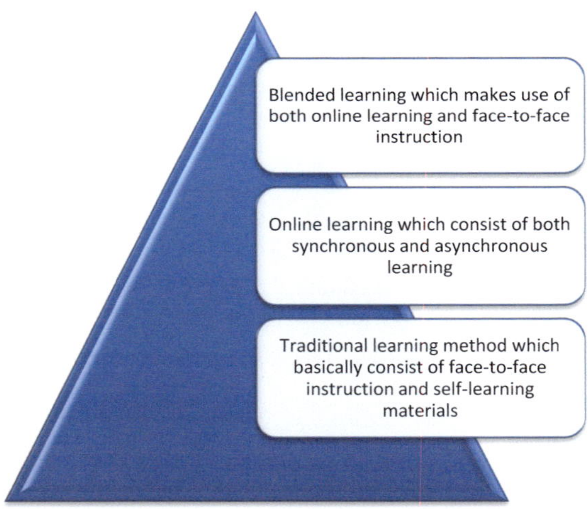

From the above diagram, it can be seen that blended learning, online learning and traditional learning are used in conjunction with one another. In fact, all three of them are interrelated.

Some of the Important New Media Technologies that Are Used on a Wide Scale by the University Have Been Exemplified in the Following Manner

(a) Provision of academic learning through the medium of community radio: The community radio of the University known as Jnan Taranga, which was launched on 20th November, 2010 broadcasts a number of community-based programmes bordering on issues like health and hygiene, rights of the children, sanitation, drug abuse and women empowerment. An Internet version of the community radio (known as e-Jnan Taranga) is also available for the benefit of the learners, whereby the different programmes can be accessed anytime and at any place.

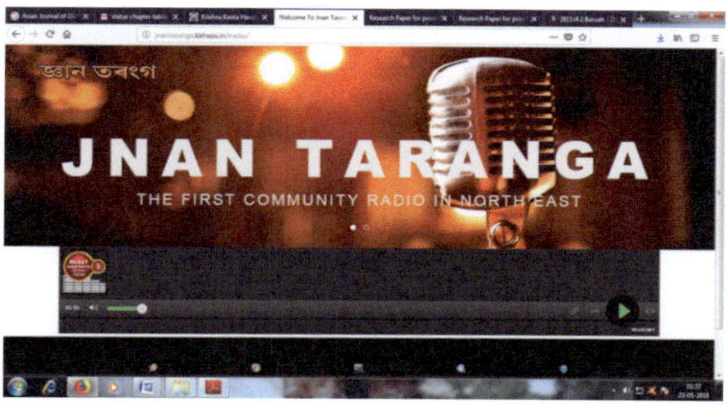

e-Jnan Taranga site: http://jnantaranga.kkhsou.in/iradio/

(b) **Provision of online resources and E-learning portal**: In order for the learners to make use of the online learning materials, the University has made provision for the availability of an E-resource portal where a number of important links to some of the websites and online journals (JSTOR, JGATE and SAGE) are readily available. The Central Library of the University maintains this database and an online search engine known as the Open Access Journals Search Engine (OAJSE-http://www.oajse.com/) is in place. This is an open access E-journal portal of the University.
The University's website serves as another important platform for acquiring knowledge and information. Home assignments, admission forms, old question papers and other important documents of the University are readily available on the website which the learners can download whenever necessary (Figs. 1, 2, 3 and 4).

(c) **Provision of SMS alert services**: The University has made provision for SMS alert facility whereby learners can subscribe for latest news and keep themselves updated. In a way, this form of mobile learning system is beneficial because it is always not possible to look at the website of the University for any news and information.

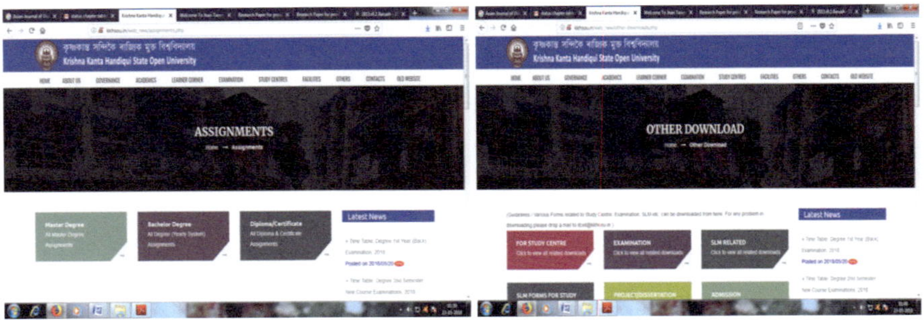

Fig. 1 Website of KKHSOU offers a plethora of materials like home assignments (http://kkhsou.in/web_new/assignments.php), old questions papers, application forms that can be downloaded (http://kkhsou.in/web_new/other-downloads.php) very easily

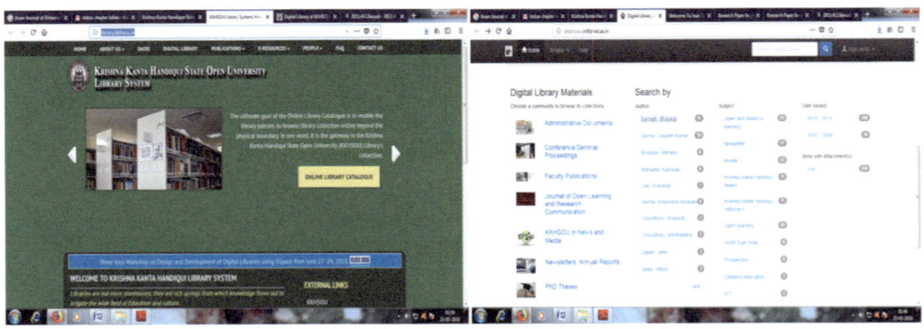

Fig. 2 Central Library (http://library.kkhsou.in/) and the Digital Library (http://dlkkhsou.inflibnet.ac.in/) of the University provides links to different resources like the OAJSE, research reports, faculty publications, video links

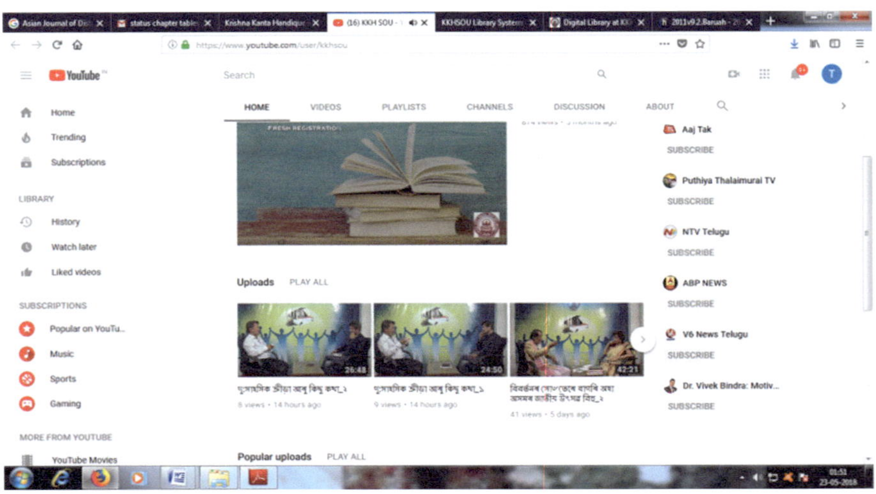

Fig. 3 Links have also been provided for the streaming of videos through YouTube (https://www.youtube.com/user/kkhsou)

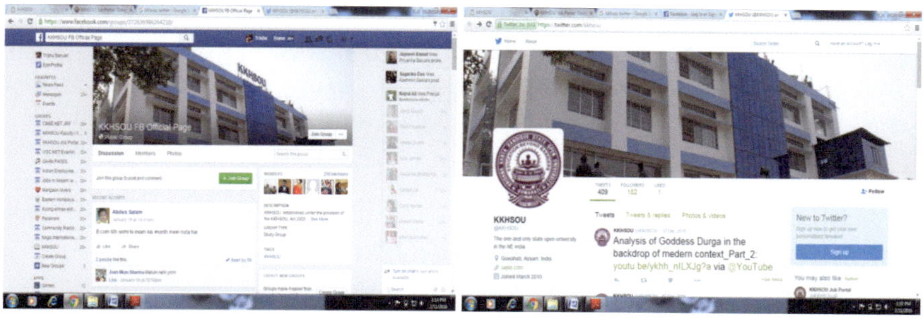

Fig. 4 KKHSOU's official home page on Facebook and Twitter

(d) **Newmedia (here emphasis is given on social media) as a medium for interaction**: Of late, different forms of new media like social media are used extensively by different educational institutions for the purpose of maintaining connectivity with the learners. KKHSOU too is also not far behind in this regard. Social networking platforms like Facebook and Twitter are used by the University to post any updated news or start a discussion with the members of the home pages.

(e) **Availability of E-SLM**: Learners can also access the self-learning materials that are provided in electronic format in the website of the University (Fig. 5).

(f) **Launch of educational television channel**: KKHSOU launched an educational television programme known as 'Ximar Poridhi Bhangi' (literally translated as 'Breaking the Barriers') from June 2018 onwards. This programme has been conceptualized in collaboration with Prag News channel of Assam and is broadcast every Sunday from 3.30 pm to 4.00 pm in the

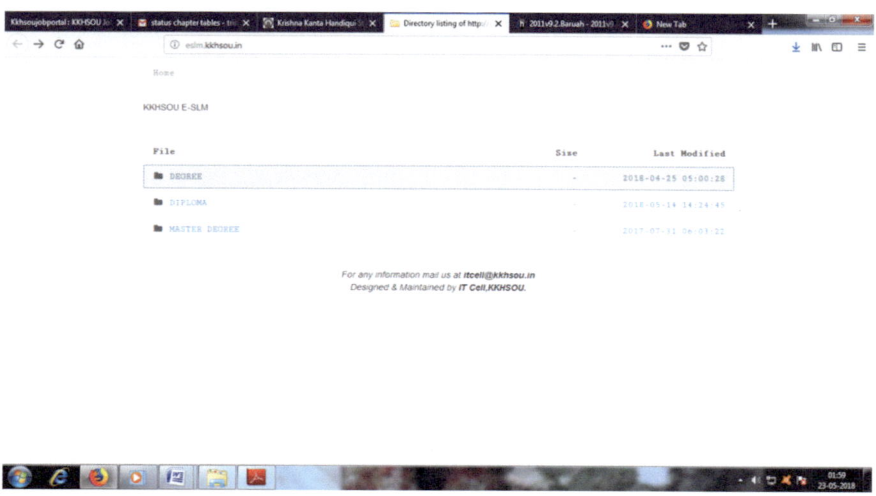

Fig. 5 Provision of E-SLM (http://eslm.kkhsou.in/)

concerned channel. The episodes can also be viewed in the YouTube platform (link to these episodes—https://youtu.be/LdgQSfMKnkg). The programme content is discussion oriented whereby the faculty members from different disciplines discuss curriculum related topics for the benefit of the learners.

Best Practices Being Followed at KKHSOU

- ***Online Admission at KKHSOU***

The University has gone one step ahead and made online admission to various courses compulsory from 2018–19 academic sessions onwards. Before applying for online admission, one has to register with the University's Online Admission System (http://online.kkhsou.in).

- ***Virtual Learning Environment under KKHSOU***

The University has introduced ICT-enabled programmes from February 2015 onwards. These programmes are offered in the field of Master of Business Administration (MBA), Master of Computer Application (MCA), Master of Science in Information Technology (MSc-IT), Postgraduate Diploma in Computer Application (PGDCA), Postgraduate Diploma in Business Management (PGDBM) and Postgraduate Diploma in Human Resource Management (PGDHRM). As far as MBA programme is concerned, learners are selected based on a written entrance test. The important features of the ICT-enabled programme are given below (Fig. 6)-

Learners who enrol in these programmes can avail the contents of the programme through online, mobile and offline platform as mentioned below—

i. **Online**: In the online system of learning, learners are given an individual Learning Management System (LMS) ID where they can access the soft copies of the study materials and other pre-recorded video lectures. Online quiz sessions have also been included under each chapter so that the learner can assess as to how much of the learning he or she was able to understand. Learners also have the option of joining a LIVE VIRTUAL CLASS as and when conducted. However, if a learner is unable to attend it, then he or she can go over the recorded version of the same. There is also the provision for the learners to participate in discussion forums.
ii. **Mobile Learning**: Learners using Android platform can download 'Lurningo' app from Play Store and access all the benefits of online learning on their mobile handset.
iii. **Offline**: University printed study materials are given to the learners. Moreover, the learners have the choice of opting for a SD (secure digital) card by paying a nominal fee. The SD card contains all the video lectures of that particular

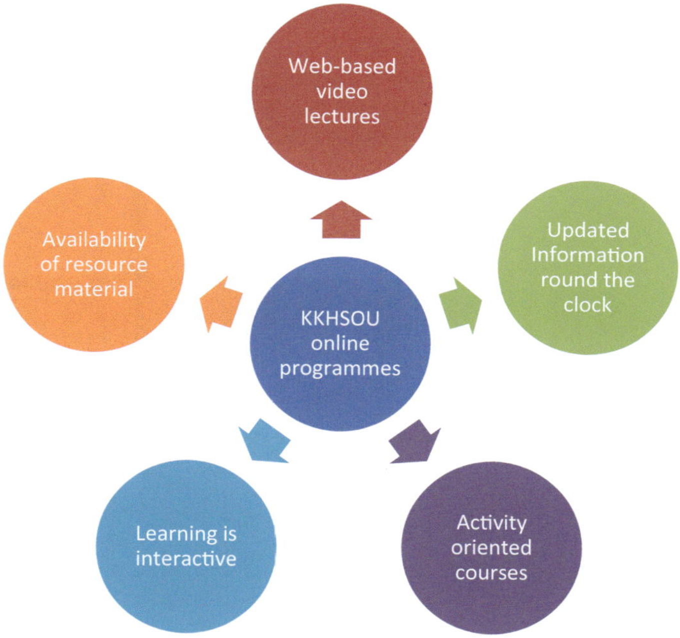

Fig. 6 Basic features of KKHSOU ICT enabled programme

semester. The learner just needs an Android/Windows phone where they can access all the videos without net connectivity.

Provision of TAB: Learners of MBA and MCA are provided with learning TABS free of cost which helps them to learn anywhere and at anytime (Fig. 7).

- ***Andriod App***: This Android app which is available free of cost from Google Play Store is another important IT tool that helps in browsing for different types of information at one click. However, this app is applicable for only Android Devices (2.3.6 and above version). This particular app has even received an award for information in 'Mobile Application as a Learner Support Services' in 2017 from IGNOU.
- ***Learner Information Management System***: Under this system, every learner (from 2013 academic session onwards) of KKHSOU have been provided with login credentials (enrolment and date of birth) which enables them to access their own personalized information.

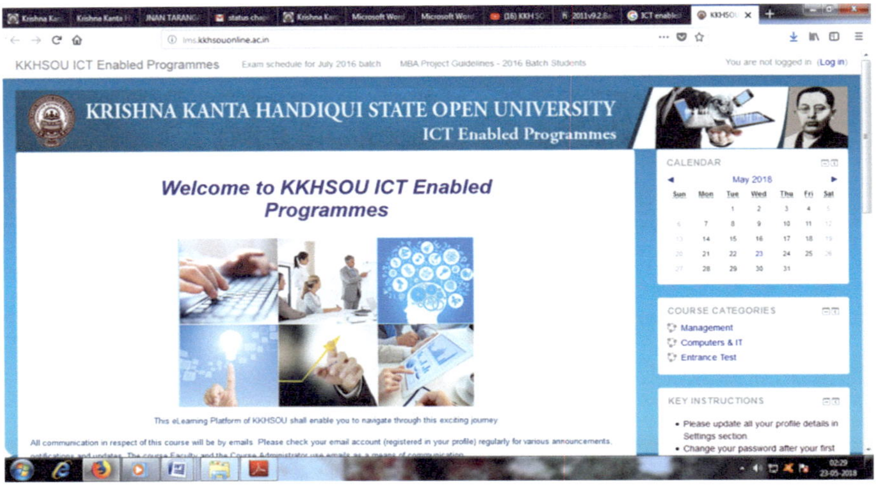

Fig. 7 Home page of ICT-enabled programmes of KKHSOU (http://lms.kkhsouonline.ac.in/)

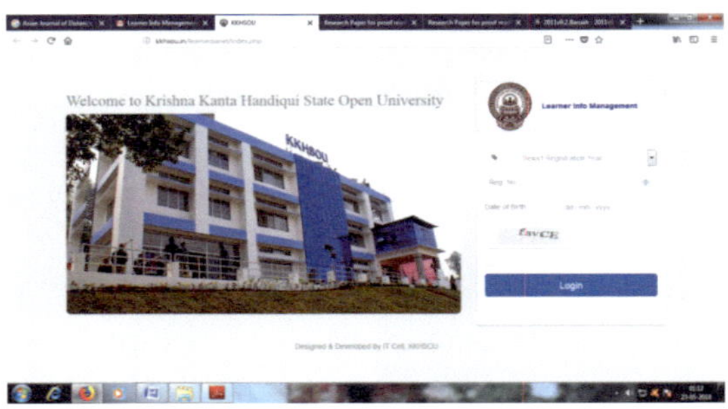

Site: http://kkhsou.in/learnerpanel/index.php

No wonder the University was able to bag the prestigious ‘Excellence for Institutional Achievement’ Award for the year 2011–13 during the 7th Pan-Commonwealth Forum for Open Learning held in Abuja, Nigeria, in 2013. Most of the universities, the world over have made sincere attempts in integrating virtual learning environment in the teaching–learning process. It won’t be long before a networked community on a global level will emerge connecting the learners, instructors and the stakeholders of the distance educational system.

Challenges Being Faced by KKHSOU in the Implementation of the New Media Technology and Its Future Prospects

It can be said without any doubt that new media technology indeed helps to make learning interesting and interactive in the field of distance education. But the question that arises is whether all the ICT-based tools and technologies are effectively being used in the distance educational system of KKHSOU? Both the new media learning tools along with the traditional instructional tools are used in conjunction with one another in order to impart learning to the learners.

Very often, it has been seen that learners have to face certain problems like power shortage, low Internet connectivity, lack of instructional guidance on how to proceed with the curriculum and finally a feeling of isolation due to lack of interaction and contact with their instructors. If one looks from the administrative point of view of the open universities, lack of infrastructure in place also poses a problem in the effective functioning of the ICT-based tools. Proper planning must be done before going for any such ambitious projects as there is every possibility of these technologies lying unused in the long run.

Plans are afoot for introducing videoconferencing facility in the next few months. This would greatly benefit the learners as they can engage in discussions with another person while being geographically separated. With the passage of time, Learners' Support Services has also been undergoing change to meet high expectations of the learners in providing qualitative services. The entire gamut of ODL delivery mechanism has been undergoing a paradigm shift from tutor counselling to technology-mediated support service system to suit quality and quantity dimensions of ODL delivery practices.

Thus, it is seen that new media tools have indeed facilitated in the delivery of Learners' Support Services which forms the crux of any distance learning system. For instance, social networking sites have emerged as major platforms of discussion for the numerous learners while the eResource portal offers a plethora of information as far as academic courses are concerned.

So, in a way, support services are provided to the learners with the aid of new media technologies.

In the coming future, the University plans to make extensive use of communication tools to support the differently abled learners. The University also plans to develop more video-based instructional materials for teaching practical skills at a distance. An effective learning management system would be of much value in the field of distance educational system and the University plans to put an effective LMS in place soon.

Virtual reality and augmented reality have taken the world by storm. It is being used on a wide scale in most of the developed countries of the world in the field of education. KKHSOU is also mulling in introducing such form of technologies for distance learning programmes so as to make learning more interesting and interactive thereby leading to an increase in enrolment and reducing dropout rates in the long run.

Conclusion

In this age of ICT, only printed SLMs will not suffice the needs of the distance learners. It has to be well supplemented by advanced information and communication tools (ICT) in order to make learning interesting and interactive. This would also ensure the timely and effective delivery of learners' support services which forms the crux of any distance educational system.

Technology is a power tool in the teaching learning process both in the case of face-to-face and open and distance education. Before infusing ICT into the distance learning network, the ODL institutions must look at the feasibility of operating it. There must be adequate funding from regulatory bodies to not only keep the communication tools in working condition but also upgrading them with technological advancement. Most importantly, well qualified instructors must be employed who would be capable of looking into the effective delivery of the support services with the help of communication tools. The learners cannot be bombarded with a large cache of ICT tools without educating them on its mode of operation. Steps must be taken on a war footing to make ICT a part and parcel of distance education especially in the rural areas.

Reference

Husain, M. (2003). *Distance education: Theory and practice*. Encyclopedia of Distance Education. New Delhi : Anmol Publications.

Use of Technology for Learner Support Services: A Case Study of IGNOU

V. Venkata Subrahmanyam

Indira Gandhi National Open University: A Preamble

India being a diverse nation, there are multiple options available for students pursuing higher education. Distance education constitutes a major part of the higher education spectrum in India. As per the reports on the Distance Education Bureau, UGC website, the share of distance education to Gross Enrolment Ratio (GER) is 22–23%. The website estimates approximately 40 lakh students enrol in distance education programs annually. Apart from the dual mode Universities (universities which offer both regular and distance courses), there are fifteen single mode open universities in India as shown below in Table 1. Among them, Indira Gandhi National Open University is a National Open University and others listed here are State Open Universities.

Indira Gandhi National Open University, the world's largest open university, was established by an Act of Parliament in 1985, "to advance and disseminate learning and knowledge by a diversity of means, including the use of any communication technology, to provide opportunities for higher education to a larger segment of the population and to promote the educational well-being of the community generally, to encourage the open university and distance education systems in the educational pattern of the country and to coordinate and determine the standards in such systems" (IGNOU 2007). It has tried to make a mark in the higher education scenario in India by offering high-quality teaching through Open and Distance Learning (ODL) mode. In 1987, the University was started with two academic programmes (Diploma in Management and Diploma in Distance

V. Venkata Subrahmanyam (✉)
School of Computer and Information Sciences, Indira Gandhi National Open University, New Delhi, India
e-mail: vvsubrahmanyam@ignou.ac.in

© Springer Nature Singapore Pte Ltd. 2018

Anjana (ed.), *Technology for Efficient Learner Support Services in Distance Education*, https://doi.org/10.1007/978-981-13-2300-3_6

Table 1 National and State Open Universities in India

SNo.	Name of the open university	National/state open university
1	Indira Gandhi National Open University (IGNOU),New Delhi	National Open University
2	Dr.B.R. Ambedkar Open University (BRAOU), Hyderabad	State Open University
3	Vardhaman Mahaveer Open University (VMOU), Kota	State Open University
4	Nalanda Open University, Patna	State Open University
5	Yashwantrao Chavan Maharashtra Open University (YCMOU), Nashik	State Open University
6	Madhya Pradesh Bhoj Open University (MPBOU), Bhopal	State Open University
7	Dr. Babasaheb Ambedkar Open University (BAOU), Ahmedabad	State Open University
8	Karnataka State Open University (KSOU), Mysore	State Open University
9	Netaji Subhas Open University (NSOU), Kolkata	State Open University
10	UP Rajarshi Tandon Open University (UPRTOU), Allahabad	State Open University
11	Tamilnadu Open University (TNOU), Chennai	State Open University
12	Pt. Sundarlal Sharma Open University (PSSOU), Bilaspur	State Open University
13	Uttarakhand Open University, Haldwani, Nainital	State Open University
14	Krishna Kanta Handiqui State Open University, Guwahati	State Open University
15	Odisha State Open University, Sambalpur	State Open University

Education) with a strength of 4,528 students. Today, it serves the educational aspirations of over 3 million students in India and other countries through 21 schools of studies, divisions and a network of 67 Regional Centres, around 2948 active learner support centres (LSCs) and 29 overseas partner institutions with 58,000 approved academic counsellors from conventional institutions of higher learning, professional organizations and industry among others. At present, the University is offering 236 academic, professional, vocational, awareness generating and skill-oriented programmes of study at the level of Certificate, Diploma, Bachelor's Degree, Master's Degree and Doctoral Degree through its schools of studies. The enrolment (fresh and re-registration) of learners in 2016–17 was 9,17,117. IGNOU has been conferred with Award of Excellence by the Commonwealth of Learning (COL), Canada. It was listed 27th in the webometric ranking of Indian Universities, based on the criterion of its presence on the Internet, in March 2013. IGNOU has lived up to the country's expectations of providing education to the marginalized and diverse sections of society, thus striving to meet its commitment of the democratization of higher education.

Authorities of IGNOU

Visitor or Chancellor of the University is *The President of India*. Next the Vice Chancellor of the University, is the Chief Executive Officer. He is the ex officio Chairperson of the *Board of Management (BOM), the Academic Council, the Planning Board, the Research Council* and the *Finance committee* of the University.

The *Board of Management* is the Chief Executive Body of the University. It is empowered by the *Statutes* to look after the management and administration, the revenue, finances and property of the University as well as conducting all academic and administrative affairs. The apex academic body which decides the academic policies of the University and gives directions on methods of instruction, evaluation and improvement of academic standards is the *Academic Council*. It also provides guidance and supervision to research activities in the University. The financial matters, fixing the limits for the total recurring and non-recurring expenditure for the year is the function of the *Finance Committee*. It also reviews the grants from government, income and resources of the University. The responsibility for the design and formulation of priorities for academic programmes offered by the University is looked after by the *Planning Board* of the University. The *Research Council* is responsible for the planning, designing, organizing and monitoring of the research programmes.

The *School of Studies* are the basic academic units responsible for the conceptualization, design and development of academic programmes. Every school has a school board that oversees the academic activities of the school. It will be chaired by the Director of the school. The officers of the University include the Vice Chancellor, the Pro-Vice Chancellors, the Directors of the Schools/Divisions/Centres/Cells/Institutes, the Registrars, the Finance Officer and the Librarian.

Schools of Studies

The academic activities of the University are mainly organized through the schools of studies. At present, there are 21 schools of studies, which are responsible for planning, designing, developing and coordinating the academic programmes and courses offered by the University. Each school has a school board, a statutory body that oversees the development, research work and academic activities of the school. The 21 schools of IGNOU are School of Agriculture, School of Computer and Information Sciences, School of Continuing Education, School of Education, School of Engineering and Technology, School of Extension and Development Studies, School of Foreign Languages, School of Gender and Development Studies, School of Health Sciences, School of Humanities, School of Inter-Disciplinary and Trans-Disciplinary Studies, School of Journalism and New Media Studies, School of Law, School of Management Studies, School of Performing and Visual Arts,

School of Sciences, School of Social Work, School of Translation Studies and Training, School of Tourism and Hospitality Services Management, School of Vocational Education and Training.

Divisions

IGNOU has *Academic Coordination Division, Administration Division, Computer Division, Construction and Maintenance Division, Finance and Accounts Division, International Division, Library and Documentation Division, Material Production and Distribution Division, Planning and Development Division, Regional Services Division, Student Evaluation Division and Student Registration Division* which perform the University's academic and administrative activities and provide support in different areas.

The *Academic Coordination Division* (*ACD*) is engaged with the management of the affairs of the Teachers and Academics and facilitation of policy formulation of all academic matters of the University in accordance with the provisions of the IGNOU Act, Statutes and Ordinances.

The *Administration Division* leverages all the academic and non-academic activities of the University in one form or the other. It provides logistical infrastructure facilities and facilitates smooth functioning of the University.

The *Computer Division* (*CD*) is the prime IT service hub and provides various computing and network services. Network services, software development, website development and maintenance, application interfacing, ERP back office, data centre maintenance, training and capacity building and users' support are some of the activities of this division.

The *Material Production and Distribution Division* (*MPDD*) is one of the major operational divisions of the University which caters to the needs of the learners in terms of material production and distribution of self-instructional material. It also undertakes the activity of synchronization of production of assignments printing and dispatching to the learners.

The *Regional Services Division* (*RSD*) of the University is entrusted with the responsibility of developing policies, systems and procedures, establishing and managing student support system of the University comprising IGNOU Regional Centres (RCs) and Learner Support Centres (LSCs). The University has set up a nationwide network of 67 Regional Centres. These include nine RCs in the North-East region, six Army-Recognized Regional Centres, four Navy-Recognized Centres and one Assam Rifle-Recognized Centre. The network of Regional Centres is managed by nearly 700 academic and administrative staff posted at RCs. The RCs being full-time offices of the University oversee the operations of LSCs within their jurisdiction and also monitor academic and administrative support to distant learners.

Student Registration Division (*SRD*) monitors the registration of students for different programmes offered by the University besides re-registration, credit transfer, re-admission and change of elective course(s), assessing equivalence of degrees, etc. The division is effectively and successfully maintaining the database of over 3.04 million active students on the rolls of the University.

Student Evaluation Division (*SED*) is the operational division which coordinates and manages the term-end examinations being conducted twice a year in June and December across the country and overseas. This division is also responsible for conducting various entrance tests for some programmes having limited seats and where admission is based on merit of these tests. The division coordinates with the RCs for the learners' data pertaining to continuous assessment, evaluation of project/dissertation work. The division has made provision for students to submit online examination forms. It prepares data sheets for all the courses on offer for term-end examinations. It is overall in charge of the process provides all the support to these evaluation centres for smooth conduct of evaluation process. It handles the declaration of the results, preparation of grade cards and made them available on the University's website. It is also responsible for overall coordination of the activities pertaining to the preparation of the degrees/certificates and conduct annual convocation of the University.

International operations are looked over by a separate division, namely *International Division* (*ID*). It is entrusted the responsibility to promote bilateral and multilateral collaborations, network with international educational institutions/ inter-governmental agencies, to serve as a single window system for the University's overseas operations, to provide capacity building through training, and to coordinate the international delegations and visits to the University.

The *Finance and Accounts Division* (*F&A*) is responsible for financial management function of the University.

Library and Documentation Division (*L&DD*) operates at three-tier structure having the central library at headquarters and libraries at RCs and LSCs. It acts as a information hub of IGNOU to provide access to books, journals, reports, theses, microforms, archives, Prof G. Ram Reddy Memorial Collection, course material and eResources. Web-OPAC and integrated search engines to its members were supported by the eResources. The library has installed LibSys software for its central library and KOHA software for Regional Centre libraries. It has provided remote login facility to authorized users within the framework of copyright laws for accessing eResources from anywhere, anytime. Central Library is a member of the UGC-INFONET, DELNET and IIPA.

A separate division, namely *Construction and Maintenance Division* (*CMD*) is responsible for the maintenance of the University Buildings and other allied services. It also monitors the construction activities of Regional Centres, administrative blocks, warehouses, extensions, residential complex, etc.

Instructional System

The University provides multi-channel, multiple media teaching/learning packages for instruction and self-learning. The different components used for teaching/learning include self-instructional materials, audio–video materials, radio, television broadcasts, face-to-face counselling/tutoring by academic counsellors, laboratory and hands-on experience, teleconferencing, web-casting, SMS support. In streams like sciences, computer sciences, nursing, medical sciences, engineering and technology arrangements have been made to enable students to attend intensive practical classes at selected learner support centres. While the traditional distance education delivery through print and study centre support is strengthened, the University is strengthening the development of interactive multimedia content and learner support through video-conferencing and web-based platforms by utilizing the Internet (Christos 2013).

Evaluation Scheme

At IGNOU, a three-tier mechanism of evaluation is followed:

- **Self-Evaluation**, through the devices built into the self-instructional material.
- **Continuous Evaluation**, through any combination of theory-based assignments, practical assignments, project work, log books and contact programs.
- **Term-End Examination**, through examinations which are conducted twice in a year during June and December.

Proportionate weightage is given to various components for calculation of the final grade.

Credit System

IGNOU follows a credit system that is based on the time factor involved in studying. One credit is equivalent to 30 study hours inclusive of all learning activities. Different programmes have different credit requirements. Students have the right to collect credits at their own pace, convenience and according to their own capability. IGNOU also provides a credit transfer facility whereby credits may be transferred from any other University to IGNOU after fulfilling the necessary requirements.

Institutes, Consortia, Centres and Chairs in IGNOU

Staff Training and Research Institute of Distance Education (STRIDE)
It is a specialized Institute for staff development in ODL. It conducts capacity building programmes for IGNOU staff as well as for all the State Open Universities, Distance Education Institutes in India and other countries. STRIDE also undertakes research studies and programme evaluation.

Inter-University Consortium for Technology-Enabled Flexible Education and Development (IUC-TEFED)
IUC-TEFED is the nodal platform for collaborative efforts amongst institutions which strives to integrate technology for qualitative improvement of the open and distance learning system.

National Centre for Disability Studies (NCDS)
NCDS caters to the educational, vocational and rehabilitation needs of persons with disabilities through academic activities, sensitization programmes aimed at their inclusion.

National Centre for Innovations in Distance Education (NCIDE)
NCIDE aims at promoting, supporting, re-engineering and disseminating innovations in ODL. Some activities include innovate learning solutions, and virtual training lounge.

National ODL Centre for Local Governance (NOCLG)
This centre has been established to catalyze the process of democratization by catering to issues related to local self-government.

Indira Gandhi Centre for Freedom Struggle Studies (IGCFSS)
This centre conducts research related to the freedom struggle. Some research areas include collection and compilation of Persian and Urdu records of First War of Independence, compilation of Nationalist Poetry in Urdu and Hindi.

Chairs

IGNOU houses eight chairs: (i) Bahadur Shah Zafar Chair, (ii) General Shah Nawaz INA chair, (iii) Shaheed Kartar Singh Sarabha chair (iv) IIBF Endowment chair (v) Bombay Stock Exchange chair (vi) Dr. B. R. Ambedkar chair (vii) Catholic Bishops Conference of India IGNOU chair (viii) Sindhi Chair. Chairs are funded/ sponsored by ministries, Bombay stock exchange, CBCI and National Council for Promotion of Sindhi (NCPSL), respectively. Objectives were well-defined for the chairs to facilitate, undertake studies and research work in respective areas.

Some Best Practices

Freedom to learn, learner-centric education, multi-channel learning, modular programmes, flexible learning environment, flexibility in entry qualifications, place, pace and duration of study, credit exemption, credit transfer, robust delivery mechanism, vast network of study centres nationwide, recognized qualifications and certification are some of the best practices the University follows. Apart from these practices, there are some unique ones as described below.

Free Education to Transgenders

The University has exempted the fees of transgender students for all its programmes.

Free of Cost Education to the Jail Inmates

Free of cost education is being provided to all jail inmates across the country.

Scheme of Fee Reimbursement to Scheduled Caste and Scheduled Tribes Students

The University is providing fee reimbursement to the students belonging to SC/ST joining all the certificate programmes, diploma programmes, BA, B.Com., B.Sc., BCA, BSW, BTS, B.Sc. (nursing), B.Ed., BLIS, MPhil and PhD under SCSP and TSP scheme.

Campus Placement Cell

The objective of this Campus Placement Cell (CPC) is to enhance and facilitate the process of gainful employment for its divergent learner population. CPC works on the premise that the right candidate meets the right recruiter. CPC's endeavour has been to evolve a mechanism to work with placement agencies on a long-term basis. This cell conducts on-campus and off-campus placement drives and employability enhancement activities at the headquarters and Regional Centres/study centres. Some of the companies in the recruiters list are British Telecom, Mahindra & Mahindra Financial Services Ltd., Genpact India Pvt. Ltd., Policy Bazaar, Convergys, Yatra.com, Goibibo.com, Delvin Formulations, Indigo Airlines, ICICI Prudential Life Insurance Pvt. Ltd., Navjoti Global Solutions Pvt Ltd., Vivahzone.com, NIIT Ltd., CarTrade.com, Frankfinn, Allsec Technologies, and Ornatuc Business Pvt Ltd..

Apart from CPC at headquarters, RCs have also been organizing placement activities to help the passed-out students get employment according to their qualification and aptitude. A no. of placement drives were held at the RCs/LSCs under the overall supervision of CPC.

Digi Initiatives

IGNOU, a system leader in Open Learning, is today at the threshold of a Digital Revolution that heralds ICT application in higher education melding teaching–learning, research, learning support services and capacity building into a coagulated whole known as Open and Digital Learning (ODeL). The implications are deep and wide. Important and popular initiatives are discussed below.

eSupport to Learners

Other than the support provided by the Regional Centres and study centres, IGNOU promotes digitalization of easy access and transparency of operations. eSupport is a learner-centric web-based online interactive digital platform developed using ICT tools to support the learners in ODL. The eSupport creates digital space for each learner to view their profile and also facilitate learners to perform various activities during their learning life cycle. Some of the significant online services made available to the learners are:

- Online registration for admission (fresh and re-registration)
- Term-end examinations (TEE) forms submission
- On-demand view/downloads (admit cards, hall tickets, grade cards, assignments, old question papers, etc.)
- Learner's eProfile
- Convocation registration
- Registrations for entrance examinations for MPhil/Phd programmes
- Registration data transfer service (RDTS)
- Learner-centric website and allied services.

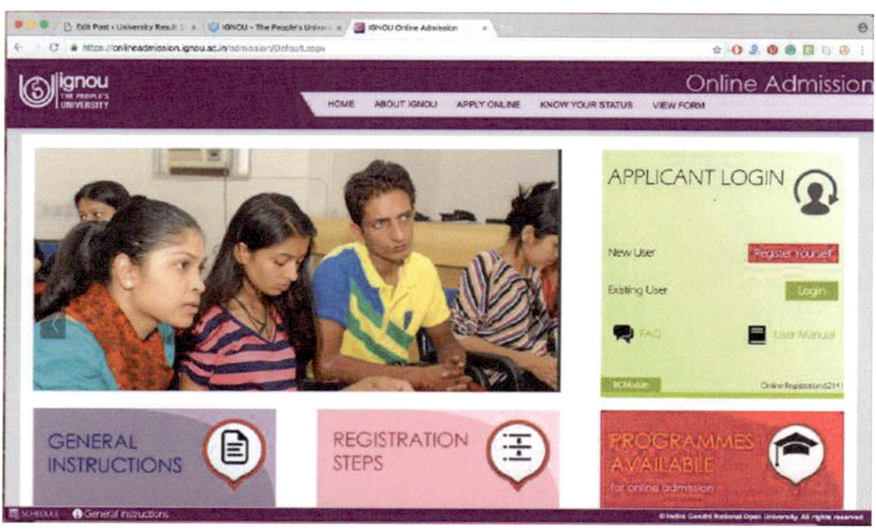

The online admission system allows the students to submit their application online, upload the relevant documents online and pay the fee through credit/debit card/net banking. They receive confirmation of their application submission instantly through email and SMS. The facility of online payment through debit/credit card and net banking has been made in the online admission system, which helps the learners in making payment without the hassle of getting a bank draft. In addition, POS machines have been installed at Regional Centres for receiving payment. The response to these initiatives has been very encouraging.

The University has received tremendous response to its online initiative which is evident from the fact that more than 371,000 applicants have already registered on the online admission system for July 2017 cycle of admission. Similarly, more than 230,000 students have submitted their re-registration form online.

IGNOU's Enterprise Resource Planning (ERP) Project for Back Office Automation

In 2008, IGNOU has integrated all the business process in back-office automation through a PeopleSoft application called ODLSOFT. For all day-to-day transactions, such as leave, medical, payroll, inventory, workforce administration and the financial and accounting transactions. The modules are extensively being used by all employees of IGNOU headquarters.

Student's Grievance Addressal

The Indira Gandhi National Open University (IGNOU) has an effective grievance redressal mechanism with a dedicated centre, namely the Student Service Centre (SSC), established in the year 1999 at the University headquarters. SSC has the mandate to provide the right information at the right time, redress student grievances at every stage, provide counselling from time to time and bridge the gap between the organization and the student. SSC constantly tries to address the causes and consequences of student grievances and works with the motto of maintaining "zero grievance" and advancing a culture of safety, transparency and justice; thereby trying to improve student experience and satisfaction. The various modes through which the University receives student grievances include face-to-face, email, letters, fax, telephone calls, portals (UGC online portal, PG portal and RTI MIS portal, iGRAM, INGRAM). SSC also handles the National and Delhi Scholarship Portals and related queries/grievances from students.

Proactive and regular follow-ups are made with Schools/Regional Centres/Divisions concerned through emails and telephone calls for attending to student queries/grievances in order to ensure minimum average disposal time'. Nodal persons have been identified at each Regional Centre/School/Division, thereby establishing/strengthening linkages in the Grievance Redressal Network of the University.

Regular updates are sent to the aggrieved students through mail. If the query/grievance lacks clarity and it appears to be urgent, the student concerned is approached on phone. To familiarize and guide the prospective students about the procedures involved before and after enrolment into IGNOU programme/s, a "Ready Reckoner" has been prepared and distributed to students. Relevant forms for various purposes are kept handy for the students online and offline. Student Support Centre is publishing Ashray, an Annual eNewsletter covering the aspects of student support services. This digital eNewsletter is circulated to all the faculty, academics and staff through email.

Academic Counselling via Gyanvani

IGNOU's Electronic Media Production Center (EMPC) has been running Gyan Vani educational FM stations across the country since 2001. After a brief interruption in transmission, Gyan Vani Delhi FM 105.6 MHz resumed its operation from 11 January 2017. Currently, the transmission of the FM station is from at 8 am to 8 pm with a bouquet of programmes ranging from interactive radio counselling to weekly education news to programmes related to culture and tradition, and other programmes contributed by various educational Institutions, ministries and government organizations.

The Interactive Radio Counselling sessions on Gyanvani are a way of bridging the gap between the teachers and the learners. As the word "interactive" suggests, it is a two-way communication wherein the learner can listen to the session and participate by asking questions or clarifying their doubts regarding the subject under discussion in real time. This is done through telephone medium or chat mode through the Internet. And if due to some reason, the learner is unable to listen to the sessions during their first broadcast, they can listen to the repeat broadcast of the sessions later in the day.

Gyandhara

Gyandhara, an Internet-based interactive web radio service for the students was started in October, 2016. It is audio streaming through the Internet. Students can listen to the LIVE discussions happening in the studios by the teachers and experts on the topic of the day and interact with them through telephone or email or through chat mode. It is a very useful and cost-effective way of reaching the students. The sessions can also be heard online through "Gyandhara" on www.ignouonline.ac.in/gyandhara.

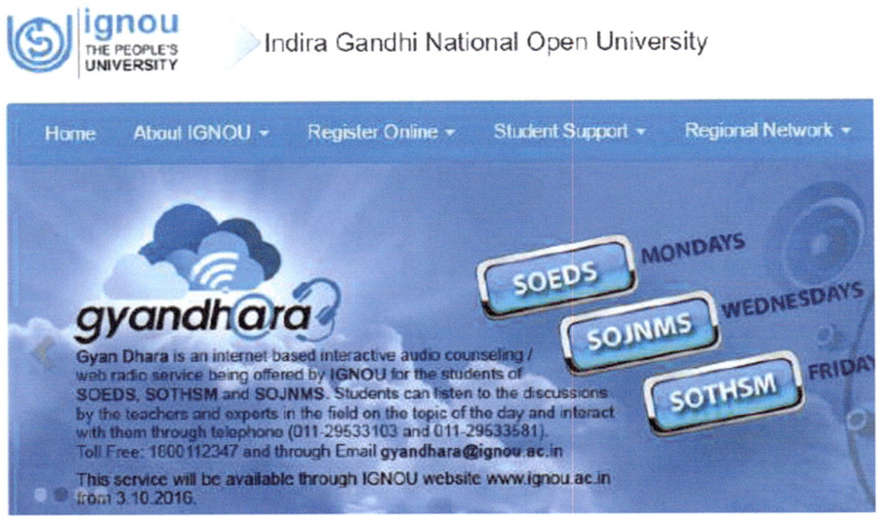

The details of the sessions for every month are being uploaded onto IGNOU Website's Education Broadcast as well as on Gyandhara. Besides IGNOU learners, Gyan Vani FM channels also find wide listenership among other general public as evident from the feedback received by the stations.

QR Code-Based SLM and OER Access

School of Computer and Information Sciences (SOCIS) made an attempt to provide QR code-based SLM and OERs access to some of its courses under the publications page of SOCIS. For each course, the course coordinator designed few pages providing the QR codes to access the SLMs, programme guide, videos, powerpoint presentations, old question papers, link to the Gyan V, etc., for the benefit of the students.

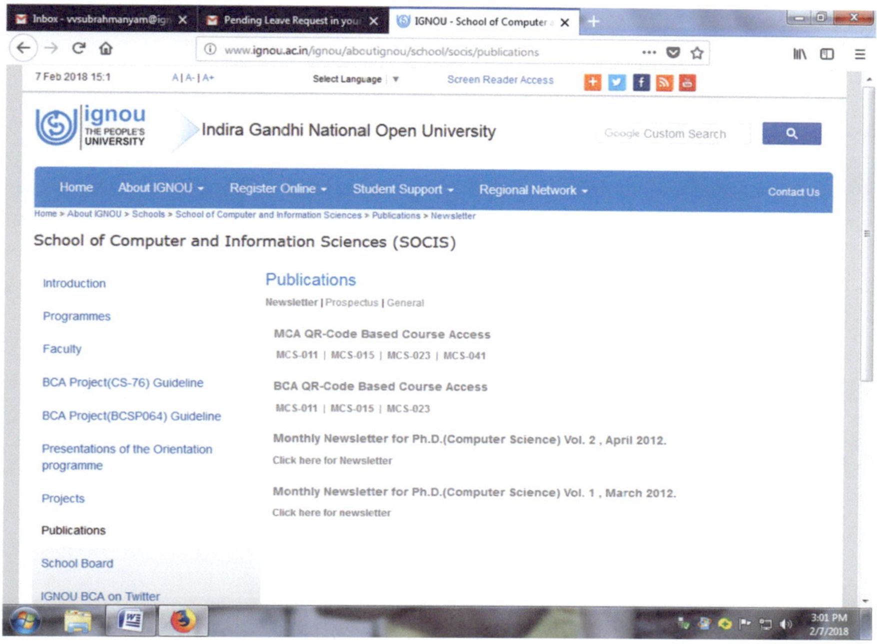

Role of Social Media in Providing the Student Support

Some of the programme coordinators of the popular programmes have started sending tweets through Twitter account. In this context, SOCIS is having the Twitter accounts for its two most popular programmes Bachelor of Computer Applications (BCA) and Master of Computer Applications (MCA).

Many of the Regional Centres have their presence on the Facebook helping students to share the important news, circulars, news clippings, short videos pertaining to the activities in their region.

Short Messaging System (SMS) Alerts

There is a provision to send SMS alerts to the students by the Regional Centres to alert students related to academic and administrative circulars/short notifications. Some of the programme coordinators also used this facility to send alerts to their students enrolled for the programme.

eGyankosh

It is a web-based digital repository of Educational Resources of IGNOU which allows access to IGNOU materials and video archives for various academic programmes. Inter-University Consortium (IUC) has been given responsibility of hosting, updating and maintaining the eGyankosh Digital Repository. This repository will facilitate the learners to search and access the content with more ease on various web-based platform. IUC is also supporting webcasting and web-conferencing facility for the University and is in process of reactivating webcasting of Gyandarshan channels.

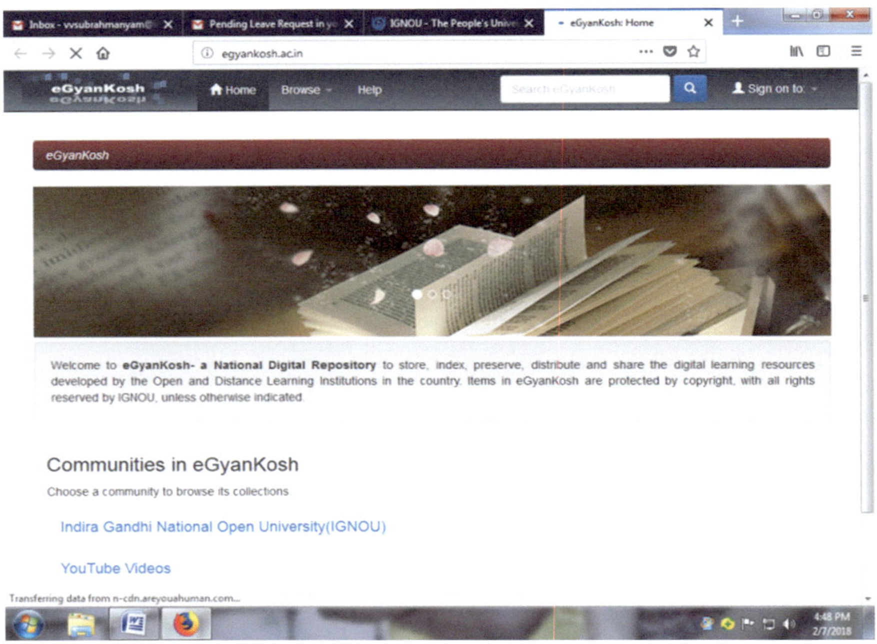

SWAYAM

The future of learning lies in massive open online courses (MOOCs), wherein not just students but any person interested in any subject of their choice can update their knowledge digitally and that too free of cost. Some of the faculty members are now engaged in developing MOOCs for some courses.

IGNOU is one of the National Coordinators among seven others for the Study Webs of Active Learning for Young Aspiring Minds (SWAYAM) programme of MHRD for offered massive open online courses (MOOCs) at certificate and diploma level. It has already launched 11 courses on SWAYAM from July 2017 (Subrahmanyam and Swathi 2016). These programmes are available free in the public domain and can be accessed by anyone in the world. The following are the MOOCs offered by IGNOU during its first run:

1. Food laws and standards
2. Technology of fermented, cheese, ice cream and by-products
3. Indian agricultural development
4. Sustainable management of biodiversity
5. Introduction to poultry farming
6. Design and facilitation of e-learning courses
7. Basics of Russian language
8. Library automation and digitization
9. Document processing and organization
10. Information sources and library services
11. Database and content management.

Many more MOOCs are in the pipeline for offering them during 2018.

SWAYAM PRABHA

SWAYAM PRABHA has been conceived as the project for using the (2) GSAT—15 transponders to run (32) Direct-to-Home (DTH) free to air channels that would telecast high-quality educational programmes on 24×7 basis. IGNOU is the National Coordinator for five channels: agriculture, humanities and liberal arts, State Open Universities, culture and teacher education.

Virtual Training Lounge

NCIDE developed a novel solution, namely Virtual Training Lounge (VTL) to provide training and capacity building of the ODL functionaries through web-based platform. This system is designed to provide not only synchronous training, but also to sustain the learning experience of the trainees online. The VTL can be accessed through personal mobile phones too. The ease of access to the VTL anytime from anywhere makes it an ideal platform for training and its sustainability.

Ennovate

This is a newsletter in electronic format in order to disseminate innovate ideas and innovative practices through various modes. This eNewsletter brought out by NCIDE is sent as an email. The eNewsletter carries articles/contributions from faculty and eminent experts.

Innovation Club@IGNOU

This innovation club was started by NCIDE in April 2015. It aims to create the culture of innovation and encourage the faculty and students to do innovations. In order to fulfil the objectives of the club, it regularly organizes various activities. In the same lines, several Innovation Clubs were started functioning at various Regional Centres also.

Navdharana

It is a system for managing new ideas and innovations through a web-based platform. New ideas need to be collected and managed in an effective manner so as to utilize them for implementation. At present, it hosts more than one hundred ideas from IGNOU, SOUs and other institutes of Distance Learning in India.

Public Information Unit

The Public Information Unit acts as bridge between the University and its various stakeholders. It helps to maintain a positive image and enhance the visibility of the University by sharing important information on new developments with wider audiences. This unit prepares and disseminates media releases related to the important events and new academic programmes, activities of various schools, centres and units of the University. It releases advertisements pertaining to admissions, appointments, tenders and other notifications. Recently it started publishing DiGi News, a digital booklet sharing the glimpses of the functions held at the headquarters of IGNOU. PIU is designing and circulating this digital booklet immediately after function is over to all the faculty, staff etc., through an email.

Future Initiatives

The University is working towards the following future initiatives whose details are given as follows:

IT Infrastructure Usage from NIC Cloud

Some of application services being offered to learners will be hosted at NIC Cloud IT Infrastructure as a secondary resource, apart from main campus for high availability and accessibility. The domain name system (DNS) was already hosted in real time and working as secondary service. Online admission service is tested and will be deployed in real time, soon. Efforts are in progress to host website and other learner support services.

Digital Locker Application

Digital Locker is a key initiative under Digital India, the Indian Government's flagship Programme. Digital Locker is a secure cloud-based platform for storage, sharing and verification of documents and certificates. The implementation of Digital Locker Application in association with DEITY, Govt. of India, is in progress. It was decided that Digital Locker Application be implemented, initially for SRD and SED as a Requester as well as an Issuer, respectively.

Learner-Centric Website Design

The learner-centric website template design and development is in progress. The new template primarily focuses on learners and their support and grievance redress services.

Strengthening of Learners' Central Database

Efforts are in progress in strengthening of existing learners' database, which is created in ORACLE and is tightly integrated with all learner application support services. It facilitates stakeholders to get information, on demand, through predefined web-interface with proper authentication and avoids duplicity and ambiguity in learners' data.

Web-Based Learner Support Services

An exclusive web-interface is in development stage for learners, Student Support Centre (SSC) and others to receive and address queries/grievances.

Campuswide Wi-Fi Connect

Most of the schools and the divisions have the WiFi connectivity in its main campus.

National Virtual Library

Now, search the availability of any book/manuscript/periodical/journal which you thought is no more available in your nearest library or a 3D image of any museum artefact with a click of a mouse. IGNOU is aiding in the initiative of Ministry of Culture under the National Mission of Libraries by way of creating a union catalogue of libraries across India which apart from books includes artefacts and other resources from libraries, museums, archives using open-source platform Koha.

DVD

The University has created a vast repository of learning resources in the form of digital content, recorded video and audio lectures. The University is planning to provide these learning resources to its learners on a DVD. This will be in addition to the printed self-instructional material to be provided to them. As an added dimension of academic support, the learners are provided teaching input through Gyandarshan and Gyanvani. In this direction, the then VC inaugurated a DVD containing the learning resources for Bachelor of Preparatory Programme on 15 August, 2017.

Challenges

Although there are several advantages in implementing the Digital Initiatives, there are some challenges which are briefed below:

- ***Technology Plan***: A proper technology plan must be in place to help guide and assist any tech integration into the applications designed for the University. When designing your technology plan, make sure to include the opinions and also its stakeholders.
- Examine Technology ***Budgets*** Frequently: Forecasting the annual budgets for hardware, software, annual maintenance contracts, professional development, and tech should be done with great care. Having a properly planned budget with adequate funds can help so if something needs to be scaled back.
- Choosing effective ***tools and devices***.
- Should tackle the ***resistance to change***.
- ***Professional development*** and ***capacity building***.
- ***Storage and backup*** procedures should be adhered to.
- University should have an approved ***IT policy*** in place.
- Should cope up with ***technological failures***.
- ***Database Security, Network security, application-level security*** should be strictly followed.
- Strict ***access*** mechanisms to the applications/database, etc., should be maintained.
- Proper ***logs*** maintenance should be there.
- ***Roles and responsibilities*** should be well-defined prior.
- ***Risk management*** and ***mitigation management*** procedures should be in place.
- There should be proper ***data-centre*** maintenance procedures.

Conclusion

In this chapter, we have seen the complete case study and best practices at Indira Gandhi National Open University along with some Digital Initiatives. Over the years, IGNOU has lived up to the country's expectations of providing education to the marginalized sections of the society. Free of cost education is being provided to all jail inmates, SC/ST students for some undergraduate programmes and transgender community across the country. Emphasis is now being laid on digital initiatives, adding value to the traditional distance education.

Foundation Stone by Sh. Rajiv Gandhi, Former Prime Minister of India

Prof. G. Ram Reddy, Founder Vice Chancellor of IGNOU

References

Christos, P. (2013). Teleconference in support of distance learning—views of educators, open education. *The Journal for Open and Distance Education and Educational Technology 9*, Number 1, 2013 Section one. © Open Education ISSN: 1791-9312.

IGNOU brochure. (2017).

IGNOU Profile. (2017). Published during convocation.

IGNOU Statutes of the University (as amended up to 31-03-2007) (2007).

UNESCO. (2002). *Open and Distance Learning: Trends, Policy and Strategy Considerations*, UNESCO, Paris.

Subrahmanyam, V. V., Swathi, K. (2016). MOOCs in the digital age learning—An Indian perspective. In *the Proceedings of Open, Online and Flexible Learning: The key to Sustainable Developmentheld on 27–30 Nov 2016 at Kaulalumpur, Malaysia*.

Web References

www.ignou.ac.in
www.ignouonline.ac.in
www.egyankosh.ac.in
http://www.egyankosh.ac.in/handle/123456789/35033 (IGNOU Video Archives)
http://www.ignouonline.ac.in/gyandhara/
http://igram.ignou.ac.in/
http://www.ignou.ac.in/ignou/studentzone/downloads/3
http://navdharana.ignouonline.ac.in/navdharana/
http://www.ignou.ac.in/ignou/aboutignou/icc/cpc/introduction

Technology-Mediated Learning Support Services at Wawasan Open University, Malaysia

Ramesh Chander Sharma

Introduction

Educational systems all over the world have some challenges: of quality, of numbers, of access, of equity and of equality, etc. ICT plays an important role in meeting these challenges by bridging the knowledge gap, increasing access to educational opportunities, faster delivery of knowledge products, massification of education and enhancing student-centred learning (ADB 2009). In educational institutions, ICT is integrated into various systems, not only to assist in teaching and learning, but also for administration and management purposes like student enrolment, course schedules, student grading, staff evaluation (UNESCO 2011). Not only in universities, ICT is used in TVET institutions for creating a skilled and ICT-capable workforce (ADB 2009). If we examine the adoption and integration of ICT into educational systems, we note some disparity, some take full advantage while some lack those. Possible reasons are lack of support from management, shortage of trained staff, uncoordinated planning and implementation, ambiguity in roles and responsibilities, staff resistance to training and reluctance for retraining and inadequate finances for developing, purchasing and implementing ICT (UNESCO 2011).

In recent times, massive open online courses (MOOCs) have been a wave of disruptive technology with many universities, governments and other institutions developing and offering MOOCs. MOOCs were reported to be next big thing in the technology development of higher education (NMC Horizon Report 2012) and then the year 2012 being declared as the year of the MOOC by the New York Times. As in open and distance education system, MOOCs also reflect the move towards openness in learning. A team of scholars at United Kingdom Open University

R. C. Sharma (✉)
Instructional Design, Ambedkar University Delhi, New Delhi, India
e-mail: rc_sharma@yahoo.com

© Springer Nature Singapore Pte Ltd. 2018

Anjana (ed.), *Technology for Efficient Learner Support Services in Distance Education*, https://doi.org/10.1007/978-981-13-2300-3_7

(UKOU) examines the pedagogical trends affecting higher education sector. The 2016 report examined new science of learning drawing from the research outcomes from neuroscience, cognitive sciences, educational and social sciences to understand the dynamics of how we learn. In this report (Sharples et al. 2016), some of the innovative technologies and pedagogies identified to have transformed education were learning through social media (using social media to offer long-term learning opportunities); learning through video games (making learning fun, interactive and stimulating); formative analytics (developing analytics that help learners to reflect and improve); translanguaging (enriching learning through the use of multiple languages); and blockchain for learning (storing, validating and trading educational reputation). The 2017 edition of the similar report from UKOU, the focus has been on online world where 'learners are faced with fake news, pseudo-science, 'post truth' and increasing tensions between some communities' (Ferguson et al. 2017, p. 6). Some of the important innovative pedagogies as per this report are open textbooks (adapting openly licensed textbooks); immersive learning (intensifying learning by experiencing new situations); student-led analytics (using data to help learners set and achieve their own goals); and big data inquiry: thinking with data (understanding the world by working with large sets of data). These developments have a significant bearing upon the ODL world. Before we examine the impact of these developments to our focused institution, let's have a brief look at distance education in Southeast Asia.

Distance Education in South East Asia

Southeast Asia (SA) (extending for around 4000 miles roughly from northwest to southeast and comprises of around 13,000,000 km^2 of land and sea) is a very interesting region as it comprises of many cultures and ecologies. It is situated east of Indian subcontinent and south of China, has two dissimilar portions: a continental projection (indicated as mainland Southeast Asia) and insular Southeast Asia (consisting of many archipelagos to the south and east of the mainland (Britannica Online Encyclopaedia 2017). The region falls into tropical and subtropical climatic zones and observes regular monsoon. Geographically the region is marked with mountains, plains and plateaus. The countries of Cambodia, Laos, Myanmar, Thailand, Vietnam and Singapore are at the southern tip of the Malay Peninsula. Malaysia is both mainland and insular. The ten member countries constitute Association of Southeast Asian Nations (ASEAN): Brunei, Cambodia, Indonesia, Laos, Malaysia, Myanmar, the Philippines, Singapore, Thailand, Vietnam. Owing to the diverse geography and cultural settings, it is important to learn something about higher education in Southeast Asia. This has been echoed well in the UNESCO Bangkok and SEAMEO RIHED (2006) Report "Higher Education in Southeast Asia" that "For constructive and productive cooperation, policy makers and practitioners must be well-informed about higher education development and trends in other countries so that they can convert such information into useful policies and practices within the confines of their national needs and circumstances" (p. 1). The ASEAN Socio-Cultural Community Blueprint 2025 lays emphasis on cooperation on human and social development in relation to among other areas, education and ICT use. For education, it specifies, "The ASEAN Work Plan on Education 2016–2020, which was adopted at the Ninth ASEAN Education Ministers meeting in Kuala Lumpur in May 2016, covers cooperation in areas including regional history and culture, education access, ICT in education, Technical and Vocational Education and Training (TVET) and lifelong learning, education for sustainable development, quality assurance, university–industry partnerships and capacity building in the education sector. Improving accessibility is a particular emphasis of the ASEAN Declaration on Strengthening Education for Out-of-School Children and Youth, adopted at the ASEAN Summit in September 2016." (OECD 2017, p. 124).

The literature is abundant to prove that open and distance education system is a very successful model to serve educational needs of masses. Distance education is an effective medium to solve the problem of accessibility of higher education when it comes to social issues and working hours, etc., in addition to increasing learning efficiency (Vasilevska et al. 2017). Calderon (2012) estimated that by 2030, globally higher education sector will observe 414.2 million enrolments, an increase of 314% from worldwide enrolment in 2000. By 2035, student enrolment in higher education worldwide is expected to exceed 520 million. On these lines, MOOCs have been tried in SA region too. The National Institute of Education (NIE), Singapore, offered a MOOC on management and school leadership in 2015. National University of Singapore and Nanyang Technological University also experimented with MOOCs (Teng 2015). Malaysia also launched MOOCs on www.OpenLearning.com platform in 2013 and currently many of the universities not only in Malaysia but other countries too use www.OpenLearning.com platform to offer MOOCs.

The establishment of UNESCO Bangkok Asia Pacific Bureau in 1961 and creation of Southeast Asian Ministers of Education Organisation (SEAMEO) in 1965 were important milestone for boosting regional cooperation in education, science and culture. This was soon followed by launch of ASEAN in 1967 (Chou and Ravinet 2017). The seriousness of the governments to higher education provisions can be noticed as ASEAM members established an ASEAN University Network (AUN) in 1992 to manage various discipline-based collaborative initiatives, projects, networks and associated mobility scholarships among 30 flagship higher education institutions (Chou and Ravinet 2017, p. 151). Southeast Asian Ministers of Education Organisation's Regional Centre for Higher Education and Development (SEAMEO RIHED) also plays a great role in higher education cooperation in ASEAN region. There are around 12 million post-secondary students studying in 6500 higher educational institutions (Morrison 2016). The region is characterised with student and programme mobility and observes innovative forms of managing and regulating transnational education; however, there is no inter-regional regulatory framework for tertiary education, credit transfer or quality assurance (Morrison 2016, p. 3).

Ramkhamhaeng University of Thailand (established in 1971) is considered to be the first open admissions university in Southeast Asia (Latchem and Jung 2007). Its purpose was to provide a platform to large number of school-leaving students to get university education because other Thai Universities were not able to accommodate large admissions. Gradually, almost all countries in the region established open universities to provide an alternate mechanism for tertiary education. This became so popular that some of them acquired the status of "super mega universities" (Ali 2012). Indonesia started an Open Junior Secondary School in 1979 initially in five locations in five provinces, later on spread to whole country to provide basic and secondary education to school-age children who were not able to attend formal schooling due to geographic, socio-economic and cultural reasons (Sadiman 2006). Open Universities were established in Thailand, Indonesia, Philippines, Myanmar, Vietnam and Malaysia, etc., to cater to not only primary, secondary and tertiary education but also teacher education. In addition, ICT has been prominently used in the region; for example, radio broadcasts were provided for primary school teachers since 1970s. Thailand started using TV broadcast way back in 1964 and then radio for distance education programmes from primary to pre-university level in 1978 (Sadiman 2006). Some of the countries adopted ICT policy (e.g., Thailand and Malaysia). This promoted use of eLearning or online education greatly in the region. Philippines has been using ICT for basic education for a long time for areas like infrastructure development, technical support, teacher training on the design, production and use of ICT-based instructional materials, research and development, technology integration in the curriculum, use of innovative technologies in education and training, and fund generation (UNESCO 2003). Not only this, there is a policy focus on reforming higher education to deliver better quality and cost-effectiveness of tertiary education in the region. For example, higher education is expanding in Myanmar with 32 institutions in 1988 to 163 in 2012 (OECD 2017, p. 237). While expanding access to university education in Myanmar, the Govt need to focus on technical and vocational education and training (TVET) because it will create more jobs. Thus, a comprehensive education sector review (CESR) was started in 2012 as a SWOT analysis and one of the recommendation was "assigning dedicated staff to teach and manage distance-education courses" (CESR Office 2014) (Table 1).

Distance Education in Malaysia

Universiti Sains Malaysia (USM) (earlier called as Universiti Pulau Pinang) was the first institution to start distance education programmes in Malaysia in 1971 in the form of off-campus academic programmes. A year later, in 1972, Universiti Teknologi Malaysia was established. Initially (in 1971) eight courses in humanities and social sciences were offered as an opportunity to working adults wanting to upgrade to university education. Later on, in 1973, courses in pure science and mathematics were also offered on the directions of Ministry of Education. The modality of student support was providing them lecture notes, supplementary readings and lists of textbooks. To provide further academic support to students as face-to-face tutorials, lecturers made visits to local study centres. Radio Malaysia

Table 1 Some of the Open Universities of the region

Country	Open University/e-University	Year of establishment
Thailand	Ramkhamhaeng University	1971
Thailand	Sukhothai Thammathirat Open University	1978
Indonesia	Universitas Terbuka	1984
Myanmar	Yangon University of Distance Education	1992
Myanmar	Mandalay University of Distance Education	1998
Vietnam	Hanoi Open University	1993
Vietnam	Ho Chi Minh City Open University	1993
The Philippines	University of the Philippines Open University	1995
Malaysia	Open University Malaysia	2000
Malaysia	Wawasan Open University	2007
Malaysia	Asia e University	2008

provided free airtime to broadcast 20 min radio programme on weekly basis. The correspondence courses were also offered by private institutions, e.g., Malaysian Correspondence College, Adabi College, Stanford College and Raffles College. A major boost to distance education came in 1990 when Mara Institute of Technology (UiTM) offered Diploma in Business Administration and Diploma in Public Administration. Soon, other universities also started offering distance learning programmes, like National University of Malaysia (1993), University of Malaya (1993), University Putra Malaysia (1994), Northern University of Malaysia (1995), Universiti Telekom (1997) and University Tun Abdul Razak (1998). Except University Tun Abdul Razak which offered programmes solely via distance or eLearning modality, other universities offered them in addition to their on-campus programmes. To strengthen distance education further, centres were established at different universities, like the Centre for Distance Education (CDE) at Universiti Sains Malaysia; the Institute for Distance Education and Learning (IDEAL) at University Putra Malaysia (UPM); the Centre for Instructional Resources Distance Education (CIRDE), at Northern University of Malaysia (UUM), the Centre for Innovations in Education (CiE) with a Distance Learning Unit at Universiti Telekom (UNETELE), the Centre for Continuing Education at ITM and the Centre for External Degree Programs with a Distance Learning Unit (CDL) at University of Malaya (UM) (Table 2).

"The Eleventh Malaysia Plan (2016–2020): Anchoring growth on people" focuses on "accelerating human capital development for an advanced nation" (Economic Planning Unit 2015). The National Vision Policy of the Govt of Malaysia (2001–2010) emphasised on the development of a knowledge-based society. From 75% literacy rate in 1970, it increased to 98% in 2015, along with 27% of labour force having access to tertiary education (Govt of Malaysia 2015). The Govt aimed at strengthening the TVET to produce more high-skilled workers. Quality of education delivery being a priority, the Malaysia Education Blueprint 2013–2025 lays stress on mastery of STEM education (Science, Technology, Engineering and Mathematics), higher-order thinking skills (HOTS), moral and

Table 2 Some of the universities offering distance education programmes in Malaysia

Name of the University/Institution	Year of establishment
Universiti Sains Malaysia (USM)	1971
Universiti Teknologi Mara (UiTM)	1990
Universiti Kebangsaan Malaysia (UKM)	1993
Universiti Malaya (UM)	1994
Universiti Putra Malaysia (UPM)	1995
Universiti Utara Malaysia (UUM)	1997
Universiti Tun Abdul Razak (UNITAR)	1998
Universiti Multimedia (MMU)	1999
Universiti Islam Antarabangsa (UIAM)	2000
Universiti Terbuka Malaysia (OUM)	2000
Wawasan Open University (WOU)	2006

religious education. With the purpose to achieve 80% graduate employability within six months of graduation, Malaysia Education Blueprint 2015–2025 (higher education) is another important strategy.

The Malaysian Education Blueprint 2015–2025 (higher education) identifies 10 shifts to achieve the targets and enhance quality, efficiency and overall performance of the system. The 10 shifts are divided into two groups: (a) outcomes: holistic, entrepreneurial and balanced graduates; talent excellence; nation of lifelong learners; and quality TVET graduates (b) enablers: financial sustainability; empowered governance; innovation ecosystem; global prominence; globalised online learning; and transformed higher educational delivery. It can be noticed that globalised online learning is identified as an enabler which will lead to outcomes as quality TVET graduates, nation of lifelong learners and holistic, entrepreneurial and balanced graduates. Osman et al. (2016) examined the mediating effect of attitude on perceived ease of use and student intention to use online learning platform among online learning institutions in Malaysia. They found that attitude is very significant within ODL institutions to the use of online learning platforms. ODL system has a significant role to realise these outcomes. Major shifts in Malaysian Higher Education System will be from focus on university education to where academic and TVET pathways are considered equal, shift from inputs to outcomes, shift from mass production delivery model to technology-enabled innovations to deliver and tailor education for all students and from a highly centralised system to a model of earned autonomy for institutions.

According to a Docebo report (2016), the eLearning market was worth USD 165 billion in 2015 and would exceed USD240 billion by 2023. Enterprises of different sizes have adopted eLearning to cater to their changing business needs and technology advancements. The traditional teaching methods are getting either replaced or improved. The Corporate Learning Network (2014) identified four technologies which facilitated adoption of eLearning solutions in institutions: social, mobile, analytics and cloud (SMAC). Out of these four factors, mobile learning has changed the way we transact in our lives. According to MarketsandMarkets 2016 Report, the global mobile market was worth USD 28.63 billion in 2016, which is expected to grow to USD 98.85 billion by 2021, at a compound annual growth rate (CAGR) of 28.1%. Mobile learning market is becoming one of the most vibrant markets in Asian region; from USD 4.5 billion in 2014, it is expected to increase to USD 7.7 billion by 2019. A report by China Internet Network Information Center (CINNIC) (2017, p. 1) the number of mobile Internet users in China was 695 million in December 2016, an increase of 75.50 million from the end of 2015. CINNIC report of 2015 showed that 195 million people in China use their phone to access mobile learning content on monthly basis. ODL institutions have realised the benefit to provide learning opportunities using mobile devices. Lim et al. (2011) highlight successful implementation of the mobile learning (initiated in 2009) via SMS at Open University Malaysia (OUM) for providing administrative and academic support, e-counselling services, learner development support and learner assessment. The authors report that this project was sustainable in terms of costs, efforts and resources, and OUM now plans to implement it for fully online courses.

Wawasan Open University (WOU)

Wawasan Open University Sdn Bhd (WOUSB) was established under the Private Higher Educational Institutions Act 1996 (Act 555) of Govt of Malaysia and registered on 15 August 2006 and formally launched on 22 September 2006. It is a private and not-for-profit university. Wawasan Education Foundation (WEF) owns the WOU. The university's vision is 'to be a vibrant learning community that inspires learning, supports innovation and nurtures all-round personal growth. First intake of 721 ODL students was done in January 2007, and more than 19,000 students have since experienced learning in an ODL environment. First batch of 38 MBA graduated in Oct 2010. Up until 2016, 1,748 first-degree students and 661 postgraduate students have graduated. Currently, a total of 42 programmes are fully accredited by Malaysian Qualifications Agency (MQA).

The course materials are developed through a stringent quality process. The emphasis is on outcome-based education (OBE). The quality assurance in programme development is ensured through two types of stakeholders (Table 3):

Table 3 Quality assurance in programme development

Internal stakeholders	External stakeholders
School Board	Advisory Peer Group
Quality Assurance, Teaching and Learning Committee	External Course Assessor
Senate	External Examiner
Management Board	External Programme Assessor
	Board of Governors

The chief characteristics of course materials are

- All courses have five study units;
- A course guide for students and a course guide for tutors is available; and
- The content is interactive, reader-friendly and pedagogically sound.

Each study unit has

- An overview
- Objectives/learning outcomes
- 2–5 sections/lessons
- Activities, videos and self-tests
- Unit summary.

In 2013, WOU introduced “On Campus Learning” (OCL) for young adults in addition to its offerings for distance learners. This transformation from a single mode dedicated Open University to a dual mode institution allowed students a facility to opt for full-time or part-time study facilities.

University has, in addition to different supports Divisions or Units, four schools, one Institute of Research, one Directorate, and two Centres:

SBA	School of Business and Administration
SST	School of Science and Technology
SHSS	School of Humanities and Studies
SELC	School of Education, Languages and Communications
CGS	Centre for Graduate Studies (established in May 2007)
PACE	Centre for Professional Development and Continuing Education
IRI	Institute of Research and Innovation
DQAER	Directorate of Quality Assurance and External Relations (Table 4).

Table 4 Academic programmes of WOU (As of July 2017 semester)

No.	Programme	Total
1	MPhil/PhD (by research)	5
2	MBA (by coursework; ODL)	5
3	Postgraduate Diploma (ODL)	2
4	Bachelor Degree (ODL + OCL)	27 + 6
5	Graduate Diploma (ODL)	9
6	Graduate Certificate (ODL)	2
7	Diploma (ODL)	1
	Total no. of programmes (ODL + OCL)	51 + 6

Note ODL = Open Distance Learning (part-time)
OCL = On-Campus Learning (full-time)

Technology-Mediated Learning Support Services

Wawasan Open University offers a vast bouquet of online services to the learners by registering for an online account. To assist them, suitable instructions are provided showing how students can activate their account and manage the password. The various online services provided to the learners are as follows:

- Learning management system
- Student portal
- Online assignment submission (OAS) system
- Digital library
- Tutor portal
- Turnitin

Learning Management System

There are two variants of LMS to provide online academic services to the learners: WawasanLearn (for part-time students) and Wawasan2U (for full-time students). Both systems have identical functionality. Students read notifications, download course materials or use forums to post their messages about course, or seeking clarification or guidance from course coordinators, tutors or peers.

The WawasanLearn variant of learning management system caters to the open distance learners. It provides access to their course materials and the updated notifications and course information. WawasanLearn enables the university to create a collaborative learning environment through multiple learning modes, for example, self-paced coursework (in the form of web links, downloadable text, audio and video contents) or group learning (online forums). Course coordinator or tutors upload lecture notes, power point slides, timetables and web links to other learning sites relevant to the course for learners.

WawasanLearn serves to assist course coordinator (CC) in organising the coursework activities and track tutors and students. WawasanLearn provides a platform for CCs, tutors and students to communicate and learn from each other through collaborative tools. There are five main forums in WawasanLearn:

1. Announcements from Course Coordinator—The course coordinators post latest information about their courses, provide content material and regularly update information.
2. Announcements from Tutor—Tutors post information about tutorial sessions by mentioning date, time, topic and URL for the online session or face-to-face tutorial. They also post information about examinations, tutor-marked assignments and other relevant information for students.

3. Tutor Contact Details—At this forum, students can find the contact details of their tutor and tutorial timetable.
4. Public Forum—This forum is used by students to raise general issues.
5. Tutorial Forum—This is the place for students and tutors and students to interact with each other to discuss tutorial related matters and assignments. Students can post their questions, doubts or concerns related to course material which the course coordinator or tutor will reply to.

Starting January 2018, the WawasanLearn has been upgraded to Moodle 3.2 which features a fresh new design and easier navigation throughout the platform. In addition, the new interface also ensures greater improvement across all devices. Some of the features of this upgraded version are

1. Enhanced interface and navigation. With improved navigation that aligns with many websites, it is seamless for students to navigate within the platform. To further boost students' learning experience, the online course resources have been structured according to the units so that students now have more space on screen to view the important course content.
2. Easy means of communication and viewing online course resources using Moodle mobile app. In response to the global increase in usage of mobile device, students can now use the Moodle mobile app available for iOS and Android devices to view online course resources and engage in a forum discussion using the app.
3. Informative dashboard—The user's dashboard now contains important information such as TMA deadlines, My Library Search widget and Guides for Online Assignment System (OAS) and Turnitin.

Student Portal (http://www.wou.edu.my/student-portal/)

Through the portal for students, they can avail following facilities:

- There are two instances of learning management system: "WawasanLearn" for open and distance learning students (ODL) and "Wawasan2u" for full-time on-campus students. Through these, students can participate in online discussions/forum by asking questions to their tutors, course coordinators and fellow students.
- A digital library provides access to books, journals and other literature for their studies.
- An "Online Assignment Submission System" (OAS) for the students to submit their assignments.
- For seeking administrative and academic support, university has established regional centres in different locations across the country at Penang, Ipoh, Johor Bahru, Kuching, Kuala Lumpur, Bandar Utama and Klang. These regional

centres provide the facility of counselling and tutorials to the students, or they can meet informally with their peer as self-help groups.

- To guide and advise the students about their studies, they are assigned a tutor. The tutor can be contacted either at the regional centre or by telephone and email. These tutors conduct face-to-face tutorials to learners to explain the course content and answering to their queries.

Online Assignment Submission (OAS) System

Students at WOU submit their tutor-marked assignments (TMAs) using online assignment submission (OAS) system. Since system is configured to allow them to submit each TMA only once, the students are advised to pay attention while uploading to have the right document for online TMA submission. The TMAs are submitted by logging in to the site: https://assignment.wou.edu.my. In case someone uploads wrong TMA, the student needs to apply for TMA resubmission from the OAS system, which is subject to approval of respective course coordinator. There may be cases when the students are not able to complete the assignment and/or upload it due to reasons of illness, accident, disability, bereavement or other compassionate grounds, the request for submission extension is also made via the OAS system. In case, student wants extension of more than seven days, application is made through OAS to the concerned Tutor who considers the case on individual basis for its validity and unexpected emergencies. Further, the tutor decides and advises the student of the revised date for submission of assignment. All such applications for extension to submit the assignment need to be lodged on or before the due date of submission. The application for extension of date for submission of assignment is done at https://assignment.wou.edu.my/onlineExtension.asp.

MOOCs Offerings

Wawasan Open University offered massive open online courses (MOOCs) of three months duration in February 2015 through its Centre for Professional Development and Continuing Education (PACE), namely “Action Research Course” and “Open Educational Resources (OER) in e-Learning”. Funding for these MOOCs came from Commonwealth of Learning and Commonwealth Educational Media Centre for Asia (CEMCA) respectively.

Online Facilitation and Interactions

The university has the provision of providing online and synchronous tutorials through videoconferencing, WizIQ and Skype. The students access the online tutorials from any place they can have access to Internet or at regional centres of the university. As a component of learner support services, face-to-face tutorials are arranged by the university at its HQs and regional centres. There are challenges of hiring competent tutors for specialised subjects. Certain courses may have very low enrolment and thus provision of a dedicated tutor may have financial implications. Due to high bandwidth requirement, video conference posed challenges of offering online tutorials. In 2010, university decided to use WizIQ as a virtual classroom tool to provide online tutorial support to the students. There are various benefits of this virtual classroom platform: providing synchronous academic and tutorial support to learners, reduced tutor costs, ability to offer tutorials to vast geographical locations, the scheduling of the online class was linked to WawasanLearn with the help of WizIQ plug-in for Moodle, effective use of multimedia like audio, video, animation, showcasing presentation or writing on whiteboard as we do it in a physical classroom, students' live participation through either voice-based or chat-enabled question–answer, and making available the recording of the tutorial session to those who could not attend live session or want to revisit the recording for further clarifications. Currently, flash version of WizIQ is being used at the university for which a third party plug-in is required to run the class. This takes lots of bandwidth and class quality also gets hamper. University is soon switching to WebRTC version of WizIQ. WebRTC is a technology where everything works on browser itself, also there is no need for any plug-in for MP4 recordings or screen sharing. Moreover, the sessions get recorded in HD audio/video. Some of the features of WebRTC features are better audio/video, screen sharing, content upload from desktop/library, chat, interactive whiteboard, code editor (for developer use), class recording, smartboard connectivity, pen tool, media player, polling, layouts, class extension, YouTube, textbox and PDF downloader.

Online Programme Commonwealth Executive Master of Business Administration (CeMBA) http://www.wou.edu.my/cemba-online-programme/

The Commonwealth Executive Master of Business Administration (CeMBA) programme has been on offer since 2008 at WOU. First batch of students graduated in 2010. Keeping in view the demand from mobile learners who wish to access the programme anytime/anywhere, CeMBA was launched as fully online programme in January 2017 using www.OpenLearning.com platform. This empowered the learners to access the programme content and resources from anywhere with an Internet connection, interaction with tutors and course coordinators and accessing digital library. Course content contained assignments, previous examination papers, course introductory and lecture videos, presentation slides and various multimedia including interactive exercises making them self-sufficient study units. A virtual classroom platform WizIQ is used to provide online tutorials to the students. The tutor schedules an online session and posts the class URL in the LMS or informs students through email. These tutorials are auto-recorded on the virtual classroom platform from where either they can be viewed online or downloaded and archived. This facility is useful to those who could not attend live session or wish to revise the discussion. The tutorials are of one hour, can be more depending upon discussion during the session. All courses have ten tutorials in a semester. Course assessment is done through two tutor-marked assignments (TMAs). There are two TMSs per course. Students upload their assignments into an online assignment submission system (OAS) which the tutor accesses to evaluate and upload results.

Open Educational Resources (OER)

Open educational resources are educational materials which are freely accessed, copied, reused, adapted and shared and available under an open licence or are in the public domain for use without paying licensing fees (UNESCO 2012). The term "Open Educational Resources" was adopted at the UNESCO's Forum on Open Courseware in 2002 when Massachusetts Institute of Technology (MIT) offered some of its courses as open courseware, and it became a hit among the students and teachers. The OER comprises of audio lessons, video recordings, photographs, lesson plans, syllabus, hand notes, lecture notes, slides, textbooks, podcasts, diagrams or simulations, etc. The Sustainable Development Goals (SDG) #4 pertains to "inclusive and equitable quality education and promoting lifelong learning opportunities for all". It lays special emphasis on access, equity and inclusion.

The Malaysia Higher Education Blueprint (MEB) 2015–2025 emphasises on five aspirations, i.e., access, quality, equity, unity and efficiency. These concerns can be well addressed by the creation, adoption and sharing of OER. WOU is leader in adoption of OER for course development and delivery. Since 2011, university has regularly conducted training for academics in search, creation and repurposing of OER for course materials development. As a result, WOU has developed around fourteen under- and postgraduate courses which are partially or fully OER based. Taking the OER movement further, WOU adopted two very important policies in 2012: (i) WOU Open License Policy and (ii) WOU OER Policy. These policies paved the way for effective and efficient way for creating awareness about OER, its use and reuse for course development and training of staff, including research on OER. Other notable initiatives related to OER at WOU are:

- Development of an OER Asia toolkit (2010)
- Formation of OER Integration Steering Committee in WOU (2011)
- Three OER training workshops (2011, 2014, 2015)

- OER Asia website hosted by WOU (2011)
- Two regional symposia on OER (2012, 2014)
- Two online OER repositories (2014, 2015).

WOU launched *OER Asia* (www.oerasia.org) in 2011 to share resources, information, research studies, guidelines and toolkits, etc., on good practices on and about OER in the Asian region.

WOU also created an *OER Repository* (http://weko.wou.edu.my) as an online collection of OER, metadata of learning objects, and other learning open resources. This repository was created using WEKO—an open-source repository software developed by the National Institute of Informatics, Japan. Currently, the repository holds around 380 resources. The site had 50,548 views during 2014–2016 with 65,909 downloads out of which more than 25% downloads were done by external agencies/individuals.

The *OER@AsiaHub Repository* (http://oerasia-repository.wou.edu.my) is another initiative of WOU with currently 21,605 records in its database.

WawasanCare

The university has very recently launched WawasanCare, an initiative to increase student engagement, to increase student enrolment and to put a check on student attrition. In this system, suitable messages are sent to all registered students of the university which pertain to themes like course content, course management, forum, tips, motivation, tutorial date and about TMA submission dates. The students have been advised to download the generic Moodle mobile app and the Wawasanlearn has been configured to be accessed by mobile app. These messages are broadcast using LMS.

WOU Press

WOU Press was set up in mid-2016 to encourage scholarly activities and provide publishing opportunities to WOU academic members. Most of the higher education institutions across Malaysia have established their own publishing department to produce and circulate their own publications related to academic research and findings. WOU Press receives support from the WOU's Institute for Research and Innovation (IRI) which provides funds and encourages research and development activities of the university. The first publication published by WOU Press is entitled "Open Educational Resources—Vignettes of Selected Asian Experience", edited by G. Dhanarajan. Second publication from the WOU Press is "Emerging Trends in Higher Education Pedagogy", edited by Santhiram Raman.

Challenges

1. **Student satisfaction and engagement**: Student learning and attainment is one of the most important aspects of educational delivery. It has a direct bearing upon student retention and attrition too. Monitoring of learning is an important challenge, and university is incorporating suitable technology to achieve this. The two types of LMS (Moodle and www.OpenLearning.com) generate lot of data about student engagement with the course content and interactions and the system generated analytics would reveal how the students are interacting with it. This area needs to be strengthened.
2. **Web Conferencing**: There are three modes of interacting with students, tutors and administrative staff in the regional centres: videoconferencing, Skype and WizIQ. Certain complaints are regularly being received from students and staff about poor connectivity, audio or video issues during using WizIQ or Skype, etc. There is a new WebRTC version of WizIQ launched which does not use Flash, and thus, it is hoped that online tutorial delivery will be smooth once the WebRTC interface is implemented.
3. **Upgrading the old hardware and software**: Since the university is venturing into multimedia resources development, there is a need to upgrade the relevant hardware and software.

Future Directions

The university developed a Base Strategic Plan (BSP) in 2016–17, which has following seven Strategic Thrust Areas (STA) for 2017–2022:

STA 1: Expand WOU products, markets and systems—making them industry relevant, going online for programmes delivery

STA 2: Increased focus on on-campus learners and its promotion, making WOU as a university of choice

STA 3: Dual mode offering of right spectrum

STA 4: Adopting University Client Charter for Service Excellence, paying attention to student and staff retention and market competition

STA 5: Exploring other income streams and ensuring cost efficiency

STA 6: Ensuring group-shared resources and services for shared benefits

STA 7: Exploring a new financial model for more funding support

In March 2017, the Board of Directors, WOU requested the development of Upside Growth Plan (UGP) to explore ways to grow beyond what was envisioned in the BSP. Six teams were constituted to work on specific areas. Table 5 shows the expected outcome of UGP teams.

Later on, UGP was superseded by the formation of the Transformation Steering Committee (initially named as Transformation Working Committee). The idea was

Table 5 Upside Growth Plan activities

Team with theme	Activity	Expected outcome
TEAM 1: "Traditional" Analysis of Existing Data	• Collect analysis that has already been done in the past • Identify major correlations and trends	• Consolidate data already existing, school wise, programme wise, region wise • Present existing analysis and trends with some extrapolation
TEAM 2: Data Mining Approach to Determine Deeper Patterns	• Do demographics drive behaviour? • Do demographics and behaviour drive outcomes? • Define data fields, extract them from databases (SIS, LMS, OAS) in correct format, combine data into single warehouse, use sophisticated analytical techniques to uncover patterns, employ data visualization techniques to communicate results	• Identify key variables across which relationships are sought to be studied • Define data needs to arrive at these relationships • Conduct analysis to arrive at relationships, trends and possible inferences
TEAM 3: Define a Whole New Level of Service	• Starting points are Client Charter project, Southern New Hampshire University example • Coordinate with attrition/retention team	• Working closely with the Client Charter recommendations, identify the key service expectations for all front line service providers, other levels for both external and internal customers • Draft outline plan to reach desired service level outcomes working with above and SARS team
TEAM 4: Attrition/ Retention Analysis	• Work with existing teams to summarize information most relevant to strategic direction • Assemble all data that we have on student feedback. • Assess lessons learnt, effectiveness of instruments • Coordinate with service level team	• Recommend ways to improve student feedback process • Recommend ways to reduce attrition based data from on current interventions • Share the findings SARS and retention study in the form of actions required to be taken within the strategic plan period • Present a clear identification of the gaps between existing service levels/practices and desired service levels/practices
TEAM 5: Delivery Technology Assessment	• Create a long-term vision and actionable plan for optimal delivery strategy that maximizes user experience, learning objectives and reach	Based on a clear overview of the available and applicable ET options, and an analysis of learners at WOU- • Present a roadmap of the delivery technologies that we may like to work with • Assess the related investment

(continued)

Table 5 (continued)

Team with theme	Activity	Expected outcome
TEAM 6: Assessing Non-Consumers	• Design approach for understanding "non-consumers" • Set up research plan to understand selected target segments of non-consumers	Based on understanding of prospective market, industry and other stakeholders • Present a view of non-consumers that fall in the category of our target market • Present an outline research plan to study the non-consuming target learner population by outlining scope, objectives, data needs, approaches to data collection and proposed analysis as well as the timelines

to integrate the best elements of UGP and BSP to focus on digital transformation, leadership, culture and talent along with process excellence and efficiency.

Conclusions

Ten years are not a long time in the history of an institution; however, the WOU has done a tremendous great job within one decade of its existence. It has been a leader for open and distance education in the region, set examples for the use and adoption of OER for course development and innovative use of ICT for learner support. Suitable strategies need to be put in place for skills transfer to huge cohort, which is currently excluded, from any form of tertiary education. Not only this, university needs to focus on retraining of existing cohort for knowledge and skills transfer through relevant pedagogy. To maintain the quality of distance learning materials, these need to be consistently revised and updated. Cost element for ICT is an important factor. This may be for infrastructure building, support learners, developing open learning materials, training and maintenance etc.

The university was accorded the SETARA Tier-5 (Excellent) rating by the Education Ministry in 2012. The Malaysia Integrated Rating for University and University College Excellence (SETARA) measures the quality of all public and private universities and university colleges, including foreign branch campuses. This is an evidence of university's compliance to well-defined and documented set of quality assurance policies and procedures which can match any international best practices. Affordable, Accessible and Flexible are the motto of the university. However, there is a matter of concern that as per SETARA-2017 Performance Report; the rating of Wawasan Open University has been rated Tier-3 (under Emerging University category) which is labelled as "Good"; however, the reason for the change from 5 to 3 may be that university now had to compete as a dual mode university with others and thus assessment done with different parameters. Malaysia Education Blueprint 2015–2025 has spelt out certain aspirations for higher education sector, and SETARA-2017 is developed to work towards these aspirations. This rating system enables the higher learning institutions in Malaysia to focus on three core functions of universities and university colleges: (i) teaching and learning, (ii) research and innovation and (iii) services to community and industry. Based on four criteria (general, teaching and learning, research and services), there are six levels of ratings, ranging from one star (poor) to six stars (outstanding). The institutions are classified into three categories: (i) mature university, (ii) emerging university and (iii) university college.

There are certain other challenges to the university, like maintaining a steady sustainable growth, learner dropouts/attrition and financial viability. The priority should be to bring innovation in designing, developing and delivering its products and services, to serve two sets of clients (ODL and OCL). Mr Klaus Schwab (President of World Economic Forum) speaks about four industrial revolutions. He says, "We are at the beginning of a global transformation that is characterized by the convergence of digital, physical, and biological technologies in ways that are changing both the world around us and our very idea of what it means to be human. The changes are historic in terms of their size, speed, and scope. This transformation—the Fourth Industrial Revolution—is not defined by any particular set of emerging technologies themselves, but rather by the transition to new systems that are being built on the infrastructure of the digital revolution. As these individual technologies become ubiquitous, they will fundamentally alter the way we produce, consume, communicate, move, generate energy, and interact with one another." (Schwab 2016).

Therefore, to meet the challenge of Fourth Industrial Revolution, staff and management needs to prepare themselves for the challenges of twenty-first century. Innovations in ICT and online pedagogy have transformed the design, development and delivery of instruction (Sharma 2018). University needs to tune in its content to suit the trends and demands for mobile and ubiquitous learning, which is the expectation of our learners too. Focusing on international affiliations and collaborations, effective research outcomes, staff capacity building, innovative pedagogy, enhanced students engagement is the need of hour for the university. There should be a strategy for implementing digitised interactive learning materials for better student success which may allow the university to achieve its mission of expanding higher educational opportunities and increasing level of knowledge through excellent teaching in Malaysia.

References

ADB. (2009). *Good practice in information and communication technology for education*. Mandaluyong City: Asian Development Bank.

Ali, A. (2012). Surviving the 21st century in Southeast Asia: open and distance learning for human capital development, SEAMEO SEAMOLEC and HOU international seminar on open and distance learning: Southeast Asian open and distance learning in the 21st century Danang city, Vietnam, held on 26–28 October 2012.

Britannica online Encyclopedia (2017). Southeast Asia. Encyclopedia entry, available at https://www.britannica.com/print/article/556489.

Calderon, A. (2012, September 2). Massification continues to transform higher education. Retrieved from University World News: http://www.universityworldnews.com/article.php?story=20120831155341147.

CESR Office (2014), Comprehensive Education Sector Review Phase (2) Report (Draft): Consultation Meeting for Development Partners (presentation), Comprehensive Education Sector Review Office, Yangon.

China Internet Network Information Center (CINNIC). (2017). The 39th Statistical Report on Internet Development in China. Available at https://cnnic.com.cn/IDR/ReportDownloads/201706/P020170608523740585924.pdf.

Chou, M., & Ravinet, P. (2017). Higher education regionalism in Europe and Southeast Asia: Comparing policy ideas. *Policy and Society, 36*(1), 143–159. https://doi.org/10.1080/14494035.2017.1278874.

Corporate Learning Network. (2014). Measuring Knowledge Investment: A Benchmarking Report from the Corporate Learning Network. 13 January 2014. https://www.corporatelearningnetwork.com/measurement-analysis/white-papers/measuring-knowledge-investment-a-benchmarking-repo.

Economic Planning Unit. (2015). The Eleventh Malaysia Plan (2016–2020): Anchoring growth on people. Malaysia: Economic Planning Unit, Prime Minister's Department.

Ferguson, R., Barzilai, S., Ben-Zvi, D., Chinn, C. A., Herodotou, C., Hod, Y., et al. (2017). *Innovating Pedagogy 2017: Open University Innovation Report 6*. Milton Keynes, UK: The Open University.

Govt of Malaysia. (2015). Speech by The Prime Minister YAB Dato' Sri Mohd. Najib Bin Tun Haji Abdul Razak for The Tabling of The Eleventh Malaysia Plan On 21 May 2015.

Latchem, C., & Jung, I. S. (2009). Distance and blended learning in Asia. London and New York: Routledge.

Lim, T., Fadzil, M., & Mansor, N. (2011). Mobile learning via SMS at Open University Malaysia: Equitable, effective, and sustainable. *The International Review of Research in Open and Distributed Learning*, *12*(2), 122–137. http://dx.doi.org/10.19173/irrodl.v12i2.926.

Markets and Markets. (2016). Mobile marketing market by solution (SMS, MMS, Push Notifications, Mobile Emails, QR Codes, Mobile Web), by User Type (SMB and Large Enterprise), by Vertical (Retail and E-commerce, Travel & Logistics, Automotive) & by Region—Global Forecast to 2021. Web report, May 2016. https://www.marketsandmarkets.com/Market-Reports/mobile-marketing-market-246836146.html.

Morrison, K. (2016). A rough guide to Southeast Asia for BC Institutions. http://bccie.bc.ca/wp-content/uploads/2016/06/ascendance-of-southeast-asia.pdf.

NMC Horizon Report. (2012). *Higher* (Education ed.). Austin, Texas: The New Media Consortium.

OECD. (2017). Economic Outlook for Southeast Asia, China and India 2017: Addressing Energy Challenges, Paris: OECD Publishing. http://dx.doi.org/10.1787/saeo-2017-en.

Osman, Z., Alwi, N. H. & Khan B. N. A. (2016). A study of mediating effect of attitude on perceived ease of use and student intention to use online learning platform among online learning institutions in Malaysia. In *Paper presented at Pan-Commonwealth Forum 'Open, Online and Flexible learning: The key to sustainable development', held from 27–30 November 2017 at Open University Malaysia, Kuala Lumpur, Malaysia, Conference abstracts* (p. 143).

Sadiman, A. S. (2006). Challenges in education in Southeast Asia. In *Paper presented at the International Seminar on "Towards Cross Border Cooperation between South and Southeast Asia: The Importance of India's North East Playing Bridge and Buffer Role*", Kaziranga, India,

16–19 November 2004. http://www.seameo.org/vl/library/dlwelcome/publications/paper/india0.
Schwab, K. (2016). *The fourth industrial revolution*. Geneva: World Economic Forum.
Sharma, R. C. (2018). *Innovative applications of online pedagogy and course design* (pp. 1–411). Hershey, PA: IGI Global. https://doi.org/10.4018/978-1-5225-5466-0.
Sharples, M., de Roock, R., Ferguson, R., Gaved, M., Herodotou, C., Koh, E., et al. (2016). *Innovating Pedagogy 2016: Open University Innovation Report 5*. Milton Keynes: The Open University.
Teng, A. (2015, November 12). NIE to offer courses on open online platform. Retrieved from Straits Times: http://www.straitstimes.com/singapore/education/nie-to-offer-courses-on-open-online-platform.
UNESCO. (2003). Synthesis of Country Case Studies, South East Asian ICT Advocacy and Planning Workshop for Policy Makers, Bangkok: UNESCO Asia and Pacific Regional Bureau of Education.
UNESCO Bangkok and SEAMEO. (2006). *Higher education in Southeast Asia*. Bangkok: UNESCO Asia and Pacific Regional Bureau for Education.
UNESCO. (2011). *ICT in higher education: Case studies from Asia and the Pacific*. Bangkok: UNESCO Bangkok.
UNESCO. (2012). 2012 Paris OER Declaration. Paris, France: World OER Congress. http://www.unesco.org/new/fileadmin/MULTIMEDIA/HQ/CI/CI/pdf/Events/Paris%20OER%20Declaration_01.pdf.
Vasilevska, D., et al. (2017). Analysis of the demand for distance education at eastern and central european higher education institutions. *Journal of Teacher Education for Sustainability, 19*(1), 106–116. https://doi.org/10.1515/jtes-2017-0007.

Technology Affordances at the Open University of Mauritius

Perienen Appavoo, Kaviraj Sharma Sukon, Abheenaye Chauhan Gokhool and Vandanah Gooria

Distance Education in Africa: General Account

Education is a rudimentary human right. United Nations stresses the education's prominence in contributing to the improvement and fulfilment of human rights and to socio-economic evolution (UNESCO 2010). The African countries have committed themselves to 'Education for All', although it is a daunting task which requires more use of open and distance learning (Udai 2010). Distance education (DE) contributes significantly to the development of higher education. In the distance learning environment, learners are free from the limitations of a time frame, and setting and on the flip side, they have adaptable learning scopes. DE proffers some benefits for Africa as it meets the challenges of 'expanding enrolment', constricted budgetary estimates, thronged classrooms, coupled with bleak career probabilities (Butcher et al. 2011). Grants and scholarships are available to encourage African students to further their tertiary education in Western states. Initially, the raison d'être of this funding was to gear and harness those aptitudes in the home country, but this has yielded a reversal outcome with more 'brain drain' (Mutume 2003). In this respect, DE is commonly regarded as a feasible option and has made a radical change, because it has allowed learners to enrol in programmes administered at low cost from outside their sociocultural environment and

P. Appavoo (✉) · K. S. Sukon · A. C. Gokhool · V. Gooria
Open University of Mauritius, Moka, Mauritius
e-mail: p.appavoo@open.ac.mu

K. S. Sukon
e-mail: ks.sukon@gmail.com

A. C. Gokhool
e-mail: a.gokhool@open.ac.mu

V. Gooria
e-mail: v.gooria@open.ac.mu

© Springer Nature Singapore Pte Ltd. 2018

Anjana (ed.), *Technology for Efficient Learner Support Services in Distance Education*, https://doi.org/10.1007/978-981-13-2300-3_8

facilitating skills reinvestment within local communities. Accordingly, DE has an auxiliary potentiality to assist and coach a specialized African manpower in line with social and professional possibilities to fortify the African labour force (Mufutumari 2010). Obviously, traditional face-to-face delivery cannot solely cater for the surging demand for tertiary studies in Africa (Goolam 2015). Open, distance and online learning are other avenues that should be considered to cater for ongoing adult and teacher training. In this prospect, the set-up of open universities in various African nations with the concomitant use of distance learning is enhancing face-to-face teaching in traditional universities. However, given that there is staggering effort to bring considerable technological development in African countries, there is less likelihood to fully accomplish the distance education prospects (Karsenti and Collin 2013). Africa does not have adequate access to computer equipment and the deficiency of high-speed Internet bases and the lack of specialized manpower to enforce and efficaciously sustain the techno-savvy teaching methodologies in the distance learning context.

Overview of Mauritius in the African Continent

Mauritius is a tiny island in the Indian Ocean, situated just east of Madagascar and the African continent (Figs. 1 and 2). Mauritius was explored by the Portuguese (1505), Dutch (1638–1710), French (1715–1810) and Britain (1810–1968), with unsuccessful attempts to transform the island into a prosperous colony. In 1968, Mauritius adopted a new constitution and became independent. It achieved the status of republic 24 years later in 1992. Mauritius has a population of 1.3 million with an annual growth rate of 0.40% as on 5 February 2018 (Countrymeters 2018) and has developed into a diversified economy. The GDP per capita in Mauritius is equivalent to 78% of the world's average. It has the seventh highest GDP per capita in Africa and is also rated as the highest among African countries for its engagement and human rights and its sustainable economic opportunity. The GDP annual growth rate in Mauritius averaged 3.90 per cent from 2001 until 2017 (Trading Economics 2018). The rapid socio-economic growth has transformed the Mauritian citizens into high literacy rates (youth 98.7%, female 62.7%, adult 90.6% in 2015 (World Data Atlas 2018). Unlike many other countries around the world, Mauritius offers free primary and secondary education for all children. Free tertiary education is also offered to a significant number of potential students. It also provides free public transport to students and the elderly and free health services to all. Internet penetration in Africa was 35.2% as on 31 December 2017 (Internet World Stats 2018). Mauritius ranks first in terms of ICT Development Index and shows significant progress towards becoming an information society. The Internet subscriptions per 100 inhabitants in Mauritius are 66.6% (2015), and 51% Mauritians make daily use of the Internet (Roussety 2015).

The educational system in Mauritius is based on the British model since its independence. Currently, Mauritius is focussing more on being the knowledge hub

Fig. 1 Location of Mauritius

in the region and consequently, the new ingenious technological development aired alongside other major incursions in the field of higher education altogether renders the knowledge market significantly competitive. With the soaring technological evolution, distance education is commonly considered as the optimum solution to cater for surging educational prospects. As on December 2015, the total number of students (part-time and full-time) enrolled on tertiary-level programmes (including distance education) was 48,970 in contrast to 50,608 in December 2014, signifying a decrease of 3.2%. The majority of students (77%) were enrolled in tertiary education locally in both public-funded institutions (44%) and private institutions (33%). The remaining 23% of the students were enrolled in tertiary education overseas (Statistics Mauritius 2016). Among other Tertiary Education Institutions (TEIs), within the five years of existence, the Open University has enrolled more than 5,000 learners despite trials, tribulations, hardships and competition. The university has vested a lot to accomplish the mission to become the national focal point for open and distance learning in Mauritius. Today, there is a great demand from those who have missed the opportunity to study, and the Open University has opened the door for adults and working people.

Fig. 2 Map of Mauritius. *Source* https://www.worldatlas.com/webimage/countrys/africa/mu.htm

Distance Education in Mauritius and Contribution of Open University of Mauritius to Higher Education in the Country

In Mauritius, the concept of distance education dates back to as the early 1972 when people studied for their A-level or followed professional courses delivered by correspondence institutions in the UK and South Africa. They were receiving printed copies of their learning materials as well as audio cassettes through the post. The national television also aired educational programmes. To meet the growing demand for education at various levels, the first government of the independent Mauritius decided to set up the Mauritius College of the Air (MCA) in the year 1971. MCA was providing education through mass media and distance education methods. It produced video and audio programmes for learners of the primary and secondary schools based on the national curriculum. These programmes were aired nationally. In fact, the MCA launched its first course in October 1972, in collaboration with the University of Mauritius (Dhurbarrylall and Dodds 1996). In 1973, MCA played a key role in providing training to primary school teachers after the introduction of New Mathematics. Blended mode was used, and this allowed teachers to meet tutors during the weekend and after school hours. Thus, after establishing the MCA as the focal point for the delivery of distance education in Mauritius, its initial focus was on upgrading the qualifications of the teachers at primary and secondary levels as well as offering the opportunities to study for A-level (Tertiary Education Commission 1994).

The year 1989 is a historic year in the field of open and distance learning as it was the year in which two major reports were published, namely Lord Young's report entitled Open Learning and its Potential in Mauritius and Sir John Daniel's report named Distance Education for Human Resource Development in Mauritius: The Way Forward (Dhurbarrylall and Dodds 1996). These reports helped to shape the provision of education through distance learning mode. They were also used in the development of the Master Plan on Education for the year 2000 that was published in the year 1991. This plan stressed the pivotal role of distance learning method in the socio-economic and cultural development of a country like Mauritius that has as its main asset its people. Undoubtedly, distance learning allows the vast majority of people to update their set of skills and competences continuously in order to remain employable in this highly competitive world fuelled by rapid advances in technology.

Already in the mid-1990s, several overseas institutions were providing courses on distance education mode. According to Leste (1997), an audit conducted in 1995 showed that sixteen such institutions were operating in Mauritius. University of South Africa (UNISA) played a prominent role in Mauritius. One of the important partners of MCA in the delivery of degree programmes has been Indira Gandhi National Open University of India (IGNOU). Several programmes were offered including MBA. MCA was also a partner of the mega pan-African e-network project financed by the Government of India. Through this project, citizens from several African countries have been benefitting several programmes including MBA freely.

In 2012, Open University of Mauritius (OU) was set up. Most of the members of staff of MCA integrated OU. As MCA did not have degree-awarding powers, it was heavily dependent on other institutions. This made it difficult to abide by the rules and regulations of different institutions. Staff had to follow different procedures for different institutions. Fortunately, the Open University of Mauritius Act of 2010 endowed OU with all the necessary powers. OU started enrolling its first students in 2013. The strategy used is blended method. It offers a wide range of courses ranging from short courses up to degree programmes including DBA and PhD.

OU has been the fastest growing public university since 2013 while being the only ISO-certified public university of Mauritius offering high-quality education. A large number of learners, mainly adults, joined OU because of the flexibility that it provides. OU made a significant difference in the lives of employees who could not be at the university on a full-time or part-time basis. Through its blended mode of learning, OU has broadened access to university education. Thus, employees can earn a qualification while working; learners can also work part-time and study; and others, including retired persons as well as people having to look after their family during the day, can study at their own pace and place. OU has been endeavouring to create affordable and high-quality blended learning materials. It has a full-fledged studio to produce audio and video materials. It has developed a strong e-learning platform Moodle. In collaboration with Imperial College London and the Royal College of Physicians, Edinburgh, several training programmes are conducted for medical doctors and specialists. This has allowed OU to be the second public university in terms of the number of students within 5 years after its establishment. OU is also nearly financially independent after 5 years of operations.

One of the key ingredients of the success of OU is its solid international partnership. Learners no more consider OU as a second choice. Today, OU attracts the largest number of learners wishing to study for the MBA. Within a short period of time after it has been set up, OU has forged a solid working relationship with partners like Imperial College London (UK); Stockholm University (Sweden); University of California, San Diego (USA); and University of South Africa. It has also benefitted from unflinching support from several international organizations like Commonwealth of Learning (COL); Association of Commonwealth Universities; Distance Education Association of Southern Africa; African Council for Distance Education; and International Council for Open and Distance Education.

Employability of its learners remains at the heart of the operations of OU. In this context, OU offers a number of employability short courses that provide the opportunity to everyone to acquire the necessary soft skills that are as important as the academic qualifications, especially in an era where knowledge is evolving rapidly. Experts from the industry are selected to form the core team to develop the study materials, after being thoroughly briefed about the development of ODL materials.

OU has also convinced employers to use blended mode of training for their employees. It has been able to attract a large number of employees from public and private sectors to follow tailor-made training.

Undoubtedly, open and distance learning is considered equal to the conventional mode of learning in Mauritius. MOOCs have certainly helped to establish the parity. It is hoped that advances in technology will help to enhance the provision of the open and distance learning further.

Technology Integration at the Open University of Mauritius—Practices and Challenges

Since day one, the Open University of Mauritius has genuinely been at the forefront of the technological revolution embedding various technological tools like e-mails, videos, Skype, tablets and the Moodle platform in different activities to provide students with the most conducive learning environment. This has been achieved to various degrees of success, leaving room for discussion, reflection and re-engineering the whole process.

Moodle Platform

The very first tool with which students have to familiarize themselves is the Moodle platform which can be described as their 'life partner' during their studies at the institution. The Moodle platform, learning-centred software, is being used in most universities, by both students and staff (Aljawarneh et al. 2010). This powerful and useful tool contains all the information that students need to assist them in their studies, like the timetable, examinations results, assignment questions and learning materials. According to Nyandara (2012), the platform is an effective way for sharing learning materials between the university and the students. At the Open University, once a student has registered for a programme, the latter is given access to all learning materials and other related information posted on the platform. A presentation of the tool is conducted during the induction exercise to explain its benefits to learners. Every learner accesses the Moodle platform using a unique password and user ID provided by the university. Both tutors and students can create discussion groups to discuss the learning materials and any other issues related to the course programme. For authors like Zainuddin et al. (2016), the Moodle platform allows tutors to be closer to their students, especially if they are abroad or cannot attend face-to-face sessions. Tutors are thus encouraged to use this interactive platform to provide maximum support to their students. Training sessions are regularly conducted at OU to empower them in the efficient use of this platform.

The use of the discussion board (DB) which is a facility offered by the Moodle platform is also being encouraged at the Open University. A research study (Appavoo et al. 2016) was carried out to investigate the acceptance of learners to use the discussion board in their study and do away with prevailing practices. The participants of this study were learners doing their master's degree at the university. They commented that the DB added value to their learning, allowing them to engage in peer tutoring, tutor/learner interaction and development of reflective and analytical skills. On the other hand, the study revealed the need for all stakeholders, including tutors and learners, to get acquainted with the affordances of the DB. This implies taking time to master the appropriate functionalities of the platform and derive maximum benefits from it. Moreover, the findings further revealed that there is a need for ODL learners to enhance their writing skills in order to maximize from the interactions taking place on this learning interface. The findings concur with some of the concepts describing the term 'Webagogy' which is an emerging science of learning on the net. Figure 3 shows how the acronym 'TELEPHONE' was used, whereby each letter describes what the authors retrieved from interviewing the learners.

The DB is also a platform which engages participants in deep thinking. During the focus group discussions, learners reported that since their posts could be accessed by any one of the platforms, they took additional time to delve into deep thinking and critical analysis before posting. The concern for learners to delve into deep thinking before posting is substantiated in the literature by Petrides (2002) and

Fig. 3 Telephone approach

Vonderwell (2003). As reported by Zhang et al. (2004), the DB proved to be a convenient venue to encourage peer tutoring and sharing of information. In some cases, learners took the role of tutors and provided the necessary mentoring and advice to their friends. It was thus concluded that the DB platform was an appropriate tool to support the ODL mode of learning offered by the university.

It is worth mentioning though that one of the key factors determining the success of the implementation of the discussion board within the learning space is the involvement of the tutors, which in turn depends on their skills and conviction of the pedagogical worth of the tool. A significant share of the assessment exercise can be accomplished using the DB where marks can be attributed for the postings and their relevance. At the Open University, our tutors are constantly reminded of the benefits of using the DB to keep learners active and fight alienation.

E-mails

E-mails are another tool commonly used by the university to sustain communication between the university and the students. According to Leh (2001), using e-mail in education is quite flexible and easy. E-mails facilitate the communication not only between students and tutors but among learners as well. Students can also send their queries to the learner support unit and to their respective programme managers. In some cases, additional learning materials can also be sent by the university to students or tutors through e-mails. One important element of using e-mails is feedback. In the context of Open Distance Education, feedback is very important, and Tao and Boulware (2002) stated that learners are motivated and are able to clear their doubts about academic issues through the use of e-mails. It has been observed that there is a tendency for students to use e-mails more than the other types of technological tools because of their convenience and accessibility. For example, a student can access his e-mail account through his/her mobile phone, anywhere and anytime to receive information about assignments, change in the timetable or still to organize collaborative learning sessions.

Skype

Another technological tool frequently being used at the Open University is Skype. The use of Skype for educational purposes is already a common practice among students (Zygouris-Coe 2012). This tool is mainly used with students who are abroad and therefore cannot attend the tutorial sessions. The Republic of Mauritius also comprises the island of Rodrigues, located some 385 miles to the east of Mauritius. A number of learning activities are facilitated by the functionalities of Skype for Rodriguans. According to Voireanu (2016), Skype does not only encourage students in group chats or debates but also help provide support and advice to them. In the case of our students from Rodrigues, they can follow lectures online, present their assignment and receive instant feedback from the tutors. Where required, Skype sessions are conducted between the tutor and the students so that they can discuss the learning content and assignments. Because of its modus operandi, the Open University resorts to resource persons and lecturers who are sometimes abroad. Their services are thus provided through the Skype platform. We have lectures and viva sessions being run with resource persons from Europe and Africa.

Tablets

Today, mobile technology including smartphones and tablets is gaining momentum to revolutionize the educational panorama. The use of technological devices like tablets, smartphones and laptops to provide education is defined as mobile learning (Traxler 2005). According to Xiang et al. (2009), tablets are easy to use. The Open University is the only tertiary institution that provides free tablets to all students enrolled on a degree course. For the first semester, all study materials are preloaded on the tablets. For subsequent semesters, students can download the relevant content on their tablets using the Moodle platform, where such documents are uploaded regularly. Students are encouraged to bring their tablets to the tutorials sessions so that they can follow the explanations of the tutors. The portability of the tool makes it very convenient for students to access learning content for study or revision work. In a study carried out by Appavoo and Koonjal (2015), the authors found that students at the Open University value the flexibility tablets offer to learn anywhere, anytime and at their own pace. In fact, the study showed that learners were regular users of technology, with many of them using the computer for more than an hour daily. Learning was found to be one of the common activities. Figure 4 depicts the major uses of tablets by OU learners. The main use of tablets was for studying the course materials. During the focus group discussions, students revealed that they found the tablet very convenient for revision purposes before the exams, as it relieved them from the burden of carrying heavy textbooks. Some learners used the tablets for other purposes such as doing their assignments, Internet search and even for interacting among themselves and with their respective tutors.

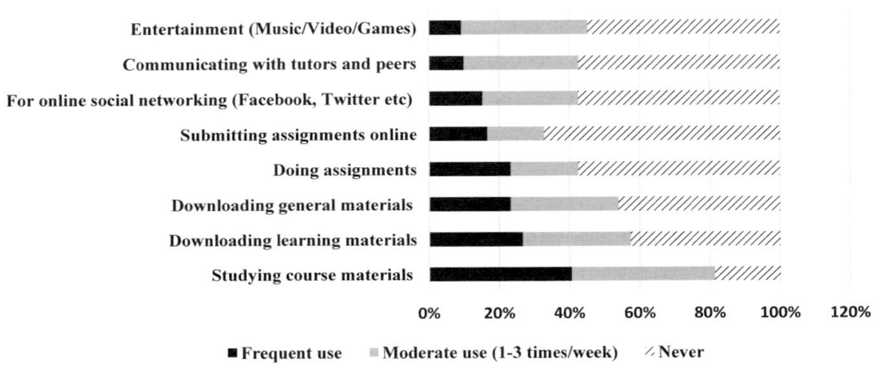

Fig. 4 Extent of tablet use by OU learners

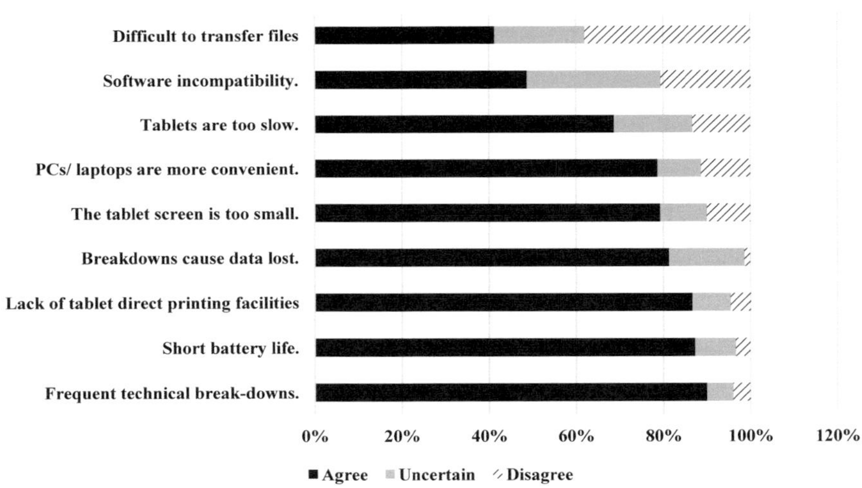

Fig. 5 Barriers to the effective use of tablets

But the use of tablets is not without difficulties. Figure 5 highlights the major barriers hindering the effective use of tablets.

Some of the barriers listed above are closely related to the cheapness of the tablet. It is therefore important to go for the more robust ones where durability, reliability and high processing power can be guaranteed. Moreover, this study confirmed that the mere provision of technology does not automatically lead to better knowledge acquisition. Kaganer et al. (2013) proposed that success with mobile learning initiatives requires a close fit between course design and the functionalities of the technology, whereby the benefits of multimedia can help understand, assimilate and process learning materials much easier. The challenge today is to empower instructional designers with skills that can blend learning materials with media components.

Videos

One of the strong pillars of the Open University is its video production unit, which captures lectures and selected tutorials and produces documentary videos to complement each of the course modules. Programme managers recruit the best lecturers, resource persons and presenters and with the help of highly skilled TV directors, design, plan and produce the most appropriate video contents. By making the latter available on the Moodle platform, students can review lectures and enhance their understanding of the subject matter. It is also a viable option for those who miss tutorials or who want to do some revision work. According to Kozma (1991), instructional videos are very powerful and rich in information. This information is presented in a consistent and attractive way, which encourages students to have recourse to them. The videos allow the students to see sequences in motion, to listen to the explanation of the tutors and also view actual objects or even realistic scenes (Zhang et al. 2006). But today, instructional videos on any topic can also be found free on the net. There are hundreds of thousands of videos on YouTube, and one needs only the right skills and necessary guidelines to locate a relevant video for a given subject matter. To that effect, Appavoo et al. (2015) proposed a set of guidelines to identify an appropriate video for a particular topic. The Open University which emanates from the erstwhile Mauritius College of the Air has a strong repository of videos on various topics. For its employability skills courses and foundation programmes, these videos have proved to be a constant catalyst for learning.

Text Messages Service

Text messages are also commonly used by the Student Affairs Unit of the Open University to facilitate communication between the university and the learners and their respective tutors. Text messages are sent to learners and tutors to remind them of the forthcoming tutorial session, or if the tutorial session has been cancelled on the eve, or still to request them to check their e-mails for more details about any other issues. The challenge with this service is that the text limit is 160 characters and the text has to be very concise and precise. Furthermore, students often change their phone numbers without informing the university.

Collaborative Learning

Studying at a distance has its challenges, and learners often find it difficult to adapt to this new learning environment and thus become easily isolated. Collaborative learning has much been privileged in the distance mode of learning and is believed to help overcome isolation and boost learning performance. According to Gokhale (1995), Dillenbourg (1999), Swain (1997, 2000) and Jacobs et al. (2002), CL is a situation in which two or more students learn, share ideas or attempt to learn something together or work among students to better understand a subject towards a common goal. Many scholarly works, such as those of Slavin (1996), Ellis (2003), Johnston et al. (2000), Maesin et al. (2009) and Jiang (2009), highlight the benefits of collaborative learning, which among others include learner motivation, better marks, promotion of social interaction and critical thinking.

With emerging technologies, there are several tools like WhatsApp, Skype and Moodle which can be used to foster collaborative learning and thus help students communicate, collaborate and learn through social interaction. Cole (2005) observed that Moodle could be used as a facilitator in collaborative learning. Through the Moodle platform, educators create several activities for learners to discuss or even share their ideas. The educators can act as a moderator of the discussion group or let the students discuss among themselves. Since Moodle has many functions, students can also use the chat function to create a group and complete their tasks such as assignments. Rabbany et al. (2013) added that Moodle indeed enables students to participate in collaborative learning. Students create forums in which they can discuss certain topics of the curriculum or address other issues concerning their studies. They can also encourage their tutors to participate and share additional notes on these forums.

According to Zygouris-Coe (2012), many students use Skype to conduct group discussion among themselves. The author found that students create their group on Skype and set up ways of conducting collaborative learning. Many authors mentioned several examples of Skype being used in collaborative learning. For example, Lan et al. (2007) reported how some students formed a learning group on Skype to complete a task which was allocated to them. Authors like Hrastinski and Aghaee (2012) explained the advantage of using Skype in collaborative learning. When using Skype, students can get instant feedback from their peers by either messages or video calls. Skype is also useful in cases where one or two members cannot attend a meeting but can go online to catch up with the rest of the group.

One of the most famous social technologies used among people nowadays is WhatsApp. People use this software for various purposes and even in collaborative learning. Amry (2014) identified several ways in which students use WhatsApp while undertaking collaborative learning. The software allows students to create specific groups in which they exchange messages, pictures, documents and videos. Students can also do video calls with each other. Chan (2005) added that WhatsApp provides opportunities for students who choose the distance education mode, to cooperate, collaborate and to share ideas and knowledge. Moreover, Preston et al. (2010) conducted a research on WhatsApp among students and found that more than 50% of students prefer to learn on groups such as WhatsApp group where they can freely discuss their academic problems.

Two effective teaching and learning tools, wikis and blogs, have been increasingly used in higher education to facilitate student collaborative learning. Kuo et al. (2017) added that blogging as a medium for CL enhances asynchronous peer interaction, reflection and positive attitudes towards academic achievement in collaborative activities. Wang (2010) in his study found that students perceived that blogs were a useful tool to reflect and interact with classmates and enlarge the resources of learning support.

Because of the relative importance of CL and its contribution to the learning experience of students, a research study (Appavoo et al. 2017) was carried out at the Open University, and it depicts how different technological tools have been embraced to facilitate this learning process.

Figure 6 shows the technological tools currently used by learners at the Open University to delve into activities related to CL. E-mails proved to be a common tool used by learners, together with WhatsApp, the telephone and the Moodle platform. While face to face remained the most preferred means of conducting CL sessions, the authors found that technological tools were taking an increasing share in promoting this activity. The figures look promising, but it is equally vital to research the smaller minority who were experiencing difficulties to tame the functionalities of these technologies for their studies. Not availing themselves of such benefits can deprive ODL learners of a prime avenue to enhance their learning. Regarding the venue for conducting CL, this study revealed that the virtual and online platform came as the second preferred option as learners found it hard to find a common meeting place at an agreed time. Learners found it convenient to fix the CL sessions just after their tutorials. But because attendance at the tutorials is optional, the online option came in as handy. This growing interest for online meeting platforms reflects today's gradual trend towards e-learning, where both synchronous and asynchronous interactions make learning a more dynamic, interactive and engaging process (Amry 2014; Kuo et al. 2017). The authors also unveiled that the availability of technological tools was a contributing factor to the holding of CL sessions as was also reported by Zhu (2012) and Amry (2014).

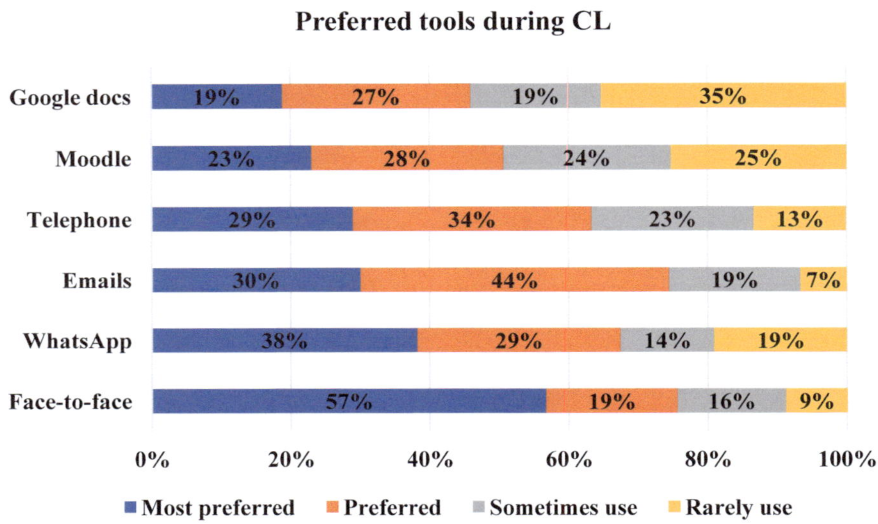

Fig. 6 Preferred tools during CL

Challenges of Using Technological Tools at the Open University of Mauritius

The previous sections have described the various technological tools used at OU. Although these tools enable the institution to perform efficiently, the integration of technology at the Open University is not without challenges, despite all the advocacies for it. As with all innovative practices, resistance is ever present because it is human to resist change. But unfortunately, change is the only constant that guarantees the survival of the business and keeps it running. Technology pessimists have always opposed the uptake of technology, especially in the educational sector. This part of the unit deals with challenges in connection with the required technological infrastructure, the technological skills of freelance tutors, the profile of the learners, running Skype sessions and the usability of videos made available to learners.

The Required Technological Infrastructure

The institution does have an IT infrastructure in place to enable the use of the technological tools. However, this is insufficient. As the number of students keeps increasing, OU faces the challenge to cater for the technological needs of these students. Because of space restrictions in the main building, many tutorial sessions are held in schools where Wi-Fi facilities are restricted. The limited computer laboratories are often reserved for IT students. Moreover, some students do not have broadband Internet access and cannot fully benefit from all interactions necessitating Internet connection.

Skills of Freelance Tutors

To conduct its activities, OU relies a lot on freelance tutors, many of whom are in their fifties or sixties. While they all demonstrate some basic computer skills, they may not necessarily master the functionalities of the latest forms of technological tools. For example, some tutors are not well versatile with the different functionalities of Moodle and are thus not always willing to upload their notes or conduct assessments on this platform. While every effort is made to encourage them to maximize on the various technological tools made available at OU, there is still some hesitation from a number of them. This can result in a low level of motivation among students looking for assistance when using these tools. To overcome this shortcoming, training sessions are regularly being organized for the tutors.

The Profile of the Learners

Most of OU learners are quite mature in terms of age and not necessarily conversant with tools such as Moodle, Skype or the tablet. For many of them, the use of such technological tools poses some problems. For example, they may lack the ICT skills required to use these tools or are simply reluctant to use them because they have always been used to traditional learning methods. This represents a major challenge for OU academics, who constantly have to address this shortcoming as more and more of the learning activities of the university are being organized around technological affordances. Special consideration is thus being given to these learners so that they are not deprived of learning opportunities.

Skype

Skype facilities often require a good Internet connection at both ends, and experience has shown that this does not always happen causing a lot of delays and frustrations. In some cases, the video mode has to be switched off so that the oral presentation can go on. However, where there are slide presentations, this can seriously jeopardize the quality of lecture or presentation. Furthermore, some tutors or students may not really know how to operate the Skype software and this can hinder the learning process of the learners who are abroad.

Videos

Videos are also provided to learners to support their studies. They can be quite helpful for students who are unable to attend the sessions, but in some cases issues can arise. For example, some videos which have a long duration can take a lot of time to be downloaded and can be a real challenge for students if they are experiencing a poor network connection or their personal computers or laptops do not support the format of these videos. At times, some videos can be boring or too long or have not been designed properly. This can create confusion for the student on what to focus.

The main challenges of using technological tools have been discussed in this part of the chapter. Although the Open University is ensuring that all its activities are being run efficiently, it should not neglect these challenges. These challenges can be transformed into opportunities in the long run if properly managed. And there is the need for the institution to devise plans to handle these challenges and continue to deliver quality education to its students.

Conclusion

In the midst of the technological era, the educational landscape of Mauritius, especially the ODL sector, is witnessing major transformations in delivery modes. The Open University has left no stone unturned to maximize on technological affordances to meet the learning needs of both digital natives and digital immigrants which characterize the profile of its learners. Much has already been achieved using tools like Moodle, Skype, e-mails, tablets and videos to closely assist and support learners in their studies. There is still some fine-tuning to be done to strengthen existing practices and improve the logistics already in place. But OU will not hesitate to venture into new avenues of technological transformation to locate such approaches that will ease the interaction between the university, the freelance tutors and the students, such that learning can happen in the most conducive environment.

References

Aljawarneh, S., AlMaghayreh, E., Alkhateeb, F., Muhsin, Z. & Nsour, A. (2010). E-learning Tools and Technologies in Education: A Perspective, E-learning. In: *The Fifth International Conference of Learning International Networks Consortium (LINC), MIT*. Cambridge, MA. Retrieved April 10, 2017, from http://people.math.sfu.ca/~vjungic/shadi.pdf.

Amry, B. A. (2014). The impact of WhatsApp mobile social learning on the achievement and attitudes of female students compared with face to face learning in the classroom. *European Scientific Journal, 10*(22), 116–136.

Appavoo, P., & Koonjal, P. (2015). Assessing tablets' adoption by ODL learners: A Mauritian CASE STUDY. In *2015 Conference on the society of Digital Information and Wireless communications (SDIWC)*.

Appavoo, P., Gooria, V., & Gokhool, A. C. (2017). *Collaborative Learning in a Blended Learning Environment*. In *The University of Kwazulu Natal's 11th Annual Higher Education Conference*. Durban, SA.

Appavoo, P., Gungea, M., Jutton, T. & Dookhun, P. (2015). Confused which educational video to choose? Appropriateness of YouTube videos for instructional purposes- making the right choice. In: *International Conference on Computing, Communication and Security (ICCCS) 2015 Conference*, pp. 1–8. https://doi.org/10.1109/cccs.2015.7374187.

Appavoo, P., Sohoraye, M., & Gungea, M. (2016).'Webagogy'—the next milestone after pedagogy and andragogy? In *IEEE International Conference on Emerging Technologies and Innovative Business Practices for the Transformation of Societies (EmergiTech)* (pp. 317–322). https://doi.org/10.1109/emergitech.2016.7737359.

Butcher, N., Latchem, C., Mawoyo, M., & Levey, L. (2011). Distance education for empowerment and development in Africa. *Distance Education, 32*(2), 149–158. https://doi.org/10.1080/01587919.2011.584844.

Chan, L. (2005). WebCT revolutionized e-learning. *UBC Reports, 51*(7).

Cole, J. (2005). *Using moodle: Teaching with the popular open source course management system*. Sebastopol: O' Reilly Community Press.

Countrymeters (2018). *Mauritius Population clock:Quick facts about the population of Mauritius*. Retrieved February 5, 2018, from http://countrymeters.info/en/Mauritius#population_2018.

Dhurbarrylall, R., & Dodds, T. (1996). *Mauritius College of the Air: A case study*. International Extension College.

Dillenbourg, P. (1999). What do you mean by collaborative learning? In *Collaborative-learning: cognitive and computational approaches* (pp. 1–19).

Ellis, R. (2003). *Task-based language learning and teaching*. Oxford: Oxford University Press.

Gokhale, A. A. (1995). Collaborative learning enhances critical thinking. *Journal of Technology Education, 7*(1), 22–30.

Goolam, M. (2015). Higher education in Africa: Facing the challenges in the 21st century. *International Higher Education, 63,* 20–21.

Hrastinski, S., & Aghaee, N. M. (2012). How are campus students using social media to support their studies? An explorative interview study. *Education and Information Technologies, 17,* 451–464.

Internet World Stats (2018). *Internet Users Statistics for Africa*. https://www.internetworldstats.com/stats1.htm.

Jacobs, G. M., Power, M. A. & Loh, W. I. (2002). *The teacher's sourcebook for cooperative learning: practical techniques, basic principles and frequently asked questions*. Corwin Press: Thousand Oaks.

Jiang, Y. M. (2009). Applying group work to improve college students' oral English. *Journal of Studies in International Education, 2*(3), 136–139.

Johnston, C. G., James, R. H., Lye, J. N., & McDonald, I. M. (2000). An evaluation of collaborative problem solving for learning economics. *The Journal of Economic Education, 31* (1), 13–29.

Kaganer, E., Giordano, G. A., Brion, S., & Tortoriello, M. (2013). Media tablets for mobile learning. *Communications of the ACM, 56*(11), 68–75.

Karsenti, T., & Collin, S. (2013). Distance education in Africa: A longitudinal study of the perceptions of 2,416 Students. *International Journal of Technologies in Higher Education, 10* (3). https://doi.org/10.7202/1035580ar.

Kozma, R. B. (1991). Learning with media. *Review of Educational Research, 61*(2), 179–212.

Kuo, Y. C., Belland, B. R., & Kuo, Y. T. (2017). Learning through blogging: student's perspectives in collaborative blog-enhanced learning communities. *Educational Technology & Society, 20*(2), 37–50.

Lan, Y., Sung, Y., & Chang, K. (2007). A mobile-device-supported peer-assisted learning system for collaborative early ELF reading. *Language Learning & Technology, 11*(3), 130–151.
Leh, A. (2001). Computer-mediated communication and social presence in a distance learning environmenT. *International Journal of Educational Telecommunications, 7*(2), 109–128.
Leste P. (1997). *Audit of DE – MCA Mauritius to host the secretariat for Africa*. Le Mauricien.
Maesin, A., Mansor, M., Shafie, L. A., & Nayan, S. (2009). A study of collaborative learning among Malaysian undergraduates. *Asian Soc Sci, 5*(7), 70–76.
Mufutumari, N. (2010). Deploying Africa's intellectual diaspora: Potentials, challenges and strategies. In D. Teferra & H. Greijn, (Eds.) *Higher education and globalization: Challenges, threats and opportunities for Africa*. Maastricht, Netherlands: Maastricht University Centre for International Cooperation in Academic Development, (pp. 89–100). http://dare.ubvu.vu.nl.
Mutume, G. (2003). Reversing African's 'brain drain': New initiatives tap skills for African expatriates. Africa Recovery, 17.
Nyandara, Z. (2012). Challenges and opportunities of technology based instruction in open and distance learning: A comparative study of Tanzania and China. In *Proceedings and report of the 5th Ubuntu Net Alliance annual conference* (pp. 130–145).
Petrides, L. A. (2002). Web-based technologies for distributed (or distance) learning: Creating learning-centered educational experiences in the higher education classroom. *International Journal of Instructional Media, 29*(1), 69–77.
Preston, G., Phillips, R., Gosper, M., McNeill, M., Woo, K., & Green, D. (2010). Web-based lecture technologies: Highlighting the changing nature of teaching and learning. *Australian Journal of Educational Technology, 26*(6), 717–728.
Rabbany, R., ElAtia, S., Takaffoli, M., & Zaiane, O. R. (2013). Collaborative Learning of Students in Online Discussion Forums: A Social Network Analysis Perspective. In A. Peña-Ayala (Ed.) *Educational Data Mining: Applications and Trends* (pp. 441–466).
Roussety, N. (2015). *Mauritius, in the race for e-commerce platforms*. Analysis Institute of Management. Retrieved February 5, 2018, from http://www.analysis.im/uploads/filemanager/Management_Barometer_2-E-commerce.pdf.
Slavin, R. E. (1996). Reseach on cooperative learning and achievement: What we know, what we need to know. *Contemporary Educational Psychology, 21,* 43–69.
Statistics Mauritius (2016). Education Statistics—2016. http://statsmauritius.govmu.org/English/Publications/Documents/EI1269/Edu_Stats_Yr2016.pdf.
Swain, M. (1997). Collaborative dialogue: its contribution to second language learning. *RevistaCanaria de EstudiosIngleses, 34,* 115–132.
Swain, M. (2000). The output hypothesis and beyond: mediating acquisition through collaborative dialogue. In J. P. Lantoff (Ed.), *Socio-cultural theory and second language learning*. Cambridge: Oxford University Press.
Tao, L., & Boulware, B. (2002). Issues in technology email: Instructional potentials and learning opportunities. *Reading and Writing Quarterly, 18,* 285–288.
Tertiary Education Commission. (1994). *Distance education in Mauritius: The present and the future.*
Trading Economics (2018). *Mauritius GDP Annual Growth Rate*. Retrieved February 5, 2018, from https://tradingeconomics.com/mauritius/gdp-growth-annual.
Traxler, J. (2005). Defining mobile learning. In *IADIS International Conference Mobile Learning*.
Udai, L. P. (2010). Distance Education: A Model for Ethiopian University of Gondar. *International Journal of Education Economics and Development (IJEED), 1*(4).
UNESCO (2010). *Trends in tertiary education: Sub-Saharan Africa*. http://unesdoc.unesco.org/images/0019/001926/192603e.pdf.
Vonderwell, S. (2003). An examination of asynchronous communication experiences and perspectives of students in an online course: A case study. *Internet and Higher Education, 6,* 77–90.
Voireanu, D. (2016). *Interaction and Guidance in Distance Education, Distance Learning*. Retrieved May 23, 2017, from http://www.distancelearningportal.com/articles/248/interaction-and-guidance-in-distance-education.html.

Wang, C. Y. (2010). Educational implications of blogs for enriching adult collaborative distance learning. *International Journal of Continuing Education and Lifelong Learning, 2*(2), 60–71.

World Data Atlas (2018). *Mauritius—Adult (15 +) literacy rate*. Retrieved February 5, 2018, from https://knoema.com/atlas/Mauritius/topics/Education/Literacy/Adult-literacy-rate.

Xiang, W., Goh, S., Pather, S., Maxwell, A., Wang, H., & Ku, H. (2009) Use of wireless tablet PCs as an effective learning and teaching enhancement tool. In *EDUCAUSE Australasia Conference 2009: Innovate, Collaborate and Sustain*, Perth, Australia.

Zainuddin, N., Idrus, R., & Jamal, A. F. M. (2016). Moodle as an ODL teaching tool: A perspective of students and academics. *The Electronic Journal of e-Learning, 14*(4), 282–290.

Zhang, D., Zhao, J. L., Zhou, L., & Nunamaker, J. F., Jr. (2004). Can e-learning replace classroom learning? *Communications of the ACM, 47*(5), 75–79.

Zhang, D., Zhou, L., Briggs, R. O., & Nunamaker, J. F., Jr. (2006). Instructional video in e-learning: Assessing the impact of interactive video on learning effectiveness. *Science Direct: Information & Management, 43*(2006), 15–27.

Zhu, C. (2012). Student satisfaction, performance and knowledge construction in online collaborative learning. *Educational Technology & Society, 15*(1), 127–136.

Zygouris-Coe, V. (2012).Collaborative learning in an online teacher education course: lessons learned. In *ICICTE Proceedings* (pp. 332–342).

Use of Technology at the Open University of Cyprus (OUC) to Support Adult Distance Learners: To What Extent Is Being Informed by the Learner-Centred Education (LCE) Paradigm?

Maria N. Gravani

Introduction

The following chapter, which is part of the book on the use of technology for efficient delivery of learner support services, aiming at understanding the ways in which technology is being used by major open universities across the world in supporting distance learners, focuses on the Open University of Cyprus (OUC) and the use of technology in its context to support adult distance learners. In particular, the chapter aims to critically explore and address the following crucial question: to what extent is the use of technology at the OUC being informed by the learner-centred education (LCE) paradigm, as opposed to the traditional teacher-centred delivery model.

As stated in the book proposal, one of the main challenges for open and distance learning providers is to ensure effective learner support system to help learners make paradigm shift from traditional teacher-centred delivery mode to mediated distance learning. It also emphasized the importance for the distance educators to take into consideration the expectations of learners in open distance learning systems and address the needs, aspirations and individual differences of the target groups. At the same time, the literature on distance learning underlines the necessity for adult learners, who are the primary audience of the open universities, to be self-directed and autonomous in distance learning environments (Holmberg 1987, 1989; Keegan 1996; Peters 1998; Li et al. 2000; Balaban-Sali 2008; Yiayli et al. 2010; Gravani 2015). Adult learners have control over their lives, have jobs, families and social commitments and hence should be solely in charge of

M. N. Gravani (✉)
School of Humanities and Social Sciences, Open University of Cyprus, Nicosia, Cyprus
e-mail: maria.gravani@ouc.ac.cy

© Springer Nature Singapore Pte Ltd. 2018

Anjana (ed.), *Technology for Efficient Learner Support Services in Distance Education*, https://doi.org/10.1007/978-981-13-2300-3_9

formulating their programme of study in distance education, as well as have control over the processes of learning (Holmberg 1989).

Nonetheless, as postulated in the literature (Keegan 1996; Peters 1998; Yiayli et al. 2010; Gravani 2015), most of the distance learning courses are not learner-centred and learners' autonomy is not guaranteed. Keegan (1996), in particular, argues that learning in distance education is teacher-centred and knowledge is transmitted from the teacher, by the means of technology and education material, to the adult learner who has a passive role in the process of learning. Distance education programmes are highly structured, prescribed and predetermined, and they are even more controlled than programmes in traditional universities (Peters 1998; Lionarakis 2001;Christidou et al. 2012). Distance education systems restrict in practice the autonomy of adult learners since both internal characteristics of the courses (aims, content, method of delivery, assessment) and external (academic schedule, deadlines, methodology, regulations for studies, technology) are decided by the institution without the involvement of the learners (Peters 1998). As a working definition for distance education in this chapter, the one proposed by Keegan (1996) is adopted which perceives this as a semi-permanent separation of teacher and learner that it is influenced by the educational organization, in both the preparation of the teaching materials and the students' support, it uses technical media, and it is a two-way process.

Following the above, the present chapter discusses the extent to which technology used in distance learning programmes at the OUC promotes learner autonomy and LCE. Such an exploration is valuable as it seeks to address the ways, the learning contexts and the conditions under which technology endorses LCE, and if not, what are the restrictions or barriers it faces. As Kollias (2017) accurately states, technologies are not culturally and politically neutral tools. They are interrelated in complex ways with what is already there, in terms of the institutions, dispositions, power relations and practices. Hence, technologies alone can never change education as it is known.

In doing so, the present chapter draws on my 10 years of experience as a faculty member and adult educator at the OUC and uses document analysis along with data from a qualitative research study with adult learners (undergraduate and graduate) and educators, both chosen opportunistically from the School of Humanities and Social Sciences. The participants embarked on a number of distance learning programmes at the OUC.

In what follows, the learner-centred education paradigm, the OUC context and the use of technology by the OUC to support adult distance learners are presented; then, the eClass eLearning Platform is described and research data on the use of the eLearning Platform are discussed. Finally, conclusions are drawn regarding the degree to which the use of technology at the OUC is informed by the learner-centred education (LCE) approach, followed by a discussion of theoretical and practical implications.

Learner-Centred Education (LCE) Paradigm

Learner-centred education (LCE), as a notion, has a long history. Elements of this can even be traced back to the ancient Greek philosophy and the teaching of Socrates. Schweisfurth (2013a) recognizes this as a "travelling policy and practice" which is promoted by international organizations within a rights framework and is used as part of the definitions they give for quality education (Schweisfurth 2013a). In the modern literature, the term is connected to the notion of child-centred education. Nonetheless, LCE is a policy and practice that extends beyond childhood. In the literature on adult and distance education, LCE is not used extensively, despite sharing common principles with andragogy (Knowles 1980), Freire's (1972) problem-based approach, experiential learning (Jarvis 2004), transformative learning (Mezirow 1997). The term emerges through approaches with different names, such as progressive education, problem-based learning, enquire-based learning, constructivism, self-directed learning, learning which promotes learner autonomy (Schweisfurth 2013b).

Problem-based approach has been introduced by Freire (1972) in opposition to the traditional teacher-centred approach. It is envisaged as a communicative and dialogic process, through which learners and educators simultaneously teach and are taught by critically reflecting on each other's views and the world around them. "Students, as they are increasingly posed with problems relating to themselves in the world and with the world, will feel increasingly challenged and obliged to respond to that challenge" (Freire 1972, p. 81). Problem-centred teaching and learning were also promoted by Knowles (1980), as one of the six principles that underlie adult education. According to him, learners prefer problem-centred activities which would assist them in realizing the practical applications of what they have just learned. The other assumptions about adult learners that Knowles (1980) identified are: the *learner's self-concepts*—adults have a self-concept, namely being responsible for their own decisions and lives; the *role of learner's experience*—adults come into an educational activity with both a greater volume and a different quality of experience than youths; *readiness to learn*—adults become ready to learn in order to perform more effectively in some aspects of their lives; *motivation*—while adults are responsive to some external motivators, their most powerful motivators are the internal ones. The sixth assumption about adult learners introduced by Knowles concerned the *self-directed* educational needs of adults. The self-directed learning of adults is part of their everyday lives and the kind of learning whose organization and systematization came from the learners themselves rather than from a teacher or a fixed curriculum (Merriam 2001). The goal of the self-directed approach to education is to constitute learners, who can assume responsibility for their learning (Brockett and Hiemstra 1991), who can critically reflect on themselves and the world (a process which suggests "…a prerequisite for autonomy in self-directed learning"—Mezirow 1985, p. 27), who can become socially active and who can engage in learning with expected emancipatory outcomes (Merriam 2001).

The chapter draws on Schweisfurth's (2013b, p. 20) working definition of LCE "as a pedagogical approach which gives learners, and demands from them, a relatively high level of active control over the contents and processes of learning. What is learnt, and how, are therefore shaped by learners' needs, capacities and interests". Schweisfurth (2013b, p. 20) sees this educational practice as existing along a continuum from less learner-centred to more learner-centred, with LCE at one end of the continuum. At that LCE end, learners have more control not just over the content of learning, but over how they learn and what is learnt and how what is learnt is based on learners' necessities. Following the above, Schweisfurth (2013a, p. 2) recognizes three justificatory narratives used to promote LCE: the *cognitive* narrative, suggesting that the learner controls the content and process of learning; the *emancipation narrative*, proposing that learners are fortified to inquire critically the society and knowledge presented to them. This second narrative echoes Freire's (1972) work on adult education. He advocated dialogue to encourage learners' reflection on and questioning of their own realities as a central aspect of the learning process. And finally, there is the *preparation* narrative, inferring that inquiry and critical thinking reinforce the growth of an effective knowledge economy (Schweisfurth 2013a).

Exploring education policy documents and existing policies on education and adult education in Cyprus, it was found that they do not explicitly talk about LCE as a pedagogical approach used in practice; nonetheless, they acknowledge the value and importance of practices and models that would place the learner at the centre of the educational process. Aspects of the LCE approach will be discussed in relation to the use of technology at the OUC. Before doing that, the Cypriot context as well as the role of the OUC in distance education in Cyprus will be presented, as it is important to have some knowledge of the broader context within which the institution operates.

The Context: Open University of Cyprus (OUC)

The Open University of Cyprus (OUC) is one of the three state universities operating in the Republic of Cyprus, part of the divided island (since 1974) of Cyprus which is located in the East Mediterranean Sea. The country, being independent the last 43 years, can be considered as a developing state in terms of its higher and distance education. Although there is a strong cultural tendency in Cyprus for general secondary education, families support young people to continue to higher education, for which there is a high demand. Yet the first university in the island, the University of Cyprus, has started its operation only 26 years ago (in 1992). Since then, two more public universities were established: the Open University of Cyprus (OUC) in 2002 and the Cyprus University of Technology in 2003; as well as five private universities: University of Nicosia, European University, Frederick University, Neapolis University, University of Central Lancashire—Cyprus. In addition, private schools of tertiary education operate providing academic and professional study cycles, part or full time (Gravani and Ioannidou 2014). The above indicate the rapid increase in higher education in Cyprus the last two decades.

As a response to this, the government established in November 2015 the Cyprus Agency of Quality Assurance and Accreditation in Higher Education (DI.P.A.E.), to ensure the quality of higher education in Cyprus and to support, through the procedures provided by the relevant legislation, the continuous improvement and upgrading of higher education institutions and their programmes of study. The agency is responsible for the: institutional, departmental and programmatic evaluation and accreditation of higher education; quality assurance in higher education, on the basis of the European standards; evaluation and accreditation of cross-border forms of education, offered by local institutions in member states or third countries; assessment of the conditions for the provision of cross-border education from foreign institutions in Cyprus; assessment of inter-institutional cooperation of higher education institutions; and the provision of information of quality assurance in higher education (DI.P.A.E. 2017). It can be gathered from the aforementioned that the agency exercises central control to all universities and university programmes in Cyprus, including distance education programmes, as an extension of the highly centralized education system that is prevalent in the state (Gravani 2015). Centralization is portrayed in every stage of education, from preprimary to higher and adult education, and extends from matters of general policy (administration, enforcement of educational laws, budget, material infrastructure for schools), to details of everyday classroom practices, curricula, syllabuses and textbooks. The operation of the OUC is not independent of this broad educational context.

The OUC is the only public university in the country dedicated to distance education. It has been operating since 2006, offering interdisciplinary, career-oriented, academically rigorous and stimulating undergraduate and postgraduate (master's and PhD) degree programmes, as well as training and vocational programmes of short duration. It is financed mainly by the university's state-funded budget and students' fees, as well as external income from various national, European and international programmes. The OUC is committed to open up education for all, assist citizens to participate in lifelong learning, which has become a priority for Cyprus, study at their own pace and obtain higher education qualifications. Adults play an important role in its strategic mission, which is to provide them with an equal opportunity to learn, irrespective of age, place and year of study, and to promote science, knowledge, learning, research and lifelong learning (Gravani 2015). Moreover, the OUC aims to establish itself as a leading distance education university in the broader area of Southeastern Europe and the Mediterranean, contributing in that way to the development of the country as an international centre of education. Recently, it was established by the Ministry of Education and Culture as the coordinator of distance education in Cyprus by offering joint degrees with all the other universities, based on the distance learning educational methodology.

Nowadays, the OUC has more than 400 part-time tutors, 22 faculty members, all PhD holders and about 6000 students from Europe, Middle East, Africa and the USA. The latter study in 27 different programmes delivered either in Greek or English language by one of the three faculties: Humanities and Social Sciences, Pure and Applied, and Economics and Management. Programmes operate on a modular degree system, and degrees are awarded through the completion of a number of ECTS credits. Degrees are fully recognized in Cyprus and the EU.

In each programme, an academic coordinator is assigned by the Dean of the Faculty. The core organizational unit of each programme is the thematic unit or module. For each thematic unit, a thematic unit coordinator is allocated by the academic coordinator in charge of coordinating tutors teaching it, and students, as well as deciding about and organizing the course content, in terms of subject knowledge and educational practices followed. For each group of students, there is a tutor that supports and guides them during the course. The tutors organize face-to-face (f2f) meetings, online meetings and teleconferences and communicate with learners via phone and e-mail (Gravani and Karagiorgi 2014). In the past 11 years, tutors did not receive any formal training on how to teach adults in a distance learning environment; it was only in 2017 that a preparatory course for all tutors has been introduced. It is now obligatory for them to attend it before taking up their post. There is no evaluation for this course yet. Tutors along with the coordinator and the academic coordinator of the course develop the "educational package" for each thematic unit. This includes printed material (books, articles, other documents, etc.) as well as digital (video and audio) educational material and self-evaluation activities, in which it is split into weeks. Learners plan their reading of the material according to a study guide which accompanies their "educational package" (Gravani and Karagiorgi 2014). At this point, it is worth mentioning a research study that analysed the printed material of two programmes of the School of Humanities and Social Sciences using the Bernsteinian concept of framing (Bernstein 1990, cited in Christidou et al. 2012). The findings reveal that the characteristics of the printed learning material are mainly oriented towards definite arrangement of instructional rules, i.e. the selection of content, sequencing, pacing and evaluation criteria. Therefore, it is indicated that self-direction is not implemented through the printed material in these contexts. By doing so, the material might undermine learners' control on diagnosing their needs, formulating their plans and objectives, and evaluating their learning, which constitute crucial aspects of adult education. This can be easily justified on the grounds of distance education and the characteristics and role that the printed material is expected to play in this context. To put it more simply, the printed material in these contexts is meant to explicitly describe and regulate the instructional rules (Dimopoulos, Koulaidis and Sklaveniti 2001, cited in Christidou et al. 2012, p. 44).

Use of Technology by the OUC to Support Adult Learners

As tutors and learners are placed in different locations, teaching and learning have to be supported by some sort of technology. In describing the educational methodology used at the OUC, Epiphaniou et al. (2015) identify as its basic components: *thematic unit* and *student group*, which are discussed above; the *group advisory meetings*, i.e. the non-mandatory face-to-face (f2f) meetings that after the deployment of the synchronous platform can be organized either completely through the Web conferencing service or by applying a hybrid model combining both f2f and Web conferencing forms; the *student assessment;* and the *educational tool*. The latter is discussed critically below. Students are assessed in the thematic units through written assignments and final exams which entail physical presence. There are specified closing dates for both the submission of the assignments and the final exams, predetermined by the OUC. Assignments are submitted, checked by the plagiarism detection service, commented and graded only through the eClass eLearning Platform (eClass) (Epiphaniou et al. 2015). The above resembles Peters' (1998) aforementioned words about the restrictions and firm context of the distance learning institutions, characteristic example of which is the above (Gravani 2015). This is also in contrast to the LCE paradigm as it does not give the space to adult learners to become agents of their learning process. Likewise, an individualized approach to learning is not adopted. Adult learners often complain about not having their own pace of learning valued, as some are good at discussions, while others can manage writing under pressure. They comment on the pressure of writing under stress and the overall idea of final summative assessment that contradicts to basic principles of adult learning such as: empowerment of learners, individualized approach that suits learners' needs and appreciates previous knowledge and experience (Brookfield 1986; Knowles 1980).

The tool that the OUC uses to implement its educational methodology is the eClass eLearning Platform. It is based on Moodle and supports both blended learning and online courses. The eLearning Platform offers to tutors, learners and university administrators the utensils to create, deliver and assess their courses. It also furnishes them with a point of entry all OUC e-learning services. It is worth emphasizing that the eClass team members of the OUC (Rodosthenous et al. 2016) comment on the hierarchical structure of the eClass, arguing that resembles the academic hierarchy of the OUC. All the thematic units have the same basic structure in eClass; therefore, tutors have to "build" their educational material on a pre-existed model. This homogeneity is considered, by the eClass team, as being constructive for students as they become acquainted with the educational setting from the first course they take. However, homogeneity, imposed by the instructional designers, implies a strictly predefined environment that in turn implies strictly predefined learning contents and replicates traditional classroom practices (Kollias 2017; Gravani 2015).

The eClass eLearning Platform comprises of numerous facilities, courses, educational content and activities. The following six are the core services, and it includes: *Asynchronous Learning* service where participants in the platform have 24 h, 7 days per week admittance to the educational material, resources and activities; *Synchronous Learning* service that enables students to enter virtual classrooms and interrelate with their colleagues and tutors; *Video Lecture and Streaming* service for capturing and recording lectures and delivering them to audience, students and others, either live or recorded; *Assignment Submission and Plagiarism Detection* service for the electronic submission and assessment of assignments, which are also checked for plagiarism; *Learning Activity Management System* (LAMS) that qualifies tutors to create visually learning activities for their thematic units; and *Mobile Learning service* which allow students to attend their thematic units and join the online activities via their tablets or smartphones (Rodosthenous et al. 2016). A technical presentation of the eLearning Platform, the offered services and its integration to the OUC's infrastructure for the library and the university's administration is given in Rodosthenous et al. (2016). In what follows, some of the most important services mentioned above will be presented and critically discussed in terms of their underlining pedagogy, as the aim of the chapter is to explore the extent to which technology used at the OUC has been informed by pedagogies that support the learner-centred education (LCE) paradigm.

EClass eLearning Platform Services and Underlining Pedagogies

Asynchronous Learning has been the first core component of the eClass. It ensures that participants in the educational process have access to knowledge and opportunities to cooperate. Educators can design their thematic units by the means of numerous tools available ranging from educational content tools (files, folders, links, Webpages) to communication and collaborative tools (forums, instant messaging and chat), as well as assessment tools (assignments, questionnaires, quizzes) (Epiphaniou et al. 2015; Christoforou et al. 2015).

Commenting on how online educators built their courses in the context of asynchronous learning service, Kollias (2017), an experienced tutor at the OUC, argues that the learning contents are strictly predefined, "presented" in a series of videos or a series of PowerPoints or a combination of different media that the learner has to "navigate" and learn from them. Students usually watch these videos or read the materials, and they are expected to exhibit their new knowledge by taking a test or by answering some questions. According to him (Kollias 2017), this is a typical situation where the expert on a subject matter, the educator, "transmits" his or her knowledge to the novices. The epistemological assumptions behind this pedagogic approach often go unnoticed and hence are seldom challenged. According to this approach, knowledge is objectively discernible, neutral and external to the knower. This is ingrained in Skinner's *behaviourist pedagogic approach*, which adopt an objectivist epistemological stance (Conole 2008). His ideas about human learning are adopted today in many online teaching/learning arrangements like the one adopted in the OUC. For instance, as Kollias (2017) points out, ideas that the online learning content should be broken down to small chunks of information presented to the individual learner in a predefined sequence, that the learner can follow this content in his/her own pace, that the learner after being exposed to such a chunk can immediately take a kind of quiz on what (s) he believes is the correct answer and gets immediate feedback and that each learner progresses to the next step only after (s) he has mastered the preceding steps are clearly rooted in Skinner's ideas.

Synchronous Learning service has been initiated from the necessity for both educators and learners to interact closer with each other. It is based on Elluminate Live! software (later Blackboard Collaborate) and creates a class-like environment for participants to chat, talk, see each other and exchange emotions. The above seems to provide ample opportunities for dialogue, a key element to pedagogies based on socio-constructivist principles, where the emphasis is on coconstruction of knowledge and support a more learner-centred approach (Conole 2008). Opposite to the behaviourist pedagogic approach, for constructivism, knowledge does not result from a mere recording of observations without a structuring activity on the part of the learner (Kollias 2017). Vygotsky's *social constructivism* or *socio-cultural approach* to learning emphasizes that the origin of knowledge construction should not be sought in the mind but in the social interaction coconstructed between individuals. Learning how to use symbol systems and tools that mediate and transform human activity, such as computers and the Internet, is a key objective of constructivist pedagogy and a distinguishing feature of human experience. Through teacher guidance to tasks within learners' *zone of proximal development*, Vygotsky's model of social constructivism leads online learners towards educational objectives designed to provide them with certain crucial forms of social and cultural knowledge (Kollias 2017).

As Kollias (2017) continues, in his critique of online pedagogies, for other constructivists the focus of concern is the construction of knowledge as a shared achievement located not in each individual's mind but in the interactions between them. Lave and Wenger (1991) argue that learning is necessarily situated, a process of participation in *communities of practice*. They emphasize the significance of shifting the focus for learning from the individual as learner to learning as participation in the social world and from the concept of cognitive process to the more-encompassing view of the social practice. In the light of the above, participation in a community of practice becomes the "potential curriculum" with the circulation of information among the participants as a "condition for the effectiveness of learning" (Lave and Wenger 1991, p. 93).

Synchronous learning service at the OUC can also be used for thesis and dissertation presentations, as well as for other demonstrations and public lectures, which can all be recorded and replicated, whenever needed.

Video Lecture and Streaming is based on the Panopto system and allows tutors to record, upload and amend videos so that their students can view them. It is also used for the broadcast of live events in the university, such as lectures, keynotes, training workshops and welcoming messages.

Assignment Submission and Plagiarism Detection has been introduced in order for students to submit their assignments and for the latter to be checked for plagiarism. There is a big repository with different sources with which assignments submitted are compared for similarities and differences.

Reflecting on how existing learning theories align with the above eClass eLearning Platform services—the technological tools used at the OUC—it can be argued that an attempt is being made on behalf of the university for the services to be mainly guided by socio-constructivist principles, which, as aforementioned, emphasize the coconstruction of knowledge and support a more learner-centred approach. Social constructivism is absolutely compatible with the adult learning principles; however, there might be difficulties to apply to online teaching, as in the case of the OUC. The social interaction and simulated forms of learning might not be conveyed accurately through the online platform. Social constructivism suggests that we learn from the action and behaviour of other people in the society. However, through the eLearning Platform learners see and hear what is broadcasted; hence, this might limit their understanding of the content. Learning can be highly mechanical and might not grasp the authenticity of learning in social settings. Moreover, learning contents and curriculum is fixed allowing very small space for learners and educators to be involved in a creative and meaningful dialogue about the learning process. Also, the absence of learners' involvement in deciding about aspects of the course and so on inhibits the endorsement of LCE via the use of technology tools in the OUC. The above, of course, is not independent from the macro-level, the highly structured policy context, within which the OUC operates, due to the centralized education system in the country. Central control is exercised via the Agency for Quality Assurance in Higher Education, the Ministry of Finance and the General Auditor—who imposes restrictions to the university's budget—to every aspect of the distance learning programmes and technology used. The above are also evident in the reported experiences and perceptions of the OUC adult learners and their educators that follow.

Experiences from the Use of the eLearning Platform

As mentioned in the introduction of the chapter, participants in the research (ten adult learners—five men and five women—and five OUC tutors—three women and two men) from different programmes of the School of Humanities and Social Sciences were asked to describe their experiences and perceptions of the use of the eLearning Platform, its functionality, the opportunities it provides for interaction and collaboration, with the aim to unveil the extent to which it supports social constructivism and a more learner-centred approach to learning.

Prior to data collection, informed consent was ensured. Participants were informed about the research aims, the semi-structured interviews employed to elicit information, interviews' tape recording, time and place. They also became aware of the right to withdraw cooperation at any time. This was done through telephone communication. Moreover, issues regarding disclosure, sensitivity and trust were firmly secured. Educators and students were promised privacy, confidentiality and anonymity. They were guaranteed that data presentation would be anonymous and that transcripts would be handed back to them allowing them to change aspects of the text which they felt misrepresented them in a way.

Research findings highlighted issues regarding the functionality of the eClass eLearning Platform (the main educational medium of the OUC that hosts a number of services, courses, educational content and activities) and the occasions it provides to adult learners and their educators for communication and partnership. Data was analysed thematically, as categories emerged according to the commonalities they shared. In what follows, some of the most key data is presented.

With regard to the use of the platform, almost all the participants in the study underlined, from the beginning of the interview, that they had not been systematically trained on how to use it. On the one hand, educators argued that they had been informed of the use of it by the eClass team at the beginning of the academic year, through a sit and get training seminar that was useful, although short and theoretical. Learners, on the other hand, noted that they were not offered at all the opportunity to participate in a training programme on the use of the digital platform tools. They were convinced that their participation in such a programme would significantly contribute to limiting their "techno-phobia" and increasing their interest in systematically exploiting the platform throughout their studies. Characteristic is the following quote from the interview with a female student. She argued:

> I think, yes, for a first year student training on how to use the platform would be very useful. Students should be located in a room with computers so that they get into the platform and obtain hands on experience. There might be functions on the platform that students don't know […] it is important to be given the opportunity, through a training programme, to get to know their use.
> (Maria, Learner)

Learners also pointed out that educators' familiarity with the platform, as well as the extent to which they gave incentives to their students to use it, had a direct impact on their practices. Thus, when students got used to systematically practise the eClass Platform, they gradually acquired great comfort in its use even if they had not attended any relevant training programme. Finally, two educators in the study estimated that training in the use of the platform is a factor that clearly could have a positive impact on their teaching practice. They stated that those who used the tool comfortably saved a great deal of valuable time in their cooperation with their students.

Commenting on the above, it can be argued that the lack of systematic training on the use of the platform prohibited the extent to which it was used to facilitate distance learning at the OUC. A basic prerequisite for an educational tool to be successfully used in supporting learner-centred education is for its users to be familiar with its functions, the opportunities it provides and so on. At the OUC, it seems that educators and learners entered the programme with a disadvantage that hindered a more energetic and engaging process of learning.

Functionality

Functionality refers to the number of functions that the eClass Platform provides. Both educators and learners talked positively about the features of the platform. Among these, they identified the possibilities for posting, "downloading" and distributing multimodal educational material, assigning activities and exercises, receiving comments and queries, submitting assignments, interacting, through synchronous and asynchronous communication, In addition, they argued that the platform is easy to use and well organized. Indicative are the words of the female educator:

> It's functional. It provides me with too many ways to interact with students [...] the chat, the elluminate, the asynchronous communication. Elluminate is amazing [...] I come in with my headphones from home. I can even see my students through the video and talk with them at the same time. I can give a lecture and answer student's questions [...] I mean, these opportunities are given, but it does not mean that the interactions are taking place.
> (Ioanna, Educator)

Commenting on the weaknesses of the platform, participants identified the following: the lack of technical support to download on their personal computer the recorded online meetings and failure to provide educators and learners with access to the educational material of other thematic units at the OUC. Educators are restricted to have access only to the thematic unit they teach, while they would prefer to be more flexible and open to learn from other colleagues, restrictions on the use of the platform imposed to the students. The latter cannot take initiatives to organize online meetings in the platform, unless the educators or administrators provide them with this possibility. This limits their freedom and flexibility; technical problems that are presented sometimes and prohibit learning; "techno-phobia" that some of the adult learner exhibit and, as a result, their learning is prevented; the lack of training on the use of the platform; and, finally, the lack of time on behalf of the educators and learner to get acquainted with the platform. The quotes illustrate some of the above:

> As a student, I cannot take advantage of the platform. I'm not free to use it as I would like to. Educators have to give me the freedom, as they are entitled to organize me on how to use it [...] There was an incitement on behalf of my teachers to use the platform, but it's just that I was afraid of [...] I have to overcome this fear [...] There are people who don't do well with electronics.
> (Kostakis, Learner)

> I would like the platform to enable both me, as an educator, and my students with the chance to have access to related modules and material […] I, for example, do not have access to the material of another thematic unit. I only have mine. Therefore, in this respect, I feel restricted. I cannot see comparatively the work of another colleague; how does he use this tool, what does he do, what is the response from the students.
> (Giorgos, Educator)

Opportunities for Interaction and Collaboration

Regarding the opportunities for interaction and collaboration that the platform provides to its participants, research findings indicate that almost all the participants in the study agreed that the platform is useful and it can bring people together. This is described in what follows:

> Its role is quite important. I can communicate with my classmates, they communicate with me […] I can use it (the platform) any time to post a question and solve a problem; I could share my questions or concerns with my fellow students, either I'm at work or home, in or out of the university; I can access the educational material.
> (Vasilis, Learner)

However, the vast majority of the learners (seven out of eight) claimed that although the platform is useful, it does not replace the face-to-face communication of the educator with the students, and, as a result, students and teachers cannot come closer. Sometimes, they even argued that the platform brings loneliness and alienation to the participants in the programme. Some extracts from the interviews are characteristic:

> The platform is a good tool. It creates some sort of communication, without being able to replace the physical contact between students and the teacher. Of course, it's better having something, rather than nothing.
> (Kleanthis, Learner)

> Okay, it was functional, but I don't think it's the "a" and "z" in the relationship between students and the educator. For me it's just a tool through which I can get and send information for my studies […] that's all. I can raise a topic for discussion but nothing more than this.
> (Katerina, Learner)

> The platform cannot replace human interaction. What is essentially missing from distance education is the communication with each other; that is not to feel that I'm alone or I travel alone in the sea. This is important […] my suggestion is for teleconferences to be an obligatory part of the programme, to be regular and frequent, so that students are not aliens; and, for f2f meetings to be more than one.
> (Froso, Learner)

Concluding Remarks

Summing up, the chapter has discussed the extent to which technology used in distance learning programmes at the OUC promotes learner autonomy and learner-centred education, as opposed to teacher-centred delivery model. Such an exploration is valuable as it seeks to address the ways, the learning contexts and the conditions under which technology endorses LCE, and if not, what are the restrictions or barriers it faces. In doing so, the chapter has critically reviewed the LCE paradigm, analysed the OUC context and its particularities, and presented the technology used at the OUC to support distance learners. Technology/eClass eLearning Platform used has then been critically discussed in the light of the underlining pedagogies. This has been accomplished with the support of the relevant literature on learning theories and institutions' documents. Then, data from a qualitative research study has been used to unveil the degree to which the platform supports LCE.

Certainly, the analysis has revealed that technology used at the OUC is not being informed to a great extent by the LCE paradigm due to all the reasons and restrictions mentioned above (centralized system, fixed curriculum, predefined aspects of the units that imply the transmission of knowledge from the educator to the learner, failure of the platform to grasp the authenticity of learning in social settings, and establish intimate relationships among participants and so on) which influenced the implementation of technology at the OUC. This also agrees with findings of previous studies contacted by the author (Gravani 2015). The chapter and the discussion developed conform to the widespread belief that new technologies did not, so far, transform formal education in profound ways. Sceptics also argue that new technologies were actually "normalized" to reproduce and amplify the power of dominant educational norms (Kollias 2017). However, the research reported is optimistic in that it does indicate some positive aspects of LCE implementation that related to opportunities for interaction and collaboration. The study finally has made a clear point that technology can be and it is useful, but as a tool that is not cultural and political neutral, in order to support adult learners in distance education, needs to be used in a context that favours learners' autonomy and respects their needs and experiences. In order for this to happen, solutions and changes need to be done on a policy macro-level, and a critical mass of actors needs to be really involved in this and takes action, rather than giving rhetorical prescriptions (Schweisfurth 2013a, p. 5).

References

Balaban-Sali, J. (2008). Designing motivational learning systems in distance education. *Turkish Online Journal of, Distance Education, 9*(3), 149–161.

Brockett, R. B., & Hiemstra, R. (1991). *Self-direction in adult learning: Perspectives on theory research, and practice*. London and New York: Routledge.

Brookfield, S. (1986). *Understanding and facilitating adult learning: A comprehensive analysis of principles and effective practices*. Milton Keynes: OU Press.
Christidou, V., Gravani, M. N., & Hatzinikita, V. (2012). Distance learning material for adult education: The case of the OUC. *Ubiquitous Learning: An International Journal, 4*(2), 33–46.
Christoforou, P., Rodosthenous, C., Epiphaniou, M., Mavrotheris, S. & Christodoulides, C. (2015) Deploying new services in the Open University of Cyprus eLearning Platform—Our experiences. In *INTED2015 Proceedings*. Madrid: IATED (pp. 6108–6116).
Conole, G. (2008) 'New schemas for mapping pedagogies and technologies, *Ariadne, 56*, Retrieved December 10, 2017, from http://www.ariadne.ac.uk/issue56/conole/.
DI.P.A.E. (2017). *Cyprus Agency of Quality Assurance and Accreditation in Higher Education*. Retrieved January 10, 2018, from http://www.dipae.ac.cy/index.php/en/dipae/foreas.
Epiphaniou, M., Rodosthenous, C., Christoforou, P., Mavrotheris, S. & Christodoulides, C. (2015) Engaging users in distance education—The case of the Open University of Cyprus. In *INTED2015 Proceedings*. Madrid: IATED (pp. 6092–6101).
Freire, P. (1972). *Pedagogy of the oppressed*. London: Penguin.
Gravani, M. N. (2015). Adult learning in a distance education context: theoretical and methodological challenges. *International Journal of Lifelong Education, 34*(2), 172–193.
Gravani, M. N. & Ioannidou, A. (2014) *Adult and continuing education in Cyprus*. Bielefeld: DIE. Retrieved December 30, 2017, from https://www.die-bonn.de/doks/2014-zypern-01.pdf.
Gravani, M. N. & Karagiorgi, Y. (2014). Underpinning principles of adult learning in face to face (f2f) meetings employed by distance-teaching universities. *Journal of Adult and Continuing Education, 20*, 53–67.
Holmberg, B. (1989). *Theory and practice of distance education* (2nd ed.). London: Routledge.
Holmberg, B. (1987). *Growth and structure of distance education*. London: Routlegde.
Jarvis, P. (2004). *Adult education and lifelong learning: Theory and practice*. London: Routledge.
Keegan, D. (Ed.). (1996). *Foundations of distance education* (3rd ed.). London: Routledge.
Knowles, M. (1980). *The modern practice of adult education: From pedagogy to andragogy*. New York: Cambridge Books.
Kollias, A. (2017) *Teaching adults on-line*. Study Guide. Nicosia: Open University of Cyprus.
Lave, J., & Wenger, E. (1991). *Situated learning: Legitimate peripheral participation*. Cambridge: Cambridge University Press.
Li, N., Lee, K., & Kember, D. (2000). Towards self-direction in study methods: The ways in which new students learn to study part-time. *Distance Education, 21*(1), 6–28.
Lionarakis, A. (2001). For which distance education ado we talk about? In Lionarakis, A. (Eds.), *Proceedings of the 1st Panhellenic Conference of Open and Distance Education*. Athens: Propobos, (Vol. 2, pp. 185–194) (In Greek).
Merriam, S. B. (2001). *Andragogy and self-directed learning: Pillars of adult learning theory*. John. Retrieved December 30, 2017, from http://umsl.edu/~wilmarthp/modla-links2011/Merriam_pillars%20of%20anrdagogy.pdf.
Mezirow, J. (1997). Transformative learning: Theory to practice. *New Directions for Adult and Continuing Education, 74*, 5–12.
Mezirow, J. (1985). A critical theory of self-directed learning. In S. Brookfield (Ed.), *Self-directed learning: From theory to practice* (New Directions for Continuing Education, No. 25. San Francisco: Jossey-Bass).
Peters, O. (1998). *Learning and teaching in distance education. Pedagogical analyses and interpretations in an international perspective*. London: Kogan Page.
Rodosthenous, C., Christoforou, P., Epiphaniou, M., Matheou G., Mavrotheris, S., & Christodoulides, C. (2016). Building an infrastructure for empowering distance education in the Open University of Cyprus. In *Online, Open and Flexible Higher Education Conference (OOFHEC)Proceedings*. Rome, Italy (pp. 719–734).

Schweisfurth, M. (2013a). Learner-Centred Education in International Perspective. *Journal of International and Comparative Education*, 2 (1), 1–8.

Schweisfurth, M. (2013b). *Learner-centred education in international perspective: Whose pedagogy for whose development?*. London: Routledge.

Yiayli, S., Yiaylis, G. & Koutsoumba, M. (2010). Autonomy in learning in a distance educational environment. *Open Education: The Journal of Open and Distance Education and Educational Technology,* 2 (1&2), 92–105.

Information and Communication Technologies (ICTs)-Based Learner Support in Distance Education in Pakistan

Irshad Hussain

Backdrop

The information and communication technologies (ICTs) are the remarkable innovations and inventions of twenty-first century with their ever-enhancing capacities and capabilities. Seemingly, the ICTs have brought about a revolution in human life by disseminating information through emerging information sharing applications (apps) like videoconferencing, social networking sites called social media, android or smartphone applications including WhatsApp, Viber, IMO. These new technologies and applications (apps) are being used for enhancing connectivity and interactions of people not only for communication but for educational and academic purpose also. Among others, distance education has become a popular endeavour which embraces all individuals of the society without any discrimination. It is a flexible and learner friendly instructional strategy, and the use of ICTs adds to its flexibility. Hussain (2005) asserted that the use of ICTs actively involves students, and they feel convenient in learning individually by using extended resources.

It is an individualized learning approach which is regarded as a mediated learning experience aiming at facilitating *"intentional acquisition of knowledge, attitudes and competencies"* (Kirschner and Valcke 1999, p. 81) of the learners. As it is learner-centred instructional strategy which completes under the guidance and tutelage of distance tutors and embraces ICTs, hence it seems an innovative learning endeavour. It is based on constructivist approach associated with technology-based interactive learning process (Bates 1995). Therefore, it [distance education] appears as ICTs-based form of education with flexibility and collaboration as its characteristics.

I. Hussain (✉)
Department of Educational Training, The Islamia University of Bahawalpur, Bahawalpur, Pakistan
e-mail: irshad_iub@yahoo.com

© Springer Nature Singapore Pte Ltd. 2018

Anjana (ed.), *Technology for Efficient Learner Support Services in Distance Education*, https://doi.org/10.1007/978-981-13-2300-3_10

Distance Education in Pakistan: A General Account

Pakistan is a developing country having three types of distance education institutions/ universities along with mainstream universities which offer on-campus programmes. These three types of distance education institutions include correspondence distance education university—Allama Iqbal Open University, Islamabad (http://www.aiou.edu.pk/); virtual education—Virtual University of Pakistan (http://www.vu.edu.pk/); and dual-mode universities which are offering distance education programmes along with on-campus programmes. Virtual University of Pakistan was established in 2002 and is imparting education by using modern information and communication technologies including Internet and its television channels.

To address the ever-increasing demands of higher education in the country, some formal universities have adopted distance education mode by offering some of their programmes through it. These are dual-mode universities. Dual-mode universities are formal education universities and are offering distance education programmes along with their on-campus programmes. There are more than one dozen public and private sector formal on-campus universities which are offering distance education programmes (including COMSATS Virtual Campus) Islamabad (http://vcomsats.edu.pk/), along with their regular programmes.

Currently, the dual-mode universities offering distance education programmes include "University of Sindh, Jamshoro" (http://usindh.edu.pk/academics/faculties-uos/education/department-of-distance-continuing-and-computer-education/); "Bahauddin Zakariya University, Multan" (https://www.bzu.edu.pk/directorate-of-distance-education-dde-bzu-multan-downloads_1845.html); "University of Peshawar" (http://thepeshawar.com/admissions/distance-education-peshawar-university-2015-2016-admissions/); "Gomal University, Dera Ismail Khan" (http://www.degu.edu.pk/); "COMSATS Institute of Information Technology, Islamabad" (http://vcomsats.edu.pk/); "University of Agriculture Faisalabad" (http://uaf.edu.pk/directorates/distance_learning/dist_overview.html), "Government College University, Faisalabad" (https://gcuf.edu.pk/directorate-distance-learning); "the Islamia University of Bahawalpur" (http://www.iub.edu.pk/department.php?id=52); "Shah Abdul Latif University (SALU), Khairpur, Sindh" (http://www.salu.edu.pk/department/directorate-distance-education-program); "International Islamic University, Islamabad" (http://www.iiu.edu.pk/?page_id=18297);"Sukkur Institute of Business Administration, Sukkur" (http://www.iba-suk.edu.pk/ibasuk/aboutiba/wpMain.aspx); "University of Balochistan" (http://application1.uob.edu.pk/de/index.php); "University of Sarhad (a private sector university": http://www.suit.edu.pk/distance-education); and "Preston University Kohat, Islamabad Campus (a private sector university": http://preston.edu.pk/dri_main.php).

However, Allama Iqbal Open University Islamabad is the mother institution of distance education in the country. Generally, it offers its courses and/or programmes through correspondence study. However, presently it is using modern technologies like Internet and its applications or tools for information sharing and extending student support services to facilitate its learners.

The Allama Iqbal Open University—the AIOU

In 1974, Pakistan embraced distance education formally by establishing the Peoples Open University in public sector in Islamabad which was renamed as Allama Iqbal Open University (AIOU) in 1977. It was established on the lines of UK Open University, and it was second university in the world and first Open University of Pakistan and South Asia which started offering its programmes and courses through distance education. It embraces learning while earning philosophy and aims to provide education to all at their doorsteps without leaving their homes and jobs. Distance education, in Pakistan, appeared as a complementary approach to formal or mainstream education system by opening up opportunities of education at all levels for millions of people who otherwise would have not been enrolled in such courses and/or programmes they have graduated. It has promoted educational opportunities, particularly, the opportunities of higher education to women and disadvantaged people, who otherwise are unable even to enrol or continue their higher studies due to social norms and cultural values in culturally restricted traditional areas like Balochistan, interior Sindh and Southern Punjab.

Objectives of the AIOU

The AIOU works in accordance with the broader principles of its act, guidelines ascertained in Education Policies particularly, the Education Policy of 1972–80 and its objectives. AIOU believes in education for all without any discrimination. It aims to facilitate masses of Pakistan by providing education at their doorstep, train teachers, and embrace innovations and modern [technologies] methods of instruction and disseminating knowledge and award degrees or diplomas after examinations (http://www.aiou.edu.pk/).

Instructional Methodology of AIOU

Instructional process of distance education is dynamic and innovative in nature. It makes it unique and progressive and enhances its capacity to accept advancements on the one hand and to accommodate ever-increasing large number of students on the other hand. Instructional process is a main characteristic of distance education which differentiates it from formal on-campus education. As distance education is learner-centred form of instruction, hence all instructional activities are designed and prepared to facilitate learners keeping in view their profile and characteristics. AIOU (http://www.aiou.edu.pk/) as a mega progressive university adopts modern approaches of instruction and instructional delivery (like Internet) along with correspondence materials including study guides and [allied] self-instructional materials, radio and television instruction and/or broadcasts, audio and video CDs offered under guidance and tutelage of tutors. The university appoints trained part-time tutors to guide and help learners in their studies. The main elements of AIOU's instructional methodology (http://www.aiou.edu.pk/) are described below.

i. ***Study Centres***

A study centre is regarded a component of distance education (Hussain 1999). It serves as a local centre established at a place where learners have easy access. A study centre is a meet-up place for distance learners where they come often in evening or afternoon according to the schedule called tutorials. Here, they discuss their study problems with their tutors and fellow learners. Meeting up with tutors and peers develops motivation and a sense of belongingness among learners.

ii. ***Radio and Television Programmes***

AIOU uses radio and television broadcasting to provide support to its learners in studying self-instructional correspondence material at their homes or workplaces. The Institute of Educational Technology (IET) prepares packages of such programmes (audio and video programmes) for their broadcasting. The students are provided with audio and video cassettes and now in CDs as supplementary instructional materials. The university presents one-hour programme daily on PTV World to facilitate a large number of distance learners.

iii. ***Latest Development in the Information and Communication Technologies***

In overall, the latest developments in information and communication technologies including Internet seemingly have modernized the entire landscape of open and distance education. AIOU is using satellite communication and Internet for instructional as well as information dissemination purpose. The ever-emerging developments are modernizing and replacing traditional tutorial and correspondence instruction.

iv. ***Tutorial***

Tutor and tutorials are regarded as the backbone of distance education system. AIOU employs part-time tutors across the country to facilitate its learners in their study. A tutor provides continuous guidance to distance learners on how to study the self-instructional material, how to prepare assignments and how to prepare for getting through the examination. Guidance is provided through correspondence, personal visits of learners to study centres and/or to the tutors for face-to-face individual or group tutorials. The tutorials are organized by the respective regional offices at a study centre in evening or afternoon hours.

v. ***Media Programmes***

Media and technology play an important role in distance education. Media and technology are used not only for information dissemination but for instructional purpose also. AIOU extends media support to its learners in terms of audio/video or non-broadcast productions for many programmes and/or courses.

vi. ***Assignments***

Assignment is an important feature of distance education. Writing an assignment develops creativity, critical thinking and analytical approach among students. There are certain compulsory assignments for each of the courses which a distance learner has to write and submit to the respective tutor according to the schedule. Generally, as a requirement, the learners have to submit two or four assignments according to the nature of the course. The tutor assesses the assignments, writes comments and sends back to the students. It is a type of formative assessment of distances for learners to record their performance continuously. The cumulative scores of assignments are credited to final evaluation of the learners.

vii. ***Workshops***

Workshops are face-to-face instructional meetings focused on achieving specific objectives of the subject(s). AIOU organizes workshops for some of its courses at study centres. The learners are required to participate in compulsory workshops for the respective courses. Workshops extend opportunities of interaction to the learners with their fellows and tutors.

viii. ***Final Examination***

AIOU holds final examination like that of public examinations for all of its credit courses at the end of semester. Generally, the ratio of assignments' component and final term examination is 30:70; i.e. 30% weightage is given to assignment component, whereas 70% consists of marks of the final term examination. However, 40% aggregate marks are required to getting through a course.

Contribution of Allama Iqbal Open University (AIOU) to Higher Education in the Country

AIOU offers its programmes at all levels of education starting from non-credit functional and basic literacy up to PhD in different disciplines. These programmes are offered by 41 academic departments under four faculties. The higher education programmes of AIOU ranging from bachelor to the doctorate in languages, applied and social sciences include almost all such programmes which an on-campus university offers in Pakistan except medicine and surgery, aeronautics and alike.

It offers degrees and diploma programmes including teacher education and training, computer and information and communication technologies, business and commerce, and also announces some innovative programmes like women studies, environmental design and community health and nutrition.

Unique Features of AIOU

Allama Iqbal Open University is extending its educational services to all individuals of the society. AIOU is one of the mega universities in the world and the largest university of Pakistan having 1.3 million enrolments in 2000 courses offered by 41 different academic departments under four full-fledged faculties. It offers non-credit (functional literacy) courses to research (Ph.D.) degree programmes. It serves all individuals of the country without discrimination including urban (42%), rural (58%) with more than half of its female students. It has a well-organized country-wide system of students' support services consisting of nine regional campuses, 33 regional centres, 138 regional coordinating offices and 1172 study centres to facilitate its learners. These centres have modern facilities of information and communication technologies. AIOU has best printing and publishing unit (house) which prints about 1.8 million books annually. The varsity is now focusing more on innovative and science and technology-related academic programmes, technology-based support services and collaboration and linkage with national and international universities and organizations to realize the needs of twenty-first century.

Students Support Services at AIOU

Self or independent study is one of the main features of distance education which distinguishes it from face-to-face (f2f) instruction. For realizing success of distance education programmes, the distance education universities and/or institutions facilitate their learners by extending necessary facilities and services to create interest and motivation among them. Such services and facilities which support distance learners to continue and complete their courses and/or programmes successfully are called learner support services (or student support services which is a widely used and familiar term in distance education) and consist of different facilities and activities which make instructional process easier and more interesting for them.

All of the supporting activities or services help distance learners to continue their studies through interaction with their faculty and fellow learners, and enhanced communication (Simpson 2000). Distance learners need support services throughout the entire course of their studies. Even providing assistance to distance learners begins before admission when university announces admission in the media. These services include and range from local study centres, counselling and/or tutorial support to the solution of administrative problem (Rumble 1992) related to studies of distance learners.

Student or learner support system in distance education is considered as a contributing factor in retention of students and their success in studies. Therefore, Kishore (1998) asserted that learner support services determine the strength or weakness of universities and/or institutions offering distance education programmes. In this regard, learner support services become more significant in creating conducive to learning environment in distance education—facilitating learners in their learning process, motivating them to continue and complete their studies, encouraging their socialization by promoting teamwork and team spirit among them and improving academic standards of the programmes. Similarly, Moaler et al. (2001) envisaged main objectives of such services as to helping distance learners in using learning package properly, making better choices of studies, reducing sense of isolation, providing access to learning resources and opportunities, and enhancing learner's interactions through technology-mediated experiences.

Effective learning takes place through two-way communication between instructor and learner, whereas student support services play an instrumental role in initiating and maintaining two-way communication in instructional process. According to Tait (1995), student support services complement instructional materials which are produced by distance education institutions massively and these also facilitate learning process. Different activities are included in student support services including advising and counselling, orientation, individual or group tutoring, promoting learning and examination skills among learners, feedback on assessment and learning progress, career guidance and solving administrative problem (Tait 1995) logically. These services distinguish distance education from private and/or correspondence study (Keegan 1990). The main objective of support services appears to be motivating distance learners, helping them select right track of study, encouraging them in making appropriate use of educational facilities and facilitating their learning process to graduate successfully. The learner support services shape the pace of distance education and are regarded to be its basic components. These help learners in accomplishing their educational objectives and realizing their academic requirements (Thorpe 2002) and learning needs. These are embedded in self-instructional materials (Hui 1989) and ensure successful learning experiences (Wright 1991). According to Simpson (2000), there are two broader areas of student or learner support services: firstly, the academic services which include tutorial support services. These facilitate students in the areas of cognition including intellectual development and knowledge building regarding particular course or courses. Secondly, there are non-academic or counselling services which support distance learners in affective domain and organizational aspects of their studies.

But Robinson (1995) viewed three components of student support services. These are the elements shaping the system, alignment of these elements and interaction between such elements and the students. The elements of system consist of interaction among students and the providers (distance education universities or institutions) of support services, individual interaction of students in f2f or other means, individual feedback to students on their learning, providing allied materials, allowing them use library, laboratory and other required equipment. However, the formation the components depends upon need and nature of the course, individual differences and learning styles of students, availability of human and material resources intentions and objectives of distance education providing institution or university. Realistic objectives, flexible course design and efficient and effective student support services encompassing modern information and communication technologies lead towards success.

However, (Manjulika and Reddy (1996) asserted that the power of information and communication technologies put forth an innovative impression of learners' support services. Limited f2f interaction may become more frequent, more effective and more efficient by using ICTs. The electronic media can transform delivery of student support services as does with instructional delivery methods.

Support Services as Need of Distance Learners

Distance learners need support services for their guidance and retention in the system. They need support services at different stages of their study including before/pre-admission stage or pre-entry into distance education, the programmes and/or course stage and the post-programme and/or course stage (Manjulika and Reddy 1996). AIOU provides better support services to its learners by using modern educational technology at all of these stages.

Support Services at Pre-admission or Pre-entry Stage

The pre-admission or pre-entry student support services facilitate prospective or potential learners and attract them to getting into the varsity. At pre-admission level, the potential learners need information on or about different programmes and/or courses offered by the distance education university or institution. They also want to know admission criteria, instructional and assessment processes, fees and dues, programme duration, etc. They need guidance on selection of academic programme (s) suitable for them and their career in future.

The potential learners need a mix of information, advice and counselling services to getting into distance education university or institution (Manjulika and Reddy 1996).

At pre-admission stage, the AIOU uses electronic as well as prints media to extend support services to its prospective learners. It uses popular media—the social media, university website, FM radio, television network (PTV Home) for disseminating information on or about programmes and/or courses to be offered—pre-admission counselling regarding selection of programmes and/or courses, information about instructional delivery, information about basic requirements for entry into a programme, fees and dues, and minimum/maximum duration of a programme or a course, etc.

Support Services at Programme and/or Course Stage

This stage begins when a potential learner becomes formally a distance learner by getting admission in a certain programme or course(s). On completion of admission process, the correspondence study materials along with questions for assignments and guidelines for studying the materials and completing and submitting assignments are dispatched to the learners on their given addresses. As it is a self, independent and individualized study, therefore, at some point during the study a distance learner may feel isolated and less motivated which may lead him/her to drop out. Some personal and non-academic problems may also arise from the situation and need facilitation. All such issues can be addressed through student support services.

AIOU has an extensive network of regional offices throughout the country to provide such services to its learners. Besides, it uses Internet, Twitter and Facebook for information sharing and enhancing interaction of its learners. Assignments and previous question papers are also found on different websites to facilitate learners. Tutors and learners use mobile phones for effective communication among them. Similarly, email medium is also used by the learners as well as the tutors to maintain communication. Information is also disseminated through television programmes and radio broadcasts. AIOU provides e-library facility to its learners. The learners formulate their groups on social media and smartphone application to exchange information and academic queries. Similarly, their tutors also share information to groups of distance learners by using modern apps like WhatsApp. They can also use conference call facility on mobile phones or Skype audio and/or video call. It creates a sense of belongingness and team spirit among the learners which motivates and inspires them to continue their studies.

Support Services at Post-programme and/or Course Stage

This stage comes when a distance learner completes all requirements of the programme and/or course(s). At this stage, the learners need communication of final result, advice regarding and future prospects, and guidance and counselling on their future education or profession. The AIOU facilitates its graduates by providing all such services through its website. The results of students are uploaded on university website. Similarly, degree form, degree verification form, duplicate degree form, reappear or resit form, and NOC form, all are available on university website for use of graduates. They can download their relevant form, fill it properly and submit to the university from their homes. The university takes appropriate action within minimum prescribed time to facilitate the graduates accordingly.

Innovations and Integration of ICTs in Student Services and Instruction

The advent of technologies particularly the information and communication technologies seemingly has revamped the landscape of education and training, and hence distance education overwhelmingly embraced it. Distance education universities and institutions are using ICTs for instructional purpose as well as for providing support services to the learners. By embracing ICTs, distance education facilitates self-learning by making it meaningful to learners instead of providing knowledge, information and enhancing interactions merely. Advancements and innovations in ICTs have geared up new possibilities and learning opportunities in distance education.

It is observed that ICTs have extended student support services in distance education. The ICTs have facilitated learners in accessing learning materials and getting information on and/or about different activities offered to them by their respective distance education university/institution.

The use of ICTs for promoting student support appears to be a popular useful strategy as it provides learner-centred services. There may be some cases where learners need group study and f2f instruction for their better learning, whereas others may prefer individualized study through online teaching or instruction. Such cases may be addressed by blending the traditional support services with ICT-based student support services. Expectedly, it would increase satisfaction distance learners and improve their learning and learning outcomes.

Use of Technology by AIOU for Extending Learner Services

AIOU as a pioneer distance education university of Pakistan extensively uses modern information and communication technologies for instructional as well as support services. It uses ICTs for effective and efficient learner's facilitation and support services along with instructional usage.

Institute of Educational Technology

AIOU is a distance education university, and it caters educational needs of over 1.3 million learners offering then facilities of studying at their own place, own pace and their own convenience. The university goes to the students at their doorsteps irrespective of the distance, location and their caste and creed. In realizing it, the Institute of Educational Technology (IET) is main pillar with its unique role. It is the media hub of AIOU. It is a production house which produces radio, television and non-broadcasted audio and visual programmes, documentaries and packages to support course at various levels of study. Such packages are offered to the students through radio and television broadcasts. Besides, it maintains recording of lectures and other educational activities for transmission on the media.

Live Media at AIOU

AIOU hosts it live media consisting of AIOU Web TV (http://iet.aiou.edu.pk/web-tv/), Voice of AIOU "FM 91.6" (http://iet.aiou.edu.pk/fm/), Video on Demand (http://iet.aiou.edu.pk/vod/). The live media disseminates important information to the learners as well as the general public. It presents documentaries and lectures, lecture notes and presentations on different topics along with entertainment. The brief account of each is given below.

Web Television (Web TV)

The IET of the AIOU during the academic year 2014–15 launched web TV in collaboration with information and communication technologies and e-learning department. A tab "VOD" (Video On Demand) is given on the Web TV portal of IET website. It provides an opportunity to the listeners and viewers to watch videos which they need for any particular course. It is an Open Educational Resource (OER), and anyone from anywhere can access these videos through AIOU website. Even so, AIOU is in process of installing its own educational television channel.

However, a 30 seconds' advertisement regarding admissions is broadcasted by National Television Channel—PTV News and private prominent TV channels including Geo News, Dunya News during admission days.

FM Radio

Radio is a major source sharing and disseminating information and knowledge among learners. AIOU has started broadcasting uninterrupted live transmission through its FM (91.6) radio. Currently, the Campus Radio of the AIOU (FM 91.6) is broadcasting educational informational programmes from 8.30 am to 7.00 pm daily. This broadcasting covers Islamabad and Rawalpindi. The students of major cities of Pakistan would be benefitting from educational programmes of AIOU by installing new transmitters.

The IET has planned to launch FM radio stations at 12 regional campuses including Lahore, Karachi, Quetta, Peshawar, Mirpur—AJK, Multan, Dera Ghazi Khan (DG Khan), Skardu, Swat, Kalat, Umerkot/Mithi and Faisalabad. Networking with other universities' campus radios across Pakistan has also been made possible. Similarly, documentation has been completed for getting satellite channel for educational purpose at AIOU.

Electronic Version of Course Books

As a part of its multimedia course repository plan which aimed at facilitating learners in getting electronic version of their respective curses thorough computer network, the AIOU launched electronic version of course books during the second half of 2015. The university started offering electronic books and other allied materials along with hard copies of the course materials. In the beginning, it started at the main library and gradually to go to the regional campus level. Similarly, the research repository of AIOU maintains about more than 4000 theses and dissertations in PDF as well as hard form for use of learners.

SMS Alert

AIOU has been using mailing services of Pakistan post and TCS (a private courier) Pakistan. But issues were reported regarding delayed information, delayed delivery of the books, roll number slips, result cards, etc. To address such issues, the university is now using SMS intimation system to inform learners about their admission, payment of fee, mailing study materials and books, etc. In Semester Spring 2015, AIOU informed about 0.35 million students through Short Message Service (SMS) regarding their fee submission and admission in respective programmes and/or courses. Similarly, the university informed them about the status of mailing/dispatch of books to them. After a successful experience, AIOU is now planning to use the same practice for communication of information about tutors, roll number slips, examination and examination centres, and results to the students.

Automation of Mailing and Tracking System

Timely mailing of books to the students has been a challenging task for the university, especially with ever-increasing enrolment. To enhance efficiency and effectiveness of support services, AIOU has started tracking system and automation of mailing system. By using this system, students now can track their books by entering their roll number and registration number on the website. Similarly, they can view their result, get provisional result card and know about the status of their degree.

Facility of Call Centre in Directorate of Students Advisory

Student support services are significant in retention of students and continuation of their studies. To make the system efficient and learners responsive, AIOU has started the facility of call centre in the Directorate of Student Advisory (DSA). In the call centre in gateway block, dedicated and motivated personnel have been deputed who receive queries and complaints from the students with patience. They guide them or help them contact the relevant department. Callers' satisfaction is realized through monitoring of the calls.

Complaint Management System

Along with telephone helpline, online complaint management system has also been activated by the university. In this system, the online-registered complaint is processed and forwarded to the relevant department under an efficient monitoring system. It ensures proper responding to the complaints.

Building E-Learning Capacity Through Multimedia Project at AIOU

According to Jung and Rha (2000), it is generally observed that technology-based instructional design appears to be flexible in courses, having speedy and repeated feedback, layouts to capture the attention of learners, and accompanying by meaningful interactions of learners boosting effectiveness of e-learning and satisfaction of the learners.

AIOU uses modern ICTs in extending student support services to its learners. The Multimedia Electronic Courseware Design Centre is an example that uses modern ICTs. It was established at AIOU in 2001 for developing and deploying multimedia materials; performing related research and development activities; and building e-learning capacity of the university personnel with its major gals.

As an objective of the project, faculty members were trained. Similarly, multimedia laboratories were established for course development purpose. Resultantly, multimedia materials were developed and delivered for ten courses. In this way, AIOU sets an example for other distance education universities or institutions to address the issues of capacity building in instructional design.

Using Online Technology Services for Enhancing Effectiveness and Efficiency of the Support Services

AIOU uses a standardized online Learning Management System (LMS) for local (Pakistani) and ELMS for international students on its website. It facilitates students in reading and downloading materials, participating in discussions, sending and receiving emails, involving themselves in live talks or chats, taking online tests and/ or quizzes, and tracking their progress in learning.

Using modern technologies, AIOU has developed an online system of open nature for extending support services to its learners. It accumulates all of the queries of learners to respond quickly. It has the capacity to handle queries through email, website, telephone, etc. Customized reporting module analyses the queries to categorize as according to criteria. The respective learner is automatically responded or intimated via email and SMS on each query (Mir 2017).

Likewise, Sangi (2005) elaborated the "Open Learning Institute of Virtual Education (OLIVE)" framework given in Fig. 1. According to him, it integrates different online activities related to instruction, research, operations and administration.

The OLIVE project appeared to be effective showing nationwide student's improved results and uniformity. It appeared to be economical for the AIOU as 33% reduced course cost was reported. It makes it feasible for international faculty to participate in instructional process through online mode. However, some problems including assessment, e-content developments were expected in the time coming ahead.

The OLIVE framework has the following models.

Model-A: The Regional Study Centre Model

It is used for small class size at a study centre established in local community and equipped with high-bandwidth Internet connectivity, laboratories, classrooms, library under supervision of faculty. The courseware is put on local server of the relevant study centre. A tutor supervises the learners during instructional process. The learners submit their assignment to their respective tutors and sit in offline examinations. However, learners have an online access to main campus. Similarly, online forums and asynchronous facilities (as provided in LMS) are ensured to the learners. Its salient features include

i. Instructional facilities including Internet are available at each study centre.
ii. Pre-produced multimedia courseware is played at the study centres.
iii. Online access to university server is provided to each student as an additional open self-learning.
iv. However, participation of students in online sessions is prohibited as they are provided instructional support at the centre.

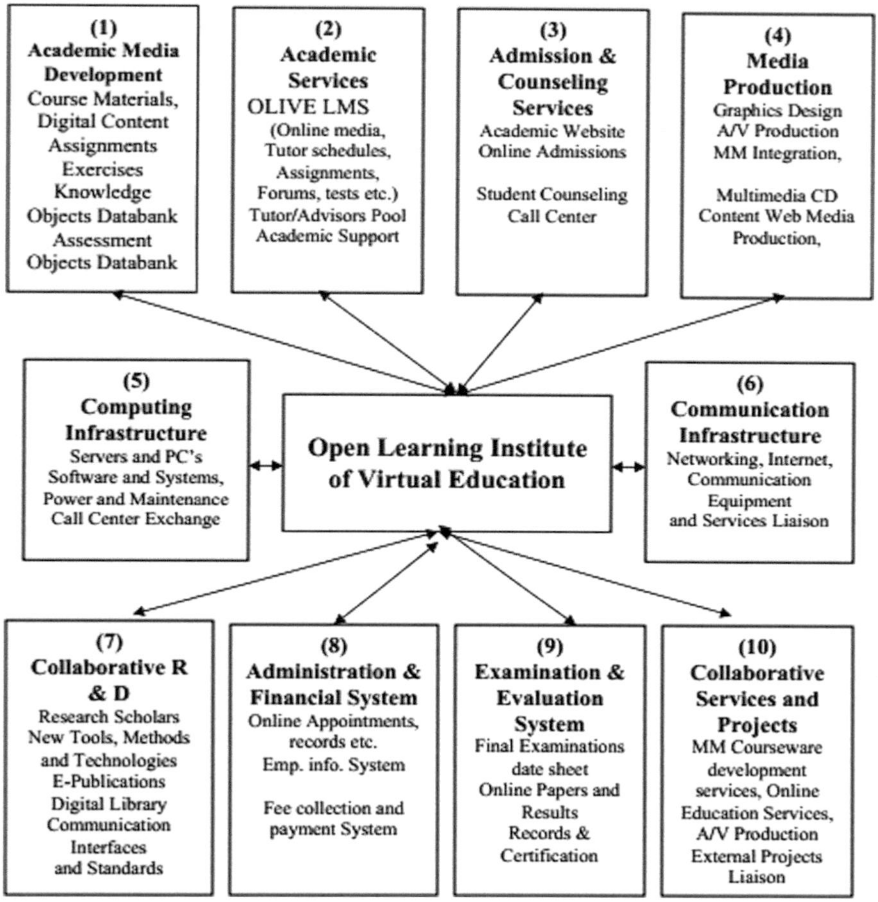

Components of OLIVE E-learning framework. Adopted from Sangi (2005).*Engineering Quality Learning through ICT: An AIOU Model for Online Education and Research. p. 4.*

Model-B: Internet-Based Model

It is feasible for those learners who use Internet at home or workplace. Its salient features consist of

i. Internet is a source of online instruction—submission of assignments, online lectures and live discussion with tutors.
ii. Students are provided access to online multimedia courses.
iii. Video-recorded lectures are also available to the students.

Model-C: The Girl at Home Model

This model addresses those learners who do not use Internet and is called "Girl at Home" model. Self-instructional multimedia courseware on CDs is provided to them. Reference material is also provided to them. Its salient features include

i. CDs of self-instructional multimedia courseware are provided to the students along with allied or reference material.
ii. Besides, the students can use Internet at main campus, study centres or some other place for submitting their assignments.

Besides, the learners have an access to the synchronous website and asynchronous LMS (Sangi 2005).

Use of Social Media—Life at AIOU

Social media has become a popular technology among the youth, particularly, the university students. Hence, AIOU is making best use of social media. It is using YouTube (https://www.youtube.com/aiou-official), Facebook (https://www.facebook.com/Life-at-AIOU-1574777979424971/), Google Plus (https://plus.google.com/u/2/106108867754106320826) and Twitter (https://twitter.com/LIFEatAIOU?lang=en).

AIOU Library

The AIOU has libraries at its main campus as well as in the regional campuses under a library system. It regulates a modern library at its main campus having the same history as that of the AIOU. It has a large number of books, journals and periodicals on different subject areas. Now, it has become a useful resource centre for dissemination of knowledge and information. Its automation has been completed by Koha software. It is providing access to the AIOU learners as well as the faculty. The Central Library of AIOU has started offering electronic services to its faculty, students and tutors who can acquire any of the available documents just by sending an email having correct bibliographic information of that document.

The AIOU has a direct link to the National Digital Library (http://digitallibrary.edu.pk/aiou.html) which provides access to scientific journals and magazines indexed in renowned databases.

Efficient Use of Technology for Effective Support Services by AIOU

AIOU makes efficient use of ICTs in extending learners' support services. It is successfully using SMS alert to intimate learners about their admission, payment of fees and mailing of books. Similarly, it has established call centre to address queries of its learners instantly educational and informational programmes for the learners particularly and the masses generally. Besides, online tracking system has been initiated along with online complaint management system. Now, distance learners can track their books, examination centre, roll number slips, results and degrees online through university website. FM (91.6) radio and Web TV are also broadcasting.

Following its charter of providing learner's friendly education AIOU has planned to become gradually an electronic university by offering Massive Open Online Courses (MOOCs) and alleviating weightage of online programmes. For the purpose, digital educational materials and automated academic services from basic literacy (non-credit courses) up to doctorate level have been planned to offer to the learners. In this way, AIOU will be the first university of Pakistan which embraces MOOCs. The learners enjoy Web-based support services and ICT-based examination or assessment. Similarly, the varsity has developed e-tutor training system as well.

Challenges Being Faced by AIOU in Implementation of Technology

In spite of its all success in promoting access to masses across Pakistan, AIOU still faces some challenges in implementation of information and communication technologies for instructional as well as extending support services to the learners. Among other, the main challenges are given below.

i. More than two-third of Pakistanis are living in rural areas where facilities even the basic living facilities are scarcely available. AIOU learners living in remote rural areas have too access to technology to use it. Even so, poverty limits such learners to benefit from modern learning technologies. It is a big challenge for AIOU to bring benefits of modern learning technologies to these learners.
ii. Similarly, information technology skills of distance learners make them use the technologies appropriately. Generally, the distance learners have experience of formal education having less ICTs skills. For getting full benefits of the ICTs, learners need to equip such skills necessary for them to use modern learning technologies.
iii. An upward trend is observed in instructional use of modern ICTs in distance education. Nowadays, the use of Learning Management Systems, computer-supported

instruction and digital libraries are must for almost every university. Blended learning with online access to courseware is becoming demanding in distance education even in developing countries. Synchronous and asynchronous learning is becoming a norm. But social learning of the students which takes place through face-to-face interaction of learners is compromised in ICT-based distance education. Lack of physical interaction for social learning of the students appears to be a challenge for AIOU which needs to be addressed properly.

iv. Similarly, the ICT-based synchronous learning is a mode of real-time instruction where all learners are "present" at the same time. It resembles traditional classroom instructional method irrespective of the geographical location of learners. In Pakistan, synchronous learning posits a greater challenge as learners from remote areas would not be able to be available online for every hour of instruction. Electricity breakdown adds to it badly and makes it less feasible.

v. Another challenge for AIOU is the high cost of the technology and technological devices on the part of the learners. Likewise, majority of distance learners are adults and on-the-job professionals having their strict commitments. It limits them to participate in the synchronous instruction. Moreover, modern ICTs demand high costs which on learners' part limits them to use such technologies.

vi. AIOU is also facing administrative challenges such as development of high-quality course content synchronous as well as asynchronous learning, online admission system, online class and course registration, availability of online library and textbook on a large scale.

vii. Likewise, providing online guidance and counselling services to the learners also appears to be a challenge for AIOU to cater their needs along with issue of online tutoring services.

Future Trends

In Pakistan, distance education has an environment which nourishes it to flourish with full bloom having social recognition and academic excellence. Distance education appears to having a vibrant and progressive future in the country. The Higher Education Commission (HEC) of Pakistan as a university regulatory body has started taking initiatives to regulate and streamline distance education programmes particularly, offered by the dual-mode universities. As the main objective of any distance education, endeavour revolves around educational needs of learners; hence, learner support services occupy a significant place in system of distance education in the country. Technology-based support services are becoming popular and common among communities of distance learners.

World-recognized innovative strategies are being adopted for the purpose; e.g. recent practices like the Massive Open Online Courses (MOOCs) have been designed to cover distance learning through interactive mode with the help of information technology in the developed countries. Likewise, some other initiatives such as edX, Coursera and Udacity which assimilate distance education to virtual education platforms are becoming popular among distance learners. The same is on upward inclination in Pakistan as efforts are being made to credit such courses.

Online support services are becoming popular among the learners as well as the distance education provider universities (AIOU 2017; 2015a).

The availability of the contents of self-instructional materials on university website is getting popularity among the learners as they can download at their homes or offices without mobility. Provision of such materials through Web, email and digital library is also becoming common. The use of audio and/or videoconferencing, Skype, Skype for learning and other Internet-based tools like social media including YouTube appears to be the top trend in distance education. Similarly, mobile phone communication including short text messages and android applications (apps) such as WhatsApp, Viber, IMO, Tango are also becoming popular tools of group as well as individualized communication, interaction and instruction in distance education.

Even so, other IT support and services like FM radio, Web TV and corporate messaging appear to be the common trends in distance education. Learning Management System (LMS) is a robust sign in extending academic support services to the learners. A state-of-the-art LMS has become a requirement for running and managing distance learning programmes. The LMS includes and also supports student portals, faculty portal and even online library (AIOU 2017).

Suggestions for ICTs-Based Student Support Services

AIOU has set an example for other (dual-mode) universities for efficient and effective provision of support services to the learners. By following AIOU, dual-mode universities can facilitate learners in a better way for their retention in the system. The following suggestion may be useful in extending effective student services to distance learners.

i. The dual-mode universities may follow the model of ICT-based student support services.
ii. Collaboration and linkage may be developed with mobile phone companies to provide state-of-the-art communication services to distance learners economically.
iii. Learning Management System (LMS) may be installed, activated and used by the learners and tutors for instructional purpose.

iv. The distance education university may arrange orientation training on how to use technology and benefit from ICTs-based support services during first week of the admission.
v. Online groups of learners may be created for their peer interaction and distributed learners. It would develop a sense of belongingness among them by eliminating sense of isolation.
vi. A massive campaign may be launched for creating awareness of the masses generally and the distance learners particularly.
vii. LMS may be hoisted by each of the distance education university with inter-university connectivity facility.
viii. All learners may be provided with opportunities for inter-learner discussions about their programme, for example through a programme discussion forum or Web-based conferencing.
ix. Detailed support services may be communicated to learner, e.g. student admission support systems, tutorials and guidelines (print or multimedia) for learning activities, student affair cell, call centre, online/offline help desk.
x. Guidelines and code of ethics on safe use of social media, other Internet tools and smartphone apps, etc., may be formulated by the AIOU for learners as well as faculty.

References

AIOU (2017, January–February). *Quarterly AIOU News and Views*, *3*(1), Islamabad: Allama Iqbal Open University.

AllamaIqbal Open University (2016, January–March). *Quarterly AIOU News and Views. 2*(1), Islamabad: AllamaIqbal Open University.

AllamaIqbal Open University (2015a, October–December). *Quarterly AIOU News and Views. 1* (5), Islamabad: AllamaIqbal Open University.

AllamaIqbal Open University (2015b, July–September). *Quarterly AIOU News and Views. 1*(5), Islamabad: AllamaIqbal Open University.

AllamaIqbal Open University (2015c, April–June). *Quarterly AIOU News and Views. 1*(3), Islamabad: AllamaIqbal Open University.

AllamaIqbal Open University (2015d, January–March). *Quarterly AIOU News and Views. 1*(2), Islamabad: AllamaIqbal Open University.

AllamaIqbal Open University (2015e, January). *Quarterly AIOU News and Views. 1(1)*, Islamabad: AllamaIqbal Open University.

Bates, A. W. (1995). *Technology, Open Learning and Distance Education.* London: Routledge.

Hui, H. W. (1989). *Support for students in a distance learning programme—an experience with a course in Fashion and Clothing Manufacture*. In Tait, A. (Ed.), Conference papers: *Interaction and Independence: Student Support in Distance Education and Open Learning.* The Open University.

Hussain, I. (2005). *A study of emerging technologies and their impact on teaching learning process.* An unpublished PhD Thesis; Islamabad, AllamaIqbal Open University.

Hussain, I. (1999). *A study of problems of distance education tutors in Bahawalpur Region.* An unpublished M.Phil Thesis; Islamabad, AllamaIqbal Open University.

Jung, I. S., & Rha, I. (2000, July–August). Effectiveness and cost-effectiveness of online education: A review of literature. *Education Technology,* 57–60.

Keegan, D. (1990). *Foundations of distance education*. London: Croom Helm.

Kishore, S (1998). Student support and quality indicators in distance learning. *Indian Journal of Open Learning, 7*(2), *205–212.*

Kirschner, P., Valcke, M., & Slujsmans (1999). Design and development of third generation distance learning materials: from an industrial second generation approach towards realizing third generation distance education. In J. V. Akker, L. M. Branch, J. Gustafsm, N. Nieveen, & T. Plonp (Eds.), *Design approach and tools in education and training*. London: Kluwer Publisher.

Manjulika, S. & Reddy, V. (1996). *Distance education in India: A model for developing countries.* New Delhi: Vikas Publishing House, Pvt. Ltd.

Mir, K. (2017). Design and development of online student support system. *Pakistan Journal of Distance and Online Learning, 3*(1), 01–08.

Moaler, R. et al. (2001). *support services for the study student, New York: The foundation of American Distance Education: A college correspondence study*. London, KoganPage.

Rumble, G. (1992). *The management of distance learning system*. Paris: UNESCO and IIEP.

Robinson, B. (1995). Research and pragmatism in learner support. In F. Lockwood, (Ed.), *Open and Distance Learning Today*. London: Routledge.

Sangi, N. A. (2005). Engineering quality learning through ICT: An AIOU model for online education and research. In *A paper presented in ICDE International Conference on Open Learning & Distance Education,* New Delhi, November 2005.

Simpson, O. (2000). *Supporting student in open and distance learning*. London: Kogan Page.

Tait, A. (1995). Student support in open and distance learning. In F. Lockwood (Ed.), Open and distance learning today (pp. 232–241). London, UK: Routledge

Thorpe, M. (2002). Rethinking learner support: the challenge of collaborative online learning. *Open Learning, 17*(2), 105–119.

Wright, S.J. (1991). Research on selected aspects of learner support in distance education programming: A review. In *The Second American Symposium on Research in Distance Education*. Pennsylvania State University.

Websites Accessed

AllamIqbal Open University, Islamabad (http://www.aiou.edu.pk/).
(http://www.aiou.edu.pk/ProgrammesList.asp?P=PHD).
(http://www.aiou.edu.pk/ProgrammesList.asp?P=MPHIL%20/%20MS).
(http://www.aiou.edu.pk/ProgrammesList.asp?P=MASTER).
(http://www.aiou.edu.pk/ProgrammesList.asp?P=BACHELOR).
(http://www.aiou.edu.pk/ProgrammesList.asp?P=PGD).
(http://www.aiou.edu.pk/ProgrammesList.asp?P=BED).
(https://www.youtube.com/aiou-official).
(https://www.facebook.com/Life-at-AIOU-1574777979424971/).
(https://plus.google.com/u/2/106108867754106320826).
(https://twitter.com/LIFEatAIOU?lang=en).

University of Sindh, Jamshoro (http://usindh.edu.pk/academics/faculties-uos/education/department-of-distance-continuing-and-computer-education/).

BahauddinZakariya University Multan (https://www.bzu.edu.pk/directorate-of-distance-education-dde-bzu-multan-downloads_1845.html).

University of Peshawar (http://thepeshawar.com/admissions/distance-education-peshawar-university-2015–2016-admissions/).

Gomal University Dera Ismail Khan (http://www.degu.edu.pk/).

COMSATS Institute of Information Technology, Islamabad (http://vcomsats.edu.pk/).

University of Agriculture Faisalabad (http://uaf.edu.pk/directorates/distance_learning/dist_overview.html).
Government College University Faisalabad (https://gcuf.edu.pk/directorate-distance-learning).
The Islamia University of Bahawalpur (http://www.iub.edu.pk/department.php?id=52).
Shah Abdul Latif University (SALU) Khairpur, Sindh (http://www.salu.edu.pk/department/directorate-distance-education-program).
International Islamic University Islamabad (http://www.iiu.edu.pk/?page_id=18297).
Sukkur Institute of Business Administration, Sukkur (http://www.iba-suk.edu.pk/ibasuk/aboutiba/wpMain.aspx).
University of Balochistan (http://application1.uob.edu.pk/de/index.php).
University of Sarhad (a private sector university: http://www.suit.edu.pk/distance-education).
Preston University Kohat, Islamabad Campus (a private sector university: http://preston.edu.pk/dri_main.php).
Virtual University of Pakistan, Lahore (http://www.vu.edu.pk/).

Role of Technology in Dissemination of Science Education

Anuradha Dubey

Introduction of ODL System

Education is a social obligation, an essential vehicle, individual empowerment, and national development (Kour 2013). Overall development of a country depends on its educational reform, because only educated manpower leads to economic development of a country.

College and universities have a decisive role to play in educating individuals to broaden their horizons. The government is also providing major funding in education sector of India. The growth of higher education in India has been exceptional and even enrollment is continuously growing.

Besides the conventional regular universities, open universities are also imparting education. The idea behind initiating open universities was to access higher education for deprived groups of population who had not got the opportunities to study in formal education system. Although open learning and distance education are different, they are complementary. Some elements of distance education are needed to be introduced in open learning system. Similarly, introduction of distance learning means open up educational opportunities to more people. Therefore, it has become common to bring these two terms together in the expression open and distance learning or ODL (Daniel et al. 2006). Open and distance learning universities were started with the objective to reach the masses of society that otherwise remain untouched in reference to higher education be it in terms of socioeconomic background, family issues, marital status, etc. A learner may be employed or unemployed in ODL universities. A teacher and learner are in regular touch via assignments and various means of ICT and have minimum

A. Dubey (✉)
Department of Botany, School of Science & Technology, Vardhman Mahaveer Open University, Kota, India
e-mail: anuradhasharma@vmou.ac.in

© Springer Nature Singapore Pte Ltd. 2018

Anjana (ed.), *Technology for Efficient Learner Support Services in Distance Education*, https://doi.org/10.1007/978-981-13-2300-3_11

face-to-face interaction in distance education. But a learner can meet teacher to solve his any kind of problem.

Distance education has value due to its ability to reach learners who are not well served by conventional educational institutions (Tony Bates 2005). It removes the barriers of learning. “Open and Distance Learning (ODL) system is a system wherein teachers and learners need not necessarily be present either at same place or same time and is flexible in regard to modalities and timing of teaching and learning as also the admission criteria without compromising necessary quality considerations” (www.mhrd.gov.in/distance-learning). In simple words, it can be said that educational system which is open for all is called open and distance learning (ODL). ODL system aims to include vast dimensions of openness in terms of flexibility, access, curriculum, course structure, learning satisfaction, and cost-effectiveness. Open and distance learning provides facility for the learners to study as per their convenience. They can learn at their own pace, place, and time. ODL system includes non-restrictive admission process; there are also no restrictions to age at the time of admission, on the number of examinations given per year, on subject combination and choice of course. ODL system is a learner-centered education. One of the great advantages of distance education is its low price and value for money (Fernandez 2008).

Research shows that people with disabilities are joining ODL institutions because ODL is convenient for them as they can study at their own pace, place, and time. There is no need to travel to campus or seek accommodation near the institution. Second, ODL offers content in various formats so learners can read, listen, or watch lectures as per their suitability. Third, ODL is more affordable as it costs significantly less than campus-based institution. Finally, ODL also provides a degree of anonymity where students with disabilities can interact without feeling discriminated (Kanwar and Cheng 2017). As per the findings of Hellman (2003), distance education is actually offering a big prospective to its students as well as facilitators.

The first open university was established in 1969 in the UK. Various international open universities like Open University of Israel (Israel), Open University of Hong Kong (China), Open University (UK), University of Southern Queensland (Australia), Western Governors University (USA) are disseminating education through ODL mode. The concept of ODL in India came into existence in the 1980s with the establishment of first Distance Education University. In India, Andhra Pradesh Open University was the first Distance Education University that was established in 1982 in Hyderabad. Later, it was renamed as Dr. Bhim Rao Ambedkar Open University in 1991. Besides, India has 12 State Open Universities such as Nalanda Open University (1987), Karnataka State Open University (1996), Netaji Subhas Open University (1997), Madhya Pradesh Bhoj Open University (1992), Uttar Pradesh Rajarshi Tandon Open University (1999), etc. One National Open University and 140 dual universities offering programs through distance mode. The National Open University came into existence in September 1985. IGNOU is India’s first National Open University. Vardhman Mahaveer Open

University (VMOU), Kota, is the third oldest Open University of India which was established in 1987. Thus, 40% of universities in India are offering education through distance mode (Kundu 2014).

It is a common belief that open and distance learning universities are only for faculty of arts and education and commerce and management, i.e., non-science stream, but with the dawn of the last century, the paradigm is shifting. Now it is becoming popular in teaching practical exercise-based courses of science and technology, agriculture, nursing, medicine, etc. In science streams not only computer science and mathematics but also subjects like botany, zoology, chemistry, physics, geography and even biotechnology which needs lots of practical hands-on training are now successfully attracting the attention of the society. More and more learners are interested in enrolling in Science–Schools/Departments of Open Universities for getting higher education in their respective fields. This practice is definitely encouraging for open and distance universities but it is a challenge to disseminate science education through ODL system and to maintain its quality as they need more attention.

Technological Advancements in Education Sector

The revolutions led due to technological advancement have widely affected all aspects of society (Nigam and Joshi 2007). Now every aspect is requiring technologically sound sector. Technology is also affecting education reform, not only in India but in the entire world. It is a useful concept in the reference to ODL education system.

As in the ODL universities, students generally do not think about classroom teaching, but in science programs, more and more interactions are needed between learner and teacher. So they have to fulfill course content with assignments, projects, camps, video lectures, question bank, e-learning texts, practical counseling sessions, etc., besides reading only books. These practices need more interactions with learner and definitely improve quality of science stream courses.

According to Thurmond (2003), interaction is explained as the involvement of learner with the subject content, the counselor, other learner and technology implemented with the course content. It creates a dialogue between each other and results in a mutual interchange of information. By interchanging information with each other, learner improves their knowledge. Eventually, interaction achieves its objective to enhance understanding of the subject matter.

There is no one best way of teaching than teaching with technology (Ansari 2002). The dusk of the last century has witnessed a swing in communication and information technology. It has broadened the horizons of distance education learning system. Computer and communication have opened the ways to formats other than pen and paper correspondence courses, and it allows for a more interactive learning environment (Jasola and Sharma 2005).

According to Bola (1994), "Educational technology consists of all modern media, methods and materials and needs to be used in a well-integrated manner of maximizing the learning experiences of students at various levels. It implies a behavioral science approach in teaching and learning and makes use of relevant scientific and technological methods and principles developed in psychology, sociology, linguistics, communication and other related areas."

Rapid expansion of the Internet is helpful in developing two-way communications between teacher and learner. The Internet has greater potential for sharing information. Development of the Internet has revolutionized the system, and now, it has become an essential component of ODL institutions. In order to participate in distance learning, learners need to have a computer system and regular access to an Internet connection.

Launching of Edusat (Education Satellite), a satellite dedicated only to education, is a milestone in this direction (Kour 2013). Satellite-based education has revolutionized the education system in India. The Internet and satellite technology is used to promote science education through distance mode. Information and communication technology is playing important role in accessing science education through open and distance learning mode. Development of technology breaks through all barriers and permits learner to pursue higher education even in the field of science programs as per their convenience.

The latest technologies are more cost-effective, easy to access, and better in term of quality. The Internet is so cheap and easy to distribute materials. Open Educational Resources are a great revolution in distance education system like MOOC. With the help of free open-source software movement, FOSS, people can work as a team to develop software for various applications and then further it is freely available for adaptation (Daniel 2005).

Print media provide the base besides video conferencing; computer conferencing are also effective means of face-to-face interactions. Teleconferencing is generally used to provide information to learner. For the purpose of providing education potential of other media like computer, artificial satellites, digital libraries, telephones, radio and television broadcasting are exploring by the institutions. The Web is an immense resource for learners, and it is already easily available (Rashid and Elahi 2012).

According to Michael (2008), technology puts the following positive effects:

- Supportive in students' achievement.
- Improve professional abilities.
- Fulfill special needs.
- Encourage continuing education.
- Provide workforce skills.

Technologically developed environment improves overall personality of learner. Use of technology boosts up their confidence. Reports of Sivin-Kachala and Biolo (2000) stated that students who are engaged in techno-friendly environments show positive and consistent patterns in their studies. They showed a significant increase and success in all their respective subject areas and better approach toward learning and greater confidence. Findings of Schacter (1999) also favor that students who have access to various technologies such as computer-assisted instruction, integrated learning systems, simulations, and different advanced software related with higher-order thinking, collaborative networked technologies, and programming technologies showed an affirmative increase in their achievements.

Success of any program running through ODL system depends on various aspects. To successfully run the science programs through ODL system, its module should include approach to reach vast number of learners, smooth and easy admission process, development of self-learning material (SLM), evaluation pattern, quick delivery of SLM to learners, intensive practical exercises, necessary instruments and special techniques to perform practical-based exercises, special study centers or infrastructure as per need of the course structure, timely declaration of results, trained academic staff, administrative support, and job-oriented nature of program.

ODL mode university has to make efforts in various aspects to successfully run a science program. Some of which are discussed here step by step.

Use of Technology by Vardhman Mahaveer Open University (VMOU) in Dissemination of Science Education

1. **Approaching Learners**

Success of any course is measured only by the number of enrollments in it, so ODL universities should try to reach unreached masses of society as much as possible. Generally, open universities have regional centers and study centers to approach a vast number of learners. VMOU has taken an initiative to approach its learner by going to their doorstep. For this approach, a schedule of orientation program for learners has been designed. It is planned prior to the admission session. Various groups of team members including faculty and supporting staff visit every district of state. Each group thus approaches learner of that particular area. At a center location, masses are collected and they are informed about the functioning of the University by these team members.

Technology is used as a tool as each group has a PowerPoint presentation among the learners. These presentations are helpful in explaining every aspect of the University in a detailed way. The visual presentation makes it more interesting for learners to understand. Audio–visual presentations are comprised of animations, demonstrations, and sound that make it more lively and simple to understand.

Use of PowerPoint presentations has avoided printing of pamphlets/leaflets, brochure, etc., which are of no use after a visit. Thus, technology has helped to prevent unnecessary wastage of paper, money, and time.

Radio talks of faculties and live radio phone-in programs are also helpful in building connections with remote learners.

2. **Admission Process**

Easy admission process is must to attract learners in distance education. Admission process should be flexible in terms of age, gender, socioeconomic background, marital status, time constraint, employed or unemployed or admission criteria, etc.

VMOU is running various programs of science, viz. physics, chemistry, mathematics, botany, zoology, geography, computer science and information technology, biotechnology in undergraduate degree programs. Learners can complete undergraduate degree programs in 3 years, and maximum duration to complete the programs is 8 years. The major advancement of the School of Science and Technology came with the launch of master's degree programs in July 2013 session in botany, chemistry, computer application, mathematics, physics and zoology. While learners enrolled in a distance learning master's degree program in science programs, they can complete it in 2 years, but maximum duration to complete it is 6 years. VMOU got great response of learners toward these courses, and it is rapidly increasing session after session.

VMOU at present is offering following courses in various subjects:

1. Master's Degree Program.
2. Bachelor's Degree Program.
3. Diploma Course.
4. Certificate Program.

Besides the above-mentioned courses, VMOU also offers lateral entry at undergraduate and postgraduate level and additional subject in the concerned graduation. This makes it easier for a student to learn more in a short span of time.

The next step ahead is making the University a center of research and excellence to promote science at the fullest.

Detailed course information of VMOU programs are provided in e-prospectus available on University's official website. VMOU offers admission twice in a year (January and July months). VMOU also has provision of lateral entry and additional entry in science programs.

In VMOU, process of admission for science programs was offline initially but has been shifted gradually to online mode. Currently in science program, only online mode of admissions is there.

But simultaneously, it was also realized that some learners especially from rural/remote areas face difficulty in filling online forms and a need of a techno-friendly person is felt to help them. To meet out this requirement of learners, VMOU has taken an initiative to adjoin its services with e-mitra.

e-mitra is an e-governance initiative of Government of Rajasthan which is being implemented in all 32 districts of the state. Government of Rajasthan is using public–private partnership (PPP) model to establish e-mitra centers. With the help of e-mitra, government is delivering various services almost at doorsteps. (Arora et al. 2008). The e-mitra is a successful effort of Government of Rajasthan for making convenience and transparency in delivering services to the citizens. VMOU is using this e-platform to provide all its information and services to rural and urban masses under one roof. Now candidates who wish to take admission in any course run by VMOU but are not techno-friendly and feel difficulty in online admission process can get access to University through e-mitra kiosk.

In VMOU, cashless transaction is preferred. Fees deposition is performed only through the net-banking. Presently in VMOU, its 90% financial working is cashless. Technology is used in developing transparency in banking services through cashless transaction.

Due to the technological advancement, admission process is totally online in VMOU.

3. **Development of Self-learning Material and Other Learning Supports**

The printed self-learning material is the most imperative aspect in the learner support system of distance education system, and it contributed the most to the overall satisfaction of quality (Chooi Sim et al. 2004). ODL system needs more cooperation of teachers, learners, and institutions to develop self-learning material and run a program in science stream. A team of faculty members develops SLM for open universities. The faculty members of a team are the subject experts who can be from other universities too. The teams develop course material in self-learning style with the language of learner's comfort zone. Basic terminology of science courses are in English so it is suitable to develop SLM in English, but sometimes, if there occurs zonal problem, then it is better to develop the course in language of learner's choice.

Different textbooks or additional sources need to be consulted for a single topic by students. To overcome this problem, VMOU provides special study materials in form of self-learning materials (SLM) to its learners. SLM are written courses that are written in a planned manner by competent academicians keeping learner in focus and are used by learners on their own. So these are learner-friendly. These are the integral part of ODL education/system for knowledge dissemination. SLM perform the role of a teacher and is easy to understand. They are self-sufficient and self-explanatory and thus promote self-learning. These are always provided with aims and objectives and are summed up with glossary and model questions. They have major emphasis on self-assessment so learner can self-evaluate by self-check exercise.

Technology is playing important role in this respect too. As during past practices, it was very tedious and time-consuming task to collect manuscripts from writers and then send them for typing, proofreading, editing, etc. But with the use of the Internet and scanning machines, written or typed material can be easily exchanged.

Technology supports make them available on the official website of the University. The softcopies are uploaded, and learner can get relevant copy of his SLM. Presently, SLM of VMOU is available in both printing form as well as online. The learner can get an access to his SLM in the way he wants. Besides providing SLM to students, VMOU is helping learners to focus their study with the help of other supporting learning aspects like video lectures, question banks. Video lectures of renowned faculties relevant to course content are also available for learners. Concerned faculty plans overall schedule for recording the lectures. These video lectures are recorded and developed by electronic media and production center (EMPC).

Even popular video lectures relevant to course content available on other websites can be made available to learners. Videos related with practical exercises can also be uploaded for the sake of distance learners.

Assignments that are important part of evaluation are available on official website of the University. Student can download the related assignment and submit it after completing it in the concerned department. Assignments are a means of two-way communication between teacher and learner. Technology has resolved the difficulty of printing and dispatching assignments to learners.

Apart from SLM and assignments, question banks of each course are also designed by team of faculty members and are available to distance learners on official website of the University. Question banks help learners in their studies by clearing their doubts. They get idea about the types of questions which can be framed from the subject content, making them prepared for the examinations.

"Student one view" is a link that is available on the University's official website, from where learners can get full information about course related to them like place and location of SLM, assignments, question bank of their choice of course, examination timetable, information about practical and theory counseling, old question papers. Hence, learners get updated due to this technological advancement.

Research students and others too can access e-journals and other learning material in VMOU library through INFLIBNET association. These practices are possible only due to the advancement of information technology.

ICT has made it possible to store all the details minutely in various formats at a single place due to its high storage capacity and that can be presented in a wide range too. The only requirement of distance learner is that he just has to be self-motivated to approach everything provided by distance university.

4. **Evaluation Pattern and Examination Cell**

For the sake of learners, evaluation pattern for ODL students are designed such that it shall be helpful to secure passing marks. Out of total marks, 20% marks are for assignments and 80% are for theory. In this, students generally prepare assignments in definite time as per given instructions and are required to submit it to relevant center. These are helpful for them for understanding course before examination, and the obtained marks are also added in term-end examination for calculating total results.

Now, all the work related to evaluation of examination, i.e., award list for assignment, practical's examination, term-end examinations, attendance list, are prepared with the help of computers, and softcopy for entering marks or attendances is available only to concerned faculty. The technology has made it easier to work as a team.

The University's Examination Department also owns an OMR sheet scanner so that courses based on multiple choices question-based pattern can be checked very speedily and even sometimes results are declared on next day of examinations.

Results of various programs are uploaded on the University's official website and even they can download their mark sheet as per their need.

5. **Delivery of SLM to Learners**

Delivery of SLM to learners should be on time so that they can go through the content before theory and practical counseling sessions. Now after validation process at regional center (i.e., final step of admission), admission lists are directly transferred to the Material Production and Distribution Department (MP&D). This direct transfer saves time and efforts and makes the dispatch faster.

Now, learner after getting his scholar number can track location of his SLM and on the date of arrival in nearby department can easily collect or know the time of delivery at home. This kind of SLM delivery prevents the loss in delivery and has reduced the heavy postage fees with no postal delays. This is possible only due to technological advancement in the system.

VMOU adopts alternative method to deliver SLM to learners. Material is sent to regional centers and study centers from where learners can collect their SLM.

6 Practical Counseling and Practical Examination

In delivering science education through open and distance learning system, a key challenge is to offer the learner a genuine and significant laboratory experience (Harsha 2017). For a science program, it is essential for a course to include practical counseling sessions apart from providing self-learning material to them (Nnaka 2016). Reports of Jason and Shin (2006) stated that practical counseling sessions include advantages of providing distance students with practical work, strengthen learner's knowledge in the subject matter, and develop activist approach, increasing relationships between counselor and learners. Practical work includes any teaching and learning activity which involves observation of real objects and materials. The term "practical work" is used in preference to "laboratory work" (Irwin 1995).

For specially science programs, practical manuals are also prepared in VMOU to describe methodology in detail to learners. A CD having videos of practical exercises can be made available to learners with SLM. During practical counseling, faculty can easily explain the scheduled practical work with the help of PowerPoint presentation and videos of related practical exercises.

As per UGC guidelines, now specific dissection exercises are totally banned in some courses. Those exercises can be explained with the aid of computer simulations. Technology is providing option to understand functioning of animals without killing them in an easy manner.

Laboratories of VMOU also have computer-assisted microscopes with digital cameras, and with the help of that, learners can see prepared slides directly on computer and can save that to study later. Still, moving, or time-lapse images can be captured, labeled, enlarged, etc., and live image of a microorganism such as a seed or analysis of pond life can be seen.

School of Science and Technology, VMOU, also has projector, and it can be used for whole-class interaction, demonstration, and lecturing.

In the subjects like biostatistics, technology is providing softwares to perform data analysis. By the use of this technology, learners can explore concepts and ideas. It is useful to enhance their knowledge.

Practical aspects in various subjects which need graphical visualization of results to find out the interpretation of experimental data can use computational softwares designed for that. Learners can make different graphs quickly and easily to represent their results. Thus undoubtedly, use of technology is facilitating learners of ODL system.

Besides above, a practical guideline is also available on official website of the University, including rules and regulations related to conduction of practical counseling and practical examinations should also be there to clear rules uniformly in each and every learning center. On this basis, academic, administrative as well as non-teaching staff can work in collaboration.

7. **Monitoring of Learning and Examination Centers**

ODL system is an easy way to reach masses for which proper monitoring of learning and examination centers are must to meet out the expectations of learners and reach out its goal.

During examination time, in VMOU, a team of teaching staff visits VMOU examination centers as an observer. Schedules of visits are planned in such a way so that most of the examination centers can be covered.

Even during practical examinations and practical counseling, faculty members visit the practical centers too. These practices are helpful in maintaining quality of education as well as control any type of malpractices.

But with the help of technology, now it became much more easier as video of daily classes can be observed by director of concerned regional center or any responsible authority. Scanned copy of learner's attendance can also be obtained from concerned study centers through mail. Recording of CCTVs can also be helpful to observe their activities. Technological improvement is providing so many ways to monitor activities of learning and examination centers and keep a check to prevent any sort of discrepancy.

8. **Research Programs in Science Stream**

Besides imparting education in undergraduate and postgraduate programs, VMOU has also started research programs from 2013 in various streams. The science-based research can be conducted in laboratory facilities available at the University headquarter. Ph.D. program run by VMOU is abided by research regulations as prescribed by UGC. Presently, School of Science and Technology is running Ph.D. program in botany, geography, and zoology.

Role of Technology in Extending Learner Support Services

As per Simpson (2000) in distance education system except for the production and the delivery of course materials, all other activities that help in the educational growth of students are the part of the learner's support system.

He classified it into two categories:

1. Academic support is assisting learner in their relevant subject issues and encourages them in improving their knowledge.
2. Non-academic support is facilitating to learners by efficient organizational dimensions of their studies related to institution.

VMOU is constantly making efforts to extend help to learners of its ODL system. This system does not have direct interaction with learners to provide access to education, so it needs Learner Support Services.

The entire process of Learner Support Services is designed, managed, and implemented by Director—Regional Services Division at headquarter. It directs working of regional centers and study centers.

Presently in VMOU, seven regional centers are functioning in the state of Jaipur, Jodhpur, Ajmer, Bikaner, Kota, Udaipur, and Bharatpur. These regional centers are headed by Director—Regional Center. These regional centers have been set up to coordinate the working of study centers (VMOU Annual Report 2015–2016).

The objective of Learner Support Services is to create a link between learner and open university. This link should be developed at local level. The local centers are known as study centers. They offer academic facilities and communication support to learners. VMOU has an extensive network of 209 study centers to extend Learner Support Services throughout the state. Study centers are basically the resource centers. VMOU study centers are mainly the academic institutions of higher education recognized by UGC. VMOU uses premises of study centers during holidays and off-hours also. All study centers are involved in educating learners on part-time basis. Activities of study centers are managed by a coordinator.

Learner Support Services generally include promotional activities, pre-entry counseling, admission process, multimedia (audio–visual) learning, library facility, assignments, induction programs, coordinating examinations, and various programs.

- Television and radio programs are best approach for promotions of academic programs running through open universities.
- Orientation programs of centers and learners can be performed by video conferencing.
- Net-banking helped in developing cashless structure in VMOU.
- Validation of student database can be done rapidly as now it is performed with the help of in-built system of the University computers (Intranet).
- Audio–video sessions of counseling can be easily organized everywhere even in the absence of counselor.

- Time schedule of practical and theory counseling sessions is announced on the University's official website.
- Faculty members may create a group of learners on social media to directly connect with them, like Whatsapp groups, blogs.
- "Student one view" link is providing direct common link for various activities related to their program.
- Learners can register their complaints online through the link to learners provided on the University's official website. Even they can see the status of their complaints regularly.
- Besides, VMOU also has a Student Affair Cell (SAC). It gives focused attention on student's problem. SAC has been performing its objective promptly. It is successfully extending all possible help to learners on various issues.
- Regional centers of VMOU are developed as model study centers having proper facilities for learner like providing information telephonically and personally; having e-mitra kiosk; helping learners to fill online admission forms and examination forms, admission validation; organizing orientation programs, practical and theory counseling sessions at suitable study center; sending SMS reminders to learners and notifications through mobile phones for submitting assignments, etc.

These practices are already discussed in detail. Here, it shall be mentioned that with the advancement of technology now distance learner has not actually remained distant from education. Technology has minimized the distance between a learner and education by literally giving education at their doorstep.

Best Technological Practices Followed By VMOU

- **Effective Use of Mobiles**

VMOU is using mobile number of students for sending mass reminders of assignment submission deadlines, examination dates, practical counseling camp dates, admission verification, etc. It is very effective and learners become aware regarding their courses. SMS text message helps learner by updating their program activities. It enables learners to receive information cost-effectively, including text messages and e-mails.

- **Educational Media Production Center**

VMOU has Educational Media Production Center. It was established in the year 1998. The objective of the center is to develop audio and video recordings of the University's different academic program (VMOU Annual Report 2015–2016). In VMOU, its role is not only limited to development of electronic media development but it is also strengthening information and communication technology in VMOU. It has upgraded software and hardware. It has developed an integrated online system, where once a learner gets admission, his entire student life in VMOU is managed.

EMPC helps in managing **student one view** on official website of the University, from where student can track all detail regarding his program like type of program, enrollment information, assignments, question banks, location and tentative date of delivery of SLM, exam timetable, information of counseling schedules, old question papers, defaulter forms, examination form, promote forms, practical camp city forms. It can be accessed by learners using their scholar numbers or name as per the choice.

Center is also working in the implementation of e-governance model for the University. The center is maintaining various ICT services including network, storage systems, servers, and many others. The center has been delivering live programs via Internet mode which has facilitated the learners (VMOU Annual Report 2015–2016).

EMPC also has a centralized server which controls LAN work of the University and monitors proper functioning in the campus.

- **E-Learning**

The e-learning refers to electronic technologies used for education. VMOU also has its own e-platform known as **e-Acharya**. VMOU has launched its online programs (Srivastava 2016), and it is also in process of developing Open Educational Resources (OERs). Research students, in particular, are intimated through e-mails for any correspondence.

- **School of Science and Technology**

School of Science and Technology coordinates overall courses running in science stream. In the states, it organizes practical counseling, theory counseling, and examinations with the help of concerned departments. Practical counseling/camps are performed on the special study centers having required infrastructure.

VMOU has its own laboratories at headquarter to perform practical counseling sessions of science learners. Here, facilities are available to conduct practical exercises from 12th to research-level programs. It has botany, zoology, chemistry, physics, geography, chemistry, and computer laboratories. These laboratories are well equipped with all necessary instruments which are needed to perform practical-based exercises for the students.

School of Science and Technology has all necessary technical facilities like computers, printers, Internet facility, scanner, photographic camera, microscopic camera, and projector. Each faculty member has laptop and mobile facility on their desk for smooth functioning of the system.

- **E-Filing**

The University has developed the file tracking system and has adopted software of NIC. Presently, it is functioning and all the official files of the University are being tracked on the file tracking system.

- **Central Library**

Central Library of VMOU has important sections like acquisition, reference, periodical, new book, technical, computer, audio–visuals. All the divisions are well equipped with basic infrastructure. Library of VMOU is automated with SOUL software. Information about 36,000 books have been entered in the library database, and it is accessible to all users within campus.

Eighteen computers are interlinked through Local Area Network (LAN) with Internet facilities. Now learner can access OPAC, e-resource everywhere in the library. The library is subscribing e-journals from renowned publishers like Springer, Wiley-Blackwell, Taylor & Francis through INFLIBNET and DELNET consortia (VMOU Annual Report 2015–2016).

Challenges Faced by VMOU in Implementation of Technology

In an organization, implementation of technology is not always easy. It is really difficult to distribute the functioning of a traditional system when the issue is about technology it can be difficult to manage.

The best practices in technological strategy implementation involve proper appreciation environment for its operation. Management shall be careful in selection of relevant technology projects, capacity building among staff through re-skilling, identification of the right technologies (Gichoya 2005). It is also necessary to involve overall staff during development.

VMOU has faced so many challenges since its establishment in terms of funding sources, employee training to enhance their knowledge and skills. The lack of awareness and fear for change were in the organization, but skilled leadership helped to come out from that.

VMOU has charted out a proper plan of action for the adoption of ICTs in their operations, and these are being executed systematically (Srivastava 2016).

Technology used by the University is implemented to better serve its learners. With the passing of time, it has offered a huge positive impact. Use of technology is benefiting everyone who is interacting with it.

Conclusion

Traditionally, ODL system is associated with the philosophy of making education easier for learners to access learning. Technology is playing a vital role in this concern, and it has become an essential component of ODL system. Information and communication technology (ICT) has made open and distance education possible for a learner to be available anywhere and everywhere. At each and every step of science program implementation and disseminating education through ODL mode, challenge can be successfully achieved by VMOU only due to the technological advancement in the present scenario.

References

Tony Bates. A. W. (2005). Technology, e-Learning and Distance Education, Taylor & Francis group-e-library. http://www.mhrd.gov.in/distance-learning.

Ansari, M. M. (2002). Best practices in open and distance learning systems in india: An assessment. *Indian Journal of Open Learning, 11*(2), 219–228.

Arora, A., Deshpandey, A. M., & Sharma, R. K. (2008). *Compendium of e-Governance initiatives in India* (pp. 236–247). Pg no: Universities Press.

Bola, B. (1994), Educational Technology with reference to multimedia approach to Distance Education. (Vol. XI). AIOU.

Chooi Sim, H. K., Atan, H. & Idrus, R. M. (2004). The learners' support system in distance education: A study of the satisfaction of quality. *International Journal of Instructional Technology and Distance Learning*, *2*(9).

Daniel, J. (2005), Towards education for all: The critical role of open and distance learning in national development. http://hdl.handle.net/11599/1536.

Daniel, J., West, P., & Mackintosh, W. (2006). Exploring the role of ICTs in addressing educational needs: identifying the myths and the miracles. http://hdl.handle.net/11599/1393.

Fernandez, L. M. R. (2008). A prospective vision for universities: The role of the technology transfer units and distance education. http://hdl.handle.net/11599/100.

Gichoya, D. (2005). Factors affecting the successful implementation of ICT projects in government. *Electronic Journal of e-Government*, *3*(4), 1–10. http://www.ejeg.com.

Harsha, T. S. (2017). Learning Science through distance education—A Challenge at Karnataka State Open University. *The Online Journal of Distance Education and e-Learning, 5*(1), 62–65.

Hellman, J. A. (2003). Distance education: Its advantages and shortcomings.

Irwin, A. (1995). *Citizen science*. London: Routledge.

Jasola, S. & Sharma, R. (2005). Open and distance education through wireless mobile internet: A learning model. *International Journal of Instructional Technology and Distance Learning*, *2*(9).

Jason, K. Y. C., & Shin, N. (2006). Students' perspective of practical work in learning sciences via distance education. *Asian Association of Open Universities Journal, 2*(1), 1–10.

Kanwar, A. & Cheng, R. (2017). Making ODL inclusive: The role of technology. http://hdl.handle.net/11599/2827.

Kour, M. (2013, September), Equal opportunity to learn through Open University System: A case study of IGNOU. *Research Journal of Educational Sciences 1*(6), 23–26,

Kundu, S. (2014). Open and distance learning education: Its scope and constraints in Indian scenario. *IOSR Journal of Humanities and Social Sciences*, *19*(4), ver. IV, 01–05.

Michael, O. (2008). The role of Technology in Education. 2003–2009 Business Knowledge source.com.

Nigam, A. & Joshi, V. (2007). Science education through open and distance learning at higher education level. *Turkish Online Journal of Distance Education, 8*(4)20–33.

Nnaka, C. V. (2016). Science education through open and distance learning at national open University of Nigeria. *International Journal of Library & Educational Science, 2*(1), 1–8.

Rashid, M., & Elahi, U. (2012). Use of educational technology in promoting distance education. *Turkish Online Journal of Distance Education, 13*(1), 79–86.

VMOU Annual Report (2015–2016), Vardhman Mahaveer Open University, Kota. (https://www.vmou.ac.in/annualreport).
Schacter, J. (1999). *The impact of education technology on student achievement: what the most current research has to say*. Santa Monica, CA: Milken Exchange on Educational Technology.
Simpson, O. (2000). *Supporting students in open and distance learning*. London: Kogan Page.
Sivin-Kachala, J., & Biolo, E. (2000). Research report on the effectiveness of technology in schools (7th ed.). Washington, DC: Software and Information Industry Association.
Srivastava, M. (2016). *Report: Status of the state open Universities of India*. New Delhi, India: Commonwealth Educational Media Centre for Asia.
Thurmond, V. A. (2003). Examination of interaction variables as predictors of students' satisfaction and willingness to enroll in future Web-based courses while controlling for student characteristics. Published Dissertation. University of Kansas. Parkland, FL: Dissertation.com. http://www.dissertation.com/library/1121814a.htm.

An Introspection of the Responses of the Ruralites and the Elderly to Information and Communication Technology in Open Distance Learning

Kajal De and Sampurna Goswami

List of Abbreviations

AV	*Audio–Visual*
DTH	*Direct-to-Home*
ICT	*Information and Communication Technology*
MOOCs	Massive Open Online Courses
MSW	Master of Social Work
NGO	Non-governmental Organisation
NSOU	Netaji Subhas Open University
ODL	*Open Distance Learning*
OER	*Open Educational Resources*
UNESCO	*United Nations Educational Social and Cultural Organization*

Introduction

Education is a lifelong activity that begins from time when an infant comes into the womb of his mother and continues till he takes his last breath. Since the advent of the Welfare Model of State, 'education' made an important place for itself in the policy realms and nation states have adopted various reforms in order to achieve a substantial level of education for their citizens. The nations have also come together in the United Nations to cooperate in the fields of education and culture; thereby, the nations set up the United Nations Educational, Scientific and Cultural Organization in 1945. One of the major objectives of the UNESCO is to strengthen ties and cooperation among the nations, so that every child and citizen in every

K. De (✉) · S. Goswami
Netaji Subhas Open University, Kolkata 700064, India
e-mail: kdedirectorsc@gmail.com

S. Goswami
e-mail: mailto.sampurna@rediffmail.com

© Springer Nature Singapore Pte Ltd. 2018

Anjana (ed.), *Technology for Efficient Learner Support Services in Distance Education*, https://doi.org/10.1007/978-981-13-2300-3_12

country have an access to quality education, that is a basic right and an indispensable prerequisite to sustainable development.[1] UNESCO believes that education is a primary human right for all throughout the life, and this right should be essentially accessed through quality. The Goal 4 of the 2030 Agenda for Sustainable Development talks about ensuring an inclusive quality education for all and promote lifelong education,[2] and the subsequent Education 2030 Framework for Action, point number 10, commits to promote quality lifelong education for all in all settings and in all levels of education. It also lays down the opportunities for harnessing science, technology, and innovations in the education sector and talks about harnessing information and communication technology (ICT) to strengthen education and accessing quality information.[3]

The concept of distance education is intertwined with the very idea of lifelong education. Distance education is a medium through which education can be provided to those sections of the society who can no longer enroll themselves in regular mode. Distance education is a teaching–learning process where the teacher and the student are physically separated. The rapid growth of distance education began in the 1990s with the advent of online technical education. However, it can be traced back to the 1800s. It began with the implementation of instruments like parcel post, radio classes and has gradually reached the extent of online interactions (Kentor 2015). Online learning system is highly innovative and best suited in regard to distance education because it uses specially designed learning materials and provides student support system and advanced methods of evaluation (Biswas 1999).

Open Distance Learning in India began with the establishment of Distance Education Council under the Indira Gandhi National Open University Act in 1985. Apart from this Central Open University, there exist other State Open Universities working simultaneously in reaching the unreached. In this context, ICT became important in delivering information and the genesis of ICT in education in India can be traced back to 1937 when the All India Radio took up educational broadcast in a systematic and regular manner in The University of Calcutta (Shamsu 2012). However, with the growth of Open Universities in India, and under the University Grants Commission's Distance Education Bureau (a restructure of the earlier system replacing Distance Education Council) ICT has become the primary basis of providing education via Internet in these ODL institutions. Audio–video lectures, chatting, live virtual classrooms have replaced the correspondence mode, to some extent in ODL institutes in India. India is one of the earliest countries to implement distance mode in her higher education sector. During 1995, there were about 57

[1]United Nations Educational, Scientific and Cultural Organisation, http://en.unesco.org/about-us/introducing-unesco (Accessed on 12 June, 2017).

[2]2030 Sustainable Development Goals, http://www.un.org/sustainabledevelopment/education (Accessed on 12 June, 2017).

[3]Education 2030, Incheon Declaration and Framework for Action for the implementation of Sustainable Development Goal 4, http://unesdoc.unesco.org/images/0024/002456/245656E.pdf (Accessed on 12 June, 2017).

distance learning institutes in India with seven State Open Universities and one National Open University (Panneer Selvam 2012). What is significant is to understand that distance education is important in India because of India's demographic structure. There is a popular saying that 'India lives in her villages' because there is a substantial rural population in India which amounts to 68.84% according to the Census Report of 2011. This rural population remains separated from the urban population in terms of its socioeconomic backwardness, social orthodoxy, and lack of education. It is also important to note here that most of the rural areas in India do not have the basic amenities, communication networks, schools, colleges, and hospitals. This is the section that is 'unreached' in terms of public goods and logistic facilities. Therefore, the distance educational institutions in India have been assigned with the role of reaching this particular section. Apart from the ruralites, there is another section within the population that have remained underprivileged in the context of education, the elderly population. Due to the development of the medical sciences, the average life span of human beings has increased substantially at the global level; as a result, people irrespective of their gender are becoming motivated to pursue higher education and take up some objective work, at a higher age. If we go deep into the socioeconomic history of India, we will find that securing government jobs in the first 20–25 years after independence was not a difficult task. India's socialistic economic policy laid down the opportunity for the youngsters to secure a government job on the very basis of a graduation degree. However, with the Liberalization, Privatization, and Globalization Policy adopted in 1991, securing a good job in India has become a much more difficult task as it had inculcated a sense of competition, not only among the individuals but also among the various enterprises. Now, this elderly population who had to leave their education at an early stage to get into a job or the womenfolk who had to give up their education for rearing their children and maintaining their household makes a substantial section who are enrolling themselves for higher education in the recent years. These are the two sections of the population that can be considered to be the target group of the distance educational institutes of India.

Information and Communication Technology in Education

With the advent of information and communication technology (ICT), the subsequent use of ICT in education has opened various areas of debates and discussions. On the one hand, ICT in education and especially in the distance education has added the modern techniques of online classrooms, on to the conventional ways of postal delivery of printed self-learning materials and the Personal Contact Programs, digital technology have also enabled teacher–to-teacher and student-to-student interactions who are otherwise separated by distance (Chandra 2005). On the other hand, it has raised many questions regarding responses it is acquiring in the rural sectors of India and from the elderly population who are used to the conventional ways of teaching–learning method. Scholars like Professor

Ramesh Chandra have pointed out that the senior citizens often find it easier to take courses online due to restricted mobility or a desire to study privately (Chandra 2005). However, he had conducted his study in United States of America (USA) but in India the infrastructure that is needed for conducting classes online is yet not developed in the rural sector although the present government has taken some initiative through its 'Digital India' scheme, and at the same time, it is also important to understand that the elderly population is not tech savvy, in the sense that they have been exposed to modern technologies much later compared to the present elderly population of the first world nations like USA or Great Britain. Rigorous research has been carried out in Europe regarding the role of instructional technology in the education sectors especially the higher education sector. In Europe, ICT in education was considered as a benchmark solution in dealing with the problem of 'discrepancies.' Francois Marchessou argues that in the 60s and 70s Europe as geographical entity was marked by the uneven development as many industries were collapsing; on the other hand, Europe also had areas that were highly isolated from the main cities and development in these fringes was in an embryonic stage (Marchessou 1999). In such circumstances, it was becoming necessary for the European Union to establish an education system that will help to build a society capable of meeting the emerging crises. As a result, instructional technology in higher and more importantly in Open Distance Learning played a pivotal role in adjusting the already imbalanced European society.

Before analyzing the effects of ICT in higher education, it is important to understand as to what do we mean by information and communication technology in education and to what extent or why there is an increasing emphasis on the application of ICT in Open Distance Learning?

The post-1990s world order can be demonstrated as a 'world without the borders'; although this withering away of territorial borders is apparent, this entire phenomenon is quite significant as it enhanced the use of technology especially the Internet and brought almost all the nations under one umbrella known as the 'globalization.' The increasing use of global networking, the World Wide Web, has made people to people contact a cliché matter. This use of technology had contributed greatly in the educational sectors as well. The increasing use of the smart class technology since the beginning of the new millennium has been a maverick move in the elementary education. Subsequently, there was a proposal to implement smart technology and instructional aides in higher educational sector as well. But the most effective and efficient results were recorded after implementing the information and communication technology in Open Distance Learning method. One of the earliest moves was adopted by the USA when the Federal Government passed the Higher Education Amendment Act in 1988, which laid down the benefits of 'high-level', Web-Based distance education programs (Chandra 2005).

When we talk about ICT in distance education, we mean the replacement of the earlier postal system of delivering study materials and the weekly classes with a more digitized version of effective delivery of study materials through Web sites and mobile application as well as the teaching–learning process and the Personal Contact Programs through virtual classrooms. ICT in ODL can also include

Audio—visual components of syllabus uploaded in the institutional Web sites, live classes through online streaming and an Internet-based evaluating system. The use of Massive Open Online Courses (MOOCs) has further enabled students from various socioeconomic backgrounds to easily access the knowledge pool; on the other hand, the use of MOOCs has also helped teachers and academicians to contribute greatly to the academic field. ICT can also be implemented in the learner support services. Information regarding classes, syllabus, examinations, and special doubt clearing and student assistive systems can be developed with the use of ICT.

The major objective of distance education is to 'reach the unreached,' and in order to fulfill this very idea of 'education for all,' ICT has contributed enormously. The use of networking has made the entire system much more easier and friendlier, and the conventional method of teaching–learning process followed in most of the ODL institutes has been replaced with a smarter and scientific version. However, what calls for attention is the fact that the benefits of ICT in ODL cannot be analyzed in a generalized format, many other subsidiary factors are responsible for its successful implementation, and one such primary factor is the degree of national development that includes social, economic, and most importantly the technological development and progress in a particular country.

ICT and India: Understanding India's 'Digitization' Program

According to the document published by the Department of Electronics and Information Technology, *Digital India program* is defined as '*A Programme to Transform India into a Digitally Empowered Society and Knowledge Economy*'.[4] This milestone in the country's governmental drive is essentially a historical one. However, there are certain doubts regarding the extent of the drive's success. The fact that 68.48% of India lives in villages and the critics of the policy are dubious about the extent to which the policy can ensure complete digitization whether in the rural areas or in the urban pockets of the Indian Territory. This calls for an in-depth analysis and discussion, but the need of the hour is to introspect the prospects and aspects of the program (Fig. 1).

Among the nine pillars of this program, the sixth pillar calls for attention in the sphere of virtual education. A lineage can be drawn in this regard: on the one hand, the swelling wave of distance education, Open Distance Learning, and the government's motivation to invest modestly on the objective of reaching the unreached, and on the other hand, the present regime's excruciating interest in providing digital access to information seems to converge and intersect each other. The scheme titled 'Access to Information' under the Digital India program raises the question that

[4]Digital India, Department of Electronics and Information Technology, Government of India, http://meity.gov.in/sites/upload_files/dit/files/Digital%20India.pdf (Accessed on 5 January, 2018).

Fig. 1 Screenshot of the NSOU official Web site. *Source* NSOU official Web site (Accessed on January 8, 2017)

does this information include educational information or not? Does this have any connection with the Massive Open Online Courses? What is necessary is to note that Massive Open Online Courses, ICT-enabled courses, and such other concepts were in use for a considerable amount of time and this essentially means that Digital India program is just a drive to enhance the potentials of digitization in education and is another way to invest more in terms of money and material to usher in greater success of virtual universities and educational institution.

In this context, it is ideal to discuss Government of India, Ministry of Human Resource Development's recent initiatives like *Swayam* and *Swayam Prabha*. *Swayam* is a Massive Open Online Course where knowledge seekers can easily access the knowledge repositories and contributors can contribute massively. *Swayam Prabha* on the other hand is a direct-to-home (DTH) television platform devoted to telecast high-quality educational programs. Both these programs were launched in the year 2017.[5] Apart from MHRD's initiatives in assuring digital access to knowledge, the various Open Universities in India have now come forward to launch their own educational repositories.

For instance, the Netaji Subhas Open University (NSOU), the premiere State Open University in West Bengal, since 2015, started its first ICT-enabled learner's support system in courses like commerce and social work. From 2016, most of the schools and departments operating within the university initiated the venture of developing the audio–video lecture series and other such e-knowledge bases. The most noteworthy achievement made by this institution is the Open Educational Resource (OER) Repository that was launched on 12 May, 2017. This institutional OER has enabled public access to the various courses and the subsequent educational information. What is also crucial in this regard is the university's alignment toward achieving a more technology-driven course structure that goes hand in hand

[5]Free Online Education 'Swayam', https://swayam.gov.in (Accessed on 5 January, 2018).

with the idea of 'digital access to information' as prescribed under the Digital India program.

The Open Educational Resource Repository allows the enrolled students of the university to access any field of Information. It is also to bring to notice that that institutional OER is a public domain; as a result, a non-enrolled knowledge seeker can also have an access to it. Apart from the OER Repository, NSOU has initiated the audio–video (AV) lecture series as shown in the above screen shot of the official Web site. The AV lecture series is another milestone in the University's digitization program. What is also maverick is the fact that the laboratory-based subjects like chemistry, zoology, physics, and geography have been portrayed in these AV lecture series. This has not only made such highly technical subjects much more visually attractive but has also made recondite concepts easier to understand for any section of students (Fig. 2).

However, there are sections of Indian population for whom access to Internet in itself is a major challenge, for instance, the rural population, the elderly population, the women folk, and the differently abled category. These categories are often considered as underprivileged categories. It is known that the Government of India has taken constructive approach in providing internet facilities by installation of WiFi in Railway Stations, Transport Depots, Village Schools and Government Institutions in Rural Areas as well as allowing the Private Entrepreneurs to invest heavily in the Networking and communication Sectors; Moreover, big business houses like Reliance, Tatas, Birlas, and other multinational companies who are considered as transnational elites and strongly influencing the Indian politics have now begun to infiltrate in the poorest of the poor regions with their 3G and 4G network spectrums to facilitate the present regime's Digital India program. But the use of technology is not always driven by facilities, what is also required is adequate skill, psychological instinct, and motivation to change one's lifestyle, and all such factors depend on age and social status of an individual. This calls for an in-depth analysis, and the need of the hour is to make a record of the responses of these categories to the newly incorporated ICT in the educational sector and especially in those institutions that have been entrusted with shouldering the responsibility of 'reaching the unreached.'

ICT in NSOU: Questioning the Future Prospects of the Drive

The intercourse between ICT and NSOU as an institution, although is at an embryonic stage, calls for greater analysis in order to understand the pattern of response to this newly incorporated structure. Although it is really difficult to record the response regarding the rate of acceptance of audio–video lecture series or the rate of accessing the institutional OER, ironically it is not really that difficult to understand the pattern of response. In order to understand the pattern of response to the ICT-enabled learner support system installed in the university, data was

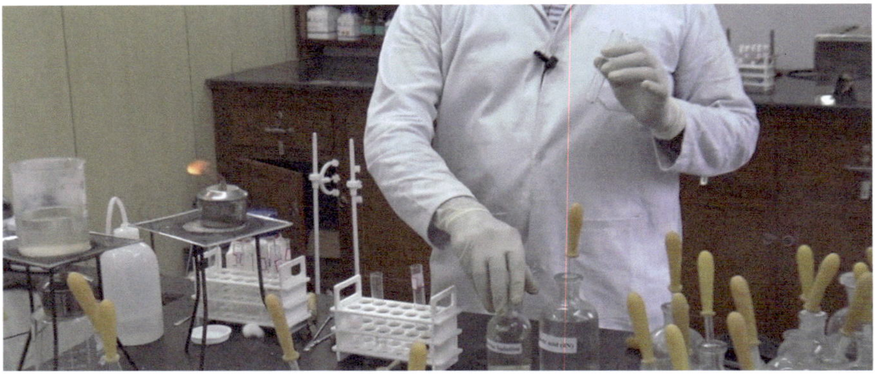

Fig. 2 Screenshot of AV lecture (BDP chemistry practical, NSOU). *Source* Audio–visual lecture program, official Web site NSOU (Accessed on January 9, 2018)

collected where the response to such support system was recorded. As already mentioned earlier, two post-graduation courses, commerce and social work, incorporated ICT-enabled learner's support system for the first time. As a result, it was feasible to analyze the pattern of responses for these ICT-enabled courses in a much more comprehensive way.

The pattern of response can be analyzed in two different ways:

- The age–gender ratio.
- The age–location (urban, semi-urban, rural) ratio.

These two parameters are crucial to analyze the way in which various sectors of the population enrolled in this particular institution are responding to the ICT that have just begun to flourish as an integral part of the teaching–learning process followed at NSOU.

The Age–Gender Ratio

In order to analyze the age–gender parameter, we have voluntarily analyzed the age-wise and gender-wise population structure responding to the various mechanisms of learner's support system followed in NSOU. The graphical representation below shows a comparative analysis of the typical responses recorded in two subsequent sessions, 2015–2017 and 2016–2018. Two underlying assumptions are needed to be taken care of: First, commerce is essentially a professional degree course; as a result, the enrollment of candidates belonging to the age group 25–40 years is the maximum. Secondly, it is a non-laboratory-based subject; as a result, the following inferences cannot be generalized and may have different results for more technical and non-technical subjects (Table 1).

Table 1 Statistical data representing the percentage of students (age- and gender-wise) enrolled in post-graduation commerce over two consecutive sessions

Sessions	Total no. of student	Age	No of student (in %)
2015–2017	503 (Male 76%, female 24%)	<25	24
		25–40	71
		>40	5
2016–2018	271 (Male 77%, female 23%)	<25	44
		25–40	52
		>40	4

Source Registrar Department, NSOU (2017)

The data above represents the admission data of post-graduation commerce for two consecutive sessions. The data clearly shows the percentage of male candidates for the years is more than that of female and the percentage of candidates belonging to age group 25–40 is maximum for both years while that of elderly learners remain negligible (Fig. 3).

The figure above shows a comparative analysis of the age- and gender-wise response to the ICT-enabled post-graduation course of commerce. The graph clearly portrays that for each age group, the response of female candidates compared to male candidates remains insignificant and quite low. On the other hand, if we take a deeper look at the age–gender ratio, for the age group 'below 25,' for both the sessions the rate of response ranges between 10 units and 100 units. On the other hand, the response for both males and females is maximum for the age group 25–40 and is the lowest for the elderly population. It can be, therefore, inferred that response to ICT is directly related to the number of candidates enrolled for that particular subject and so the response is maximum for the age group 25–40 years and nadir for the elderly section. However, what is necessary is to note that the female candidates are either not sufficiently empowered to use technology as a source of knowledge or are not that well informed about the alternatives available at their disposal (Table 2).

The data above represents the admission data of post-graduation social work for two consecutive sessions. The data reveals that the enrollment of female candidates is more than that of male candidates, and mostly, the middle-aged candidates have enrolled for acquiring post-graduation degree in social work (Fig. 4).

The data above represents the response (age–gender ratio) of the candidates enrolled for Masters of Social Work (MSW). The graph shows that there is a parity between the rate of response to ICT between the male and female candidates. Like commerce, social work is also a professional course and therefore the candidates mostly belong to the age group of 25–40. What also draws one's attention is the fact that in some cases responses of the female candidates have overseeded that of the males. The responses of the elderly learners remain meager. In case of a subject like social work, one can consider it to be obvious that enrollment of women candidates will be high; at the same time, the younger students do not consider social work to

Fig. 3 Graphical representation of response to ICT for post-graduation commerce over two consecutive sessions (age–gender ratio). *Source* Registrar Department, NSOU (2017)

Table 2 Statistical data representing the percentage of students (age- and gender-wise) enrolled in post-graduation social work over two consecutive sessions

Sessions	Total no of student	Age	No of student (in %)
2015–2017	1464 (Male 45.5%, female 54.5%)	<25	20
		25–40	74
		>40	6
2016–2018	1133 (Male 40%, female 60%)	<25	40
		25–40	56
		>40	4

Source Registrar Department, NSOU (2017)

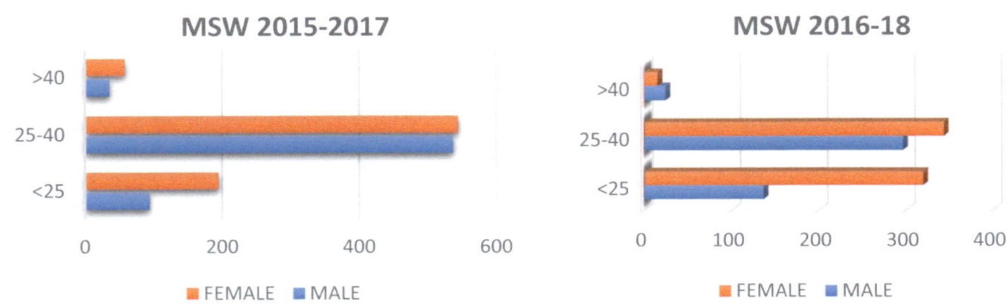

Fig. 4 Graphical representation of response to ICT for post-graduation social work for two consecutive sessions (age–gender ratio). *Source* Registrar Department, NSOU (2017)

be a career, unless they want to get associated with Social Welfare Organizations and non-governmental organizations (NGO). However, the responses of the females in all categories have overseeded that of the males; this shows that the rates of responses are related and determined by the nature of the subject and the course.

The Age–Location (Urban, Semi-urban, Rural) Ratio

Apart from the gender-wise analysis of the responses recorded for ICT-enabled learner's support system at NSOU, it is also important to understand the responses of the various sections of the population (defined in terms of their location). Taking into account India's digitization program and the present political regime's special emphasis on digitizing the rural pockets, it becomes essential to understand the rate of response of the ruralites and the semi-urban population. As a result, a modest attempt was taken to understand this ratio and analyze the parities and the disparities regarding the rate of responses from the different sectors of the population in West Bengal (Table 3).

The data clearly depicts the percentage of candidates belonging to the Urban, Semi-Urban, and Rural Areas, enrolled for Post-Graduation Commerce in the two consecutive sessions. The data shows that most of the candidates belong to the rural pockets of West Bengal and few hails from the semi-urban pockets. This shows that NSOU is able to meet its objective of reaching the remotest area of the state (Fig. 5).

The most distinguishing feature revealed by both the graphs is a very high response to ICT from the rural areas. The lowest response comes from the semi-urban areas and a somewhat sophisticated response is recorded from the urban pockets. Since the candidates in post-graduation commerce mostly belong to the

Table 3 Statistical data representing the demographic background of the students enrolled for post-graduation commerce in NSOU over two consecutive sessions

Sessions	Urban (%)	Semi-urban (%)	Rural (%)
2015–2017	39	9	52
2016–2018	32	11	57

Source Registrar Department, NSOU (2017)

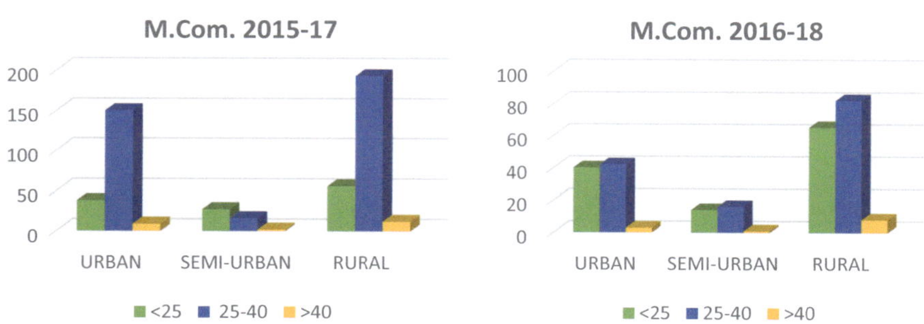

Fig. 5 Graphical representation of the response to ICT for post-graduation commerce for two consecutive sessions [the age–location (urban, semi-urban, rural) ratio]. *Source* Registrar Department, NSOU (2017)

age group 25–40 years, therefore highest response to ICT is recorded from this particular age group inhabiting in both rural and urban pockets. What also draws one's attention is the use of technology and communication networks in the rural pockets of West Bengal. A deeper look at the response recorded from the elderly learners, which remains insignificant in all the cases shows a sophisticated feedback from the rural areas. This high response from ruralites depicts that the digitization program and the subsequent digitization of the rural pockets of India have been a success story till date, and it also proves that ICT is being highly accepted by the most underprivileged section of the Indian society. However, what needs to be noted is the fact that the elderly population is not really accepting ICT as a medium of communication and information. Elderly response to ICT remains negligible whether the population belongs to the urban or the rural area (Table 4).

The picture portrayed in the above statistical data shows that maximum amount of candidates belongs to the rural areas, when it comes to post-graduation social work. In 2016–2018 session, 93% of the candidates enrolled were ruralites while very few candidates belong to the urban and semi-urban pockets. The case is the same for the previous session, where 86% of the candidates enrolled were rural (Fig. 6).

The above graphical representation shows the percentage response of the candidates to ICT-enabled course of post-graduation social work. The picture

Table 4 Graphical representation of the demographic background of the students enrolled for post-graduation social work in NSOU over two consecutive sessions

Sessions	Urban (%)	Semi-urban (%)	Rural (%)
2015–2017	8	6	86
2016–2018	4.50	2.50	93

Source Registrar Department, NSOU (2017)

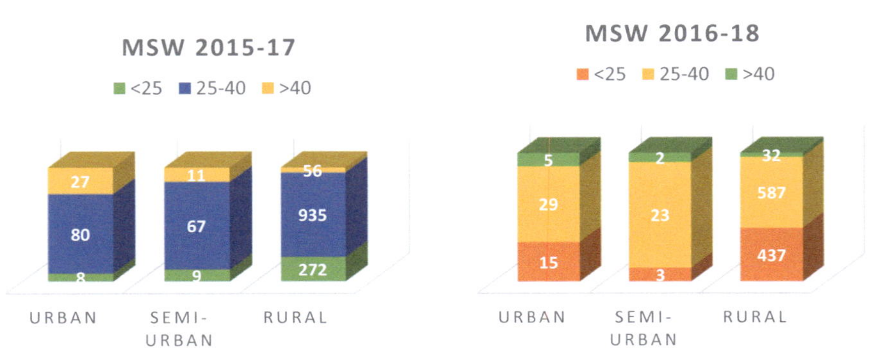

Fig. 6 Graphical representation of the response to ICT for post-graduation social work for two consecutive sessions [the age–location (urban, semi-urban, rural) ratio] *Source Registrar Department, NSOU (2017)*

resembles the disparity between the urbanites' response and the ruralites' response to ICT. The story here is somewhat similar to that of Masters of Commerce. Highest response is recorded from the candidates inhabiting the rural areas, and similarly, lowest response is recorded from the semi-urban pockets. For both the sessions, the regular students (age group below 25 years) show a poor response to ICT whereas the response of the elderly learners to ICT is comparatively better than that of commerce. What draws one's attention is the fact that in spite of the presence of an underlying assumption, that commerce and social work being professional degree courses attract middle-aged learners and so the response to ICT from this particular section of the batch is the highest; the negligible response from the elderly learners and the youths portrays a demeaning picture. There can be three reasons behind such a low response: first, the lack of motivation and the lack of temptation to achieve something better for the elderly generation of students; secondly, especially in the case of the elderly learners, the uncomfortableness of the candidates with smartphones and computers and their detachment from the use of computers for a long period of time; and thirdly, the fact that the younger generation does not consider degree in social work a potential career option and therefore does not enroll, unless they opt for NGO jobs. Moreover, in most cases it is often found that the elderly population, with few exceptions, suffers from a psychological setback in their failure to use Internet successfully; as a result, they restrict themselves from using laptops and smartphones and enjoy using conventional technologies.

From the statistical analysis of these two ICT-enabled courses, it is quite clear that the ICT incorporated learner's support system in NSOU has remained a success story as of now. Whether it will bring out some concrete positive results or whether it will be cost effective or whether it will accomplish the basic objective of the institution that is 'reaching the unreached' are matters of debates and discussions. But apparently it seems that ICT in education and especially distance education has played an important role in meeting the immediate objectives of the State Open University. What calls for necessary action is the elevated response from the ruralites, and this in general should play the pivotal role in making NSOU a more technology-driven educational institution. The goal of reaching the unreached, to put it more directly, the goal of promulgating education to rural population can be achieved more comprehensively through the inclusion of ICT as a potential mode of knowledge delivery.

Apart from these data analyses, an impersonal and informal interaction with the students of post-graduation history and post-graduation political science was arranged. The contrasting feature of these two courses with the other courses in the university drew the attention. Firstly, most of the enrolled candidates were rural, and secondly, there was a substantial amount of elderly candidates enrolled for both the courses. An interaction with this mix of students brought out some striking revelations regarding the newly incorporated ICT-enabled course delivery system. Most of the candidates from the young lot used smartphones and were successful in accessing the institutional OER and the series of audio–visual lectures. However, they pointed out that the university should immediately arrange for offline mode of the OER and audio–visual lecture series. Eight out of every ten candidates claimed that accessing the institutional Web site and the other support systems required Internet connectivity and claimed that they are deprived of mobile data connectivity due to lack of mobile tower installations in their locality. Apart from this younger lot, the other section of the student population belongs to the elderly category and it was observed that the entire section is comfortable when not using smartphone technology, let alone Internet and Web sites.

This informal observation helped us to realize that the response to ICT and the structure of the candidates enrolling in the university varies in accordance with the courses. For the earlier instances, as mentioned already, the courses were professional courses where middle-aged people enrolled the maximum. In spite of a substantial amount being ruralites, the response to ICT was sophisticated. This shows that such courses are mostly taken up by persons with some professional aptitude even those inhabiting in the rural sectors of West Bengal. This section is pretty acquainted with smart technologies, and being professionals and mostly associated with a professional career have learnt to access the Internet and arrange for connectivity irrespective of the degree of infrastructural development available at their disposal. On the contrary, out of the stereotypical conscience considering the subjects to be less recondite, those enrolling for history or political science are candidates who are of utmost backward in terms of the academic orientation. It can be assumed that they are unknown about the available alternatives regarding connectivity, they lack the motivation of ardently and devotedly concentrating on the academics, and this may be a reason for such a poor response to ICT from these courses.

Conclusion

Since the emergence of the concept of ICT in education, most of the universities whether regular or distance have begun to incorporate ICT in their mode of delivery. For regular universities, more emphasis is laid on features like smart classrooms and application-based software that enable access to information. But the entire process is challenging for open and distance learning institutes. The very definition of Open Universities includes the characteristic of the apparent absence of face-to-face contact between the teachers and the students. This absence of direct communication forces these institutions to depend highly on information technology. What distinguishes these distance learning institutions from the regular universities are the lesser amount of classroom lectures, the eclectic background of the learners, and the scattered location of the study centers. In order to deal with all such problems, ICT as a method of delivery of lectures and study materials is not only a logical idea but is actually one of the most effective tools in terms of cost and quality.

The success of the ICT-enabled learner's support system at NSOU has compelled the administrators and academicians associated with the institution to rethink about the prospects and benefits of ICT. Since 2016 the university has enhanced its efforts to include ICT in all its courses. As already mentioned earlier, the biggest breakthrough was the launch of Open Educational Resource Repository and the launch of the audio–video lectures. ICT as a tool empowers teachers as it proves to be effective instructional aide; it empowers the students as they can easily access the educational resources, but the greatest benefit is reaped by the institution itself as it makes the task of propagating knowledge in the remotest of the remote areas, a facile task. However, the increasing demand for offline accessibility of the OER Repository and the audio–visual lecture series should be given a thought. What is important is to note that Open Universities due to their flexibility has an access to students with eclectic background. Hence, while designing the course structure as well as the support systems and instructional aides, it is important that the authorities take into account all feasible measures in order to ensure that each and every student get the opportunity to avail all the viable options of accessing knowledge.

However, the inexplicable response to ICT from the rural areas for certain courses shows that the digitization program has had a tremendous effect in the rural pockets of the country but for a selective majority only. The assumption that smartphones are in great use among the ruralites now seems to be a fact although one can be skeptic about the degree to which Internet is being used in the rural areas. The study presented above shows a consistently contrasting picture regarding the response of the ruralites to ICT. But the problem lies with the semi-urban and the urban pockets. It is important to understand that the urbanites are exposed to technology for a greater period of time and being used to the pros and cons of the technology they are no more enthusiastic to use ICT as a means to access knowledge. What is also important is to note that the urban and the semi-urban population are exposed to a number of other MOOCs and OERs and therefore are not solely dependent on the institutional sources. In case of the elderly population, the rate of enrollment of the elderly learner's at NSOU as of now is negligible. Hence, excessive effort in promoting ICT as an aide for this particular section of the population should not be the primary target, rather enhancing the capabilities of the university and investing more time, energy, and money in developing ICT as the core method of delivering knowledge, and targeting the ruralites should be the primary objective of NSOU in particular and other Open Universities of the country in general.

However, effective use of ICT as a method of instruction requires knowledge and skill on the part of the faculty members. Special orientation programs for the faculties of science subjects are required, as science is a technical field which requires extensive and excruciating laboratory work. While using ICT as a means of instruction, high-level skill and technical knowledge should be at disposal to deal with complexities of the laboratory-based discipline. What also needs to be introspected is the prospects of creating a mobile application. Carrying laptops are now outmoded. More user-friendly and portable devices like tablets and smartphones with high-class operating system are in use. Hence, Web sites, although can be accessed through these devices, mobile applications are much more appropriate and simple.

ICT in distance education was essentially a breakthrough approach. In this context, the government's action and motivation to launch Digital India program and the subsequent development of *Swayam* and *Swayam Prabha* under University Grants Commission, Ministry of Human Resource Development, Government of India, seems to act as a catalyst in the process of digitizing education. The United Nation's objective of promoting lifelong learning has acquired a new dimension since the incorporation of ICT in education and especially in third world countries like India where the rate of illiteracy and population is so high that a welfare state like India cannot provide education as a basic social good. However, the success and failure, the pros and cons, the drawbacks and benefits of ICT in education will surely be revealed in the near future, but as a fledging concept, ICT seems to override the conventional mode and bring about an iconoclastic change in the educational orientation of the nation.

References

Biswas, P. K. (1999). Freshers in IGNOU: A study of their awareness, interests and motivation. *Indian Journal of Open Learning, 8*(3), 273.

Chandra, Ramesh. (2005). *Technology use in open learning system* (p. 4). New Delhi: Kalpaz Publications.

Kentor, H. E. (2015). Distance education and the evolution of online learning in united states. *Curriculum and Teaching Dialogue, 17*(1) & (2), 273.

Marchessou, F. (1999). From instructional technology (IT) to open and distance learning (ODL): A brief overview of educational technology in Western Europe. *Educational and Technology Research and Development, 47*(1), 114.

Panneer Selvam, S. K. (2012). *Distance Education as a Dynamic Role*, (p. 4). New Delhi: Random Publications.

Shamsu, S. (2012). Emerging paradigm of information and communication technologies in education: The Indian context. *Indian Journal of Open Learning, 21*(3), 211.

Tackling Challenges for Higher Education: Learner Support Services for Distance Learning for Sustainable Collaborative Learning Communities

Suma Parahakaran

Introduction

Distance learning has encouraged more learners to engage in flexible learning. To create an engaged and sustainable learning group of learners, it takes more effort as it involves creating supportive groups of learners so that learning becomes meaningful and motivating.

There are many challenges in the developing countries that are constraints for the sustenance of big groups in online learning. A successful institution can facilitate support from external experts for their contribution where learning is concerned. A few important factors that emerged during the review of studies are listed below in this chapter. These factors have a direct or indirect impact on learner support for distance learning.

- External contribution from experts
- Peer support and skill support (affective skills)
- Financial stability
- Knowledge- and experience-based learning
- Community-based support services (research and practices)
- Social forums/informal forums
- Technical assistance
- Library services
- Expert lecturers/tutors
- Delivery services (administrative support)
- Service learning
- Subject-specific academic counselling
- Assignments and examination preparation through counselling.

S. Parahakaran (✉)
Wawasan Open University, Georgetown, Malaysia
e-mail: sumjayan@gmail.com

© Springer Nature Singapore Pte Ltd. 2018

Anjana (ed.), *Technology for Efficient Learner Support Services in Distance Education*, https://doi.org/10.1007/978-981-13-2300-3_13

The success of online learning depends on the support services provided by the universities. Support services include administrative support, technical assistance when needed and orientation for learners on the use of technology. Distance learning has different learning platforms. An example is the learning management systems which require students to engage in formal discussions. The technical issues in universities and the initial orientation needed to log on and use the system require the learner to acquire skills which should be supported by the university. The datelines of assignments, technical operations and logistics are other obstacles students face when they are working adults that cause them learner anxiety. Their learning and anxiety issues can be solved if learners have easy access to peers for solutions and learn skills from them. The collaborative skills are enabled when learners can contact their peers and the facilitator facilitates these skills.

Mohanachandran and Ramalu (2013) stated that the increasing trend using online distance learning has been encouraging and learners have to keep up as the management of quality assurance is developed and maintained. As a result, learners have to plan and manage their learning as they continue their working life. According to the researchers, apart from the programmes that the learner has to learn there are skills such as writing, using computers and English language skills that have to be upgraded. Malaysian Open Universities or distance learning universities have seen a rise in student enrolment, exceeding 100,000 students according to Mohanachandran and Ramalu (2013). Their review stated that the retention rate of students is a huge challenge. The reasons are because they have to work and learn at the same time and they have to motivate themselves to continue learning. ODL learners are usually isolated from their peers and tutors, and a lack of immediate help from their tutors impacts learners. Learners from ODL are far from their peers. Some of the factors that learners reported state that they feel lazy and they have too much work at office and accessing libraries after office hours. These factors according to the researchers cause high student retention.

Informal discussion forums will play a very important role in student learning. Peer discussions take place in the form of social media, mobile text communications and during group meetings. As a facilitator, the role of the lecturer becomes important to bridge connections between students and the lecturer after he or she has oriented students in their roles as a learner. The author is an online tutor, and it was noted that in many instances text messages on mobile helped students to interact with each other especially when the facilitation was on an informal basis. Students who lack confidence will communicate personally rather in the group chat. Learner anxiety is mostly due to either not knowing how to prepare for examination or the assignments. The author as a tutor had to remind students that the process of learning is more important than the end results. This is the most crucial aspect that impacts student learning, and hence, learning communities are important for long-term success of students. When competent online graduate learners were asked what additional support they required using Whatsapp mode, their responses were; extra materials to be provided to learners either through email or LMS systems, more activated discussion (emphasise sharing and caring), providing them more Web site to gain specific materials for more content knowledge, more communications with the tutors, to know more of specific techniques related to the subjects. In addition, learners added that the assignments provided required learners to collaborate with another partner. This project was successful with six pairs, and two of the learners found it challenging as one of them did not know how to use the online platform for submission of assignments and was less competent in English. Motivation and techniques are required to guide learners to examination techniques and for assignments. These findings were obtained and are used for an ongoing study by the author.

The different reviews of contributions on student support services revealed that there are two outstanding ideas which will improve student support services. They are teaching and support services which must be aligned together and to know that there are technologies to help all learners, fulfilling to achieve aims and objectives, both general and specific needs (Gil-Juarena 2014). For example, according to Olivier (2016) the study with 1015 learners to investigate the impact of face-to-face sessions and online discussion forums on academic performance of learners provided a number of findings. The unique setting of Africa and its socio-economic conditions of learners could have contributed to the low attendance of contact sessions. This resulted in the late submission of assignments, less contact with their lecturers and preparing late for their examinations. The other finding was that the attendance of learners for contact sessions and the utilisation of online discussion forum by learners were extremely low. There should be more contact sessions with tutors or expert teachers so that the assignments and examination results can be better.

Roberts (2004) stated that although institutions face financial constraints for funding learners, learners will not drop out at a larger rate if they are supported. It would be logical according to Roberts to allocate more funds for learner support. The survey conducted by WICHE Cooperative for Educational Technologies (WCET) surprisingly found that learners were charged equal to or more to study online and the costs increased when new technology was integrated (Straumsheim 2017). There is limited information on this in developing nations, and hence, learners are not aware of the differences in the cost compared to learning in normal classrooms.

Gao (2012) in a study of six ICT-based distance educational institutions summarised the findings related to learner support. The distance learners from the six ICT-based educational institutions preferred to have better administrative support services compared to interactivity-related support services. The learners have very low rate of interactivity or group work, and they had only surface approach to learning. Therefore, it was concluded that the whole process of learning for learners did not prescribe to deep learning or higher-order thinking skills. Learners expected that the input from tutors was preferable compared to inputs from peer learners. From the literature, it was also found that small group work helped learners to practise collaborative work which could be extended to their working lives. The culture of collaborative group learning depends on the design of the curriculum, assessment or evaluation. According to Gao (2012), the curriculum must be designed for collaborative learning and assessment tasks to be prepared accordingly as the current ways of assessment to assess the learner without collaborative task will result only in shallow learning approaches. The external contribution from experts is an important aspect for quality learning in higher education. Distance learning although supports academic learning; it does not guarantee practical knowledge unless the support systems enable facilitation of knowledge with projects. Lessons learnt from case studies by the OECDE reinforce that there has to be innovative approaches and practices for meaningful learning that extends to workplaces (Hénard and Roseveare 2012).

> There is a strong drive to build and create knowledge together with an understanding of working life and reformulate the concept of knowledge in learning situations. Tighter connections with working life through different academic projects provide authentic opportunities to learn both generic and professional competencies as well as to build networks and pathways for employment after graduation (Hénard & Roseveare 2012, p. 8).

Henard and Roseveare (2012) asserted that delivery of contents is not just the priority of this time and it has to move towards other skills if learners are to progress in their learning. Furthermore, other mediated experiences are interwoven as real-life skills required for their working life are met.

Similar issues were noted with learners who learnt in Zimbabwe Open University. The study by researchers revealed findings that stated that they had lack of sufficient time for study, difficulties in accessing and using ICT, lack of study materials and feedback (Musingafi et al. 2015). The service quality is found to be of utmost important which has an impact on the success of the institution (Hamid and Yip 2016).

Lack of student participation in student forums in developing countries is due to either lack of time, lack of confidence or lack of sufficient competencies to use the language. Adult learners who are working or students in higher education do not continue with the same peers as in school, and hence, there is a need to facilitate communicative capacities with isolated learners to enable collaborative learning communities to be successful. It is through communication and discussion of issues that experiential learning occurs of contexts of the topics and the processes that take place related to it. Learners can then access data collection without much difficulties.

According to the report of reviews from University of Wisconsin-Green Bay (Hanover Research 2014), first-year seminars at UW Green Bay incorporated competencies as a part of their programmes for learners such as oral communications, data analysis and critical thinking skills. Class size was small, and learners were introduced to sessions such as interactions with faculty members, use of resources and co-curricular activities. The participants who took part in the seminar had a 10% higher retention rate compared to the 2010 cohorts. The Florida State

University with 32,500 undergraduate learners had provided extra attention to retention rates, and they found six strategies to support retention. They are expanded academic service, a structured programme to encourage those learners who were undecided, bi-weekly coaching for students, expanding tutoring services and special programme to assist students (Hanover Research 2014). These support systems retain students, but the universities have to extend their goals of education to relate to learner's long-term development which helps them to persevere and continue without doubts in the faculty that they enrol in.

In order that the learner is supported, apart from allocation of scholarships for students, the platforms in the Open Universities can allow learning communities to contribute their work to societies as a part of their project work in areas learners are interested in gaining experiential skills. Where assignments and project delivery are concerned, learners require external network with organisations and field experts. Lack of affective skills (communicative capacities, collaborative attitudes, positive interaction) has an impact on their level of success with their work when they are placed in employment. When such opportunities are provided, learner's retention rate will be low and the projects they are involved in engage them in real-life contexts.

Vicky Philips in the USA, the leading customer advocate for online students, provided a number of reviews from students who took up online distance learning. Common issues were about missing or disengaged professors, poor customer service and advising, dislike the group assignments and team projects, poor quality control and course designs (Philips 2017) (https://www.geteducated.com/elearning-education-blog/5-things-real-students-hate-about-online-learning-degrees/).

What Matters at the End of University Education?

The university is seen as a place where there are complex processes occurring within a teaching and learning environment which is knowledge-based to meet the goals of higher education.

The assessment criteria focus more on knowledge and experiential learning in specific fields for higher education. The Consensus Study Reports that the competencies leaders in higher education were targeting were intrapersonal competencies (ethics and lifelong learning) and intrapersonal competencies such as teamwork and intercultural understanding. These were the desired outcomes that were seen as significant for work and lifelong learning once graduates left university as reported in the Consensus Study Reports published by the National Academies of Science (National Academies of Sciences, Engineering and Medicine 2017, p. 19).

In the developing countries, many learners have taken up TESOL courses for distance learning. Some of the required skills learners are required to know before they start teaching are skills related to collaborative learning. A few examples are identifying skills based on a variety of sources, matching the skills to language objectives, learning how to integrate current technologies into instruction such as e-portfolios, collaborative networking, collaborative projects and social networking. These different skills are required, and learner collaboration with tutors and peers as well as people from their network is essential skills (Thacher, n.d). In varied disciplines, the skills required are different and a learner can no longer learn in isolation.

Community Service and Lifelong Learning

Currently, there is a disconnect between student learning and lifelong learning because of the diverging views of individual universities and there is less collaboration among universities. The issues in society are solved by experts without integrating knowledge of common expertise into a common platform for future use. Students can learn through experiences directly when they work with issues in local and global contexts from online educational resources. This will enable building of collaboratively informed knowledge which can be used for solving issues and increase their skills, knowledge and professional experiences over time. These integrated approaches help towards building a sustainable community. In Africa, the ABET department also encouraged more group discussions, tutorials and radio (added tutorials) (Phineas 2012). The new research outputs especially where technology is concerned such as STEM education have become popular in the education industry. However, there is a need to collaborate with external agencies to understand what is the necessity of the community. The solutions to various issues and innovative practices now require the knowledge and competencies which are interdisciplinary, technological assisted and require honest communications. The online learning platforms have become powerful but yet have not been tapped for collaborative dissemination of knowledge of research findings on broader issues such as health, economy, medical and social issues. The lack of collaboration within universities to serve community is lacking and works independently because of competitions among universities and the fight for survival.

Stoll, Bolam, McMohan, Wallace and Thomas (2006) stated that as collective capacities increase, such learning will lead to sustainable lifelong learning. According to the researchers, their research review reported features such as shared values and vision, collective responsibility, reflective professional enquiry and collaboration (Parahakaran 2015). In developing countries, the universities face issues related to cutting costs with the implementation of online learning and wider use of technology. In addition, there is an increase in marketing by higher institutions for higher student intakes and a struggle to retain students.

Importance of Learning Communities, Research and Development

The rise of online learning, co-curricular learning through projects and assignments of "learning to do" will lead to a rise in learning communities and specific specialised courses. With the rise of STEM for Science and Technology, more learning assignments will require external and industry linked support. Online educational resources are available, and the open access system has enabled more people to have access to reading materials where developing countries are able to access. High-quality materials are available in specialised journals, and these are not accessible to common man for research and development except for educators and students from universities who have access to them. This is a setback for developing countries who do not have access to the materials because of the high costs to access quality journal articles. It is imperative that universities tie up with organisations whose curriculum is aligned with similar targets and goals which the organisations work for. For example, universities that work with tourism can align their goals and vision and tweak their curriculum with tourism sectors locally and globally. They can support tourism industries, and the research conducted on real-life contexts can lead to supporting such industries to do better. The two-way benefits will enable a better transition for students to enter the work field. Research in developing countries can be disseminated to as many people as possible.

An example of learning to do project that was successful was the collaboration of higher education institutes (HEIs) in the United Arab Emirates (UAE) and a public-sector organisation (PSO) to promote heritage, history and culture in the tourism sector. The partnership was formed in 2012. The projects started off with PSO being able to use the available resources and creativity of HEI. The cross-discipline and joint marketing project was developed to also rewire the curriculum and PSO needs. By June 2013, all students were involved in projects which led to recommendations and resources to support PSO by increasing awareness and number of clients. The projects were not easily manageable as different disciplines had their own approaches but the staff found that the experience increased student motivation, personal development and overall learning experience. The study findings provided values that inform and highlight the importance of technology and informal relationships through collaborations (Minhas and Perret 2017).

Another project undertaken by students was the experiential learning opportunities in food systems. According to researchers, their findings through surveys, case studies and analysis, student learning outcomes provide motivation and contribute to academic achievements. Students had valued experiences which supported them to acquire jobs and careers. The learning experiences include developing practical skills for problem-solving, increasing critical skills, enhanced awareness from critical thinking and reflections from shared experiences. These reflective experiences and dealing directly with life issues help foster understanding of life and its challenges beyond school curriculum. The knowledge thus obtained can help students to develop new innovations and face difficulties in life which is beyond their life challenges in institutes (Kaplan et al. 2016). These different developmental processes become part of students' co-curricular learning and assignments for projects.

Kalam and Srijan (2015) from India stated that industries treat research as a burden and not as an investment. Hence, these sectors, of research and industry, have to be combined to increase the economy of any country. In 2012, China's contribution to research and development was 296 billion dollars, which was under 2% of its gross domestic product, while USA spent 405 billion dollars, 2.7% of its gross domestic product. Japan and South Korea spent more, which was 3.7% and 4.4%, respectively, of their gross domestic production and on research and development (Parahakaran 2015).

The quality of research (taking into account ethics, stakeholder's contribution, criteria for policymakers and criteria for strengthening communities) will depend on political agendas. With the use of open access online resources by researchers from universities, organisations and NGOs, it is possible to move into lifelong learning and reduce costs of establishing new avenues and laboratories for implementing projects. The model provided below will give a conceptual view of sustainable learning communities. The issues of plagiarism, use of resources without permission, utility costs, staff payment for laboratories or practicum hours are issues on the side of the coin which universities have to be responsible for. An example is the issues of unethical ways of the use of IT in a study of two countries, conducted in 2012 by Chatterjee et al. (2012). The unethical ways technology was used were because of complex interwoven factors (social, moral, technology facilitation). Other issues can be related to the ways staff uses information from the Internet, falsification of data, misuse of resources, etc.

According to the reviewers, from case studies in Melbourne, their findings proposed that partnerships between communities, universities and private sector will be on the rise. The universities see the partnerships with the other universities and non-public sectors as boosting the social prosperity apart from increase in the status of economy (The Economist Intelligence Unit 2008, p. 12).

There are ways by which documenting solutions to community issues from the research conducted by universities and community practices to the public can support the community on what works and what does not work. Furthermore, it increases the competencies of non-profit organisations to conduct their own research and implement such programmes. The supportive partnerships between the results in the growth of community capacities increased access to higher education institutions and its resources, solving of issues within the communities and the collaboration with a university which provides sustainable learning to communities around them (Pasque et al. 2005).

Documentary analysis by Brown, Anderson and Murray (2007) revealed that e-learning policy and strategies from 2000 to 2005 in nine countries and six states and e-learning initiatives place a larger emphasis on formal education. The emphasis on formal education has not enabled them to access information of real-life issues related to both financial and social services. Similar situations resonate with e-learning in Asian countries. This is reflected from review of the use of technology below by The Economist Intelligence Unit.

> Although university participants view these changes as having a largely positive impact, many institutions struggle with the twin challenges of rising information technology (IT) costs and the need to avoid technological obsolescence. In addition, insufficient resources, a lack of adequate instructional design staff and other technological support issues can also impede the adoption of new technologies. Despite these challenges, most believe that technology will become ever more interwoven into the fabric of academic life (The Economist Intelligence Unit 2008, p. 5).

New Model for Sustainable Education

This section of the chapter emphasises that higher educational practices leading to self-development and community development can lead to sustainability of low-cost distance learning, experiential learning, ethical competencies that will be far reaching compared to the current trends. When learners are required to complete a research on their own, they have to propose a topic which would otherwise be channelled to solve a common problem in society. When they are aware of the issues in society through community, service learners are able to question when and why certain issues occur and would be able to conduct research on those topics beneficial to the community. A recent issue with STEM education and the outcome of STEM education depicted that there is a disconnect between learning, research and community.

Linking Research, Learning and Community Projects

Some of the questions asked by partnering bodies are provided below.

What is required by society?

What knowledge exists related to the needs of the society?

What kind of field experts can provide support to distance learning and experiential learning?

What is the expected outcome?

Who will the knowledge be disseminated to?

What are the ethical aspects to be considered during communications, practices and preparation for the research?

Who are the people learners have to report to?

What are the services required for learners to complete tasks related to learning, research and community services?

What policies are in place and how practices can be carried out?

Who does the negotiations and how would it be win-win situation for the universities and the organisations linked to it?

What kind of technological help or laboratory assistance is needed for such research to be completed?

Firstly, tertiary education institutions could include community service (service learning) as part of their programmes so that students undertake experiential learning on issues relevant within their local contexts.

As learners work with partnering institutions, field experts, public services, they are able to gain skills and competencies which will help in the development of the communities. Learners will also learn ethical ways of conducting research as they will be trying to solve issues of the community rather than just gaining enough knowledge and access to data to complete their degree courses.

In order that education prepares them for developing the nation, open access information or knowledge management have become possible with online learning resources (OERs). These OERs have to be fine-tuned and integrated with values and ethics course component that focuses on current issues in both local and international contexts. The integration will help community development and enhance social responsibility in citizens. With the rising number of NGOs and corporate social responsibility projects, it is evident that the support is possible for universities to move forward (Parahakaran 2015). The issues related to social, economic, health and environmental fields can be supported with peer to peer as well as networking at different levels with online learning systems. A sustainable model would help societies in the long run. Learning communities consist of learning which includes knowledge management, critical thinking skills required to solve issues or create innovative ideas and networking. Research approaches will include service learning in both local and global contexts so that they become reflective practitioners. As mentioned earlier, the research output can be contributed to the body of knowledge through online educational resources.

Learner Support Through Partnerships, Educational Practices and Fundamental Goals of Higher Education for Community Development

Learner support for personal and community development depends on the practices obtained from higher education. Unless the university provides platforms for learners to understand real-life contexts and help them to learn about issues in their own communities and prepare learners to develop their own competencies, the developing countries will have issues. The resulting issues occur when more new technologies are developed and the cost rises.

As stated in the above sections, the issues of learner support are challenging but learners are looking for courses worth their time and money so that they have access to jobs. Distance learning should support easier organisations and completion of tasks easier although there are arguments by stakeholders that with rising costs of technology, and costs to cover their learning, the fees for courses are almost similar to face-to-face tutorials. The discontinuity between learners' learning goals and their job placements, rising costs of tuition fees and their struggle to meet up with demands of assessment is challenging. The rising issues with today's jobs which have integrated technology in almost spheres of working life have a lot to contribute to this.

An investigation of unethical use of information technology using a tested model (Chatterjee et al. 2012) with young adults in the USA and Finland revealed that the unethical use of IT is influenced by social, situational and technological aspects. Mazurkiewicz and Poteralska (2017) explored the technology transfer barriers and challenges by research and development organisations. The researchers reported that there are different orientations existing between the technology provider (research and development) and business sectors. There are imperfect communications between the technical information transmission between the R&D and the business world at the initial stages of development. In addition, the kind of technology created by R&D may not be suitable or adaptable to the market outside, thus focusing more on research results and not how suitable it is for the market. The differences arise when researchers from the science department have stable processes in the way academics work while the industry outside is ever changing in their demands. The researchers state the most significant point that key projects which contribute to the economy must be evaluated by experts with the highest practical understanding of how things work actually in society.

The divide between research and development and the business markets outside, unethical use of technology, learners' retention rates and the cost of technology call for more partnerships between research and participants who use them for economical purposes for the market outside. An example is the case of a weed-killing robot developed by the Queensland University that would cut the cost of weed control by 90%, which would save the farm sector 1.3 billion dollars a year. The robotic weed killer is capable of killing weeds using artificial intelligence, using a 3 million investment from the government and hoped to be solar powered. Mr. De Paoli, managing director of Austchilli, largest farm in Australia, stated that he would not be ready to purchase it until he is convinced to buy the robot. He would rather work with his commercial people and people who work everyday with the problems before he ventures into buying the robot. He also stated that unless the real world and the research world experiences are aligned he would not purchase it regardless of the benefits for farming the robot demonstrated. The differences between technology and research and development not only cost the people who invest money but become deterrents between the R&D and the public. It is all the more important that the learners who are future entrepreneurs and who will enter the technical fields have a hands-on approach to the issues in real-life contexts during their study in higher education. They will also be motivated to learn as they gain experience to practically learn skills and will not drop out of the universities (http://www.abc.net.au/news/rural/2016-10-21/weed-killing-robot-could-save-billions/7954680).

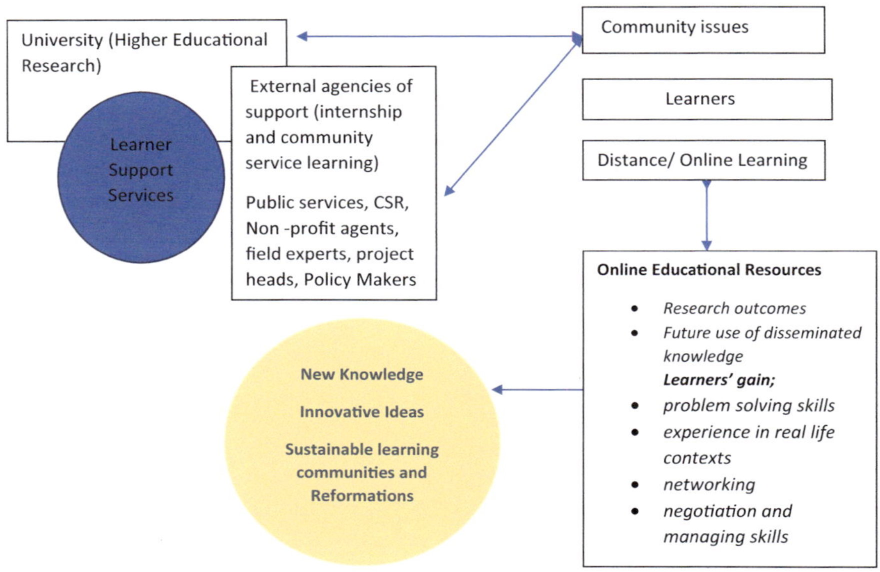

Learner Support Through Partnerships, Educational Practices and Fundamental Goals of Higher Education for Community Development

The goal of higher education is seen as an avenue for learners to be educated with knowledge and skills required for civic engagement.

Universities' efforts to educate learners should allow innovative practices to flourish. When learning is integrated with discovery learning, learners can suit learning for serving society's needs and community partnerships help universities to achieve their fundamental purpose (Fitzgerald et al. 2012). These experiences increase learners' skills to increase their capacities. When institutions of higher learning focus on solving real-world issues and they work with communities, their aims of educating learners for citizenship enable them to contribute to society (Pasque et al. 2005).

Basaza et al. (2010) reflected on their findings in Uganda with distance education in Uganda. They stated that the factors impacting distance education are poor infrastructure, high cost of an education, irrelevant curriculum, insufficient expertise in distance education and lack of motivation towards distance learning. The authors also stressed that without the collaboration of government, educational institutions and business communities the success rate will be very minimal. The difficulties can be solved if there is collaboration between people and communities.

Currently, the focus of the university has no fixed goals for serving the community. Partnerships with public services, NGOs and outside agents support the growth of interns and provide learners opportunities for learning more of their specific fields of interest. Learning communities thus formed will help learners to gain competencies in decision making, communication and teach skills through experiential learning. In addition to this, learners are able to understand the working conditions, the code of ethics followed in the companies they are attached to. In reality, learners require to know how the market works and the complex issues and they have to be communicable as well as practical in all their endeavours. The opportunities to conduct research based on their working contexts and with real-life issues help learners understand how their local contexts work. With such opportunities, the research outcomes can be disseminated in open access through a collaborative approach. Such learning communities will work for the common good and help communities they work using new knowledge created and practically implementable innovative ideas.

James L. Madara who is the CEO of the American Medical Association stated the following.

From ineffective electronic health records, to an explosion of direct-to-consumer digital health products, to apps of mixed quality, [these products are] the digital snake oil of the early twenty-first century (Madara 2017).

Madara also added that the digital tools in medicine unlike digital tools used in other industries are not efficient enough (Madara 2017).

Sustainability of Learning Communities for the Future

As the world is becoming smaller, the range of technologies is wider with multiple apps and gadgets conquering the tasks generations had been struggling with. When artificial intelligence and technology dominate by replacing human tasks, learners will be required to work with collegiality and information has to be networked. The learning communities may dominate the future, and the universities will have to adapt to such situations. When research is connected to community development, the outcome is new knowledge and learners gain experiential support. The challenge according to the researchers is to provide scholarship, and civic learning should play a significant role in faculty's professional work (Mallory 2005).

> The concern that community engagement means more work for the faculty assumes that engagement involves a separate set of activities distinct from the core professional work of research and teaching. In reality, however, community engagement is not distinct from, but is integral to, all other professional work: it motivates and contributes to research and scholarship, teaching and learning. Community engagement does not impose an additional burden on the faculty but changes and redirects the conduct of inquiry and the process of learning (Mallory 2005, p. 24).

Conclusion

The developing nations while struggling with the budget controls in universities will have to adapt to new ways of communications and coordination by maximising funds for the benefit of the society and providing learning skills which will enhance learners' expertise in professional development. Partnerships and collaborations between universities and future workplaces that results in learners' skill development will retain learners and strengthens the capacity of the university to retail learners unlike what the current situation in universities.

The future of the universities depends on quality services they provide and the new and innovative policies they integrate within the framework of their curriculum. Educators and technologists, industries, schools and NGO's partnerships will in the long term bring about sustainable learning communities. This way the burden of budget allocation is reduced, and collaborative groups demand less effort from their instructors as peer tutoring, and expert help is sought from the community around them. Such significant changes will result in research outputs which are more aligned to needs of the communities, and the university is able to negotiate with users.

References

Basaza, N. G., Milman, N. B., & Wright, C. R. (2010). The challenges of implementing distance education in Uganda: A case study. *The International Review of Research in Open and Distributed Learning [IRRODL], 11*(2). Athabasca University. Retrieved from http://www.irrodl.org/index.php/irrodl/article/view/833/154.

Brown, M., Anderson, B., & Murray, F. (2007). E-learning policy issues: Global trends, themes and tensions. In *ICT: Providing choices for learners and learning*. Proceedings ascilite Singapore 2007. http://www.ascilite.org.au/conferences/singapore07/procs/brown-m.pdf.

Chatterjee, S., Valacich, J., & Sarker, S. (2012). *HICSS '12 Proceedings of the 2012 45th Hawaii international conference on system sciences* (pp. 3017–3080). Washington: IEEE Computer Society. https://doi.org/10.1109/hicss.2012.621.

Fitzgerald, H. E., Bruns, K., Sonka, S., Furco, A., & Swanson, L. (2012). The centrality of engagement in higher education. *Journal of Higher Education Outreach and Engagement, 16* (3), 7–28.

Gao, S. (2012). *Learner support for distance learners: A study of six cases of ICT-based distance education institutions in China*. Stockholm University.

Gil-Juarena, I. (2014). Student support services in open and distance education. *Open Praxis, 6*(1), 3–4.

Hamid, S. F., & Yip, N. (2016). Service quality in distance education using the Gronroos model. *The Social Sciences (Medwell Journals), 11*(Special issue 6), 7199–7025. Retrieved from http://docsdrive.com/pdfs/medwelljournals/sscience/2016/7199-7205.pdf.

Henard, F., & Roseveare, D. (2012). Fostering quality teaching in higher education: Policies and practices. OECD, IMHE (Programme on Institutional Management in Higher Education). Retrieved from http://www.oecd.org/edu/imhe/QT%20policies%20and%20practices.pdf.

Kalam, A. P. J., & Singh, S. P. (2015). Advantage India: From challenge to opportunity. *Building the human resource: From Demographic dividend to actual advantage* (p. 66). India: HarperCollins.

Madara, J. (2017). Future challenges of digital healthcare. Newsletter. By Linda Brookes, M.Sc. Published Wednesday 26, April 26, 2016. Retrieved from https://www.medicalnewstoday.com/articles/317022.php.

Mallory, B. L. (2005). Reflections on the wingspread experience. In *Higher education collaboratives for community engagement and improvement*. University of Michigan. Retrieved from https://files.eric.ed.gov/fulltext/ED515231.pdf.

Mohanachandran, D. K., & Ramalu, S. (2013). Work and schooling challenges of open distance learning: Case study. *Research Journal of Social Science and Management, 2*(10). Retrieved from www.theinternationaljournal.org.RJSSM.

Maxwell, C. C., Musingafi, M. C. C, Barbra Mapuranga, B., Kudzai Chiwanza, K., & Zebron, S. (2015). Challenges for open and distance learning (ODL) students: Experiences from students of the Zimbabwe open university. *Journal of Education and Practice, 6*(18). Retrieved from https://files.eric.ed.gov/fulltext/EJ1079750.pdf.

Minhas, W., Perret, J. (2017). A UAE case study: Experiential learning through effective educational partnerships. *Journal of Applied Research in Higher Education, 9*(2), 304–312. https://doi.org/10.1108/JARHE-09-2014-0078.

Mazurkiewicz, A., & Poteralska, B. (2017). Technology transfer barriers and challenges faced by R&D organisations. In *7th International Conference on Engineering, Project, and Production Management. Procedia Engineering, 182*, 457–465. Retrieved from https://www.sciencedirect.com/science/article/pii/S1877705817312705.

National Academics of Sciences, Engineering and Medicine. (2017). Supporting students' college success: The role of assessment of intrapersonal competencies. Washington, DC: The National Academics Press.

Olivier, B. H. (2016). The impact of contact sessions and discussion forums on the academic performance of open distance learning students. *International Review of Research in Open and Distributed Learning, 17*(6). University of South Africa. Retrieved from http://www.irrodl.org/index.php/irrodl/article/view/2493/3963.

Parahakaran, S. (2015). Designing and evaluating collaborative projects in learning communities: Innovative practices and strategies. *International Journal of Advanced Corporate Learning (iJAC)*. New York: ICELW.

Pasque, P., Smerek, R., Dwyer, B., Bowman, N., & Mallory, B. (Eds.). (2005). Higher education collaboratives for community engagement and improvement. University of Michigan, School of Education: National Forum on Higher Education for the Public Good. Retrieved from https://files.eric.ed.gov/fulltext/ED515231.pdf.

Phineas, B. G. (2012). Learner support in open and distance learning context: A case study of ABET programmes at the University of South Africa. University of South Africa (UNISA). Doctoral thesis. Retrieved from http://citeseerx.ist.psu.edu/viewdoc/download?doi=10.1.1.1016.4400&rep=rep1&type=pdf.

Roberts, D. (2004). Learner support in South African distance education: A case study. University of South Africa. Retrieved from http://citeseerx.ist.psu.edu/viewdoc/download?doi=10.1.1.618.4794&rep=rep1&type=pdf.

Websites

Brooks, L. (2017). Future challenges for digital healthcare. Published 26 April. Retrieved from https://www.medicalnewstoday.com/articles/317022.php.

Philips, V. (2018, August). 5 things real students hate about online learning degrees. GetEducated.com; Approved Colleges. Retrieved from https://www.geteducated.com/elearning-education-blog/5-things-real-students-hate-about-online-learning-degrees/.

Straumsheim, February 17, 2017). Online education costs more, not less. Retrieved from https://www.insidehighered.com/news/2017/02/17/study-challenges-cost-and-price-myths-online-education.
Thacher, M. (n.d). 21st Century Skills-What do teachers need to know? Retrieved from http://www.tesol.org/attend-and-learn/tesol-academies-conferences-symposiums/upcoming-tesol-academies/21st-century-skills-what-do-teachers-need-to-know-(c-5).
Weedlaying robot could save farmer sector $ 1.3 billion a year. Retrieved from http://www.abc.net.au/news/rural/2016-10-21/weed-killing-robot-could-save-billions/7954680.

ICT for Learner Support Services in ODL System in Developing Countries: Challenges and the Road Ahead

Moumita Das and Prabir Kumar Biswas

Introduction

There has been a tremendous change in the social, economic and political environment of the developing countries in the past couple of decades. With the rapid globalization, the international market has opened up. The international players are seen in the national markets. This fundamental global change has brought about a lot of competition in the domestic markets of the developing countries. Today, in order to survive, the developing countries have to be competitive in the international market. This has a direct bearing on the higher education in these countries as to maintain the competitiveness in the international market, they have to have an extremely skilled workforce that is suitable for international jobs.

It needs to be mentioned here that the demand of Open and Distance Learning (ODL) courses has been increasing day by day. It is not only a matter of personal learner requirement, but also an important national requirement as education is the key to a country's socio-economic progress. Therefore, the demand for higher education cannot be undermined.

Having examined the demands, when we look at the supply of higher education, we find that it is grossly inadequate in the developing countries. In these countries, the number of potential learners in higher education runs into millions. And to cater to these millions of learners simultaneously in a short span of time, there is lack of

M. Das (✉)
National Centre for Innovation in Distance Education,
Indira Gandhi National Open University, New Delhi, India
e-mail: moumitadas@ignou.ac.in

P. K. Biswas
Staff Training and Research Institute of Distance Education,
Indira Gandhi National Open University, New Delhi 110068, India
e-mail: pkbiswas@ignou.ac.in

© Springer Nature Singapore Pte Ltd. 2018
Anjana (ed.), *Technology for Efficient Learner Support Services in Distance Education*, https://doi.org/10.1007/978-981-13-2300-3_14

infrastructure. Obviously, the existing traditional universities alone cannot meet the ever-growing educational needs of the millions.

It is known to us that the traditional mode of education comprises the classroom teaching method employed in the colleges and the universities. This mode has a fixed curriculum, and the learning is imparted in the classrooms using the face-to-face lectures. The timing of examination is fixed, and certificates are issued after the student passes the examination successfully. The traditional system has been able to cater to only a fraction of higher education needs of the population in the developing countries.

The ODL system comprises the independent Distance and Open Universities and the traditional university-dependent directorates of distance education. These impart education to the learners through a combination of print material sent through post, audio, video, Web or Internet-based and face-to-face counselling sessions. The Open Universities have a wide reach and cater to learners who reside in remote areas, thereby providing access to the unreached. For example, the Indira Gandhi National Open University in India has about three million learners in India and other countries through 21 schools of studies and 67 regional centres, around 2,667 learner support centres and 29 overseas partner institutions (www.ignou.ac.in). The learner is able to learn at his/her own pace and place. There is flexibility in terms of age for admission, and time and space of study and examination. Further, the curriculum is learner-centric, where the learner has a choice from various optional courses. Considering the huge demand, the ODL system is well equipped to impart higher education to the millions of learners of the developing countries.

The concept of teaching through the distance mode usually pertains to the physical distance between the teacher and the learner. It means that since there is very limited face-to-face classroom interaction, the learner gets less opportunity to meet the teacher. In distance education, the learner could be at one end of the country and the teacher at another end. Therefore, there is a physical distance between the teacher and the learner. This distance causes a lack of flow of information. This lack results in the learner facing certain barriers that he/she needs to overcome. He/she might have many queries related to different aspects of his/her study or might need counselling on administrative, technological, psychological or career issues (Dillon et al. 1992; Kumari 2012; Kumar et al. 2000). The learner support services are designed to help the learners to overcome these barriers during the course of their study. The support aims at reducing the dropout rates, enhancing performance and facilitating meaningful learning experience and career guidance (Gil-Jaurena 2014). Learner support ensures the success of the ODL learners and remains an integral part of an effective distance education system (Gaskell 2012).

The ICT tools are used to deliver instruction and administrative services to the learners. The ICT tools bring the distance learners closer to the teacher, administrators and the peer group. The ICT tools are being increasingly used in all areas of learner support services right from the pre-admission stage to the certification stage and even beyond.

The success of ICT in learner support depends on several factors. An important factor is the awareness and knowledge of the learners. Their study habits, ICT skills, learning styles play a vital role in designing ICT-based services. The knowledge of these attributes of learners will determine how he/she is going to use the technology, how receptive he/she is towards the services provided through ICT and how useful these ICT-based services would be to the learner. The next important factor is the type of services that are provided to the learners. The factors of availability and accessibility of ICT among the teachers and staff and the learners are also important. The developing countries are in a state of transition in adopting ICT for education. Their ICT readiness is an important factor in devising appropriate learner support service systems. Many of the challenges faced by the learner support systems in the developing countries could be solved through appropriate policies, institutional arrangements, effective planning and management and innovation. In the subsequent sections of this chapter, an attempt is made to examine all these factors in detail.

The Learners of the ODL System and Their ICT Readiness

Traditionally, learning is perceived as a teacher-centric activity. However, in the last decade, the focus has gradually moved to learner-centric approach. In this context, the flexible nature of ODL system provides a complete autonomy to the learners to choose the courses and continue the study at their individual pace and place of study. With the emphasis on self-regulatory skills, the learner is expected to support himself/herself on his/her own, rather than depending on the teacher. In this changing scenario, the role of the teacher is gradually evolving towards facilitator of knowledge. They are more like a mentor who participate in the learning process and gently guide the learner. Thus, the counsellors have a major role to play in the contemporary ODL system. Furthermore, the learners are encouraged to engage in collaborative learning which promotes peer-to-peer interaction, peer-to-teacher/counsellor interaction and foster community interaction.

ICT-based interventions designed to be learner-centric would be extremely helpful in catering to the learner needs. However, the readiness of the learner to use ICT is a determining factor in the implementation of ICT-based interventions (Coopasami et al. 2017). Some studies on the ICT readiness of the learners of the ODL system in the developing countries, such as Africa (Kabonoki 2008; Mafenya 2013) or South America (Mantilla and Lewis 2012), indicate that the learners show a low degree of ICT readiness so far as computers are concerned, but the readiness is high in case of mobile learning (Chaka and Govender 2017). However, the ICT readiness is moderate in Lithuania (Vilkonis et al. 2013), Egypt (Ali 2016), Saudi Arabia (Shorfuzzaman and Alhussein 2016) or India (Suprabha et al. 2017), and good in Iran (Changiz et al. 2013). Some recent studies have found that the learners are strongly attracted to mobile learning in the developing countries (Awadhiya et al. 2014; Lamptey and Boateng 2017).

Although there is a paucity of research studies related to the ICT readiness of the learners in most of the developing countries, some studies, as mentioned above, indicate that the learners are gradually orienting themselves towards the use of technology in education. Clearly, more effort is needed to be taken by the governments and universities in this direction.

The knowledge of ICT readiness of the learners gives an idea of how the learner would use the various ICT interventions when provided to them by the university.

Types of Learner Support Services and the ICT Tools Used

Learner support, as defined by Garrison (1989), "is concerned with a range of human and non-human resources to guide and facilitate the educational transaction". Tait (2000) enumerated the following typical learner support services being offered by the ODL universities:

- Enquiry, admission and pre-study advisory services,
- Tutoring,
- Guidance and counselling services,
- Assessment of prior learning and credit transfer,
- Study and examination centres,
- Residential schools,
- Library services,
- Individualized teaching,
- Record keeping, information management and other administrative systems,
- Differentiated services for learners with special needs,
- Materials which support the development of study skills, programme planning or career development.

It is expected that the learners develop organizational skills, (reading and writing skills) and learning skills effectively through learner support services (Simpson 2002, 2012). According to Simpson, the learners also value affective and organizational support in addition to course-specific support. Essentially, there are two types of learner support services: (i) academic support services and (ii) administrative support services (Usun 2004).

Academic Support Services

The academic support services include the activities of tutoring, advising or counselling. As the learner in the ODL system is expected to learn on his/her own, he/she needs to develop good study skills. Tutoring involves imparting study skills and monitoring and conveying the academic progress of the learner to help them grow. Counselling is provided in areas related to the learner's study and career. There could be diverse types of problems the learners may face in this area, such as study-related problems, lack of motivation, inability to complete assignments/ projects, inability to manage time or plan for the future, anxiety while appearing in examination after a long gap. The counsellor helps the learners to:

- Be aware of their strengths,
- Provide them information,
- Solve problems on their own,
- Keep them motivated throughout the course,
- Support them in developing new skills and
- Plan their career.

Administrative Support Services

The major activities of administrative support services include promotion of the programmes, dissemination of information on time, facilitating the admission and registration process, delivery of study materials and ICT-based materials, provide prompt response to learner queries, and redress grievance (Somayajulu and Ramakrishna 2008). These requirements of the learners are taken care of by the administrative support services through the activities of informing, advising, developmental counselling and problem-solving counselling.

ICT Tools Used by the ODL System

The ODL system uses a variety of ICT tools, which can be used efficiently for educational purposes. These ICT tools can be divided into (i) one-way media and (ii) two-way media. One-way media comprises radio, audio tapes or CDs or files, TV (live and pre-recorded), videotapes or CDs or files, and computer-based learning. Two-way media comprises interactive radio, live interactive TV, video-conferencing and computer-mediated communication.

The advent of the Internet has facilitated the seamless dissemination of education. The Internet or the World Wide Web (www) provides a huge resource base for the learners of distance education at their own pace and time. Further, the Internet enables easy communication and interactivity with the teachers and other learners of their group. This enhances their learning process. The strengths of the Internet include: (i) a huge database in information sources, (ii) multimedia support, (iii) ease of use, (iv) fast and up to date and (v) affordability.

Mobile phones also are increasingly being used for providing information and other types of learner support services. The pedagogy of mobile learning is still evolving.

The computer-based and web-based teaching–learning have enabled a wide array of choices that could be made to impart learner support services. Education software, such as virtual classrooms, learning management systems and content management systems, applications, such as quick response codes, learner analytics, combined with social media are being used in many universities in the world to provide learner support services.

Advantages of the ICT Tools in Learner Support Services

The most obvious use of the ICT tools in learner support services is that these save enormous *time* in terms of cutting down the duration of the communication process compared to the postal era. Tait (2004) reminisces "…remember the speed of organisational communications through the post: the writing of the letter by hand; its typing up; its being posted and one or two days its being delivered … waiting to be read. A reply then being written by hand; being typed; being posted and being delivered the next day or the day after … waiting to be read. That simple exchange represented probably more than a week". Today, this process can be completed in a matter of minutes through ICT tools. Further, the information is sent in a timely manner. The learners can not only receive the information on time, but also send any required information to the university on time. The learners are able to access a variety of learner support resources (counselling, job opportunities, etc.) that are made available to them and thereby get benefitted. Thus, the ICT tools have increased the pace of learner support services and many diverse requirements of the learners are met on time.

The use of ICT tools minimizes the *cost* of investment in essential infrastructure and resources of the university to a large extent. The digitization of documents, their storage and the ease of dissemination has drastically reduced the costs incurred for storage space and manpower. The learners also are able to communicate with the university at a cost, which may not be prohibitive for them.

The ICT tools enable the universities to provided attention to the individual need, thus ensuring a *personalized learning* experience.

The ICT tools used by universities often contain facilities for *interaction* between groups of learners or between the teachers and learners or between the administrators and the learners. In these scenarios, discussions and deliberations happen between the learners, teachers and administrators. This interaction through the social media provides a psychological support to the learner who is at a distance from his or her university.

With the new and emerging ICT tools, the possibilities of *innovation* in learner support services are increasing. New devices, new software applications and new models of data-driven learner support services are being ushered in with exciting times ahead in distance education.

Use of ICT in Learner Support Services in the Developing Countries

The developing countries are mostly situated in Africa, Asia and Latin America and the Caribbean region (Gulati 2008). Since the ODL systems in the developing countries are dependent on their current ICT infrastructure, these systems can make use of only the available ICT tools to impart instruction and learner support. Indeed, there are several pioneer ODL universities, which have made excellent use of the available ICT tools. It is beyond the scope of this chapter to discuss all the open universities in the countries of Africa, Asia and Latin America and the Caribbean. However, an attempt is made below to provide a glimpse of the use of ICT in providing learner support services in select ODL universities in a few of these developing countries.

In the African continent, the 49 countries of sub-Saharan Africa have been using various ICT tools for student support, but print remains the mainstay (CoL 2002). However, there are some universities that have been using different ICT tools for student support since their inception. The University of South Africa, Pretoria, the first ODL system of the world, provides learner support through emails, Web portal, social media and radio (Phineas 2012; Arko-Chemfour 2017; UNISA 2017). The National Open University of Nigeria, Lagos, has ICT tools as the mainstay of student support. The directorate of learner support services of this university uses audio and video media, telephone and the Internet for learner counselling from the stage of application to the stage where the learner successfully graduates (Rotimi 2010). Mention must be made of the African Virtual University which has PAN African jurisdiction with 19 countries as its members. It has more than 53 partner institutions in 27 countries. It offers its programme through Massive Open Online Courses (MOOCs). For learner support, it has a MyAVU Virtual Classroom online platform which provides an individual web page for every learner. This personal web page contains information, resources and individualized services (African Virtual University 2017).

In the Asia-Pacific region, ICT penetration has fostered the development of ODL initiatives. In the rural areas of South Asia, people are being reached through computers, the Internet and audio-visual technology through the National Research and Education Networks. In Central Asia, in more than 500 institutions in Kazakhstan, Kyrgyzstan, Tajikistan, Turkmenistan and Uzbekistan the ICT infrastructure is being significantly improved by the Central Asian Research and Education Network (Apikul 2014). The Philippines Open University, since 1952, has been using radio for learner support. With new ICT tools emerging with time, the university has begun using mobile phones, computers and the Internet to provide learner support services (dela Peña-Bandalaria 2007). The Open University of China (formerly known as the Radio and Television University of China) offers learners' support in diverse areas using ICT tools. These include online tutoring, and consultation on the various learner issues of registration, study skills, employment guidance, psychological issues, and many other services (OUC 2017). The Universitas Terbuka (UT), also known as the Open University of Indonesia, uses social media, such as Facebook and Twitter. Learners and tutors form study groups in these media, and the learners can go to the group page and interact with other learners and tutors. The university also uses Office365 service that combines social media tools with productivity applications (Prasetyo and Belawati 2014). The Open University of Sri Lanka supports its learners through various ICT tools including television broadcasts (Jayasuriya 1992), interactive multimedia (IMM) techniques (Wattegama 2014) and a virtual university (myOUSL) (OUSL 2017). The Indira Gandhi National Open University (IGNOU), India, has been using a variety of ICT tools for learner support since its inception in 1985. A case study of IGNOU is presented elsewhere in this chapter.

To address the challenge of providing education to Bangladesh's growing population, Bangladesh Open University (BOU) makes use of ICTs (computers and the Internet) as well as old ICTs (cassette tapes and CDs) to ensure that education is accessible to all. These are also broadcasted on radio and television. At BOU, audio–videoconferencing technology is available to reach out to learners in remote areas (Al Ahsan and Khanam 2014).

In Latin American countries, ICT tools, such as audio–video aids and telephone, have been used for learner support (ICDE 1991). With the emergence of ICT, there has been a steady rise in the availability of e-learning and virtual learning in these countries. The National University of Quilmes in Argentina offers a virtual university programme for bachelors and foundation degrees, with ICT-enabled learner support. The Federal University of Santa Catarina in Brazil offers specialized learner support through the use of Internet, videoconferencing and satellite teleconferencing. The National Open and Distance University of Colombia provides learner support through videoconferencing, virtual libraries and virtual educational centres (OECD 2015). The countries of the Caribbean region provide distance education through the dual-mode universities. The University of West Indies Open Campus offers its courses in 17 countries of the Caribbean region. The university provides ICT-based learner support to its learners through online platforms and other Internet-based modes (University of West Indies Open Campus 2017).

The use of ICT for learner support services is on the rise in the developing countries. There is, of course, heterogeneity in the availability of ICT infrastructure in these countries. However, with the installation of mobile network infrastructure gaining momentum, these countries have bypassed the fixed-line infrastructure and its associated services and are increasingly using e-learning and the Internet tools for providing learner support services.

ICT-based learner support services at IGNOU

The Indira Gandhi National Open University (IGNOU) is one of the largest Open and Distance Learning (ODL) Universities of the world, catering to about three million learners. With its headquarters in New Delhi, its jurisdiction extends to the whole of India through its network of regional centres and study centres. It also has an international jurisdiction with a network of partner institutions in several developing countries.

The university provides learner support using multiple information and communication technology (ICT) tools. These include audio-visual material aids, interactive radio, teleconferencing, *e-Gyankosh* and Web-based services.

The Electronic Media Production Centre (EMPC) produces and coordinates the audio-visual programmes. It has several studios and production units to develop and broadcast these programmes. It coordinates the broadcasts mainly through *Gyan Darshan* and *Gyan Vani*. *Gyan Darshan* channels are a bouquet of four direct-to-home (DTH) channels that have a reach of more than ten million homes in India. *Gyan Vani* is a group of 27 FM radio stations across India.

The audio-visual materials contain audio and video compact discs (CDs) prepared by the university. These contain content to supplement the course material to facilitate the understanding of the learners. These audio and video CDs are either sent to the learners on their request or sent to the study centres for group listening or viewing by the learners. One video programme is approximately of 25–30 min duration. These video programmes are also telecast through *Doordarshan*, the national television network, and *Gyan Darshan* channels.

The audio programmes are also broadcast through the national radio, All India Radio and *Gyan Vani* (www.ignou.ac.in).

Interactive Radio Counselling (IRC) is being offered to the learners of IGNOU through the *Gyan Vani* and select All India Radio stations. The aim of IRC is to provide on-the-spot counselling or advice to the learners. The audio studio at the EMPC coordinates this activity.

IGNOU has an education broadcast website that offers an internet audio counselling service named *Gyan Dhara*. The learners can listen to the teachers and experts and interact with them through telephone or through chat. The website also broadcasts *Gyan Darshan* channel programmes (IGNOU 2018).

IGNOU has developed a knowledge repository, *e-Gyankosh*, to facilitate not only its learners and faculty members, but is free and open to all. The repository makes available more than 2,200 courses and 2,000 video lectures online. The print-based contents of the courses are available as PDF files and video programmes and are provided through a special channel of IGNOU on YouTube.

The website of IGNOU headquarters provides a wide range of information to its learners right from the announcement of the dates of admission and examination to the availability of various programmes of study, the associated schools of study and the relevant regional centre and study centre. The enroled learners are provided the access to the site to download their I-cards and examination cards and view their grade cards and other details.

The admission process has been made online, and re-registration also can also be done online through the IGNOU website. In addition to the above major learner support services at the headquarters, the regional centres have their own websites to cater to the informational and other administrative needs of the learners. There is an increasing use of emails, mobile phones and mobile apps for providing learner support services. Several regional centres have developed mechanisms to provide important information to the learners through mobile short messaging services or emails. Many mobile apps are being developed at the regional centres to cater to learners' queries.

Challenges in the Way of ICT in Learner Support Services

The learner support services in the ODL system in the developing countries face several challenges in terms of skills, infrastructure, resources and policies.

The knowledge and skills of accessing and using ICT are lacking in a large number of teachers and learners in the developing countries, and they require training (Adeoye et al. 2013; Sife et al. 2007). The unskilled teachers or counsellors are unable to communicate through ICT tools with their learners. Although they possess the necessary skills to tutor or counsel the learners, they are unable to design appropriate ICT-based solutions that would enable them to reach the learner easily on time and provide him or her their individualized attention. Similarly, the learners cannot connect to the teachers or officials of the university through ICT. They are, thus, deprived of the benefits of ICT-enabled learner support services.

Infrastructure for ICT in the developing countries is not uniform and mostly limited. Telephone connectivity is lacking, and electric supply is erratic in these countries. The socio-economic and technological situation in many of these developing countries is such that ICT tools have not been used at the same rate as in the industrialized countries (Sife et al. 2007). In the developing countries, print material and letters by post have been the mainstay in learner support services of the ODL system (Sim et al. 2005). This is because in these countries there is a shortage of financial resources, erratic power supply, limited internet access, a lack of trained teachers and a lack of proper policies. Most of the learners do not have direct access to the ICT tools. Also, many teachers and learners do not possess the necessary skills to use these tools (Gulati 2008; Musingafi et al. 2015). According to an estimate, in 30 June 2017, the Internet was used by 50% of the population in Asia, 10% in Africa and 10.4% in the Caribbean and Latin American countries (Internet World Stats 2017a). In Africa, due to poor quality and scarcity of fixed-line infrastructure, mobile networks are the predominant (more than 90%) means of the

Internet access. Also, there is diversity in mobile penetration in different countries of Africa. Southern Africa and a few North African countries have a higher penetration, while the countries of Central Africa have low penetration (50%) of mobile networks (Lancaster 2015, 2016). In Latin American and the Caribbean countries, the infrastructure is considered to be robust and there is a penetration range of 5–32% in these countries (Statista 2017). Mobile network penetration in many South American countries is high, except Paraguay, Peru and Venezuela, where the infrastructure is being developed (Internet World Stats 2017b). In Asia, fixed-line penetration is low in countries, such as Bangladesh, Pakistan and Timor Leste, and is on the downslide in many countries that once had high penetration due to increasing availability of the mobile networks. Internet penetration has diversity with countries like Afghanistan having low penetration (13%), Turkmenistan (17%) and Laos (19.5%) to high penetration in China, Malaysia and India (Internet World Stats 2017c).

Resources in the ODL system in the developing countries are in short supply (Sharma 2003; Sife et al. 2007). Financial resources are scarce, and teacher resources are inadequate or unskilled to some extent. The ODL universities in the developing countries are mostly publicly funded, and a part of the fund comes from the learners' fees (Djalil et al. 1994). More often than not, the fund is not sufficient to be utilized for developing ICT infrastructure and human resources, and implement the ICT solutions. Skilled human resources, such as teachers, programmers, administrative staff, are required to develop appropriate e-content and software platforms for learner support (Arko-Chemfour 2017). In the absence of such skilled personnel, there is no generation of ICT-based quality content and delivery mechanisms (Souter et al. 2012). The resources that are available, such as libraries, laboratories, audio–video materials, are not properly utilized (Gulati 2008).

Policies related to the use of ICT in education are related to the e-governance policy of a country. For e-governance to be successfully implemented, a range of rules, policies, laws and legislative changes to support the activities of electronic signatures, electronic archiving, freedom of information, privacy, data protection, cyber crime, intellectual property rights and copyright issues is required (Ndou 2004; Basu 2004).

The Road Ahead

Considering the advantages of the ICT-based learner support services and challenges it faces in the developing countries, appropriate steps need to be taken to pave the road ahead. The existing condition of the learner support services in these countries needs a lot of improvement. There is a need for each and every stakeholder to participate to bring about a positive change. There is a need of clear policies, ICT infrastructure and budgetary provisions at the government level. At the university level, there should be institutional arrangements, planning and management. This will create a favourable environment for ICT-based learner support services.

Policies: There is a need for government policies that are clear about the use of ICT in education. The developing countries are still behind in e-government readiness (UN 2016). These countries need to put in place their e-government policy and the associated policies of freedom of expression, privacy, intellectual property rights, cyber laws and other associated legal provisions (Mohammed et al. 2016).

ICT infrastructure: There is a need to bridge the digital divide within the country. This entails establishment of ICT networks, ensuring availability of services and appropriate devices at low cost, ensuring electricity supply for ICT infrastructure, educating the people about the benefits of ICT to remove cultural barriers and ensuring training of human resources to use and support ICT. These are some of the efforts the governments could make to ensure ICT uptake (Postnote 2006; Souter et al. 2012).

Budgetary provisions: The government policies should have inbuilt budgetary provisions to facilitate the implementation and maintenance of ICT-based services (Souter et al. 2012).

Institutional arrangements: The institutes should have proper arrangement for learner support in place. Most ODL universities, such as IGNOU, have a three-tier system comprising the headquarters, the regional centres and the study or learner support centres. Some universities, such as the Open University Malaysia, have a two-tier structure with headquarters and learner support centres. These centres are equipped to offer various ICT support services. There are other scenarios in case of online universities and dual-mode universities where ICT-based learner support services are provided (Srivastava 2012). These institutional arrangements need to be reviewed and improved from time to time. Capacity development of the tutors, counsellors and staff should be emphasized (Somayajulu and Ramakrishna 2008) and carried out from time to time.

Planning: Planning is important to achieve the quality in learner support services. The planning must address the objectives. The process of planning involves forecasting, strategic planning and operational planning. Forecasting involves projecting today's trends into the future forms are integral part of forecasting. It means that looking at the present ICT consumption pattern and areas of demand, what ICT-based learner support services are likely to be in greater demand in the future. While forecasting, the uncertainties of future have to be taken into account such as economic depression, political turmoil or new technologies that may affect the current ICT devices and services. *Strategic planning* involves formulation of strategies and includes (i) information analysis or reviewing the performance of the university in offering ICT-based learner support services, (ii) making the strategic choice or determining the directions based on the information analysis and (iii) setting specific goals with time targets. For strategic planning, the knowledge of the university, its capacities and capabilities is a must. From time to time, strategic planning has to be revisited. This is because the aspirations of the stakeholders may change, the university environment may change or the current strategy may fail to deliver. *Operational planning is undertaken* when the broad picture of goals and strategies are clear. Operational planning is carried out in the operational areas, such as production, marketing, finance, research development. The planning mainly addresses the current problems, such as constraint in resources, existing efficiency levels, information management, university culture.

Innovation: There is a huge scope for innovations in ICT-based learner support services (Jung 2007). Efforts should be made to identify the gap areas of the learner support services, and suitable interventions should be devised. The ODL system should create an environment of innovation wherein innovative ideas could be incubated and new prototypes could be developed for implementation. Efforts should be made for adaptation of innovations in ICT-based learner support services, which would undoubtedly enhance the quality of the services.

Conclusion

Learner support services are the backbone of any ODL system. It is the only way to reach out to the distant learner of the ODL system. The use of ICT in learner support services has been present in varying degrees since the inception of the ODL system. In today's world, ICT-based learner support services are effective in not only reaching out to the learners and help them in completing their study, but also helping the learners to connect them with the university and their peer groups, allowing them to express their viewpoints and enabling them to make decisions, thereby enhancing their personality, which is the goal of education. ICT-based learner support services face many challenges in the developing countries. These countries have been using ICT-based learner support services sporadically, but they need to strengthen it through various measures. This will help in the development of their learners, human resources and overall society.

References

Adeoye, Y. M., Oluwole, A. F., & Blessing, L. A. (2013). Appraising the role of information communication technology (ICT) as a change agent for higher education in Nigeria. *International Journal of Educational Administration and Policy Studies, 5*(8), 177–183.

African Virtual University. (2017). Welcome to MyAVU classroom. Retrieved November 28, 2017, from http://www.avu.org/virtualclassroom/.

Al Ahsan, H., & Khanam, F. (2014). Country case studies: Bangladesh. Open and distance learning in Asia and the Pacific. United Nations Asian and Pacific Training Centre for Information and. Communication Technology for Development. ICTD Case Study 3. www.unapcict.org/ecohub/apcict-case…open-and-distance-learning…/attachment1.

Ali, W. G. M. (2016). Nursing Students' Readiness for e-Learning Experience. *Gynecol Obstet (Sunnyvale), 6,* 388. https://doi.org/10.4172/2161-0932.1000388.

Apikul, C. (2014). Introduction. open and distance learning in Asia and the Pacific. United Nations Asian and Pacific Training Centre for Information and Communication Technology for Development. ICTD Case Study 3. p 10. www.unapcict.org/ecohub/apcict-case…open-and-distance-learning…/attachment1.

Arko-Achemfuor, A. (2017). Student support gaps in an open distance learning context. *Issues in Educational Research*, *27*(4), 658–676. http://www.iier.org.au/iier27/arko-achemfuor.pdf.

Awadhiya, A. K., Miglani, A., Gowthaman, K. (2014). ICT usage by distance learners in India. *Turkish Online Journal of Distance Education-TOJDE, 3*(18). Retrieved September 1, 2018, from http://tojde.anadolu.edu.tr/yonetim/icerik/makaleler/995-published.pdf.

Basu, S. (2004). E-government and developing countries: An overview. *International Review Of Law Computers & Technology, 18*(1), 109–132.

Chaka, J. G., & Govender, I. (2017). Students' perceptions and readiness towards mobile learning in colleges of education: A Nigerian perspective. *South African Journal of Education, 37*(1), 1–12.

Changiz, T., Haghani, F., & Nowroozi, N. (2013). Are postgraduate students in distance medical education program ready for e-learning? A survey in Iran. *Journal of Education and Health Promotion, 2,* 61. https://doi.org/10.4103/2277-9531.120862.

Col. (2002). Distance Education and Open Learning in Sub-Saharan Africa: A Literature Survey On Policy And Practice. Retrieved September 12, 2017, from http://oasis.col.org/bitstream/handle/11599/183/02DEinSSA_LiteratureSurvey.pdf?sequence=1&isAllowed=y.

Coopasami, M., Knight, S., & Pete, M. (2017). e-Learning readiness amongst nursing students at the Durban University of Technology. *Health SA Gesondheid 6*, 300–306. Retrieved September 1, 2018, from http://www.sciencedirect.com/science/article/pii/S1025984817300807.

dela Peña-Bandalaria, M. (2007). Impact of ICTs on Open Distance Learning in a Developing Country Setting: The Phillipine Experience. *The International Review of Research in Open and Distributed Learning*. *8*(1). Retrieved November 24, 2017, from http://www.irrodl.org/index.php/irrodl/article/view/334/792.

Dillon, C. L., Gunawardena, C. N., & Parker, R. (1992). Learner support: The critical link in distance education. *Distance Education, 13*(1), 29–45.

Djalil, A., Musa, I., Kesuma, R., & Damajanti, N. S. (1994). The financing system of the Universitas Terbuka. In Ian Mugridge (Ed.), *The Funding of Open Universities* (pp. 21–28). Commonwealth of Learning: Vancouver.

Garrison, D. R. (1989). *Understanding distance education: A framework for the future*. London: Routledge.

Gaskell, A. (2012). Changing models of learner support: The role and cost of online resources. *Open Learning: The Journal of Open, Distance and e-Learning, 27*(2), 99–102.

Gil-Jaurena, I. (2014). Student support services in open and distance education. *Open Praxis, 6*(1), 3–4.

Gulati, S. (2008). Technology-Enhanced Learning in Developing Nations: A review. *International Review of Research in Open and Distance Learning, 9* (1). Retrieved November 27, 2017.

ICDE. (1991). Latin America and The Caribbean: A survey of distance education in 1991. A study conducted by the International Council of Distance Education. And the International Centre of Distance Learning. Retrieved November 29, 2017, from http://unesdoc.unesco.org/images/0009/000920/092060eb.pdf.

IGNOU, 2018. Gyan Dhara and Gyan Darshan. Retrieved February 19, 2018, from http://www.ignouonline.ac.in/gyandhara/.

Internet World Stats (2017a). Internet users in the world by regions-June 2017. Retrieved November 28, 2017 http://www.internetworldstats.com/stats.htm.

Internet World Stats (2017b). South America market research: Telecommunications market reports. Retrieved November 28, 2017, from http://www.internetworldstats.com/south2.htm.

Internet World Stats (2017c). Asia Telecommunications: ICT research reports. Retrieved November 28, 2017, from http://www.internetworldstats.com/asia2.htm.

Jayasuriya, D. G. (1992). The Open University of Sri Lanka. In *Perspectives on Distance Education: Student Support Services: Towards More Responsive Systems. Report of a Symposium on Student Support Systems. Ontario: Commonwealth of Learning* (pp 76–77). Retrieved November 28, 2017, from http://www.c3l.uni-oldenburg.de/cde/support/readings/sweet75-100.pdf.

Jung, I. (2007). Innovative practices of distance education (including e-learning) in Asia and the Pacific. *International Journal for Educational Media and Technology, 1*(1), 48–60.

Kabonoki, S. K. (2008). Access to technology and readiness to use it in learning. *Open Learning: The Journal of Open, Distance and e-Learning, 23*(2), 113–121.

Kumari, S. (2012). Factors affecting students' retention and attrition in the open and distance learning system. *Indian Journal of Open Learning*, *21*(1), 19–40 (2012).

Kumar, J. P., Rao, D. B., & Rao, G. S. (2000). *Open University: Student support services* (pp. 15–16). New Delhi: Discovery Publishing House.

Lamptey, H., Boateng, R. (2017). Mobile learning in developing countries: A Synthesis of the past to define the future'. World Academy of Science, Engineering and Technology, International Science Index 122. *International Journal of Social, Behavioral, Educational, Economic, Business and Industrial Engineering*, *11*(2), 443–450.

Lancaster, H. (2015). Africa—Mobile Voice and Mobile Broadband Statistics. Retrieved November 28, 2017, from https://www.budde.com.au/Research/Africa-Mobile-Voice-and-Mobile-Broadband-Statistics-tables-only.

Lancaster, H. (2016). Africa - Fixed Broadband Market - Statistics and Analyses. Retrieved November 28, 2017, from https://www.budde.com.au/Research/Africa-Fixed-Broadband-Market-Statistics-and-Analyses/?r=51.

Mafenya, P. N. (2013). An investigation of first-year students' pedagogical readiness to e-learning and assessment in open and distance learning: An University of South Africa Context. *Mediterranean Journal of Social Sciences, 4*(13), 353–360.

Mantilla, G., & Lewis, K. O. (2012). Determining faculty and student readiness for an online medical curriculum. *Medical Science Educator., 22*(4), 228–243.

Mohammed, A. M., Aboobaider, B. M., Ibrahim, H., Abdullah, H. A., Ali, M. H., Jaber, M. M., et al. (2016). E-government and its challenges in developing countries: Case study, Iraqi e-government. *The Social Sciences*, *11*(17), 4310–4319. Retrieved September 12, 2017, from http://docsdrive.com/pdfs/medwelljournals/sscience/2016/4310-4319.pdf.

Musingafi, M. C. C., Mapuranga, B., Chiwanza, K., & Zebron, S. (2015). Challenges for Open and Distance learning (ODL) Students: Experiences from Students of the Zimbabwe Open University. *Journal of Education and Practice*. *6*(18). Retrieved November 24, 2017, from https://files.eric.ed.gov/fulltext/EJ1079750.pdf.

Ndou, V. D. (2004). E-government for developing countries: opportunities and challenges. *The Electronic Journal on Information Systems in Developing Countries, 18*(1), 1–24.

OECD. (2015). Country snapshots of distance education and e-learning in Latin America. In *E-Learning in Higher Education in Latin America*. Paris: OECD Publishing. http://dx.doi.org/10.1787/9789264209992-7-en.

OUC. (2017). Learner Support. Retrieved November 28, 2017, from http://en.ouchn.edu.cn/index.php/learner-support.

OUSL. (2017). Accessing the Open University Student Portal–MyOUSL. http://www.ou.ac.lk/home/images/Faculty_and_institute/HealthSciences/Downloads/MyOUSL_Access_Details.pdf.

Phineas, B. G. (2012). Learner Support in Open And Distance Learning Context: A Case Study Of ABET Programmes At The University of South Africa. Ph.D Thesis. University of South Africa. Retrieved November 24, 2017, from http://citeseerx.ist.psu.edu/viewdoc/download?doi=10.1.1.1016.4400&rep=rep1&type=pdf.

Postnote. (2006). ICT in developing countries (Vol. 261, pp 1–4) Parliamentary Office of Science and Technology. Retrieved September 12, 2017, from https://www.parliament.uk/documents/post/postpn261.pdf.

Prasetyo, D. A. & Belawati, T. (2014). Country Case Studies. Indonesia. Open and Distance Learning in Asia and the Pacific. United Nations Asian and Pacific Training Centre for Information and. Communication Technology for Development. ICTD Case Study 3. www.unapcict.org/ecohub/apcict-case…open-and-distance-learning…/attachment1.

Rotimi, O. (2010). Use of technology for supporting and developing the National Open University of Nigeria. *Edo Journal of Counselling, 3*(2), 240–255.

Sharma, R. C. (2003). Barriers in using technology for education in developing countries. In 2003 Proceedings of the International Conference on Information Technology: Research and Education, ITRE 2003. (pp. 512–516).

Shorfuzzaman, M., & Musaed Alhussein, M. (2016). Modeling Learners' Readiness to Adopt Mobile Learning: A Perspective from a GCC Higher Education Institution. *Mobile Information Systems*, Article ID 6982824, 10. https://doi.org/10.1155/2016/6982824.

Sife, A. S. Lwoga E. T. & Sanga. C. (2007). New technologies for teaching and learning: Challenges for higher learning institutions in developing countries. *International Journal of Education and Development Using ICT, 3*(2). Retrieved November 27, 2017, from http://ijedict.dec.uwi.edu/viewarticle.php?id=246/&layout=html.

Sim, H. K. C., Atan, H. & Idrus, R. M. (2005). The Learners' Support System in Distance Education: A Study of the Satisfaction of Quality. Retrieved November 24, 2017, from http://www.itdl.org/Journal/Sep_05/article02.htm.

Simpson, O. (2002). *Supporting students for success in online and distance education*. New York: Routledge.

Simpson, O. (2012). *Supporting students for success in online and distance education*. New York: Routledge.

Somayajulu, B. K., & Ramakrishna, T. (2008). Distance Learners and Support Service: Current Trends and Prospects, Access to Learning for Development. The Fifth Pan Commonwealth Forum on Open Learning. London: Commonwealth of Learning.

Souter, D., Adam, L., Butcher, N., Sibthorpe C., & Tusubira, T. (2012). ICTs for Education in Africa. In E. Yonazi, T. Kelly, N. Halewood, and C. Blackman, C. (Eds.), *eTransform Africa: The Transformational Use of ICTs in Africa.* A Report by World Bank and African Development Bank. Retrieved September 12, 2017, from http://siteresources.worldbank.org/extinformationandcommunicationandtechnologies/resources/282822-1346223280837/Education.pdf.

Srivastava, M. (2012). Support services: institutional arrangements and models. In *MDE 413, Learner Support Systems and Services. STRIDE: IGNOU* (pp. 56–70).

Statista. (2017). Fixed-line telephony penetration rate in selected countries in Latin America in 2016. Retrieved November 28, 2017, from https://www.statista.com/statistics/218147/fixed-line-penetration-in-latin-america-by-country/.

Suprabha, B. S., Shenoy, R., Rao, A., Rao, A., & Naik, D. G. (2017). Readiness and utilization of computer-assisted learning among dental students and faculty. *Dental Hypotheses, 8*(4), 87–93.

Tait, A. (2000). Planning student support for open and distance learning. *Open Learning: The Journal of Open, Distance and e-Learning, 15*(3), 287–299.

Tait, A. (2004). On institutional models and concepts of student support services; The Case of the Open University UK. In J. E. Brindley, C. Walti, & O. Zawacki-Richter (Eds.), *Learner support in open, distance and online learning environments* (pp. 283–293). Oldenburg, Germany: BIS-Verlag der Carl von Ossietzky Universität.

UN. (2016). Data Center. E-Government Knowledge Database. Retrieved September 12, 2017, from https://publicadministration.un.org/egovkb/Data-Center.

UNISA. (2017). Learner Support. Retrieved November 24, 2017, from http://www.unisa.ac.za/sites/myunisa/default/Learner-support-&-regions/Learner-Support.

University of West Indies Open Campus. (2017). About the University of West Indies Open Campus. Retrieved November 29, 2017, from http://www.open.uwi.edu/about.

Usun, S. (2004). Learner Support Services in Distance Education System (A Case Study of Turkey). *Turkish Online Journal of Distance Education-TOJDE, 5*(4). Retrieved September 01, 2018, from http://www.acarindex.com/dosyalar/makale/acarindex-1423932504.pdf.

Vilkonis, R., Bakanovienė, T., & Turskienė, S. (2013). Readiness of adults to learn using e-learning. *M-learning and T-learning Technologies, Informatics in Education, 12*(2), 181–190.

Wattegama, C. (2014). Country Case Studies. Sri Lanka. Open and Distance Learning in Asia and the Pacific. United Nations Asian and Pacific Training Centre for Information and. Communication Technology for Development. ICTD Case Study 3. www.unapcict.org/ecohub/apcict-case…open-and-distance-learning…/attachment1.

MIX
Papier aus verantwortungsvollen Quellen
Paper from responsible sources
FSC® C105338

If you have any concerns about our products, you can contact us on
ProductSafety@springernature.com

In case Publisher is established outside the EU, the EU authorized representative is:
Springer Nature Customer Service Center GmbH
Europaplatz 3, 69115 Heidelberg, Germany

Printed by Libri Plureos GmbH
in Hamburg, Germany

HOLZ – OFEN – FEUER

PRAXISWISSEN FÜR EFFIZIENTES, SICHERES UND UMWELT-FREUNDLICHES HEIZEN

ANTHONY BAILEY

Leopold Stocker Verlag
Graz – Stuttgart

Umschlaggestaltung, Satz: DSR – Werbeagentur Rypka, A-8143-Dobl/Graz
Titelbild: Charnwood
Bildnachweise siehe Seite 125

Titel der englischen Originalausgabe: Anthony Bailey:
The Woodburner Handbook – a practical guide to getting the best from your stove.

Text © Anthony Bailey, 2015, 2025.
Copyright in the Work © GMC Publications Ltd, 2025
This translation of The Woodburner Handbook ISBN 978-1-78494-719-4 is published by arrangement with GMC Publications Ltd.

Aus dem Englischen übertragen von Nina Schön.
Der Inhalt des Buches wurde vom Verlag und vom Autor nach bestem Wissen geprüft, eine Garantie kann jedoch nicht übernommen werden. Die juristische Haftung ist daher ausgeschlossen.
Bibliographische Information der Deutschen Nationalbibliothek:

Die Deutsche Nationalbibliothek verzeichnet diese Publikation in der Deutschen Nationalbibliographie; detaillierte bibliographische Daten sind im Internet über http://dnb.d-nb.de abrufbar.

Hinweis: Dieses Buch wurde auf chlorfrei gebleichtem Papier gedruckt.
Die zum Schutz vor Verschmutzung verwendete Einschweißfolie ist aus Polyethylen chlor- und schwefelfrei hergestellt. Diese umweltfreundliche Folie verhält sich grundwasserneutral, ist voll recyclingfähig und verbrennt in Müllverbrennungsanlagen völlig ungiftig.

Auf Wunsch senden wir Ihnen gerne kostenlos unser Verlagsverzeichnis zu:
Leopold Stocker Verlag GmbH
Hofgasse 5 / Postfach 438
A-8011 Graz
Tel.: +43 (0)316/82 16 36
Fax: +43 (0)316/83 56 12
E-Mail: stocker-verlag@stocker-verlag.com
www.stocker-verlag.com

ISBN 978-3-7020-2332-4
Alle Rechte der Verbreitung, auch durch Film, Funk und Fernsehen, fotomechanische Wiedergabe, Tonträger jeder Art, auszugsweisen Nachdruck oder Einspeicherung und Rückgewinnung in Datenverarbeitungsanlagen aller Art, sind vorbehalten.
Kein Teil dieses Buches darf in irgendeiner Weise zum Zweck des Trainings von Technologien oder Systemen der künstlichen Intelligenz verwendet oder reproduziert werden.
© Copyright by Leopold Stocker Verlag, Graz 2026

Fragen, Wünsche oder Anregungen?
Kontaktieren Sie uns!

www.stocker-verlag.com/holz-ofen-feuer-feedback/

Hier finden Sie auch weitere Informationen über unser Programm und können sich für unseren Newsletter anmelden.

INHALT

EINLEITUNG

Die meisten Menschen lieben ein offenes knisterndes Kaminfeuer. Es sieht schön aus, wie es im Ofen brennt und das Flackern der Flammen ist ein Widerhall alter Zeiten. In der Praxis ist ein offenes Feuer allerdings langsam und ineffizient und seine Heizleistung kann enttäuschend sein. Hier kommt ein relativ modernes Gerät, der Holzofen, ins Spiel. Als effiziente Wärmequelle, die schnell Hitze erzeugt und ohne Risiko betrieben werden kann, ist er weit entfernt von unseren Vorfahren, die Stöcke aneinanderrieben, um durch die Reibungsenergie winzige Funken zu erzeugen. Es ist der moderne „Weg der Flamme".

Jeder, der die richtige Immobilie und den richtigen Standort hat, kann einen Holzofen einbauen und sowohl die praktischen Vorzüge als auch die Zufriedenheit genießen, die damit einhergeht.

Es ist daher nur logisch, dass immer mehr Menschen sich für die Unabhängigkeit und Behaglichkeit entscheiden, die der Besitz eines Holzofens mit sich bringt. Holzöfen sehen nicht nur einladend aus und liefern als die Seele des Hauses angenehme Wärme, sondern erreichen auch eine beeindruckende Heizleistung. Jeder, der die richtige Immobilie und den richtigen Standort hat, kann einen Holzofen einbauen und sowohl die praktischen Vorzüge als auch die Zufriedenheit genießen, die damit einhergehen.

Rechts: *Ein Holzofen verbindet das Beste aus beiden Welten: den warmen wohligen Schein eines Holzfeuers und die Bequemlichkeit und Kontrolle moderner Heiztechnologie.*

DIE FREUDEN DES HOLZOFENS

Das Herz eines Holzofens ist, dass er als Wärmequelle, die sich vollends kontrollieren lässt, das Grundbedürfnis nach Wärme in uns stillt, anstatt dass wir den Launen der Energieanbieter oder einem Leistungsverlust aufgrund von schlechtem Wetter unterliegen. Aber die Investition lohnt auch noch aufgrund von zahlreichen weiteren Vorteilen.

NIEDRIGERE STROMRECHNUNGEN

Die laufenden Kosten für eine Zentralheizung sind hoch, ganz besonders in den Wintermonaten. Mit einem Holzofen können Sie sich eine beachtliche Menge Geld sparen, indem Sie Klaubholz sammeln und Ihr Brennholz von allen möglichen Quellen beziehen und lagern. Wenn Sie dann noch den Tipps aus diesem Buch folgen, können Sie sicher sein, dass Ihr Ofen immer so effizient wie möglich läuft und Sie somit kein Geld verschwenden.

VIELSEITIGKEIT

Ein freistehender Holzofen* ist nicht nur gut zum Heizen. Auf so manchem Modell steht auch ein dampfender Teekessel und das Kochen auf einem Holzofenherd ist absolut machbar. Selbst ein kleines Exemplar bietet Platz für ein paar Töpfe und auf mittlerer Hitze ist er perfekt, um einen Eintopf darauf simmern zu lassen. Wenn Sie sich für einen Ofen mit einem Rauchabzug an der Rückseite entscheiden, ist die gesamte Oberseite frei zum Kochen.

Ein etwas weniger dekorativer Nutzen eines Holzofens besteht im Trocknen von Wäsche. Die Hitze ist wunderbar effektiv darin, Stoffen die Feuchtigkeit zu entziehen – ganz besonders wenn die Wäsche nahe der Decke hängt, wo die Wärme aufsteigt und zirkuliert – ein Deckentrockner ist hier ideal. Die Sicherheitsregel ist allerdings, dass nichts so nahe am Ofen sein darf, dass es eine Brandgefahr darstellt, insbesondere wenn es sich um synthetische Fasern oder leichtes Gewebe handelt – beides ist hitzeanfälliger.

*im englischsprachigen Raum üblich, in Deutschland und Österreich selten.

Oben: *An grauen, kalten Tagen gibt es nichts Besseres als einen Holzofen für eine warme, gemütliche Atmosphäre. Er verleiht dem Heim einen Mittelpunkt und ein schlagendes Herz. Im Gegensatz zur seelenlos wirkenden Zentralheizung sorgt ein Holzofen für ein behagliches Wärmekissen, das sich im gesamten Haus ausbreitet.*

Links: *Einige Holzöfen verfügen über eingebaute Backrohre. Auch ohne diese Besonderheit können Sie die Ofenoberseite zum Kochen nutzen. Viele Holzofenbesitzer schwören darauf, dass es besser schmeckt als eine auf dem Gas- oder Elektroherd gekochte Mahlzeit!*

EIN „GRÜNERER" LEBENSSTIL

Jede sehr schnelle Oxidation – oder Verbrennung – führt zur Freisetzung von Kohlendioxid in die Atmosphäre. Ist ein Holzofen also tatsächlich eine umweltfreundlichere Art, unser Zuhause zu heizen? Die meisten Umweltschützer glauben, dass die Freisetzung von fossilen Kohlenstoffen (z. B. Kohle, Öl oder Erdgas aus unterirdischen Quellen, die vor Millionen von Jahren aus Wäldern entstanden sind) schlecht für die Umwelt ist. Erneuerbare Kohlenstoffe – etwa aus nachwachsenden Wäldern – sollten jedoch sinnvoll und mit Bedacht bewirtschaftet und geerntet und das geschlagene Holz möglichst effizient genutzt werden. Bäume, Sträucher und Unterholz werden zu einem wilden Dickicht, das sich selbst erstickt. Die Verbrennung von Holz ist hingegen Teil eines natürlichen Kreislaufs: Sie nutzt gefällte oder umgestürzte Bäume und macht Platz für neugepflanzte Bäume. Anders als fossile Brennstoffe oder Mineralien ist der Nachschub dieses Heizmaterials unerschöpflich, solange wir unsere Bäume pflegen. Allerdings ist trockenes Holz für eine saubere und effiziente Verbrennung unerlässlich. Es ist wichtig, Holz zu verwenden, das zuvor gespalten, geschlichtet und in einer geeigneten Umgebung getrocknet wurde und einen geringeren Feuchtigkeitsgehalt als 20 % aufweist.

Die Energie wird nicht aus einer Hunderte oder gar Tausende Kilometer entfernten Quelle geliefert, sondern mit eigener Hände Arbeit erzeugt.

EIN GEFÜHL DER ZUFRIEDENHEIT

Wenn unser Holzofen brennt, gehe ich regelmäßig zum nächsten Holzstoß an der Hintertür, hole einen neuen Sack Holz und leere ihn in den Holzkorb. Dann hole ich eine Tüte mit Anzündholz und einige Zeitungen. All dies geschieht jeden Tag, manchmal sogar mehrmals am Abend, je nachdem, wie gnadenlos das Wetter draußen ist. Dieser Holzvorrat wird Woche für Woche mit der Schubkarre aus einem der anderen weiter entfernten Holzlager am Ende unseres sehr langen Gartens aufgefüllt. Man könnte das alles als mühsam empfinden, die Plackerei ist jedoch nicht mehr so groß, wenn man bedenkt, welchen Nutzen man davon hat. Die Energie wird nicht aus Hunderten oder Tausenden von Kilometern Entfernung geliefert, sondern mit den eigenen Händen erzeugt. Für mich und viele andere ist das mit einem tiefen Gefühl der Zufriedenheit verbunden, das die körperliche Anstrengung mehr als wettmacht.

EINE PRAKTISCHE LÖSUNG

Ich besuche viele Tischlereien und die meisten, wenn nicht fast alle, haben entweder einen Holzofen oder eine Heizung, die mit Pellets aus Holzabfällen oder Holzresten selbst betrieben wird. Es wäre auch in der Tat merkwürdig, wenn sie ihr überschüssiges Holz nicht auf diese Weise verwerten würden.

Für kleinere Werkstätten empfehle ich grundsätzlich geschlossene Heizsysteme, um nicht der Gefahr durch Staubexplosionen ausgesetzt zu sein. Nicht jeder ist sich dessen bewusst, dass jeder Staub, egal wie träge er sein mag, unter bestimmten Umständen zur Explosion gebracht werden kann. Dennoch muss man zwischen „liegendem" und „fliegendem Staub" unterscheiden. Eine geringe Menge Staub und Späne auf dem Boden stellen keine Gefahr dar, also kann in dieser Situation ein Ofen genutzt werden; achten Sie aber darauf, brennbare Materialien wie Holz, Lacke und Polituren sowie Tücher davon fernzuhalten.

Hausboote, Wohnwagen und Campingbusse brauchen Wärme für den Komfort und zum Kochen – oft ist der Holzofen die einzige praktische Lösung. Es gibt tatsächlich kleinere Öfen, die für Hausboote und Narrowboats, eine kleinere englische Spezialbootsklasse für die Kanalschifffahrt, gedacht sind. Zu den wesentlichen Sicherheitsmaßnahmen gehören ein abgedichteter Rauchfang, ein fester, ebener Untergrund (z. B. eine Betonplatte) und ein Kohlenmonoxidmelder.

Oben: *Gut gepflegte Wälder sind eine Quelle für erneuerbare Energie – so geerntetes Holz macht Platz für frisch gesetzte Bäume.*

Oben: *Ein Holzofen ist oft die einzige praktische Lösung, um in einer Werkstatt, in einem Wohnwagen, Wohnmobil oder einem Hausboot zu kochen und zu heizen.*

Oben: *Im Gegensatz zu einem offenen Feuer ist ein Holzofen sehr leicht zu anzuzünden, gibt schnell viel Wärme ab und das Feuer lässt sich einfach regulieren und aufrechterhalten.*

Oben rechts: *Das Holzhacken für Ihren Ofen ist eine gesunde, zufriedenstellende Arbeit im Freien und ein gutes Gegenmittel für all die Zeit, die wir sitzend drinnen verbringen.*

ZEIT IM FREIEN

Der Holzofen entspricht unserem Wunsch nach einem einfacheren, bodenständigeren Lebensstil. Er bringt selbst in das hektischste Arbeitsleben ein Naturelement ein – etwas, was der alltäglichen Zentralheizung per Knopfdruck niemals gelingen wird. Wenn Sie gerne draußen sind, haben Sie hier die perfekte Ausrede, um auf Brennholzsuche zu gehen. Mit einem Baum, der mit der Kettensäge gefällt und in Scheite gespalten wurde, lernen Sie, wie sich das Holz am besten und effizientesten spalten und im Freien unter einem Dach trocknen lässt, damit es dann einsatzbereit ist. All dies macht sehr zufrieden und die Bewegung tut Ihnen gut. Dann, nach einem harten Arbeitstag an der frischen Luft voller Holzhacken und -schlichten können Sie sich auf ein langes, heißes Bad freuen, gefolgt von Entspannung vor ebendiesem Ofen, der verantwortlich für all die harte Arbeit zuvor ist.

Wenn Sie das Leben im Freien mögen, kaufen Sie sich einen Holzofen und nutzen Sie ihn ausgiebig; der Lohn überwiegt die investierte Zeit und Mühe um ein Vielfaches!

HOLZÖFEN VERSTEHEN

FUNKTIONSWEISE VON ÖFEN

Holzöfen sind geschlossene Systeme. Sie bestehen aus einem Korpus aus Gusseisen oder Stahl, der für gewöhnlich auf Füßen steht, mit einer verglasten oder massiven Metalltür vorne und einem Rauchabzug an der Ober- oder Hinterseite. Grundsätzlich befinden sich Klappen und Regler zur Luftzufuhr über und unter der Tür, die sich öffnen und schließen lassen. Im Inneren befindet sich ein Rost (der sich bei Allesbrennern*, die für unterschiedliche Brennstoffe geeignet sind, herausnehmen lässt) und darunter das Aschefach, in dem die Asche zur Entsorgung gesammelt wird. Der Brennraum verfügt an den Seiten über wärmespeichernde Steine (Schamottsteine) und eine Prallplatte an der Oberseite.

Der s-förmige Luftstrom im Ofeninneren ist viel effizienter und leichter kontrollierbar als ein offenes Feuer, was zu einer besser vorhersehbaren Verbrennungsrate und zu geringerer Rauchentwicklung führt.

Der Ofen arbeitet mit einem zweistufigen Verbrennungsprozess (siehe nebenstehende Abbildung), bei dem die Luft durch die untere Luftzufuhr und durch den Brennraum strömt (dies wird Primärluft genannt), um die Verbrennung anzuheizen. Der teilweise verbrannte Rauch gelangt dann unter die Prallplatte, wo er heiß bleibt und dann ein zweites Mal verbrennt, bevor er über den Rauchabzug wieder austritt (dies wird auch Sekundärluft genannt). Die oberen Regler werden verwendet, um die Verbrennungsrate zu kontrollieren. Dieser s-förmige Luftstrom ist effizienter und lässt sich leichter kontrollieren als ein offenes Feuer, was zu einer besser vorhersehbaren Verbrennungsrate und geringerer Rauchentwicklung führt.

*im englischsprachigen Raum üblich, in Deutschland und Österreich selten.

DER ZWEISTUFIGE VERBRENNUNGSPROZESS

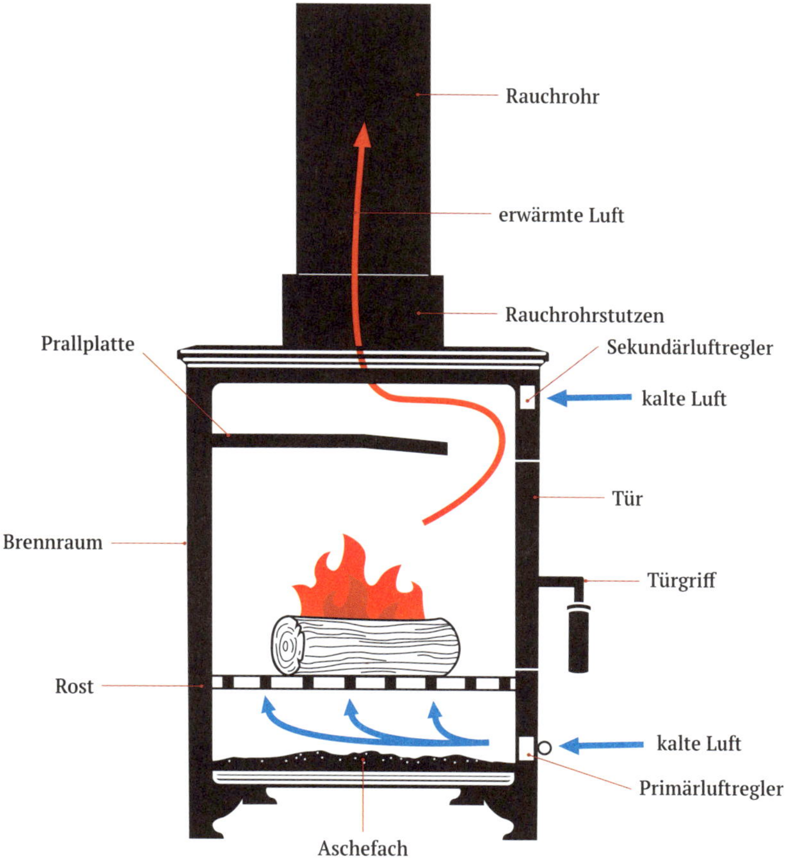

TIPP

Achten Sie darauf, dass der Schornstein oben nicht blockiert ist. Ein großer, überhängender Baum kann beispielsweise verhindern, dass der Rauch frei abziehen kann. Dies kann dazu führen, dass der Rauch zurück in den Raum gedrückt wird, wenn der Ofen geöffnet wird. Wenn der Schornstein zu niedrig ist, kann er möglicherweise nicht gut ziehen, weil zu wenig Auftrieb entsteht.

ARTEN VON ÖFEN

Moderne Öfen sind in einer Vielzahl von Größen und Ausführungen erhältlich. Einige sind nur für die Verbrennung von Holz ausgelegt, während andere mit Pellets betrieben werden oder mehrere Brennstoffe verbrennen können. Sie können freistehend sein oder in der Wand verbaut werden. Öfen können mehr als nur heizen – man kann mit Herden Mahlzeiten kochen, während wasserführende Öfen nicht nur das Haus heizen, sondern auch Warmwasser liefern.

PELLETÖFEN

Diese Öfen nutzen Holzpellets, die aus gepresstem Sägemehl hergestellt werden. Hierfür wird Sägemehl durch eine Hochdruckpresse gepresst, was zu kleinen Pellets mit einem Durchmesser von 6–8 mm führt. Sie können in einem in den Ofen integrierten Trichter (sog. Pellets-Hopper) gelagert werden, der händisch befüllt werden muss, oder in separaten Silos oder Behältern, die den Ofen durch ein automatisiertes System beschicken. Diese Möglichkeit der Schüttgutlagerung führt zu Kosteneinsparungen und minimiert den Aufwand im Umgang mit den Pellets. Die Verwendung von Pellets ist weniger energieeffizient als Scheitholz, aber effizienter verglichen mit fossilen und nicht erneuerbaren Energiequellen.

ALLESBRENNER

Allesbrenner werden auch als Mehrstoff- oder Multibrennstoff-Öfen bezeichnet. Sie sind zum Heizen mit verschiedenen Brennstoffen gedacht, darunter Steinkohle, Holz und Holzbriketts. Ihr Vorteil liegt in ihrer Vielseitigkeit: Wenn die Holzbestände niedrig werden, kann man auch alternatives Brennmaterial nutzen.

FREISTEHENDE ÖFEN

Freistehende Öfen werden von Beinen oder einem Podest gehalten und sind in unterschiedlichsten Formen und Größen zu haben. Sie sind am beliebtesten, weil sich der Ort, an dem sie aufgebaut werden sollen, frei wählen lässt. Sie sind meist rechteckig oder kastenförmig. Wenn es schon einen offenen Kamin gibt, kann ein traditioneller, kastenförmiger Ofen in die Öffnung gestellt werden. Weitere Optionen sind runde und ovale Modelle sowie Öfen auf Sockeln.

Oben: *Kaminkassetten werden direkt in einen Kamin eingebaut und brauchen weniger Platz. Sie sind im deutschsprachigen Raum wenig verbreitet.*

KAMINKASSETTEN UND KASSETTENÖFEN

Mit ihrem schlichten, minimalistischen Aussehen sind diese Öfen kompakter als die freistehenden Modelle, weshalb sie bei begrenzten Platzmöglichkeiten praktisch sind. Kaminkassetten sind so gebaut, dass sie direkt in einen Kamin oder ein Kaminsims eingebaut werden können. Für gewöhnlich haben sie einen eingebauten Luftschlitz, weshalb sie nicht so viel Platz rundherum benötigen wie ein Freisteher. Kaminkassetten können genauso effizient sein, auch wenn sie eine kleinere Oberfläche haben. Kassettenöfen sind so gebaut, dass sie plan mit der Wand abschließen, um einen „Feuerfenstereffekt" zu kreieren. Sie sind rundherum mit einem Metallrahmen ausgestattet, der als Luftschlitz dient, damit der Ofen die Luft aus dem Raum ziehen kann. Die meisten Modelle haben außerdem eine externe Luftversorgung: ein kleines Rohr, das frische Luft von draußen ansaugt. Einige sind für einen verbesserten Luftstrom mit einem eingebauten Ventilator ausgestattet.

FESTBRENNSTOFFHERDE

Auch wenn ihre Hauptaufgabe das Kochen ist, dienen Herde oft als einzige Wärmequelle in größeren Küchen. Ursprünglich für den Gebrauch von Kohle konzipiert, wurden diese Geräte dazu entwickelt, eine Vielzahl an Brennstoffen zu nutzen, darunter auch verschiedene. Holzherde wurden für das Verbrennen von Holzscheiten entwickelt. Die im Brennraum erzeugte Hitze zirkuliert durch den Ofen und liefert so eine stabile und zuverlässige Ofentemperatur. Einige Herde sind mit integrierten Boilern ausgestattet, sodass Koch-, Heiz- und Warmwasserfunktionen kombiniert werden können.

WASSERFÜHRENDE ÖFEN

Als weitere Option, die Warmwasser und Heizung gleichermaßen liefert, können wasserführende Öfen an ein Heizungs- und Warmwassersystem angeschlossen werden. Die Wärme, die durch das Verbrennen des Holzes entsteht, wird durch das Haus gepumpt. Da die Hauptfunktion wasserführender Öfen das Aufheizen von Wasser ist, erzeugen sie typischerweise nur minimale Wärme für den sie umgebenden Raum. Wasserführende Öfen gibt es generell in zwei Kategorien: Einschubkessel und Mantelkessel (Mantelboiler).

Einschubkessel können in bereits bestehende Öfen eingebaut werden: Dabei handelt es sich um einen dünnen, rechteckigen Metallkasten, der die Schamottsteine an der Ofenrückseite ersetzt. Die durch das Feuer erzeugte Wärme erhitzt das Wasser im Einschubkessel, das dann durch die Heiz- und Warmwassersysteme zirkuliert. Einschubkessel liefern für gewöhnlich genug Wärme für den privaten Warmwasserbedarf und können auch noch einen Heizkörper unterstützen.

Ein Ofen mit Mantelkessel hat einen in den Brennraum integrierten Kessel. Er führt entlang der Seiten und der Rückseite des Brennraums. Diese Bauart vergrößert die Kesseloberfläche, wodurch er eine größere Wärmemenge an das Wasser abgeben kann als der Einschubkessel – und oft genügt, um ein ganzes Haus zu heizen.

Oben: *Wasserführende Öfen produzieren sowohl Warmwasser als auch Heizwärme.*

VORSCHRIFTEN FÜR HOLZÖFEN

Dies ist eine überblicksmäßige Auswahl an rechtlichen Vorgaben – ohne Anspruch auf Vollständigkeit.

RECHTLICHE ANFORDERUNGEN BEI ANSCHAFFUNG UND INSTALLATION EINES HOLZOFENS (EU, ÖSTERREICH, DEUTSCHLAND)

PRODUKTHAFTUNG UND EU-ÖKODESIGN

Industriell hergestellte Holzöfen müssen für den freien EU-Binnenmarkt zugelassene und gekennzeichnete Geräte sein. Sie müssen die Anforderungen der EU-Ökodesign-Verordnung erfüllen, insbesondere bezüglich Emissions- und Effizienzgrenzwerten (Staub, Kohlenmonoxid [CO], Stickstoffverbindungen [NOx] und organisch gebundene Kohlenstoffe) sowie Energieeffizienzangaben in der Produktbeschreibung enthalten. Hersteller und Händler müssen entsprechende technische Unterlagen und Warn-/Sicherheitsinformationen bereitstellen.

BAUGENEHMIGUNG UND ANZEIGE DURCH BAUHERRN

In Österreich gilt: Jede wesentliche bauliche Änderung oder Neuerrichtung einer Heizungsanlage, einschließlich eines Holzofens, ist der zuständigen Baubehörde (i. d. R. Bürgermeister) schriftlich anzuzeigen; lokale Ausnahmen gelten z. B. für Kleinfeuerungen unter einer Nennwärmeleistung von 4 kW. Unabhängig davon muss die Überwachungsstelle (meist der Rauchfangkehrer) über die Neuinstallation, wesentliche Änderung oder Wiederinbetriebnahme informiert werden. In Deutschland ist grundsätzlich eine bauordnungsrechtliche Genehmigung nicht bei allen Anlagen verpflichtend; jedoch können je nach Kommune und Gebäudetyp (z. B. denkmalgeschützte Gebäude, Wohnungsbau) zusätzliche Genehmigungspflichten oder Meldungen bestehen.

VORSCHRIFTEN FÜR HOLZÖFEN

UMWELT- UND IMMISSIONSSCHUTZ

In Deutschland regelt die 1. Bundes-Immissionsschutzverordnung (1. BImSchV) den Betrieb von kleinen und mittleren Feuerungsanlagen. Neugeräte müssen die aktuellen Emissions- und Wirkungsgradgrenzwerte einhalten. Für ältere Anlagen gelten Fristen und Übergangsregelungen; nicht konforme Geräte müssen nachgerüstet, ersetzt oder stillgelegt werden. In Österreich sind ähnliche Grenzwerte durch nationale Heizungs- und Luftreinhaltegesetze sowie technische Normen (z. B. ÖNORM) umgesetzt; dies betrifft vor allem Emissionswerte, Mindestwirkungsgrade und Abgasführung.

ABNAHME UND ÜBERPRÜFUNG

Vor Inbetriebnahme ist die Anlage durch eine autorisierten Schornsteinfeger/in bzw. Rauchfangkehrer/in abzunehmen. Diese prüft insbesondere die Eignung und den Zustand des Rauchfangs, die sichere Abgasführung, eine ausreichende Zuluftversorgung sowie die Einhaltung von Sicherheits- und Brandschutzabständen.

SICHERHEITS- UND BRANDSCHUTZANFORDERUNGEN

Die Installation muss den bau- und feuerungstechnischen Vorschriften entsprechen (z. B. Sicherheitsabstände zu brennbaren Materialien, feuerfeste Unterlage, geeignete Schornsteinhöhe). Die Herstellerangaben und einschlägige Normen (z. B. ÖNORM B 8311) sind verbindlich zu beachten; Abweichungen bedürfen einer gesonderten Abnahme.

BETRIEBSPFLICHTEN UND BRENNSTOFF

Sie sind verpflichtet, nur geeignete Brennstoffe zu verwenden (z. B. trockenes, unbehandeltes Holz) und die Anlage ordnungsgemäß zu betreiben. Unsachgemäßer Betrieb kann ordnungs- oder haftungsrechtliche Konsequenzen nach sich ziehen (z. B. Nachbarschaftsstörungen, Umweltauflagen).

STANDORT IM HAUS

Der Standort Ihres Ofens spielt höchstwahrscheinlich eine Rolle bei der Wahl von Größe, Stil und Ausstattung. Wenn Sie ihn beispielsweise in der Nähe oder gar direkt in der Küche aufstellen möchten, fällt die Wahl vielleicht auf ein Modell mit guter Kochmöglichkeit. Wenn Sie einen großen Raum oder das Glück haben, ein Haus oder einen Anbau nach Ihren eigenen Vorstellungen bauen zu können, dann könnte ein Modell, das von allen Seiten betrachtet werden kann, genau in der Mitte des Raumes aufgestellt werden. Für einen großen, offenen Raum wollen Sie wahrscheinlich einen Ofen hoher Leistung, um den Raum ausreichend beheizen zu können. Ein kleiner Raum hingegen erfordert nur einen kleinen Ofen.

Für ein besseres Verständnis müssen Sie beachten, wie sich die Wärme von einem Ofen ausbreitet. Sobald sie in die Luft um den Ofen herum gelangt, entsteht eine Konvektionsströmung. Wie wir in der Schule gelernt haben, steigt Wärme nach oben, weshalb die erwärmte Luft nach oben steigt. Wenn Sie sich auf eine Trittleiter stellen, werden Sie merken, dass sich sehr viel wärmere Luft in Deckennähe befindet, wo sie nicht besonders nützlich ist. Dieser Vorgang ist daher, wie die meisten konventionellen Heizungen, ineffizient. Die heiße Luft kühlt aus und sinkt wieder nach unten. Sie strömt in einem Kreislauf zurück zum Boden, um dort wieder erwärmt zu werden und erneut zur Decke aufzusteigen. Der Begriff „Konvektion" beschreibt diesen gesamten Zirkulationsprozess – ein kontinuierliches Muster, über das wir wenig Kontrolle haben. Darüber hinaus strahlt der Ofen in alle Richtungen im Raum Wärme ab, weshalb zwei Heizeffekte gleichzeitig stattfinden, nämlich Konvektion und Strahlung.

TIPP

Der Einbau eines Schornsteins in einem niedrigeren Haus als die typischen ein oder zwei Stockwerke oder auch das Nachrüsten in einem Haus ohne Rauchfang kann gegen Bauvorschriften und -auflagen verstoßen. Sprechen Sie zuerst mit den Nachbarn über etwaige Einwände und wenden Sie sich an die örtliche Baubehörde.

Oben: *Wenn Ihr Raum keinen Schornstein hat, bedeutet das nicht zwingend, dass Sie keinen Holzofen nutzen können; vielleicht lässt sich das Problem ja durch einen aufgesetzten Edelstahlschornstein beheben. Lassen Sie sich von einem Hafnerfachbetrieb beraten.*

Aufgrund der Art und Weise, wie warme Luft zirkuliert, kann es sein, dass es im Raum mit dem Ofen sehr heiß ist, während es nebenan viel kühler ist, selbst bei offenstehender Tür. Um dem entgegenzuwirken, können große Lüftungsschlitze oben und unten an der Trennwand eingebaut werden. Noch besser geeignet sind Raumteiler, die sich nach hinten öffnen lassen, damit die warme Luft zirkulieren kann. Im Idealfall steht der Ofen in einem offenen Bereich ohne Wände oder Türen, die die Luftbewegung im Erdgeschoss und bis hinauf in den ersten Stock beeinträchtigen können. Ist dies nicht möglich, können Sie Lüftungsschlitze in den Decken anbringen, damit die warme Luft das obere Stockwerk erreichen kann (vorbehaltlich der Genehmigung durch Ihre örtliche Baubehörde).

LUFTZIRKULATION VON RAUM ZU RAUM MIT LÜFTUNGSSCHLITZEN IN DER TRENNWAND

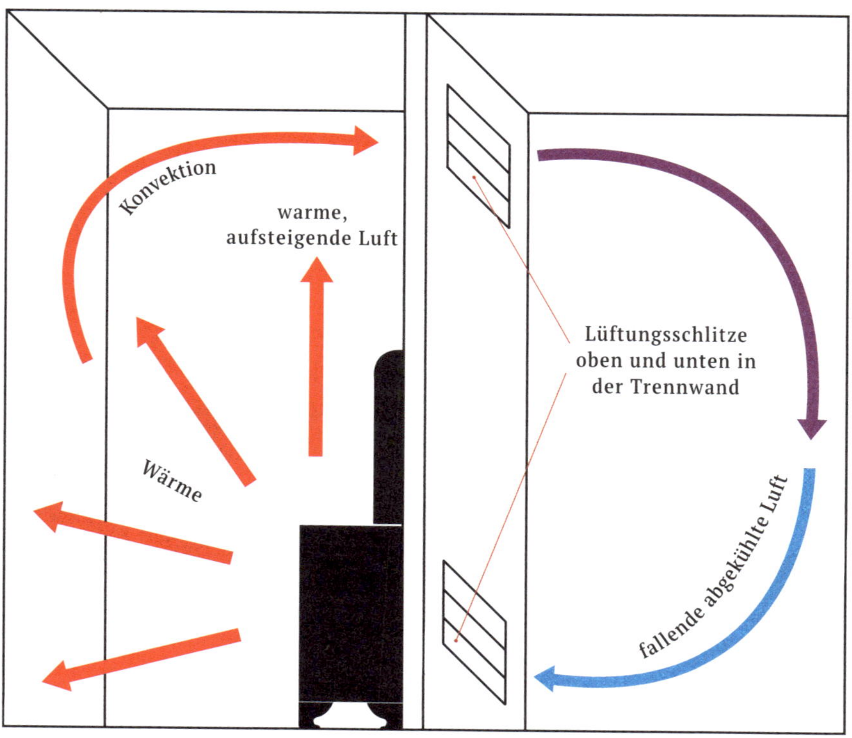

LUFTZIRKULATION VON EINEM STOCKWERK IN DAS NÄCHSTE MIT LÜFTUNGSSCHLITZEN IN DER DECKE

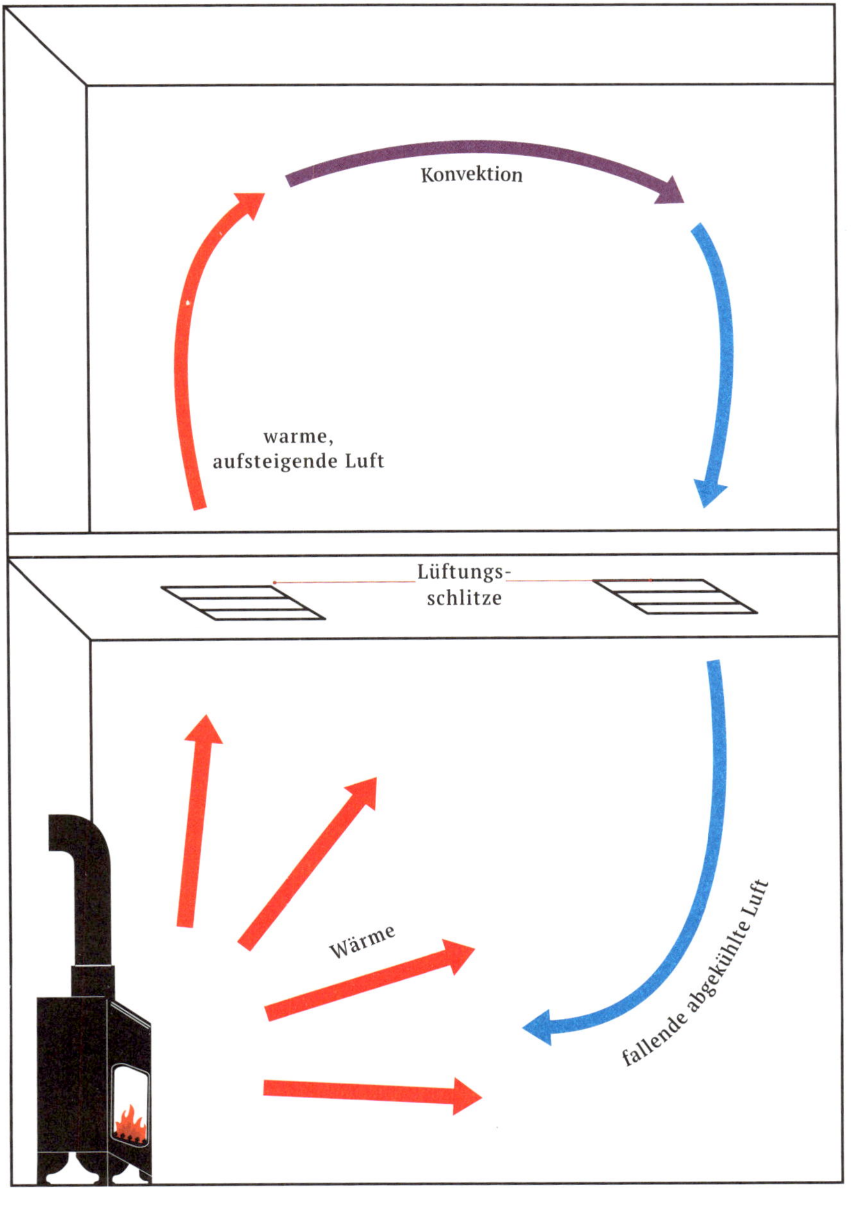

DIE RICHTIGE GRÖSSE WÄHLEN

Überlegen Sie sich, was Sie mit Ihrem Ofen erreichen möchten. Möchten Sie damit Ihr ganzes Haus heizen? Werden sie für Wärme nur auf ihn angewiesen sein? Oder wollen sie ihn nur zusätzlich zu einer bestehenden Zentralheizung und den Ofen nur für den dekorativen Effekt nutzen?

Für letzteren Fall sollten Sie beim Kauf bedenken, dass der Ofen im Notfall groß genug sein sollte, um beim Ausfall Ihrer primären Wärmequelle einspringen zu können. Es ist beruhigend zu wissen, dass man ein Backup hat, wenn die Zentralheizung ausfällt oder Schwierigkeiten mit Extremwetterlagen hat.

Allerdings bringt ein größerer Ofen auch einen Nachteil mit sich: In einem kleinen Raum wird es stickig. Zur Orientierung: Ein Ofen mit einer Leistung von 5 kW entspricht zwei großen Heizstrahlern zu je 2.500 Watt, was – ich denke, da können Sie mir zustimmen – schon eine recht hohe Heizleistung ist. In einem kleinen Raum neben dem Ofen zu sitzen, fühlt sich für die meisten Menschen drückend an. Selbst wenn Ihr Zimmer sehr geräumig ist, kann sich ein großer Ofen ohne passende Lüftung unangenehm anfühlen, insbesondere wenn Sie eine Doppel- oder Dreifachverglasung haben.

TIPP

Die nominale Heizleistung eines Holzofens sollte nur als Anhaltspunkt herangezogen werden. Die tatsächliche Wärmemenge wird von der Einstellung der Luftzufuhr, der Verschmutzung des Rostes und dem Brennstoff bedingt. Viel hängt davon ab, wie feucht oder trocken das Holz ist. An einem windigen Tag kann das Feuer besser ziehen, wenn die Luftzufuhr nicht teilweise geschlossen wird, um dies zu kompensieren. Vor einer endgültigen Entscheidung lohnt sich eine professionelle Beratung.

Oben: *Dieser Ofen ist nicht groß, aber seine Heizleistung ist für einen mittelgroßen Raum völlig ausreichend. Ein größerer Ofen könnte zu stark sein.*

***Oben**: Ein großer Ofen wie dieser liefert genug Heizleistung für einen offenen Raum mit hoher Decke. Außerdem verleiht er einem minimalistischen Raum eine dramatische Note.*

Als Faustregel gilt, jeder Holzofen mit einer Heizleistung über 5 kW benötigt eine zusätzliche Luftzufuhr. Dazu können Sie eine Lüftung am Fenster nutzen, die permanent oder zumindest in der groben Anheizphase offenstehen muss, was bei kühlem oder windigem Wetter kontraproduktiv ist, wenn Sie versuchen, den Raum warmzuhalten. Der beste Weg, um Zugluft zu vermeiden, ist daher eine spezielle Luftzufuhr, möglicherweise unter den Dielen, die vor dem Holzofen entlüftet.

Als Faustregel brauchen Sie 1 kW Heizleistung je 14 m^3 durchschnittlich isolierter Fläche, um eine Raumtemperatur von 22 °C bei einer Außentemperatur von 0 °C aufrechtzuerhalten. Sie müssen also die Größe des Raums, den Sie beheizen wollen, eruieren, bevor Sie sich für die richtige Größe des Ofens entscheiden. Wenn Sie sich unsicher sind, kann Sie jeder seriöse Energieberater unterstützen.

RAUMBERECHNUNGEN

Um das Kubikvolumen zu messen, multiplizieren Sie Länge und Breite des Raumes mit der Raumhöhe. Misst ein Raum zum Beispiel 3,5 m x 4 m, beträgt die Bodenfläche 14 m^2; ist der Raum 3 m hoch, beträgt das Volumen 42 m^3.

Selbst wenn Sie Ihren Ofen hauptsächlich zu Dekorationszwecken nutzen, ist es beruhigend, ein Backup zu haben, wenn die Zentralheizung ausfällt oder mit besonders schlechtem Wetter nicht zurechtkommt.

Gibt es Hindernisse, wie etwa eine verkleidete Treppe, berechnen Sie zuerst das Volumen des gesamten Raums, messen dann den verkleideten Teil aus und ziehen ihn von der größeren Zahl ab.

TIPP

Es gibt heutzutage einige sehr raffinierte Laser-Messgeräte, die (wenn Sie den Dreh einmal heraushaben) das Vermessen eines Raums zum Kinderspiel machen. Wenn Sie einen Fachmann zu Rate ziehen, nutzt dieser höchstwahrscheinlich ebenso ein Gerät.

AUSSEHEN UND EIGENSCHAFTEN

Es gibt viele zusätzliche Eigenschaften, die einen Ofen attraktiver machen können. Diese können funktional sein, wie etwa die Art der Luftzufuhr (siehe S. 26 f.), die Eignung auch in einem Immissionsschutzgebiet (siehe S. 23) oder die Möglichkeit, damit zu kochen (siehe S. 11). Sie können aber auch kosmetischer Natur sein, wie etwa die Farbe oder die Scheibengröße in der Tür. Vor allem müssen Sie entscheiden, ob Sie einen Ofen haben möchten, den man mit verschiedenen Brennstoffen beheizen kann oder einen, der nur für Scheitholz geeignet ist.

Eine oder mehrere verglaste Türen ermöglichen Ihnen, den Blick ins Feuer – und wenn es hübsch aussieht, dann verstärkt dies das Gefühl der Wärme, das von dem Ofen ausgeht.

ALLESBRENNER ODER HOLZOFEN

Diese Frage ist meiner Meinung nach keine Überlegung wert. Auch wenn es nützlich sein mag, den Brennstoff wechseln zu können, ist die Wahrscheinlichkeit groß, dass Sie bei einem bleiben werden – und am einfachsten ist der Umgang mit Holz. Kohle und raucharme Brennstoffe (z. B. raucharme Kohlebriketts) sind schmutzig in der Handhabung und brauchen einen Ort, wo sie trocken gelagert werden können – also einen Kohlenkeller. Holz kann auf verschiedene Arten gelagert werden. Es lässt sich leichter stapeln und arrangieren und kann immer noch einigermaßen vorzeigbar oder sogar eindrucksvoll aussehen. Ich bin nicht so sicher, ob ich schon einmal von jemandem gehört habe, der versucht hat, seine Besucher mit der Größe seines Kohlenkellers zu beeindrucken …

Oben: *Ein kleiner antiker Ofen wie dieser hier wäre eine hübsche Bereicherung für jeden Raum, entspricht aber wahrscheinlich nicht modernen Sicherheitsstandards.*

Kohle und raucharme Brennstoffe erzeugen ein verschmolzenes Material, das Schlacke genannt wird. Es ist etwas mühsam, sie vor der Entsorgung abzutrennen und zu entfernen (sie kann auf unbefestigte Wege oder in den Müll geworfen werden, wenn es nicht zu viel ist). Bei der Verbrennung von Holz zerfällt die Asche meist bei jedem Heizvorgang und fällt natürlich durch den Rost. Bei der Entfernung und Entsorgung ist Vorsicht geboten, um nichts zu verschütten, aber das ist nach meiner Erfahrung sicherlich leichter als die Alternative.

IMMISSIONSSCHUTZGEBIETE

Es gibt sowohl in Österreich als auch in Deutschland Gebiete (z. B. Grazer Becken, Stuttgart etc.) mit einer Einschränkung oder einem befristeten Verbot der Verbrennung herkömmlicher Brennstoffe (z. B. Naturschutzgebiet) aufgrund von erhöhten Luftverschmutzungen. Ihre örtliche Behörde kann Ihnen Auskunft darüber geben. Ist dies der Fall, müssen Sie eventuell nachweisen, dass Ihr Holzofen geeignet ist.

STAHL ODER GUSSEISEN?

Viele der heutigen Öfen werden eher aus Stahl statt aus traditionellem Gusseisen hergestellt. Stahlöfen können mit weniger Gewicht gefertigt werden, weshalb sie nicht so lange zum Aufheizen brauchen, und der geschweißte Aufbau sorgt für eine exzellente Luftabdichtung. Selbst wenn eine der Schweißnähte undicht wird, lässt sich dies für gewöhnlich reparieren. Stahlkonstruktionen sind vielseitig und erlauben aufwendigere und fantasievollere Gestaltungsmöglichkeiten.

Gusseisen hingegen strahlt viel länger Wärme ab als ein Stahlofen. Es ist weniger anfällig für Verformungen und Korrosion durch Verbrennungsprodukte.

DIE WAHL DER TÜR

Der Stil der Türen ist wichtig. Glastüren erlauben Ihnen, den Anblick des Feuers zu genießen – und wenn sie schön sind, trägt das zu der Behaglichkeit bei, die die Wärme abgibt. Wenn Sie den richtigen Platz haben, könnten Sie Ihren Ofen auch in die Mitte des Raums stellen, wo es sich lohnen würde, Glastüren auf jeder Seite zu haben. Eine solide Metalltür ist eine Option, wenn Sie es nicht als notwendig empfinden oder nicht mögen, das Feuer auf dem Rost zu beobachten, ich bin mir allerdings keines großen Vorteils hinsichtlich Kosten oder Effizienz bewusst. Einige Doppeltüren lassen sich öffnen, dürfen jedoch im deutschsprachigen Raum nicht offengelassen werden (selbstschließende Türen sind vorgeschrieben), während der Ofen arbeitet – bedenken Sie, dass darüber hinaus die Wärmeeffizienz so sinkt und die Brandgefahr steigt, da viele Holzarten Funken sprühen (siehe S. 58).

FACHBEGRIFFE

Wenn Sie sich nach Öfen umsehen, stolpern Sie vielleicht über einige technische oder herstellereigene Begriffe. Schlagen Sie die Definitionen auf den Herstellerwebseiten nach oder besprechen Sie sie mit den Händlern; hier ist ein knapper Leitfaden zu einigen der Hauptbegriffe, auf die Sie wahrscheinlich treffen werden.

Scheibenspülung: Diese Funktion soll die Scheibe sauber halten (auch wenn ich finde, dass dies von der korrekten Nutzung der Luftzufuhr abhängt).

Heizeinsatz mit Wassertasche/Wärmetauscher: Dies bezieht sich auf einen eingebauten Wasserheizkreislauf.

***Unten links:** Dieser Stahlofen hat ein schlankes, modernes Design und nimmt bemerkenswert wenig Bodenfläche ein.*

***Unten rechts:** Wenn Sie den Luxus eines großen Raums haben und den Ofen in dessen Mitte setzen können, lohnt sich die Wahl eines Modells, das an mehr als einer Seite verglast ist.*

Emissionsarme Öfen: Diese Öfen sind so konstruiert, dass sie möglichst wenig Rauch entwickeln. Es gibt spezielle, für Umweltzonen zugelassene Modelle.

Warmluftöfen: Sie geben warme Luft durch eine spezielle Öffnung ab, um die Bildung von Konvektionsströmen (siehe S. 26 f.) zu fördern. Ihre Hitze ist schneller spürbar als die anderer Öfen.

Anheizen: Je schneller es zu einem schönen Flammenbild im Ofen kommt, desto schneller baut sich die gewünschte Thermik auf und umso besser zieht der Schornstein ab.

Raumluftunabhängige und raumluftabhängige Luftzufuhr: Diese Begriffe werden nicht immer konsistent genutzt, aber einige Hersteller unterscheiden zwischen externer Luftzufuhr (raumluftunabhängig), wo die Luft von außerhalb des Hauses in den Ofen geleitet wird, und raumluftabhängiger Luftzufuhr, wo die Luft die aus dem Rauminneren gezogen wird. Ein gut isolierter Raum, der gegen Luftzug abgedichtet wurde, liefert eventuell nicht genug Sauerstoff ohne externe Luftzufuhr.

WELCHEN STIL MÖGEN SIE?

Holzöfen sind nicht nur funktionell, sondern auch dekorativ. Es gibt sie in vielen Farben, Formen und Größen – von sehr traditionell bis ultramodern. Das traditionelle Erscheinungsbild ist nach wie vor beliebt und fügt sich überraschend gut als Kontrast in modernste Einrichtungsstile ein. Stöbern Sie in Einrichtungszeitschriften nach Ideen und recherchieren Sie dann online, was in Ihrem Budget liegt, ordern Sie Kataloge und besuchen Sie Fachhändler.

TIPP

Wenn Sie sich für einen Ofen entschieden haben, müssen Sie ihn nicht gleich kaufen. Vielleicht finden Sie das gleiche oder ein ähnliches Modell anderswo zu einem besseren Preis oder mit geringerer Liefergebühr.

Oben: *Die geschwungenen Linien der Tür verleihen diesem kleinen Ofen ein drolliges, fast schon freundliches Aussehen. Fast, als wäre er Teil der Familie!*

ZUBEHÖR

Ihr Ofen sollte mit den folgenden Teilen geliefert werden – wenn nicht, müssen Sie sie besorgen, bevor Sie Ihren Holzofen benutzen können:

- ein Türöffner für sicheres Öffnen der Ofentür;
- ein Gerät zum Bewegen des Rüttelrosts (bei Feststofföfen/Allesbrennern);
- einen Ascheschieber oder Kaminbesteck, um das Aschefach sicher und sauber aus dem Holzofen zu ziehen und zu entleeren;
- spezielle hitzebeständige Handschuhe mit rauer Struktur zum Schutz der Hände und Unterarme. Ich habe meine kürzlich gebraucht, als die Prallplatte heruntergerutscht war und sich verklemmt hatte, während der Ofen brannte. Es war eine echte Krisensituation: Ich musste brennendes Holz entfernen und das Feuer löschen, damit ich die heiße Metallplatte herausheben und wieder richtig einsetzen konnte, sobald die Temperatur im Ofen niedrig genug war. Halten Sie die Handschuhe immer griffbereit für alle Fälle, man weiß ja nie!

Die folgenden Feuerwerkzeuge sind ebenfalls unverzichtbar:

- eine Zange, um Glut, die gelegentlich durch den Rost fällt, herauszuholen und um Holzscheite umzudrehen, damit sie auf der anderen Seite brennen, während die glühende Seite nach vorne zeigt;
- eine kleine Schaufel für die Asche und um kleine Glutstücke wieder zurück in den Rost zu befördern;
- ein Schürhaken, um Holzscheite zu verschieben oder zu zerkleinern, wenn sie durchgehend angebrannt sind,
- ein Besen aus Naturfasern, um Asche auf die Schaufel zu kehren und zum Reinigen des Bereichs um den Ofen. Er muss aus Naturfasern und nicht aus Kunstfasern bestehen, damit er nicht schmilzt, sondern nur sehr leicht versengt.

Oben: *Sorgsam gewähltes Kaminbesteck kann selbst schon als attraktive Wohndekoration dienen. Ein eleganter Ständer lässt es noch stilvoller aussehen und ist praktisch, damit man alles zur Hand hat, wenn man es braucht.*

MONTAGE-METHODEN

Der Einbau eines Ofens ist nicht schwierig. Online gibt es viele Informationen darüber, wie das funktioniert. Sie sollten es allerdings nicht allein versuchen, außer Sie sind entsprechend zertifiziert. In Österreich sind die örtliche Baubehörde und der beauftragte Rauchfangkehrerbetrieb dafür zuständig, Ihr Vorhaben zu beurteilen und den daraus resultierenden Holzofen zu überprüfen. Fachpersonal mit dem Aufbau zu betrauen, kann zudem auch für Gebäudeversicherungen erforderlich sein, um zu belegen, dass alle Installationen sicher und korrekt durchgeführt wurden. Gehen Sie kein Risiko ein, ignorieren Sie diese offiziellen Schritte nicht! Die Installation sollte immer nach professionellen Standards ausgeführt werden und Sie sollten dann durch ein Dokument, das belegt, dass Ihr Holzofen diese erfüllt, geschützt sein. Ein qualifizierter Fachbetrieb kann Sie auch hinsichtlich der Praxistauglichkeit der Installation und der besten Aufbaumethode sowie der Schornsteinarten beraten. Ein professioneller Aufbau kann binnen eines Tages fertiggestellt werden.

STANDORT

Sie müssen darauf achten, Ihren Ofen in einer feuerfesten Umgebung aufzustellen, die keinerlei immanente Gefahren wie etwa Staub, Gas oder flüchtige Elemente mit sich bringt. Die direkte Umgebung von Ofen, Rauchabzug und Schornsteinanschluss muss komplett feuerfest sein, etwa aus Stein, Beton oder was auch sonst als feuerbeständig und sicher gilt. Dort, wo der Ofen ste-

TIPP

In der Theorie dürfte ein Holzofen niemanden mit Atemproblemen wie Asthma beeinträchtigen, da er hinter geschlossenen Türen und mit einem geschlossenen Rauchabzug arbeitet. Dennoch kann sich sowohl während der Verwendung als auch beim Entfernen der Asche eine gewisse Menge an Staub in der Luft entwickeln. Wenn Sie glauben, dass Sie damit ein Thema haben könnten, schauen Sie sich Holzöfen in Betrieb an und prüfen Sie, ob dies eine Reaktion hervorruft, bevor Sie sich festlegen.

Oben: *Dieser Ofen wurde vor einem bestehenden Schornstein aufgestellt, ohne den ursprünglichen Kamin zu nutzen, der verschlossen wurde. Das Rauchrohr wird als dekoratives Element genutzt.*

hen soll, brauchen Sie eine gute Belüftung, um den Holzofen einerseits mit Sauerstoff zu versorgen und – das ist am wichtigsten – sicherzustellen, dass Sie gut atmen können.

NUTZUNG EINES BESTEHENDEN SCHORNSTEINS

Wenn Sie einen bereits bestehenden Schornstein verwenden möchten, muss ein qualifizierter Fachbetrieb ihn auf Eignung überprüfen. Möglicherweise ist es notwendig, gemauerte Schornsteine durch einen zertifizierten Betrieb sanieren zu lassen. Alle damit verbundenen Dacharbeiten sollten am besten gleichzeitig von einem professionellen Dachdeckerbetrieb ausgeführt werden.

Wer einen offenen Kamin hat, geht auch immer potenziell das Risiko eines Schornsteinbrandes ein, was ziemlich beängstigend sein kann – und zwar buchstäblich, wenn Sie die Feuerwehr zum Löschen rufen müssen. Ein Holzofen steigert dieses Risiko aufgrund des effizienteren, heißeren Verbrennungsprozesses erheblich, zudem kann jedes Austreten von Kohlenmonoxid durch das Mauerwerk zum stillen Tod werden. Darum ist ein intakter Rauchfang für vollständige Sicherheit obligatorisch.

Man kann einen Kamin sanieren, indem man eine betonartige Masse eingießt, durch die ein Stöpsel gezogen wird. So werden sämtliche Fugen und Ritzen verschlossen. In größeren gemauerten Schornsteinen kann auch ein Edelstahlinnenrohr eingezogen werden. Das Anbringen biegsamer Schornsteinauskleidungen ist im deutschsprachigen Raum nicht erlaubt.

TIPP

Noch vor der Installation des Ofens sollte ihr registrierter Monteur den Schornstein aus zwei Gründen reinigen: einerseits, um ihn auf Verstopfungen zu überprüfen, andererseits, um Schmutz und potenziell brennbaren Ruß und andere Ablagerungen zu entfernen. Vergewissern Sie sich, dass dieser Arbeitsschritt durchgeführt wird.

MONTAGE EINES EDELSTAHLSCHORNSTEINS

Wenn Sie keinen bereits bestehenden Kamin verwenden, ist die Alternative ein Edelstahlschornstein, der auf den Ofen aufgesetzt wird. Auch seine Installation ist nichts für Heimwerker. Außerdem ist eine Genehmigung durch die Baubehörde und die Abstimmung mit dem zuständigen Rauchfangkehrer erforderlich. Die Arbeit muss in Übereinstimmung mit Baubestimmungen erfolgen; bei einem Rauchrohrknie muss eine Putzöffnung vorhanden sein. Die Montage ist zwangsläufig mit einem Eingriff in das Mauerwerk und die Dachziegeln oder -platten verbunden, weshalb diese Arbeit so erfolgen muss, dass kein größerer Schaden entsteht oder die Witterungsbeständigkeit des Gebäudes beeinträchtigt wird. Verläuft der Schornstein durch potenziell entflammbare Stoffe wie Holz oder Isoliermaterial, muss er zur Gewährleistung der Sicherheit mit einer hitzebeständigen Manschette ummantelt werden. Wo ein Schornstein durch das Dach führt, ist eine witterungsbeständige Dachdurchführung notwendig, um den Eintritt von Regenwasser zu verhindern. Hierfür gibt es spezielle Lösungen.

KAMINDACH

Hierbei handelt es sich um das letzte Stück auf dem Schornstein. Es erfüllt mehrere Funktionen: Es kann Regen abhalten und Vögel am Nisten hindern. Die Schornsteinabdeckung ist nicht unbedingt notwendig, wenn der Regen ohnehin nicht den Kamin hinuntertropft und wenn der Rauchfang vor der Verwendung gekehrt wurde, sind auch Vogelnester kein Problem. Allerdings haben Sie mit einer Abdeckung in beiden Fällen Ihren Seelenfrieden.

Ein versierter Fachmann wird Sie hinsichtlich des korrekten Schornsteindurchmessers für Ihren Ofen und des Platzes beraten.

Rechts: *Die besten Kamindächer scheinen die mit einem käfigartigen Gitter rundherum und einer Abdeckung an der Oberseite zu sein. Wenn der Schornstein gereinigt wird, können Sie die Bürste des Rauchfangkehrers sehen, wenn er in den Aufsatz eintritt.*

SCHORNSTEIN OHNE BESTEHENDEN KAMIN

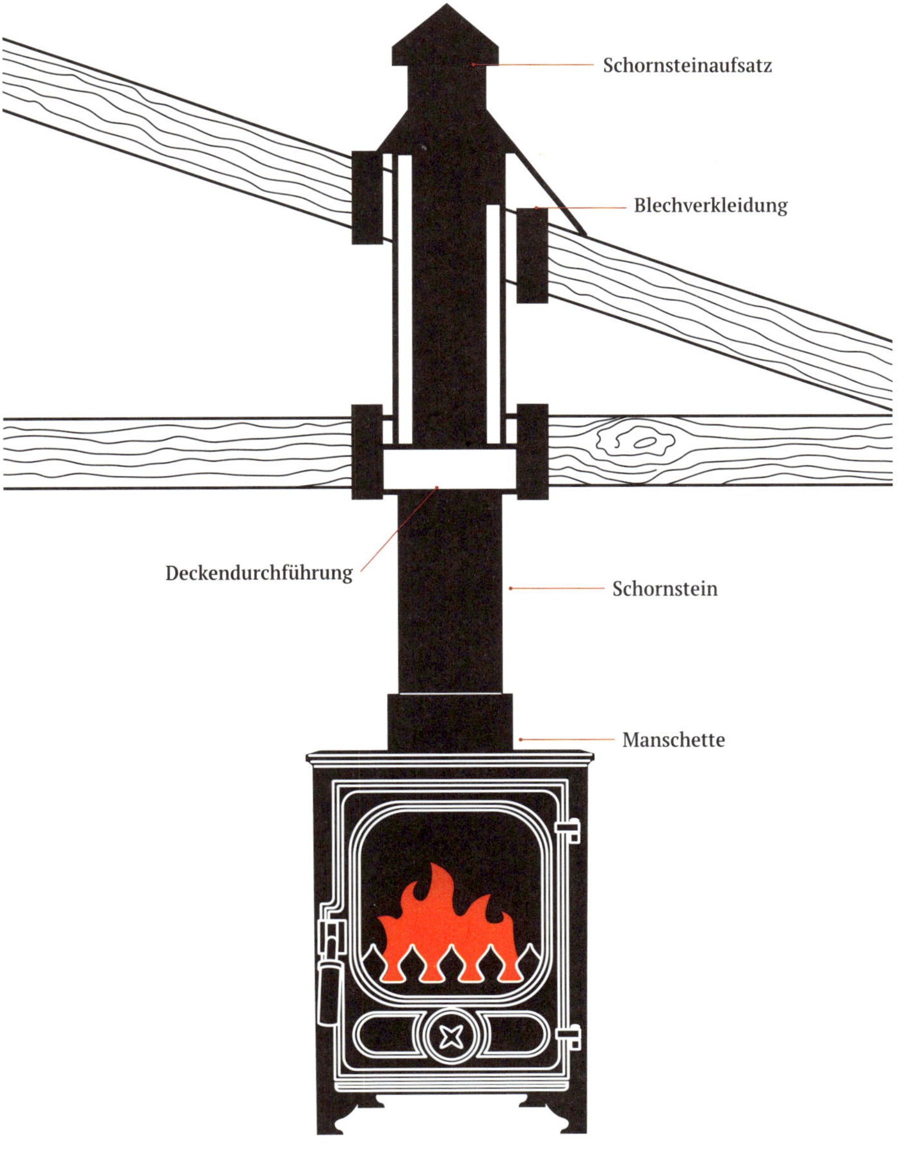

WAHL DES BRENNSTOFFS

BRENNSTOFF-ARTEN

Für mich ist Holz der Brennstoff der Wahl. Es ist leicht verfügbar, recht günstig, brennt gut, kann leicht gelagert werden und ist dekorativ und umweltfreundlich. Vielleicht besitzen Sie jedoch einen Allesbrenner oder denken über eine entsprechende Anschaffung nach. Möglicherweise leben Sie auch in einer Umweltzone und müssen sich auf raucharme Brennstoffe beschränken. Hier sind also die Fakten über die verschiedenen Optionen, die Ihnen offenstehen:

STÜCKHOLZ

Dies ist das Standardheizmaterial für einen Holzofen und wird in großer Menge benötigt, wenn Sie planen, Ihren Ofen häufig zu nutzen. Sie können es von einem Händler oder einem Holzfäller beziehen (siehe S. 62). Es gibt viele Gründe, das Holz zu spalten. Ungehackt verlangsamt die Rinde das Trocknen des Holzes oder verhindert sogar ein vollständiges Trocknen, weshalb das Spalten den Trocknungsvorgang stark beschleunigt. Das mitunter beste Holz stammt aus großen Baumstammstücken, die niemals in den Ofen passen. Durch mehrmaliges Spalten lassen sie sich daher auf handliche Größe zerkleinern. Die Rinde fungiert als Versiegelung und Isolierung. Ein rundes Holzscheit kann daher nicht schnell brennen, da die Rinde es schützt.

WARNUNG

Einige exotische und heimische Harthölzer (z. B. Eiche, Buche) sind riskant in der Handhabung, da der Hautkontakt und/oder Holzstaub eine allergische Reaktion hervorrufen kann. Falls Sie allergisch sind oder glauben, es zu sein, kann das Hantieren mit jedem Holz ein Risiko bedeuten. Feinstaub ist der schlimmste Übeltäter, da Partikel, die kleiner sind als ein Mikrometer, in die Haut und das Lungengewebe eindringen und auch die Nasengänge und Atemwege reizen können.
Der Staub von Teakholz kann beispielsweise Nasenbluten verursachen. Tragen Sie beim Sägen und im Umgang mit reizenden Hölzern stets geeignete Schutzausrüstung.
Beachten Sie, dass der einzige legitime Grund, exotische oder spezielle Hölzer zu verbrennen, sein kann, dass es sich um Werkstattabfälle oder um Holz aus einem ausgebrannten Haus handelt. Niemand heizt mit derlei Hölzern um des Heizens Willen, da es viel zu teuer ist – und einige Arten auf der Liste der geschützten Holzarten des Washingtoner Artenschutzübereinkommens (CITES) stehen.

Oben: *In kleinen Mengen können Holzscheite in Innenräumen getrocknet werden. Sie sollten allerdings in sicherer Entfernung zum Ofen gelagert werden.*

HOLZABSCHNITTE

Als Holzbearbeiter gehören Holzreste zwar zum Leben dazu, aber wenn ich mein Holzlager zusammenräume oder finde, dass ich zu viele unterschiedliche Abschnitte von Brettern habe, die zu kurz sind, um etwas mit ihnen anfangen zu können, verbrenne ich sie, solange sie nicht gestrichen oder behandelt sind. Normalerweise landen sie in meinem kleinen, geschlossenen und belüfteten Schuppen, damit sie trocken bleiben. Ich finde, jede Holzart ist dazu geeignet (siehe jedoch den Hinweis zu Allergien auf S. 48), aber je dicker die Abschnitte, umso besser, da diese langsamer und länger brennen, was vorzuziehen ist, auch wenn die Heizleistung dadurch geringer ist.

HOLZBRIKETTS

Hierbei handelt es sich um künstlich hergestellte Holzscheite, die durch das Pressen von Sägemehl hergestellt werden, wobei die natürlichen Öle und Harze im Holzstaub als Bindemittel dienen, das sie zusammenhält. Sie sind so groß wie Holzscheite, manchmal massiv, manchmal mit Loch in der Mitte, damit Sauerstoff und Flammen für eine effizientere Verbrennung auch von innen eindringen können. Sie brennen gut und sind eine effektive Art der Nutzung eines natürlichen Nebenproduktes der Holzverarbeitung. Sie liefern eine konstante Heizleistung und somit eine gute Heizwirkung.

Allerdings bringen sie zwei Nachteile mit sich: Einerseits sind sie teuer (was sich beim Kauf großer Mengen etwas verringert), andererseits müssen sie zu 100 % trocken gelagert werden. Wenn Sie dies nicht tun, zerfallen Ihre zuverlässigen künstlichen Holzscheite zu Staub, wodurch ihre Brenneffizienz gegen null sinkt – genauso wie Ihre finanzielle Investition.

Unterschiedliche Holzabschnitte von Brettern, die zu kurz sind, um etwas mit ihnen anzufangen, landen im Feuer.

KOHLE

Bestehend aus alten Bäumen, Farnen und anderer Vegetation, die unter aufeinanderliegenden Schichten aus Schlamm und Gestein unter großem Druck und bei hohen Temperaturen gepresst wurden, ist Kohle bereits „halb gebacken". Ähnlich wie Holzkohle enthält sie große Mengen an Kohlenstoff sowie Wasserstoff- und Sauerstoffatome – und andere Elemente. (Diamanten, Öl und Erdgas

Oben: Hartholz-Briketts brennen länger als Weichholz und erzeugen nur minimal Asche bei der Verbrennung.

Oben: Raucharme Brennstoffe sind umweltfreundlicher als Kohle, aber dennoch weniger gut zu unserem Planeten als die Verbrennung von Holz.

sind alle Produkte desselben Prozesses.) Kohle wird als „fossiler Kohlenstoff" klassifiziert, was bedeutet, dass durch die Verbrennung dieses Materials Kohlenstoff in die Atmosphäre freigesetzt wird und zur globalen Erwärmung beiträgt. Außerdem ist sie teuer, schmutzig in der Handhabung und man braucht einen eigenen Keller für eine vernünftige Lagerung. Sie kann in einem Standardholzofen nicht verbrannt werden, da man den Rost rütteln (also von unten harken) können muss, um ihn freizuhalten; Holz hingegen verbrennt am besten auf einem Bett aus Asche und muss nicht gerüttelt werden. Steinkohle zum Heizen darf außerdem in Deutschland, Österreich oder Großbritannien nicht verkauft oder verbrannt werden.

KOHLEBRIKETTS

Sie sind akzeptabler als Kohle, da sie einen Prozess durchlaufen haben, der die leichteren Kohlenwasserstoffe, die sonst bei der Verbrennung von Kohle in die Luft gelangen, entfernt. Dadurch sind sie weniger sichtbar schadstoffhaltig, aber es entweichen immer noch kleinere oder unsichtbare Elemente in die Atmosphäre. Zum Lagern benötigen Sie einen Kohlenkeller und der Rost muss von Schmutz (sog. Schlacke) befreit werden, was kein Spaß ist. Auch die Kosten sind ein Thema und Sie brauchen einen Allesbrennerrost; sie sind jedoch eine praktische Ergänzung, besonders, wenn Sie sie ordentlich in den Plastiksäcken aufbewahren, in denen sie geliefert werden. Es gibt zwei Sorten von Kohlenbriketts: natürlich raucharme Steinkohle und künstlich hergestellte Briketts aus Koks oder Steinkohle. Fragen Sie Ihren Händler, welche der verschiedenen Marken am besten zu Ihrem Ofen passt.

PAPIERBRIKETTS

Altpapierbriketts dürfen im deutschsprachigen Raum nicht als Brennstoffe verwendet werden! In England etwa ist deren Einsatz jedoch erlaubt. So

Oben: Eine Zeitungspapierbrikettpresse.

Oben: Eingerollte Papierbriketts; für ihre Herstellung gibt es mehr als nur ein Gerät.

wird es gemacht: Sie fertigen einen nassen Block aus gepressten Zeitungen in einer Brikettpresse und lassen ihn trocknen. Sie brauchen Zeit, jede Menge Zeitungen und einen Ort, wo Sie diese durchnässten Teile zum Trocknen aufbewahren können.

Für den Versuch ist eine Brikettpresse relativ günstig. Weichen Sie die Zeitung in einer Schüssel mit Wasser ein und lassen Sie sie eine Weile stehen, damit die Fasern aufweichen. Dadurch verbindet sich das Papier besser. Wenn Sie eine Weile darauf verzichten können, ist eine Badewanne mit etwas Wasser bestens geeignet, um eine große Menge Zeitungspapier einzuweichen. Reißen Sie das durchnässte Papier in kleinere Stücke und schieben Sie es in die Brikettpresse, bis diese voll ist und drücken Sie dann den Griff nach unten, um das Wasser herauszupressen. Vielleicht müssen Sie mehr Papier dazugeben, um die richtige Dicke zu erreichen und den Vorgang wiederholen, bis das Brikett groß genug ist, um aus der Presse geschoben zu werden. Zum Trocknen auf ein Brett legen; ein sonniger Tag eignet sich am besten, da Sie so eine ganze Holzbrikettcharge im Freien trocknen lassen können. Diese Arbeit müssen Sie natürlich weit im Vorfeld erledigen, bevor Sie die Briketts brauchen, da sie eine ganze Weile trocknen müssen, um gut zu brennen. Die Verbrennungseffizienz ähnelt der schnell brennender Holzscheite.

PAPIERSCHEITE

So wie Papierbriketts ist deren Einsatz als Brennstoff im deutschsprachigen Raum nicht erlaubt! Es gibt aber z. B. in England auch ein paar Geräte zum Rollen des Papiers zu runden Scheiten; sie werden fest mit Draht zusammengebunden, der nach dem Verheizen wiederverwendet wird. Er soll verhindern, dass diese Scheite während des Verbrennens auseinanderfallen und so dafür sorgen, dass leichte Asche die Nachbarschaft belästigt.

Oben: *Fichtenzapfen sind gutes Anzündholz und sehen in einem Korb neben dem Ofen noch dazu hübsch aus. Ein Waldspaziergang zum Zapfensammeln kann ein Spaß für die ganze Familie werden.*

ANZÜNDHOLZ

Um Ihr Feuer zu entzünden, brauchen Sie Anzündholz, das aus kleinerem, feiner gespaltenem Holz und sehr trockenen Zweigen, bereit zum Anzünden, besteht. Anzündholz muss man nicht kaufen. Vielleicht bleiben auch – wie bei mir – unbehandelte Holzabfälle von Heimwerkerarbeiten übrig. Auch das Zurückschneiden von Bäumen und Büschen im eigenen Garten kann Anzündholz liefern, wenn es einmal getrocknet ist. Zeitungen und Pappe sollen nicht zum Anzünden verwendet werden, weil sie Flugasche erzeugen, die auf den ebenen Zugflächen liegen bleibt. Auch trockenes Moos ist dazu bestens geeignet – ohne die Erde darunter, selbstverständlich.

WAS SIE NICHT VERBRENNEN SOLLTEN

Ich könnte Ihnen eine ellenlange Liste mit Dingen aufzählen, die nicht zum Verbrennen in einem Ofen geeignet sind, also ist ein gewisses Maß an gesundem Menschenverstand notwendig. Dennoch folgt hier ein kurzer Leitfaden.

Sperrholzreste sind nicht ideal, da die einzelnen Lagen mit einem Harz verklebt sind, das dem Schornstein schaden könnte. Ich verbrenne keine Spanplatten, weil sie so einen hohen Klebstoffanteil im Sägemehl haben. Dasselbe trifft auf MDF-Platten zu, die aus verklebtem Sägemehl bestehen und Formaldehyd enthalten, das wiederum schädlich sein kann.

Mit einigen Ausnahmen verbrenne ich gerne altes oder wiedergewonnenes Holz, das vielleicht auch Schrauben oder Nägel hat. Einige Holzbehandlungen sind giftig und verschmutzen die Atmosphäre, weshalb ich alles vermeide, wovon ich weiß, dass es mit etwas Schädlichem behandelt worden ist. Dasselbe gilt für sehr altes gestrichenes Holz wie etwa Tischlerarbeiten aus einem alten Haus, weil ältere Farbschichten, sofern sie noch original sind, Blei enthalten können. Blei kann nicht zerfallen oder sich auflösen und ist für Menschen und Tiere sehr gefährlich; es kann Entwicklungsprobleme bei Kindern hervorrufen, weshalb heutige Fahrzeuge auch bleifreies Benzin tanken.

TIPP

„Sauberes" Massivholz kann zugeschnitten und verbrannt werden. Sperrholzabfälle werden verbrannt, weil sie nicht so viel Harz enthalten, aber Spanplatten sind ein No-Go aufgrund des hohen Chemikaliengehaltes. Ebenso wird lackiertes oder behandeltes Holz nicht verbrannt. Das bringe ich stattdessen zu unserer örtlichen Entsorgung, um es zu häckseln und zu Verbundholz usw. weiterzuverarbeiten. So wird es nicht verschwendet und das, was ich nicht verbrennen kann, bekommt noch einen Nutzen, so wie es sein sollte.

***Rechts:** Dieses wiedergewonnene Holz mag wie eine vielversprechende Brennstoffquelle aussehen, aber riskieren Sie es nicht – die Farbe enthält höchstwahrscheinlich gesundheitsschädliches Blei.*

Holzöfen sind nicht zur Abfallverbrennung gedacht. In ihrer Gemeinde geschieht dies sicherlich weit effizienter in einer Verbrennungsanlage, die Strom aus Müll erzeugt.

Karton oder Pappe werden wegen der Flugasche zum Einheizen nicht empfohlen und Zeitungsbriketts sind hierzulande als Brennstoff nicht erlaubt; zudem ist das meiste bedruckte Papier mit Chemikalien beschichtet und brennt nicht so gut, weshalb es besser in den Altpapiermüll sollte. In jedem Fall fliegt verbranntes Papier durch den Schornstein und kann störende Ascheablagerungen bei Ihren Nachbarn verursachen.

Natürliche oder synthetische Fasern wie etwa Textilien sollten nicht verbrannt werden. Obwohl erstere viel mit Holz gemeinsam haben, ist die Verbrennungsrate viel zu schnell. Synthetisches Material verhält sich beim Verbrennen wie jedes andere Plastik: Es verbrennt viel zu schnell und erzeugt viel zu viel giftige Verschmutzung und ist somit ein absolutes No-Go.

Flüchtige Stoffe wie Paraffinöl, Benzin, Terpentin, Universalverdünnung, Farben und Lacke dürfen niemals und unter keinen Umständen ihren Weg auf den Rost eines Ofens finden. Selbst eine kleine Menge, die beispielsweise auf einen Lappen geträufelt wurde, könnte tödlich sein. Die Möglichkeit einer Feuersbrunst oder gar einer Explosion bedeutet, dass diese Substanzen völlig unsicher sind. Wenn Sie ein widerspenstiges Feuer entfachen oder anfeuern wollen, weil es tief in den Rost gesunken und ohne sichtbare Glut ist, wählen Sie eine sichere Methode wie Kaminanzünder – und haben Sie außerdem Geduld!

HOLZARTEN

Die Wahl der Holzarten ist weit weniger wichtig bei einem Holzofen als bei einem offenen Feuer. Ich kenne jemanden, der mit einem holzbeheizten Kessel das gesamte Haus heizt: Heizkörper, Warmwasser und alles weitere. Er schneidet seinen eigenen Kastanienwald zur Niederwaldbewirtschaftung. Kastanienholz wird, wie Kiefernholz, von jedem mit einem offenen Kamin mit Argwohn beäugt, da es dazu neigt, Funken zu sprühen. Das ist bei dem System meines Freundes kein Problem – und ebenso wenig bei einem Holzofen. Viele der Hölzer (siehe S. 58) schlagen Funken, aber da die Holzofentüren geschlossen sein sollten, dürfte dies kein Problem darstellen. Wenn die Türen des Ofens offenstehen müssen, vermeiden Sie funkensprühende Arten und verwenden Sie einen Funkenschutz.

Verschiedene Brennstoffe können je nach Brennwert, also der Energiemenge, die durch die Verbrennung einer festgelegten Brennstoffmenge freigegeben wird, klassifiziert werden; für unsere Zwecke sind die Kommentare in der Tabelle jedoch nützlicher.

Einige Hölzer, vorwiegend Weichhölzer (Holz von Nadelbäumen wie etwa Kiefern und Fichten) verbrennen schnell, also brauchen Sie mehr davon, um das Feuer in Gang zu halten. Harthölzer (Holz von Laubbäumen) brennen in der Regel länger.

Die Trocknungszeiten in der Tabelle beziehen sich auf Rundholz, das in der Mitte gespalten, dann geviertelt und unter einer trockenen, offenen Abdeckung gelagert wird. Scheite, die rund gelassen werden, brauchen ungefähr doppelt so lange zum Trocknen. Bedenken Sie jedoch, dass Holz ein natürlicher Stoff ist und sich nicht immer so verhält, wie man es sich erwartet.

Oben: *Brennstoff aus Nadelbäumen verbrennt schneller als Harthölzer – Sie benötigen also mehr davon.*

ART	TROCKNUNGS-ZEIT	KOMMENTARE
Apfelbaum (*Malus* spp.)	1 Jahr	Kein Funkenflug; muss gut abgelagert sein
Bergahorn (*Acer pseudoplatanus*)	1 Jahr	Brennt gut
Birke (*Betula* spp.)	6 Monate	Brennt hell; Rinde eignet sich gut zum Anzünden
Buche (*Fagus* spp.)	15 Monate	Keine Funkenbildung; muss gut abgelagert sein; bestes Brennholz
Eibe (*Taxus* spp.)	18 Monate	Brennt langsam
Eiche (*Quercus* spp.)	18 Monate	Bestes Brennholz; brennt langsam
Erle (*Alnus* spp.)	3 Monate	Brennt schnell; minderwertiges Brennholz
Esche (*Fraxinus* spp.)	15 Monate	Bestes Brennholz; leicht zu spalten
Fichte (*Picea abies*)	6 Monate	Schnelle Wärme, kurze Brenndauer
Hainbuche (*Carpinus* spp.)	1 Jahr	Brennt gut
Hasel (*Corylus* spp.)	1 Jahr	Brennt schnell; kein Funkenflug
Kastanie (*Castanea* spp.)	18 Monate	Funkenflug; brennt gut
Kiefer (*Pinus* spp.)	6 Monate	Brennt schnell; hinterlässt ölige Rußspuren
Kirsche (*Prunus* spp.)	1 Jahr	Kein Funkenflug; muss gut abgelagert sein
Lärche (*Larix* spp.)	1 Jahr	Funkenflug; hinterlässt ölige Rückstände
Tanne (*Abies* spp.)	6 Monate	Gutes Anzündholz, brennt schnell ab
Stechpalme (*Ilex* spp.)	1 Jahr	Kann teilgetrocknet verbrannt werden
Weide (*Salix* spp.)	6 Monate	Brennt schnell, muss aber gut gelagert werden
Weißdorn (*Crataegus* spp.)	1 Jahr	Gutes Brennholz

GRÜNHOLZ VS. TROCKENHOLZ

Welche Holzart Sie auch als Brennstoff nutzen, sie wird nicht so gut oder schnell brennen, wenn sie nass ist. Ein hoher Feuchtigkeitsgehalt verlangsamt den Verbrennungsprozess und reduziert die Brennleistung, da mehr Energie für das Trocknen des Holzes auf dem Rost gebraucht wird, während es brennt. Es könnte auch den Verschleiß des Ofenrohrs beschleunigen, was bedeutet, dass es früher als erwartet ausgetauscht werden muss.

Holz trocknet schneller in kleineren Stücken. Beachten Sie dies, wenn Sie den Trocknungsvorgang beschleunigen wollen.

Das Holz eines frisch gefällten Baumes ist innen feucht, sofern der Baum nicht vor der Fällung bereits tot war. Bäume sind auf das Wasser angewiesen, das von den Wurzeln, durch den Stamm und hinauf in die Blätter und Früchte über Millionen kleiner röhrchenartiger Zellen transportiert wird. Laubbäume (die ihre Blätter im Herbst verlieren) „verschließen" sich im Winter, wenn es kalt ist, bis zum Frühling – ein guter Zeitpunkt zum Fällen, aber bis dahin abzuwarten, ist nicht immer praktisch, weshalb meist das ganze Jahr über gefällt wird. Das Resultat ist feuchtes Holz, auch Grünholz genannt, das typischerweise einen Feuchtigkeitsgehalt von ca. 50 % aufweist. In einem Extremfall habe ich auch schon erlebt, wie Wasser aus den abgeschnittenen Enden eines Eukalyptusstammes gelaufen ist wie aus einer undichten Regentonne. In diesem Zustand ist Holz eindeutig nicht zum Verbrennen geeignet. Ob also nun gekauftes oder gefundenes Holz – es braucht seine Zeit an einem gut belüfteten Lagerort, wo es ausreichend trocknen oder „reifen" kann, sonst versuchen Sie einfach nur, Wasser zu verbrennen. Wenn Sie Brennholz kaufen, sollte der Verkäufer ehrlich über den Trocknungsgrad sein. Normalerweise ist es "luftgetrocknet", was bedeutet, dass es monatelang unter einer trockenen Abdeckung im Freien gelagert wurde, sodass ein Gutteil, nicht aber das ganze Wasser verdunstet ist.

TIPP

Während Harthölzer wie Eiche ein Jahr oder länger zum Lufttrocknen benötigen, kann Kiefernholz schon nach sechs Monaten bereit sein. Eine geringe Restfeuchtigkeit kann helfen, die schnelle Verbrennung zu hemmen, die durch die faserreiche Beschaffenheit und die Öle und Harze verursacht wird – sie flammen gut auf und steigern die Wärmeleistung.

Dieses Holz hat wahrscheinlich einen Feuchtigkeitsgehalt von 20 % und hat einen wesentlich höheren Brennwert als Grünholz.

„Luftgetrocknetes" Holz wurde oft monatelang unter einer trockenen Abdeckung im Freien gelagert, sodass ein Gutteil des Wassers verdunstet ist.

Das Problem ist nicht so groß, wie es klingt. Wenn Sie Ihr Holz richtig lagern (siehe S. 94 ff.), damit es trocken bleibt oder trocknen kann, falls es beim Kauf feucht war, und es dann nach und nach in kleinen Mengen ins Haus bringen, erledigt die Wärme im Haus den Rest und reduziert den Feuchtigkeitsgehalt noch weiter. Außerdem trocknet in kleinere Stücke gespaltenes Holz schneller – denken Sie daran, wenn Sie den Vorgang beschleunigen möchten. Es ist erwähnenswert, dass Tischler, Schreiner und Möbelhersteller kammergetrocknetes Holz mit maximal 8 % Feuchtigkeit brauchen und dass derart trockenes Holz den höchsten Heizwert hat. Wenn Sie Abschnitte bekommen können, brennen diese hervorragend neben Ihrem Stückholz – vorausgesetzt, sie wurden nicht mit etwas Feuergefährlichem behandelt.

Oben: *Aufgrund des verminderten Funkenflugrisikos können Besitzer von Holzöfen eine größere Bandbreite an Holzarten nutzen als jene, die lieber ein offenes Feuer haben.*

Oben: *Sie können einen Feuchtigkeitsmesser kaufen, um zu überprüfen, ob Ihr Holz trocken genug zum Verbrennen ist. Das ist vor allem dann nützlich, wenn Sie Grünholz kaufen oder Ihre Bäume selbst fällen.*

Oben: *Stadien der Feuerholzproduktion vom Baumstamm bis zum Scheitholz. Das Entfernen der Rinde hilft beim Trocknen.*

EINEN HOLZ-HÄNDLER FINDEN

Einen Holzhändler zu finden, ist ein schwieriges Unterfangen. Es gibt zahlreiche Quellen, aber woher weiß man, wem man trauen kann? Das alte Sprichwort „Wer billig kauft, kauft teuer" bewahrheitet sich bei Brennholz wie überall sonst auch. Ein Schnäppchenpreis für eine „Menge" Holz (siehe S. 64) ist wahrscheinlich am Ende gar kein Schnäppchen. Das Holz könnte innen noch feucht sein, vielleicht gibt es unsortierte Holzarten und merkwürdige, nicht verwendbare Größen. Sobald es als chaotischer Haufen in ihrer Einfahrt liegt, beginnen Sie sich vielleicht zu fragen, ob Sie einen Fehler gemacht haben. Der Verkäufer wird nicht mehr an einer Rücknahme interessiert sein, nachdem er Ihr Geld bekommen hat! In dieser Situation ist das Beste, was sie tun können, alle Übergrößen kleinzuhacken und langfristig gut belüftet zu lagern, damit das Holz trocknen kann.

Können Sie zweifelsfrei sagen, ob es sich um gutes Holz handelt? Den meisten von uns fällt dies bei stehenden Bäumen schon schwer, ganz zu schweigen von gefällten und in unerkennbare Stücke zerteilten Bäumen. Um also sicherzugehen, das Richtige zu bekommen, ist es wichtig, einen Lieferanten mit einem guten Ruf auszuwählen. Nein, der ist meist nicht der billigste, aber und das ist wichtiger, ehrlich mit Ihnen. Er sollte Ihnen sagen können, was er liefert, was oft ein Mix aus Eiche, Esche und so weiter ist. Das ist in Ordnung, da diese Holzarten sich gut verbrennen lassen. Außerdem sollte er Ihnen etwas über den ungefähren Trocknungsgrad des Holzes sagen können.

Die beste Art, einen zuverlässigen Holzlieferanten zu finden, ist über Mundpropaganda. Ein guter Anfang ist das Gespräch mit Freunden und Bekannten, die bereits Stückholz für ihre Kamine oder Holzöfen kaufen. Holzöfen sind viel pflegeleichter als offene Feuer; wenn das Material also gut genug dafür ist, genügt es auch für Ihre Zwecke. Die nächstbeste Art sind Anzeigen in lokalen Zeitungen und dem Internet. Vergewissern Sie sich, dass Sie verstehen, welche Menge und Holzart unter welchen Bedingungen geliefert wird.

Oben: *Diese Wagenladung Holz wurde bereits zu Scheiten gespalten, die bereit zum Verbrennen sind.*

Holzscheite variieren unvermeidbar in der Größe – Holz ist ein Naturprodukt, weshalb Form und Größe nicht konstant sind. Das Entscheidende ist, dass die Scheite nicht zu lang sein dürfen, um in den Brennraum zu passen. Man kann sie immer in Maserungsrichtung spalten, wenn sie zu breit sind, aber das Kürzen ist harte Arbeit. Fragen Sie Ihren Lieferanten also nach einer Größe, die zu ihrem Holzofen passt. Es ist praktisch, ein paar kleinere Scheite zu haben, die größenmäßig zwischen Anzündholz und Stückholz liegen; mit ihnen können Sie das Feuer aufrechthalten oder wieder entfachen, wenn es niedergebrannt ist und etwas Unterstützung braucht.

WAS IST EINE LADUNG?

Traditionell wurde Hol zin Großbritannien, aus dem dieses Buch stammt, in „Cords" verkauft. Ein Cord ist die Menge Holz, die ordentlich gestapelt und angeordnet einem Stapel von 8 x 4 x 4 Fuß oder einem Volumen von 128 Kubikfuß (3,6 m^3) entspricht.

In Kontinentaleuropa sind Sie beim Kauf von Brennholz mit unterschiedlichen Maßeinheiten konfrontiert, am häufigsten werden Ihnen dabei Festmeter, Raummeter und Schüttraummeter begegnen. Diese drei Einheiten beschreiben jeweils einen Kubikmeter Holz, wobei der Festmeter (fm oder F) genau einem Kubikmeter fester Holzmasse entspricht – ohne Lücken, die sich aus dem Schichten von Scheitholz ergeben. Der Raummeter (rm, historisch auch „Ster") entspricht einem Kubikmeter geschichtetem Holz. Dieses Holz kann gespalten oder ungespalten sein und zwischen den einzelnen Stücken darf sich Luft befinden.

Da das Stapeln für den Handel und den Transport oft unwirtschaftlich ist, greift man hier auf den Schüttraummeter (srm) zurück. Dabei handelt es sich um einen Kubikmeter Holz, der durch einfaches Schütten (und somit mit deutlich mehr Luft zwischen den einzelnen Holzstücken) befüllt wurde.

ZUR ORIENTIERUNG UND UMRECHNUNG NIMMT DER HOLZHANDEL IN DER REGEL FOLGENDE RICHTWERTE ZUR HAND:

FESTMETER	RAUMMETER	SCHÜTTRAUMMETER
1,0 fm	1,4 rm	2,0 srm (Fichte) – 2,2 srm (Buche)
0,7 fm	1,0 rm	1,6 srm (Fichte) –1,4 srm (Buche)
0,4 fm	0,6 rm	1,0 srm

Oben: *Diese Stämme wurden in verwendbare Größen zugeschnitten, müssen nun aber unter Dach gebracht werden, damit sie trocknen können.*

KLAUBHOLZ SAMMELN

Es liegt nahe, bei einem Spaziergang nach Klaubholz zu suchen und es nach Hause mitzunehmen. Allerdings sind die Besitzverhältnisse des Gebietes und ob Sie das Recht haben, herabgefallenes Holz zum Heizen abzutransportieren, ein Thema. Dies variiert je nach Wohnort; es gibt keinen entsprechenden Rechtsanspruch – wenn Sie also beschließen, diesen komischen toten Ast vom Boden aufzuheben und diskret mitzunehmen, seien Sie sich bewusst, dass Sie auf Gegenwehr stoßen könnten.

Wo Wälder sind, gibt es in der Regel auch Sonderrechte für die Menschen, die dort leben und diese könnten auch das Recht der Entnahme einer bestimmten Holzmenge zum Eigengebrauch beinhalten. Wenn Sie also jemanden sehen, der einen Anhänger mit Klaubholz füllt, gehen Sie nicht davon aus, dass Sie das Recht haben, es ihm gleichzutun, da Sie vielleicht in diesem Wald leben. Andererseits könnten Sie auch einen Waldbesitzer kennen, der recht glücklich damit ist, dass Sie seinen Wald ordentlich halten, indem er lästige Äste und umgefallene Stämme loswird. Wenn ich in Gesprächen erwähne, dass ich einen Holzofen besitze, ergibt es sich oft, dass mir mein Gegenüber Holz zum Verbrennen anbietet.

Angenommen, Sie haben tatsächlich berechtigterweise Zweige zum Verbrennen gefunden, müssen Sie überlegen, ob es das Plündern wirklich wert ist: Ist das Material fest und schwer oder ist es sehr leicht und durchgefault? Wenn das Holz keine Substanz hat, ist es wenig sinnvoll, es mitzunehmen, da es keine fünf Minuten auf dem Rost liegenbleibt.

Es ist fest, aber voller Schlamm? Das ist besser, aber der Matsch muss weg. Man wird beim Bewegen des Holzes schmutzig und man braucht eine Kunststoffplatte oder -plane, um den Kofferraum des Autos zu schützen – und sollte alte Kleidung tragen, falls man etwas von dem Schlamm abbekommt. Wenn es das Holz dann nach Hause geschafft hat, müssen Sie den Schlamm

Oben: *Herabgefallenes Holz sieht vielleicht einladend aus, aber gehen Sie nicht davon aus, dass Sie ein Recht darauf haben, ohne zu fragen. Dieser Wald sieht aus, als wäre er sich selbst überlassen, aber es ist möglich, dass er für diesen Zustand sorgsam gepflegt wird.*

abwaschen. Verbleibender Schlamm kann eisenhart werden oder in der Struktur der Rinde steckenbleiben. Das alles ist zwar etwas lästig, kann es aber wert sein, wenn Sie einen Ort haben, an dem Sie das Holz trocknen lassen können, damit es bereit zum Spalten und Verbrennen wird.

Sobald Sie brauchbares Holz gefunden haben, heißt es, sich entsprechend mit wetterfester Sicherheitskleidung und -schuhen auszurüsten. Eine ordentliche Astsäge kann mittelgroße Äste bewältigen und Sie können damit gefundene Äste ablängen oder Seitenäste entfernen, damit sie in das Auto passen. Auch ein Dachträger kann eine Option sein. Äste sind selten gerade, weshalb es schwierig werden kann, sie sicher zu befestigen. Lange Äste lassen sich eventuell zwischen die Vordersitze schieben, solange sie sicher verwahrt sind und Sie nicht bei der Fahrt beeinträchtigen.

Wenn Ihr frisch gefundener Schatz einmal zuhause ist, kann dieser auf mehreren Sägeböcken liegen, damit Sie ihn mit der Astsäge oder einer Baumsäge in kurze Stücke schneiden können. Wenn Sie jemanden kennen, der eine Kettensäge bedienen kann, könnten Sie ihn freundlich bitten, den Zuschnitt für Sie zu erledigen. Lassen Sie sich nur bloß nicht dazu verleiten, es selbst zu versuchen, wenn Sie dies nicht wirklich gelernt haben und über ein entsprechendes Zeugnis verfügen!

Oben: *Die Investition in eine scharfe Astsäge lohnt sich.*

Oben: *Trockene Äste sind exzellentes Anzündholz.*

Oben: *Einfachste Sägeböcke halten das Holz während des Zurechtschneidens.*

WALDBESITZ

So unwahrscheinlich es auch scheinen mag, so ist es durchaus möglich, sich ein eigenes Stück Wald zu kaufen. Sie müssen nicht zum Großgrundbesitzer werden und wenn Sie etwas Geld beiseitegelegt haben, könnten Sie sich vielleicht ein Grundstück kaufen.

Wie man sich vorstellen kann, fällen sich die Bäume nicht von selbst; es ist ein langer Weg, Bäume zu setzen, zu ernten und das Holz in brauchbare Stämme zu verwandeln. Die Bäume müssen der richtigen Art angehören, damit ein Verbrennen sich lohnt. Die Waldparzelle muss sich an einem guten Ort befinden, damit die Bäume gesund wachsen, der Boden ordentlich entwässern kann und sich das Wasser nicht staut. Sie müssen lernen, sicher mit einer Kettensäge umzugehen und brauchen einen Anhänger sowie ein passendes Zugfahrzeug. Das ist nicht jedermanns Sache, aber ich kenne einige Menschen, die dies als lohnende Investition empfunden haben und nicht länger abhängig von ihrem Holzlieferanten sind.

Mit dem Waldbesitz gehen rechtliche Pflichten nach dem Forstgesetz einher. Sie dürfen Bäume im Rahmen nachhaltiger Forstwirtschaft fällen, benötigen bei größeren Flächen jedoch eine behördliche Genehmigung und müssen wieder aufforsten. Ein Bewohnen des Waldes sowie das Abstellen von Wohnwagen oder Zelten ist strikt verboten; bauliche Anlagen sind im Außenbereich meist nicht genehmigungsfähig. Es ist ratsam, sich bei Forstbehörden und Interessensvertretungen (z. B. Forstabteilung der Landwirtschaftskammer) zu den regionalen Vorkaufsrechten und Bewirtschaftungspflichten beraten zu lassen.

TIPP

Es gibt eine Reihe an Anlaufstellen, die sich mit dem Verkauf von Wald befassen und Ihnen mit Rat und Hilfe dienen können. Die Homepages der Forstbehörden und gemeinnütziger Vereine wie dem Waldverband Österreich (und anderen Organisationen in anderen Ländern) bieten unparteiische Beratung und Informationen an. Eine der besten Gelegenheiten für Beratung ist der Besuch einer Landwirtschaftsfachmesse, wo sich für gewöhnlich mindestens ein Stand mit Themen wie dem Kauf von Wald beschäftigt. Sie können sich hier persönlich mit jemandem unterhalten, der Ihnen alle Details erklären und all Ihre Fragen beantworten kann (etwa, welche Art Wald zu Ihnen passt und was eine Eigentümerschaft bedeutet), ohne dass Sie unter dem Druck stehen, kaufen zu müssen.

Oben: *Der Besitz eines Stücks Land ist nicht so unwahrscheinlich wie Sie glauben – bedenken Sie aber, dass damit auch Verantwortung einhergeht.*

WIE VIEL LAND BRAUCHT MAN?

Die Grundstücksgröße hängt von vielen Faktoren ab. Wie viel Geld möchten Sie inklusive aller Abgaben ausgeben? Ist das Land stark bewaldet oder hat es eher schlechteren Waldboden? Gibt es Brandschneisen, Wegerechte, Bäche, Felsformationen oder andere Faktoren, die es weniger ideal machen? Welche Baumarten wachsen gerade dort und wie alt sind sie? Stehen einzelne Bäume unter Naturschutz? Sind die Bäume in dieser Gegend ideal zum Heizen? Ein spezialisiertes Forstunternehmen kann Sie zur richtigen Entscheidung führen. Meist stellt man fest, dass ein bestimmter Grund einen Fixpreis hat, den man nur akzeptieren oder ablehnen kann.

WIE SCHNELL REGENERIERT SICH DER WALD?

Einige Arten regenerieren sich schnell; Birke ist ein Beispiel dafür. Eiche hingegen braucht viel mehr Zeit, um zu reifen und kann daher geschützt sein und somit nicht für eine Holzernte zur Verfügung stehen.

Die Papier-Birke erreicht ihre Reife nach etwa 60–70 Jahren, ist aber bereits nach 40 Jahren als Feuerholz nutzbar. Sie ist ein relativ schnellwachsender Baum, es gibt also keine schnelle Lösung, wenn Sie stetig Feuerholz brauchen. Eine gute Forstwirtschaftspraxis umfasst Aspekte wie die Abstände zwischen den Bäumen, die Regeneration durch Stockausschlag (für Arten wie die Hasel) oder Versäen (wie etwa die Birke) und ob ein Kahlschlag eines Standorts notwendig ist, damit Setzlinge gedeihen können. Es lohnt sich auf jeden Fall, sich professionelle Beratung zu diesem zweifellos komplexen Thema einzuholen.

STOCKAUSSCHLAG

Stockausschlag oder “auf den Stock setzen” meint die alte und universelle Praxis, einen Baum zu fällen, aber den niedrigsten Teil (den Stock) stehenzulassen, damit er neu austreiben kann. Dies verhindert, dass der Baum zur Gänze abstirbt und erlaubt in der Folge, dass nützliche Holzprodukte gezüchtet und wieder geschnitten werden. Birke kann beispielsweise in einem Drei- bis Vierjahreszyklus für Strauchholz (Reisigbündel) genutzt werden, während reife Eichenbäume nach etwa 50 Jahren geerntet werden können, um Feuerholz zu erhalten. Auf dem Stock ausgeschlagenes Holz hat viele praktische Anwendungsmöglichkeiten, etwa zur Herstellung von Zäunen oder Körben, ist aber nicht unbedingt als Feuerholz geeignet.

Oben: *Bäume mit Stockausschlag sind leicht an ihren schlanken Trieben aus einem einzigen Stamm zu erkennen.*

RECHTLICHE ASPEKTE

Mit dem Landbesitz geht Verantwortung einher. Wenn Sie im Sinn haben, eine Parzelle Wald zu kaufen, lassen Sie sich zuerst rechtlich beraten. Abgesehen von der Transaktion selbst müssen Sie sich auch über andere Aspekte informieren, etwa gegebenenfalls den Schutz von Bäumen, das Sauberhalten von Flüssen und Bächen, das Gestatten des Zugangs auf öffentlichen Wanderwegen und Artenschutz, der übrigens auch Wildblumen ebenso betrifft wie Vögel, Fledermäuse und Säugetiere.

WARNUNG

In den falschen Händen sind Kettensägen tödlich. Wenn Sie eine zum Fällen und Zuschneiden Ihrer Bäume verwenden wollen, ist die einzige Option das Absolvieren einer ordentlichen Ausbildung. In Österreich und Deutschland ist es Personen grundsätzlich erst ab 18 Jahren erlaubt, Kettensägen zu benutzen, zu kaufen oder zu mieten. Außerdem müssen Sie die richtige Sicherheitskleidung tragen.

WAHL VON KETTENSÄGEN UND ÄXTEN

EINE KETTENSÄGE AUSWÄHLEN

Der professionelle Holzfäller nutzt seine Kettensäge Tag für Tag über Stunden hinweg das ganze Jahr über, weshalb er eine Säge benötigt, die leistungsstark und robust genug für diesen intensiven Einsatz ist.

Das bedeutet, dass eine Säge für den professionellen Gebrauch Eigenschaften aufweist, die Sie nicht bei jenen Exemplaren finden, die der örtliche Baumarkt anbietet. Diese Sägen müssen stärkere Motoren haben sowie mit einer stabilen Kurbelwelle und einer längeren Kettenführungsschiene (Schwert) ausgestattet sein, weniger Lärm und Vibration entwickeln und für eisige Arbeitsbedingungen sogar beheizte Haltegriffe haben.

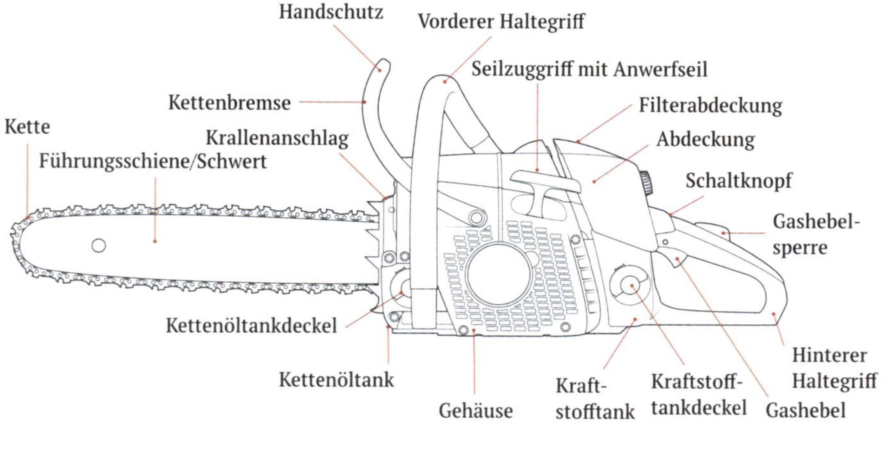

Bestandteile einer Kettensäge

Oben: *Eine gut ausbalancierte Kettensäge ist unerlässlich für einen Holzfäller, der das Gerät Tag für Tag über Stunden hinweg verwendet.*

HAUPTELEMENTE EINER KETTENSÄGE

AUSGEWOGENES DESIGN

Eine Kettensäge für den professionellen Einsatz hat ein ausgewogenes Gehäuse. Es ist länger und schmaler als das einer gewöhnlichen Kettensäge, mit dem Motor direkt hinter der Kettenführungsschiene in einem geneigten Winkel. Das gut ausbalancierte Design sorgt dafür, dass die Säge über die lange Zeit, die der Holzfäller im Wald ist, angenehm in der Hand liegt.

GRIFF AN DER OBERSEITE

Professionelle Holzfäller setzen auf Kettensägemodelle mit Griff an der Oberseite. Diese Bauweise ist im Vergleich zu jener mit Griff an der Hinterseite kompakter, wodurch sie in beengten Arbeitsbereichen angenehm im Handling ist. Durch ihr geringes Gewicht und ihre Griffposition eignen sie sich zum Schneiden von Ästen und Zweigen sowohl bei geringem Platzangebot als auch dann, wenn ein Abwärtswinkel beim Schnitt erforderlich ist.

LANGE FÜHRUNGSSCHIENE

Das Fällen von Bäumen mit großem Durchmesser erfordert eine Kettensäge mit einer überdurchschnittlich langen Führungsschiene. Das längere Schwert ermöglicht einen tiefen Schnitt in den Baum. Geschicklichkeit und Sorgfalt sind nötig, um sicherzustellen, dass der Schnitt korrekt ist.

SCHARFE KETTE

Alle Kettensägen brauchen eine scharfe Kette, aber der Profi braucht eine hochwertige und sogar ein oder zwei als Ersatz im Fall eines Bruchs. Darum muss die Kette regelmäßig durch häufiges Schärfen gewartet werden. Eine scharfe Kette verbessert nicht nur den Schnitt, sondern ist auch sicherer in der Verwendung.

RÜCKSCHLAGSICHERUNG

Kettensägen können äußerst gefährlich sein. Eine ihrer tückischsten Eigenschaften ist der Rückschlag, wenn die Schwertspitze in einen Schnitt geführt wird. Die Säge kann zurückspringen, sich am Griff drehen und, wenn sie nicht gestoppt wird, das Schwert mit der scharfen Kette in den Bediener drehen. Um dies zu verhindern, legt sich der vordere Handschutz bei einem Verdrehen der Säge auf den Arm des Bedieners. Durch leichten Druck durch den Kontakt mit dem Arm wird die Bremse ausgelöst und die Bewegung der Kette sofort gestoppt.

MARKE

Jeder hat seine Lieblingswerkzeugmarke, da sind Kettensägen keine Ausnahme. Bei den meisten Händlern kann man Werkzeug für einen Tag testen, also probieren Sie die Sägen aller Produzenten, um sich ein Bild von Leistung, Eigenschaften und Haltbarkeit zu machen. Dieser Praxistag ist unbezahlbar, um die Marke und das Modell zu finden, das am besten zu einem passt.

GARANTIE

Die meisten Profi-Kettensägen haben eine gewerbliche Garantie, die zwei Jahre abdeckt. Vergewissern Sie sich, dass Ihre dies hat, da Sie Ihre Kettensäge viele anstrengende Stunden und Tage nutzen werden und die Wahrscheinlichkeit eines Defekts höher ist als bei nicht-professioneller Nutzung. Die Garantie verschafft Ihnen ein sicheres Gefühl, wenn Sie diese Art Werkzeug unter extremen Bedingungen verwenden.

WAHL EINER AXT

Obwohl die Axt ein altes Handwerkzeug ist, das von den frühesten Holzfällerinnen und Holzfällern verwendet wurde, hat sie noch immer ihren Platz in der modernen Werkzeugsammlung. Da sie durch Menschenkraft funktionieren, bringen sie den Vorteil mit sich, dass sie keinen Treibstoff brauchen, um zu funktionieren. Das kann in abgelegenen Gebieten, in denen Kraftstoffquellen rar sind, nützlich sein. Für den geschickten Bediener ist die Axt

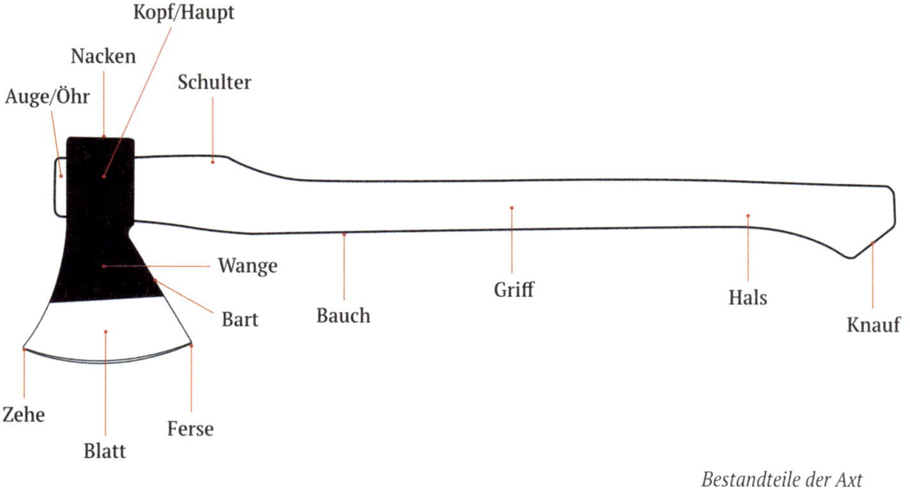

Bestandteile der Axt

eine schnelle Möglichkeit, Trennarbeiten zu erledigen, ohne dafür eine Kettensäge oder andere strombetriebene Werkzeuge hervorholen zu müssen.

Es gibt viele verschiedene Arten von Äxten, zum Beispiel Tomahawk-Äxte, Spaltäxte, Spalthämmer, Fälläxte, Forstäxte (zum Entasten), Zimmermannsäxte, historische Streitäxte und viele mehr.

Der Hauptunterschied liegt dabei in der Schneide. Einige Axtköpfe sind dicker als andere und dafür ausgelegt, Holzfasern zu spalten, etwa beim Holzhacken. Dünnere Axtköpfe dienen dazu, die Holzfasern zu durchtrennen, um Bäume zu fällen und zu entasten. Meistens verläuft die Schneide bündig in Bewegungsrichtung und parallel zum Stiel.

AXTARTEN

FORSTÄXTE (ZUM ENTASTEN)

Diese Äxte fallen in die Kategorie der Hacken und sind zum Entasten gefällter Bäume gedacht. Diese kompakten Äxte wiegen für gewöhnlich um die 0,9 kg mit einem Griff von etwa 60 cm. Beim Entasten von Bäumen ist der Platz oft begrenzt, da andere Äste im Weg sein können, die den Schwung der Axt einschränken; die Forstaxt ist ein guter Kompromiss zwischen Größe und Hackkraft. Wenn der Raum beengt ist, kann sie mit einer Hand geführt werden, bei genug Platz kann sie mit beiden Händen für einen langen, kraftvollen Schwung gehalten werden.

FÄLLÄXTE, SPALTÄXTE UND SPALTHÄMMER

Fälläxte sind Hackäxte. Sie sind zum Fällen von Bäumen und zum Spalten für Stämme und Rundhölzer gedacht. Für gewöhnlich sind sie 80–90 cm lang und wiegen 1,4 kg oder mehr. Sie sind keine kompakten Universalwerkzeuge, die sich leicht verwenden lassen. Dennoch kann ein geübter Anwender auch eine Fällaxt zum Spalten von Feuerholz und für viele weitere Trennarbeiten nutzen – auch wenn sie eher im Holz stecken bleibt als ein Spalthammer. Der Umgang mit der Fällaxt erfordert große Geschicklichkeit und Ausdauer.

Die Spaltaxt ähnelt der Fällaxt, ist aber breiter, sodass sie das Holz auseinandertreiben kann. Man kann sie zum Hacken in Bäume verwenden, weshalb sie auch eine gute Universalaxt darstellt.

Spalthämmer sind größer und schwerer als Spaltäxte und bringen mehr Energie zum Spalten großer, dichtfaseriger Scheite auf. Sie können bis zu

1 m lang sein und bis zu 3,2 kg wiegen. Die Form des Axtkopfes ist breit wie bei einem Vorschlaghammer, was bedeutet, dass der Spalthammer das Holz auseinandertreibt, anstatt es zu schneiden. Er taugt nur zum Holzspalten, versuchen Sie nicht, Bäume damit zu fällen. Das Holzspalten kann leichter werden, wenn man Keile verwendet: Mit einem Spalt beginnen, einen Keil hineinstecken und dann die Rückseite des Spalthammers zum Einschlagen des Keils verwenden.

AXTKONSTRUKTION

Wenn Sie die Materialien wählen, aus denen Ihre Axt sein soll, können Sie Ihre Wahl auf Robustheit, Haltbarkeit oder persönliche Vorlieben ausrichten. Der Axtkopf muss aus hochwertigem Stahl mit einer scharfen Schneide bestehen. Es gibt verschiedene Optionen für den Griff, je nach Vorliebe. Einige Bediener ziehen einen hölzernen Griff vor, der bei der Arbeit ein gutes Feedback liefert. Manche Profis schleifen den Lack vom Griff, um einen besseren Halt zu erzielen. Holzgriffe haben den Nachteil, dass sie sich abnutzen und brechen können, sind aber ebenso einfach zu ersetzen. Verstärkte Plastikgriffe sind leichter und robuster als Holzgriffe, aber wenn sie kaputtgehen, bedeutet dies meist, dass die Axt nutzlos geworden ist und Sie eine neue kaufen müssen, Sie können sogar Äxte kaufen, die gänzlich aus Metall bestehen, äußerst robust sind und ein Leben lang halten; sie sind allerdings auch sehr schwer und somit unhandlich zu verwenden.

Oben: *Eine Axt kann zum Kopf hin oder mit beiden Händen gehalten werden, wenn ein guter Schwung erforderlich ist.*

KETTENSÄGEN & ÄXTE SCHÄRFEN

Scharfes Werkzeug ist das tägliche Brot aller Holzfäller.Sie müssen wissen, wie sich ihre Werkzeuge schärfen lassen und sicherstellen, dass die Schneidkante möglichst lange hält. Scharfes Werkzeug schneidet nicht nur besser und effizienter, sondern ist auch sicherer. Präzisionsschnitte sind leichter auszuführen, wenn die Schneidkante schneidet, wo sie soll, anstatt durch das Holz zu wandern, wie stumpfes Werkzeug dies zu tun pflegt.

SCHÄRFE VERSTEHEN

Ich bin mir sicher, dass Sie schon einmal zum Messer oder Meißel gegriffen haben und dann feststellen mussten, dass das Werkzeug nicht wirklich so schnitt, wie es sollte. Kurz: Es war stumpf. Aber was bedeutet das?

Um den Unterschied zwischen Schärfe und Stumpfheit zu verstehen, müssen wir ein wenig über Geometrie nachdenken. Wenn Sie zwei einander schneidende gerade Linien auf Papier zeichnen, ergibt sich dort, wo die beiden Linien einander treffen, eine Spitze. Wenn nun Linien in flache Ebenen umgewandelt werden, entsteht dort, wo die beiden sich treffen, eine gerade Linie. Dieses Konzept ist grundlegend, um zu verstehen, was Schärfe wirklich bedeutet.

Wenn man diese Illustration noch etwas weiterdenkt, sollten etwa beim Blick auf ein Messer oder einen Meißel die flachen Ebenen, die die Schneidkante bilden, in der Theorie eine Linie der Schärfe ergeben.

Mit der Zeit (und der Verwendung) nutzt diese scharfe Kante sich ab und wird abgerundet. Wie schnell diese Schneidkante stumpf wird, hängt von einigen Faktoren ab, darunter das Material, das geschnitten wird, die Stahlsorte der Klinge und wie das Werkzeug verwendet wird.

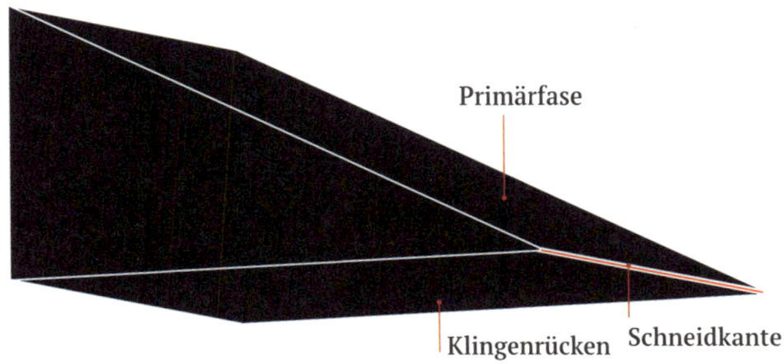

Oben: *Eine einzige Linie bildet sich als Schnittlinie zweier Ebenen.*

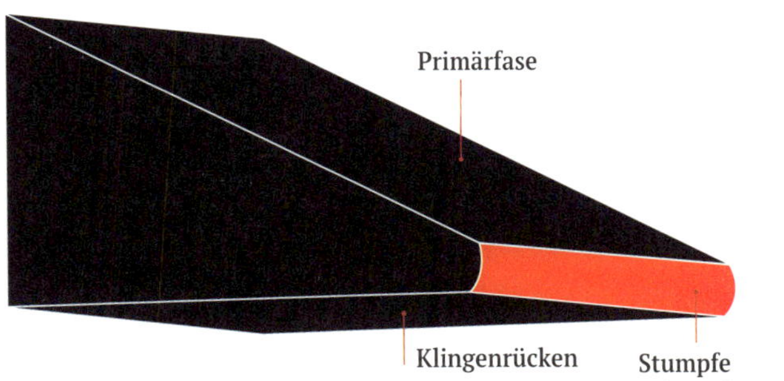

Oben: *Eine Schneidkante wird stumpf, wenn sie sich abnutzt und eine abgerundete Kante bildet.*

***Oben:** Beidseitig geschliffenes Messer (zwei Fasen)*

***Oben:** Einfach geschliffenes Messer (eine Fase)*

STUMPF IST GEFÄHRLICH

Vielleicht haben Sie schon einmal gehört, dass ein stumpfes Werkzeug gefährlicher als ein scharfes ist. Es rutscht eher ab, anstatt in den Gegenstand, den Sie bearbeiten, hineinzuschneiden. Die abgerundete Fase kann nicht „greifen" und keinen sauberen Schnitt machen. Stellen Sie sich vor, sie versuchen, beinahe ohne Druck durch die Haut einer Tomate zu schneiden. Wenn die Schneidkante stumpf ist, quetscht sie die Tomate eher, bevor sie zu schneiden beginnt. Manchmal gleitet die Messerklinge auch über die Oberfläche der Tomate anstatt durch sie hindurch und Sie können sich schneiden. Die Verwendung eines scharfen Werkzeugs ist immer leichter vorherzusehen und sicherer als ein stumpfes.

FASENWINKEL UND IHRE FUNKTION

Die Fase des Messers ist die Oberfläche, die die Schneidkante bildet. Bei genauem Hinsehen sieht man einen leichten Winkel an einer oder beiden Seiten des Messers. Ist dieser auf beiden Seiten, ist das ein beidseitig geschliffenes Messer. Fasen können in verschiedenen Winkeln geschliffen sein. Je kleiner der Winkel, umso schärfer ist das Messer in der Regel. Ein spitzer Fasenwinkel, zum Beispiel 15 Grad, erzeugt eine scharfe Schneidkante. Messer haben typischerweise spitze Winkel, die die Schneidkante erzeugen. Der dünne Stahl eines Messers mit doppelter Fase sorgt für eine rasiermesserscharfe Schneidkante, ideal zum Schneiden. Werkzeuge zum Hacken, wie Hackmesser und Äxte, werden für gewöhnlich aus härterem Stahl und mit weniger scharfer Schneidkante gefertigt. Dadurch entsteht eine stärkere Schneide, die besser für die beim Hacken auftretenden Stöße geeignet ist, durch die die Kante einer dünneren Klinge Schaden nehmen könnte.

Das gleiche Konstruktionsprinzip gilt auch für Holzbearbeitungswerkzeuge. Einige Stemmeisen sind dazu gedacht, mit dem Hammer geschlagen zu werden, um Werkstücke zu spalten und Abfall zu entfernen. Sie haben starke Schneidkanten mit weniger spitzen Fasen. Schälbeitel sind hingegen dazu gedacht, nur mit der Hand verwendet zu werden, und eignen sich hervorragend zum Abtragen von Holzfasern in dünnen Scheiben. Der geringere Fasenwinkel erzeugt eher eine Messerkante, die diese Aufgabe im Gegensatz zu herkömmlichen Meißeln erleichtert.

ÄXTE UND KETTENSÄGEN SCHÄRFEN

Tragen Sie bei Schärfarbeiten immer Arbeitshandschuhe und eine Sicherheitsbrille!

ÄXTE

Die Axt hat eine doppelte Fase und ist ein großes Werkzeug, das aggressiv geschärft werden muss. Machen Sie sie nur nicht zu scharf, da sie sonst zu viele Holzsplitter verursacht; eine mittelscharfe Axt ist am besten. Ein Schleifbock mit einer Schleifscheibe mit mittlerer Körnung sorgt schnell für die richtigen Fasenwinkel. Arbeiten Sie in einer fließenden Seitwärtsbewegung in einer Drehung, um den richtigen Winkel und die korrekte Rundung an der Schneide der Axt zu erhalten. Wenn die Fase aufgebaut ist, kann die Schneidkante an einem Schleifstein abgezogen werden. Nutzen Sie dabei dieselbe Technik wie beim Schleifbock. Der Spalthammer wird auf dieselbe Weise geschärft, allerdings sind die Fasenwinkel größer, da diese Art Axt hauptsächlich zum Holzspalten und weniger zum Schneiden genutzt wird.

In der freien Natur können Sie Ihre Axt mit einem Wetzstein oder einer flachen Handfeile schärfen. Führen Sie die Feile in langen, gleichmäßigen Strichen über eine Schneidkante und drücken Sie die Feile in eine Richtung. Merken Sie sich, wie viele Striche Sie gemacht haben und wiederholen Sie diesen Vorgang auf der anderen Seite der Axt mit gleich vielen Strichen.

***Oben**: Mit einem Schleifbock sowie den korrekten Winkeln und Bewegungen sind die Fasen am Axtkopf schnell geschliffen.*

***Oben**: Eine scharfe Axt verursacht fliegende Holzsplitter.*

KETTENSÄGEN

Die Kette einer Kettensäge besteht aus Kettengliedern mit Sägezähnen, die abwechselnd in entgegengesetzten Winkeln angeordnet sind. Zwischen diesen Zähnen befinden sich kleinere Vorsprünge, die sogenannten Tiefenbegrenzer, die kontrollieren, wie tief die Zähne in das Holz eindringen.

Sie wissen, dass Ihre Kettensäge geschärft werden muss, wenn die Kette sich nicht länger in das Holz frisst, die Kettensäge springt, nur Sägemehl entsteht oder die Säge nur noch in einer Richtung schneidet.

• Die Kette vor dem Schärfen gründlich reinigen.

• Die Sägezähne mit einer runden Feile schärfen. Ein Schärfgitter oder eine Feillehre verwenden, um die Feile im richtigen Winkel zu halten.

• Die Tiefenbegrenzer einstellen. Mit der Feillehre den Abstand zwischen den Zähnen und den Tiefenbegrenzern überprüfen. Sollten sie überstehen, feilen Sie sie mit einer geraden Feile, bis sie auf der Lehre zu liegen kommen.

• Mit einer Bürste oder mit Luftdruck Metallspäne von der Säge entfernen. Die Spannung der Kettensäge gegebenenfalls nachjustieren.

Oben: *Zum Schärfen der Zähne wird eine Rundfeile verwendet.*

Oben: *Im Uhrzeigersinn von oben: zwei Spaltkeile, ein Spalthammer, eine Spaltgranate und ein Vorschlaghammer.*

HOLZHACKEN

Wenn man Holz auf traditionelle Weise mit einem Spalthammer hackt, ist das harte körperliche Arbeit. Der Kopf des Spalthammers ist auf der einen Seite wie ein Vorschlaghammer geformt, auf der anderen wie eine Axt. Für gewöhnlich hat er einen Haken an der Rückseite, der das Holzspalten erleichtert.

Sie können Holz entweder mit der Axtseite hacken oder mit der Vorhammerseite einen Spaltkeil oder eine „Spaltgranate" einschlagen. Letztere Option wird für gewöhnlich beim Spalten von Stämmen mit großen Durchmessern verwendet.

Sie benötigen einen großen Baumstumpf als „Amboss", auf den Sie jedes Holzstück legen können, das Sie spalten wollen. Der Hackstock darf nicht wackeln, sondern muss fest auf dem Boden stehen. Sobald die Spitze des Spaltkeils oder der Holzgranate im Stamm ist, kann der Spalthammer erhoben werden und klug und mit etwas Kraft auf die Oberseite geschlagen werden. Mit etwas Übung trifft bald fast jeder Schlag, ohne zu verfehlen.

Eine scharfe Klinge muss nicht sein; rohe Gewalt wirkt besser.

Sollte die Klinge in Ihrem Hackgut steckenbleiben, ist es besser, das Werkzeug samt Holz anzuheben, um es mit voller Kraft auf den Hackklotz zu schlagen, damit das Holz auseinanderbricht, anstatt es mit Gewalt von der Axt zu ziehen. Heben Sie sie niemals über Ihren Kopf! Ich finde, dass die Arbeit mit eher stumpfen Spaltgranaten dieses Problem gut umschifft, da der Spalthammer immer frei zur Verwendung bleibt – nur die Granate bleibt im Holz stecken und wiederholte Schläge sorgen dafür, dass das Holz auseinanderfällt.

Wenn Sie eine Spaltaxt oder die Axtseite eines Spalthammers verwenden, ist es erwähnenswert, dass eine scharfe Schneidkante nicht erforderlich ist. Dies scheint gegenläufig zur üblichen Idee zu sein, dass eine Schneidkante scharf sein sollte, aber was hier wirklich gebraucht wird, ist rohe Gewalt. Das funktioniert besser und man muss sich nicht um mühsame Schärfarbeiten sorgen.

Es gibt außerdem manuelle, elektrische und benzinbetriebene Holzspalter, die diese Arbeit leichter und sicherer machen. Das elektrische Modell ist natürlich nur dann nützlich, wenn ein Stromanschluss in der Nähe ist, aber wenn Sie viel Holz selbst spalten wollen, mag ein benzinbetriebenes Gerät eine gute Investition sein.

VERWENDUNG VON KEILEN ZUM HOLZSPALTEN

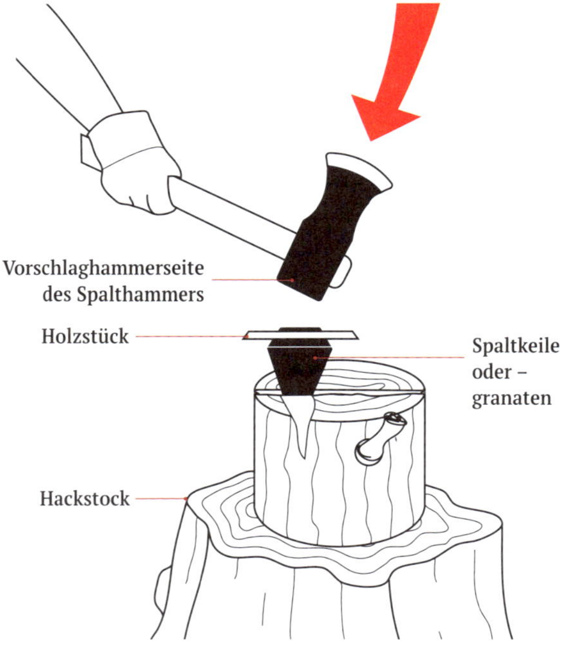

TIPP

Ein Holzstück zwischen Spaltkeil und Hammer verhindert, dass Metall auf Metall schlägt, was angenehmer für den Arbeiter ist. Zwei Spaltkeile sind immer besser als einer. Schlagen Sie sie abwechselnd ein, bis das Holz sich öffnet. Bleibt einer stecken, kann der andere zu seiner Rückholung verwendet werden.

Oben: *Eine Handaxt kann als Alternative zu Spalthammer oder Vorschlaghammer und Spaltkeil dienen.*

Holzhacken mag zwar anstrengend sein, muss aber nicht gefährlich sein, wenn sinnvolle Vorsichtsmaßnahmen getroffen werden:

- Unabhängig vom verwendeten Werkzeug benötigen Sie die korrekte Kleidung und Sicherheitsschuhe. Sie brauchen eine Sicherheitsbrille, ein paar verstärkte Lederhandschuhe und Sicherheitsstiefel mit Stahlkappen und durchtrittsicherer Sohle. Beim Holzhacken gilt es, sich vor dem Start ordentlich vorzubereiten. Beginnen Sie nicht ohne entsprechende Sicherheitskleidung und sinnvolle Arbeitskleidung.
- Machen Sie ein paar Aufwärmübungen, berühren Sie zum Beispiel Ihre Zehen, laufen Sie auf der Stelle usw., um die Muskeln aufzuwärmen und zu lockern, bevor Sie sich anstrengen.
- Nach einiger Zeit wird Ihnen heiß, halten Sie also eine Flasche Wasser oder ein Erfrischungsgetränk bereit, um nicht zu dehydrieren und halten Sie ein Handtuch parat, um sich die Stirn abwischen zu können. Ich trage gerne richtige Arbeitshosen, aber oben nur ein T-Shirt, damit ich nicht überhitze und nicht zu viel schwitze.
- Überprüfen Sie, dass der Kopf der Axt oder des Spalthammers sicher ist. Eine Klebekonstruktion sollte sicher sein.
- Stellen Sie sicher, dass niemand sonst in Ihrem Bewegungsbereich ist, um nicht getroffen zu werden und dass es auch sonst keine anderen Hindernisse gibt.
- Machen Sie keine halbherzigen Schläge, da diese oft nur schwer zu kontrollieren sind. Ich führe sehr besonnene Schläge, stehe dabei recht ruhig und hacke entschlossen – seien Sie nicht wütend auf das Holz!
- Vermeiden Sie es, vor oder hinter das Hackgut zu schlagen. Wenn Sie sich so hinstellen, dass der Kopf der Spaltaxt angenehm auf dem Hackgut ruht (siehe nächste Seite) zeigt dies die Distanz an, aus der Sie das Holz treffen sollten.
- Um Ihren Rücken zu schonen, sollten Sie Ihre Treffgenauigkeit verbessern, um dort zu treffen, wo Sie wollen, anstatt zur Seite hin abzurutschen.

TIPP

Teilen Sie sich Ihre Kraft beim Holzhacken ein – versuchen Sie nicht, durch eine Riesenmenge zu hetzen, da Sie dies wahrscheinlich eher ermüdet und empfänglicher für Fehler macht. Folgen Sie den Ratschlägen, aber akzeptieren Sie, dass Sie mit der Zeit Ihre eigene Methode und das Werkzeug finden werden, die zu Ihnen passen. Meist bestimmen die Holzscheite oder der Baum, was am besten funktioniert, da manche sich leicht spalten lassen und andere sich wehren, insbesondere wenn der Spalthammer oder die Axt nahe an einem großen, harten Ast steckenbleibt und nicht ohne großen Kraftaufwand herausgezogen werden kann. Versuchen Sie, jedes Hackgut zu „lesen" und suchen Sie sich noch vor dem Zielen den geradesten Weg ohne Äste oder Knoten hindurch.

KORREKTE HALTUNG BEIM HOLZHACKEN

WIE VIEL HOLZ BRAUCHE ICH?

Es gibt keine feste Regel zum Ausrechnen Ihres Brennstoffbedarfs. Dieser kann stark variieren und hängt von einigen Faktoren ab: von der Größe des Holzofens, seiner Effizienz, wie oft Sie ihn nutzen und welches Holz Sie verbrennen. Weichhölzer verbrennen schnell – davon brauchen Sie eine Menge; Harthölzer verbrennen langsam und halten länger (siehe S. 58 für mehr Informationen über die verschiedenen Holzarten und ihre Eigenschaften).

Wenn Sie sich hauptsächlich auf die Zentralheizung verlassen und den Holzofen nur nutzen, um den Raum am Wochenende angenehmer und einladender zu machen, brauchen Sie nicht viel Holz. Das geht so lange gut, bis es einen Stromausfall gibt und Ihre Heizung nicht mehr läuft, denn das ist der Moment, in dem Sie sich wünschen, Sie hätten viel mehr trockenes Scheitholz. Sich plötzlich Feuerholz zu beschaffen, wenn die Vorräte niedrig sind, kann teuer sein. Vorausschauend zu kaufen und zu lagern kann die Kosten verteilen und das Holz ist sofort einsatzbereit – eine Versicherung, die sich bezahlt macht!

Am anderen Ende des Spektrums steht ein junges Paar mit Kind, das ich kenne. Sie heizen ihr Haus über die Wintermonate nur mit dem Holzofen, einschließlich Heizkörper und Warmwasser. Bei besonders bitterer Kälte bringen sie eine Tonne Holz im Monat durch.

Letztlich müssen Sie ein Auge dafür entwickeln, wie lange Ihr Holzofen im Durchschnitt oder auch im Ausnahmefall braucht, um eine gewisse Holzmenge zu verbrennen. Mit der Zeit geht Ihnen dies in Fleisch und Blut über.

HINWEIS

Ein wasserführender Ofen, an den Heizkörper angeschlossen sind, braucht deutlich mehr Holz als einer, der für sich allein steht.

Oben: *Stückholzlagerung zum Trocknen an der freien Luft. Beachten Sie den trockenen, befestigten Untergrund, auf den die Holzscheite gestapelt werden.*

BRENNHOLZ STAPELN UND LAGERN

Zuerst einmal brauchen Sie einen trockenen, gut belüfteten Lagerort. Alles andere als das würde all Ihre Mühen zunichtemachen. Holz, das feucht bleibt oder wird, lässt sich schwerer verbrennen. Es ist voller Pilze und Asseln und kann sogar gefräßige Borkenkäfer und Holzbohrer beherbergen.

Man könnte annehmen, dass ein komplett geschlossener Lagerraum ideal wäre. Tatsächlich ist es jedoch sinnvoller, den Holzstapel im Freien lediglich nach oben hin abzudecken, um ihn vor starkem Niederschlag zu schützen, während die Vorderseite offen bleibt. So kann die Luft zirkulieren und die beim Trocknen entstehende Feuchtigkeit ungehindert entweichen. Das Brennholz sollte vom Boden abgehoben (z. B. längs gestapelt auf zwei schienenartig quer liegenden Holzstangen) gelagert werden, damit es trocken bleibt und nicht morsch wird. Der Stapel sollte ordentlich und stabil geschichtet sein und gleichmäßigen Luftzug ermöglichen. Bei nassem Wetter kann eine hinunterklappbare Plane als Nässeschutz verwendet werden; rollen Sie diese jedoch bei besserem Wetter wieder hoch, damit sich darunter keine Feuchtigkeit staut.

Es gibt verschiedene Lagerungsarten und Sie entscheiden, was für Sie praktisch ist. Das Beste jedoch ist ein Holzstoß, der mit Abstand zur Wand steht, damit die Luft leicht herumströmen kann.

TIPP

Es ist am klügsten, jeden praktischen Raum draußen so zu bauen oder anzupassen, dass das Holz dort gelagert werden kann. Beginnen Sie mindestens ein Jahr vor Ihrem Bedarf, das Holz zu kaufen oder zu sammeln. Wenn Sie neu im Holzverbrennen sind, nehmen Sie Holzabfälle und Ökoscheite, um ein langfristiges Brennholzlager zu bauen, das den letzten Trocknungsvorgang für die nächste Heizsaison erledigt.

Oben: *Holzscheite trocknen unter Dach. Dieser Brennholzstapel verfügt über den Luxus eines dauerhaften Dachs.*

Oben: *Ein Unterbau mit Holzdach hält die Holzscheite trocken.*

***Oben:** Eine weniger dauerhafte, jedoch ähnlich wirkungsvolle Anordnung; beachten Sie, wie das Holz etwas über den Boden angehoben wird, um es vor aufsteigender Nässe zu schützen.*

Diese Art des Stapelns kann in Reihen oder Gängen erfolgen. Falls Sie den Platz haben, sind Gänge zwischen den Reihen ideal, damit Sie sich dort bewegen können, um Scheite zu stapeln oder zu entnehmen. Üblicher ist es jedoch, das Holz in einem Unterbau mit schrägem Dach regengeschützt zu lagern. Dies sorgt zwar nicht für denselben Grad der Luftzirkulation, ist aber vollkommen ausreichend.

Das eigentliche Problem bei Holzlagern ist, dass man nie auch nur annähernd genug davon hat. Alles, was Sie tun können, um mehr Stauraum zu bekommen, ist hilfreich, da Sie dann Holz kaufen, wenn es gerade verfügbar und vielleicht auch billiger ist und sichergehen können, dass es trocken und bereit zum Verbrennen ist, wenn Sie es brauchen. Es ist auch eine gute Idee, einen kleinen Holzstapel im Haus zu haben, damit die Scheite, die Sie bald verbrennen wollen, noch etwas besser trocknen können.

NUTZUNG UND PFLEGE IHRES OFENS

ENTZÜNDEN DES OFENS

Wenn man einen neuen Holzofen das erste Mal anzündet, sollte man ihn langsam brennen lassen, damit er sich setzen kann – das Gusseisen, der feuerfeste Zement und die wärmespeichernden Schamottsteine müssen sich erst einmal „aufwärmen". Sie brauchen außerdem für einige Tage viel Luftzufuhr, da Dämpfe, aus dem Metall und anderen Komponenten austreten können. Diese Nebenprodukte des Herstellungsprozesses können unangenehm riechen und Kopfschmerzen verursachen, stellen Sie also sicher, dass die Fenster einen Spalt geöffnet bleiben, bis die Dämpfe abgezogen sind. Ofenlack oder andere Oberflächenbehandlungen können ebenso Dämpfe bei einem neuen Ofen absondern.

Am besten eignet sich in Harz getränkte Holzwolle. Formen Sie sie zu handgroßen Bällen und werfen Sie sie auf den leeren Rost. Sie werden sich ein wenig öffnen, aber das macht nichts. Sie sollen als Anzündmaterial dienen. Da sie dünn und trocken sind, füttert Sauerstoff die Flamme, mit der das Material durch ein Streichholz entzündet wurde. Alternativ können Sie auch Kaminanzündwürfel verwenden.

Stellen Sie sicher, dass der obere und der untere Regler zur Luftzufuhr geöffnet ist, damit sich die Luft ungehindert durch den Ofen bewegen kann. Legen Sie etwas Anzündholz auf die Holzwolle. Ich lege es gerne kreuz und quer darauf, um in der Mitte darunter Platz zu haben, um an das Anzündmaterial zu reichen. Die Flamme züngelt dann nach oben an das Anzündholz.

TIPP

Bedenken Sie, dass Sie bei der ersten Verwendung Ihres Holzofens einen völlig leeren Rost haben, was ein Ofen nicht mag. Ein Bett aus Asche, auf dem das Holz liegen kann, funktioniert viel besser, da es den Luftzug positiv einschränkt und eine warme Unterlage für das frisch platzierte Holz erzeugt. Natürlich lässt sich ein leerer Rost auch später nicht immer vermeiden, da eine gelegentliche Reinigung nötig ist, wenn die Asche zu hoch wird und den Platz für neues Holz einschränkt.

1 Trockenes Anzündholz auf den Rost legen.

2 Kreuz und quer aufgelegtes Anzündholz, das die Luftzirkulation hindurch und darunter erlaubt.

3 Anzünden der Holzwolle. An mehreren Stellen anzünden, da es nicht zwingend beim ersten Versuch Feuer fängt.

4 Das Anzündholz brennt, die Tür kann teilweise geschlossen werden, um den Venturi-Effekt zu fördern (siehe nächste Seite)

5 Das Feuer mit dem Anzündholz kräftig brennen lassen, bevor Sie Holzscheite hinzugeben.

TIPP

Es ist auch möglich, in umgekehrter Reihenfolge zu stapeln - also das Anzündmaterial oben, kleineres Holz darunter und die großen Scheite unten. Damit brennt das Feuer von oben nach unten. Erste Studien zeigten sogar Vorteile bezüglich der Emissionen.

Oben: *Geschafft! So sollte es aussehen, wenn das Feuer entfacht ist. Die Luftzufuhr über die Lüftungsschlitze zu kontrollieren, sorgt für ein langsameres und gleichmäßigeres Verbrennen.*

Entzünden Sie Ihr Streichholz und halten Sie es nicht nur an das Material in der Mitte des Rosts, sondern auch an andere Stellen, bevor es ausgeht. Ich zünde grundsätzlich drei Stellen an, bevor ich das Streichholz in den Rost werfe. Das sollte reichen, um das Anzündholz in Brand zu stecken.

DAS FEUER IN GANG BRINGEN

Als Nächstes wird die Tür bis auf einen kleinen Spalt geschlossen. Der Grund hierfür ist das Erzeugen eines Venturi-Effekts. Dieses allgemein bekannte physikalische Phänomen entsteht durch die Begrenzung des Luftstroms – und bewirkt, dass dieser tatsächlich schneller wird. Das mag nicht logisch erscheinen, aber es funktioniert und hilft dabei, dass das Anzündholz Feuer fängt.

In diesem Stadium können Sie das Feuer nicht allein lassen, da es noch schwach ist und etwas Arbeit erfordert. Wenn die Holzwolle und das Anzündholz ordentlich brennen und das Holz an den Rändern teilweise glüht, müssen Sie ein paar „echte" Holzstücke in das Feuer legen. Sie müssen so platziert werden, dass sie die junge Flamme nicht unter sich ersticken. Sie brauchen schmale Holzscheite, die leicht Feuer fangen können. Runde, mit Rinde bedeckte Scheite brennen nicht so bereitwillig. Lassen Sie die Tür ein wenig offen wie zuvor, und schließen Sie sie sicher, sowie das Feuer sich gesetzt hat. Ein Vorteil einer Glastür ist, dass Sie nicht nur die Flammen sicher hinter Glas beobachten können, sondern dass Sie auch beurteilen können, wie gut das Feuer brennt. Wenn das Holz einen hellgelben Schein entwickelt, ist es Zeit, die untere Luftzufuhr etwas herabzuregeln, um den Luftstrom einzuschränken. Die Luftzufuhr gänzlich zu schließen, würde zu viel Sauerstoff entziehen und zu einer unvollständigen Verbrennung und somit zur Freisetzung größerer Schadstoffmengen in die Atmosphäre und zu Glanzrußbildung im Schornstein führen. Lassen Sie also genug Luft herein, dass sowohl das Holz als auch die leichteren Elemente verbrennen und durch den Schornstein entweichen können. Jeder Ofen samt Einstellungen ist unterschiedlich und die richtige Balance zu finden, erfordert ein wenig Üben nach dem Prinzip „Versuch macht klug". Mit der Zeit bekommen Sie bei Ihrem Ofen den Dreh raus.

Mit einer Glastür können Sie nicht nur die Flammen sicher hinter Glas beobachten und den Vorgang bewundern, sondern auch beurteilen, wie gut das Feuer brennt.

Oben: *Es lohnt sich, extralange Streichhölzer zu kaufen. Sie gelangen bis an die Rückwand Ihres Holzofens und sind sicherer in der Verwendung.*

Wenn die Luftzufuhr ganz geöffnet ist, brennt das Feuer normalerweise hellgelb auf dem Rost. Wird sie hingegen teilweise geschlossen, verebben die hochschlagenden gelben Flammen und eine gleichmäßigere Verbrennung findet statt. Wenn es ein gutes Aschebett mit einem großen Scheit gibt, glüht dieser orange-rot. Die Asche verhindert ein zu schnelles Verbrennen.

DAS FEUER IN GANG HALTEN

Nachdem Sie ein Feuer in Gang gebracht haben müssen Sie gut genug nachlegen, damit es sich für längere Zeit hält. Gut abgelegenes, hochwertiges Holz hilft Ihnen dabei. Das Ziel ist ein gutes Aschebett mit heißer, rotglühender Glut auf dem Rost. Ein Anstoßen mit dem Schürhaken lässt diese auseinanderfallen und sich ausbreiten. Legen Sie nun ein oder mehrere Scheite darauf und schließen Sie die Tür. Versuchen Sie, die neuen Scheite eher in Richtung Ofenrückseite zu legen, wo das Feuer heißer ist, und legen Sie sie längs hin, damit eventuelle Funken aus dem Hirnholz nicht gegen das Glas fliegen. Der Rost sollte niemals überfüllt sein: Wenn Sie zu viel Holz hineinstopfen, wird die Prallplatte verschoben. Nur wenn das Feuer sich nach einer Weile immer noch nicht ausbreitet, sollten Sie ein bisschen am Rost rütteln, um etwas mehr Luft hindurchzulassen; sonst lassen Sie es einfach langsam niederbrennen.

Experimentieren Sie mit den Einstellungen der Luftzufuhr: Die Primärluft unten versorgt das Feuer mit Sauerstoff, während die Sekundärluft oben den sekundären Verbrennungsvorgang beschleunigt (siehe S. 16 f.). Ein komplettes Verschließen beider Luftzufuhren erstickt das Feuer und bewirkt, dass sich Glanzruß im Schornstein bildet. Beachten Sie, dass die untere Luftzufuhr normalerweise Teil der „Scheibenspülung“ ist, die teils dazu gedacht ist, einen kühlen Luftzug von draußen über die Glasrückseite zu führen. Dies fördert die Verbrennung der Bestandteile, die Kohlenstoff produzieren und das Glas verdunkeln würden – wodurch dieses hoffentlich sauber bleibt. Wenn Sie diesen Regler vollständig schließen, kann es dazu führen, dass es qualmt, mehr umweltschädliche Stoffe ausgestoßen werden und das Glas sich schwarz verfärbt. Auch jedes zu nah am Glas liegende Holz kann diese Verkohlung verursachen. Es ist ratsam, das Glas möglichst sauber zu halten – nicht nur weil es schöner aussieht, sondern weil Sie sich so ein häufiges Reinigen ersparen (siehe S.110 ff.).

Oben: *Ein hell brennendes Feuer hinter sauberem Glas – was könnte gemütlicher sein?*

Oben: Das Zerstoßen und Ausbreiten der Glut als Vorbereitung, um frische Holzscheite nachzulegen.

Oben: Die Asche muss einmal die Woche entfernt werden. Das Feuer ausbrennen zu lassen, erleichtert diese Arbeit.

FEUER ÜBER NACHT

Das mag nach einer guten Sache klingen, aber Sie müssen das Feuer beinahe verebben lassen, was in Sachen Brennleistung nicht so gut ist. Wenn es draußen richtig kalt ist, lege ich spät am Abend noch einmal nach, um dem Feuer einen „letzten Schub“ zu verpassen, bevor wir alle zu Bett gehen. Allerdings kann zu viel Wärme in der Luft für eine zu trockene und unangenehme Raumatmosphäre sorgen, wenn alle schlafen, weshalb es besser ist, die Luft etwas auskühlen zu lassen. Man kann sich ja immer noch in eine dickere Decke packen und die kühlere Luft ist besser für alle, die nachts Atembeschwerden haben, insbesondere bei einer Erkältung oder einer Grippe.

Der weitere Vorteil, den Holzofen über Nacht ausgehen zu lassen, ist, dass man den Rost am Morgen sicher rütteln und gegebenenfalls auch das Aschefach ausleeren kann. Ich erledige dies ungefähr einmal wöchentlich – es bietet eine Chance zu einem frischen Start und lässt zu, dass sich der Sauerstoffgehalt im ganzen Haus regenerieren kann. Sie brauchen das Feuer, aber bedenken Sie auch, dass das Feuer Luft verbraucht, die Sie mit Ihm teilen.

Bei der Verwendung raucharmer Brennstoffe sollte der Rost jeden Morgen gerüttelt und das Aschefach geleert werden, da sich Schlacke bildet, die die Luftzirkulation um und unter den Rost verhindert.

DEN WÄRMEFLUSS VERBESSERN

Alle Holzöfen arbeiten weitgehend mit Konvektion (siehe S 26 f.), aber jene, die als Warmluftöfen gehandelt werden, sind am effizientesten in der Hitzeverteilung, weil sie speziell dafür entworfen wurden, warme Luft so abzugeben, dass sie zusätzlich dazu, dass sie Hitze abstrahlen, die Bildung von Konvektionsströmen fördern. Aber abhängig davon, was für einen Ofen Sie haben, können Sie einige Dinge unternehmen, um den Wärmestrom zu verbessern.

Nutzen Sie den Ofen immer nur mit geschlossenen Ofentüren. Die Effizienz sinkt recht stark, wenn sie offenstehen, da ein leistungsstarker Betrieb auf dem auf den Seiten 16–17 beschriebenen s-förmigen Verbrennungspfad fußt, bedingt durch die höhere Luftzirkulation im Ofeninneren, wenn die Tür oder die Türen geschlossen sind.

Die Leistung des Holzofens fällt stark ab, wenn die Türen offenstehen, da der effektive Betrieb von dem höheren Luftstrom abhängt, der durch die Luftzirkulation im Ofeninneren entsteht, sobald die Tür oder die Türen geschlossen sind.

Versuchen Sie es mit einem Bimetall-Ventilator. Dieses schicke kleine Gerät steht einfach auf dem Holzofen und nutzt die Ofenwärme, um eine Reaktion im Metall am Ventilatorfuß hervorzurufen; dies erzeugt genug Elektrizität, um den kleinen Ventilator anzutreiben. Er ist dazu gedacht, zusätzlich die warme Luft vom Ofen in den Raum zu verteilen. Er sieht aus wie ein Gimmick,

Oben: *Das Betreiben dieses kleinen Ventilators kostet nichts, da er von der Ofenhitze in Gang gebracht wird. Stellen Sie es in Richtung Ofenvorderseite auf, damit die Hitze von hinten gezogen wird. Betreiben Sie den Ofen nicht so heiß, dass der Ventilator nicht beschädigt wird.*

Oben: *Offene, an einen Ofen angebrachte Blechdosen können die Wärmeverteilung erhöhen.*

funktioniert aber wirklich. Wenn Sie Ihre Hand davorhalten, können Sie fühlen, wie die warme Luft nach vorne geschoben wird, anstatt nur nach oben zu ziehen. Für einen recht geringen Preis lohnt sich der Kauf.

Bei einigen Öfen, die ein geeignetes Oberprofil mit Kante haben, kann der Strahlungseffekt verstärkt werden, indem man offene Blechdosen oben um den Rand herum verdrahtet, um die Wärmeverteilung zu vergrößern (siehe Seite 107 rechts) – das ist nicht elegant, aber überraschend effektiv.

SICHERHEITSASPEKTE

Sicheres Handeln ist bei Feuer immer wichtig, daher finden Sie hier einige Sicherheitshinweise, die Sie befolgen sollten.

KOHLENMONOXID

Wenn Ihr Ofen falsch installiert wurde oder sich in einem Raum mit unzureichender Belüftung befindet, besteht das Risiko einer unvollständigen Verbrennung, die toxische Gase in die Luft abgibt. Kohlenmonoxid ist ein geruchloses, giftiges Gas, das bei der Verbrennung bei mangelnder Belüftung in die Atmosphäre entweicht. Es kann sowohl den Tod als auch langanhaltende Gesundheitsprobleme verursachen, weshalb man es nicht auf die leichte Schulter nehmen sollte. Darum ist ein Kohlenmonoxidmelder unerlässlich, um einen Holzofen sicher zu betreiben. Diese Geräte sind kostengünstig und einfach zu installieren.

Um sicherzugehen, dass der Kohlenmonoxidmelder richtig arbeitet, gibt es einen Testknopf, der etwa einmal pro Woche gedrückt werden sollte. Ein ohrenbetäubendes Piepsen verrät Ihnen, dass er funktioniert. Das Gerät kann fix verbaut oder einfach an einer geeigneten Stelle platziert werden, vorzugsweise recht hoch, wo die zirkulierende Luft vorbeizieht. Ein Melder in dem Raum, in dem der Holzofen steht, ist das absolute Minimum. Er sollte staubfrei gehalten werden, um seine Funktion nicht zu beeinträchtigen.

WARNUNG

Im unwahrscheinlichen Fall, dass Ihr Ofen einen Hausbrand verursacht, gießen Sie kein Wasser auf den Ofen selbst, wenn er aus Gusseisen ist, da dies dazu führen könnte, dass er explodiert. Löschen Sie stattdessen die ihn umgebenden Bereiche, die in Brand stehen.

KAMINBRAND VERMEIDEN

Regelmäßiges Schornsteinfegen ist unerlässlich (siehe S. 118 ff.). Es ist ratsam, den Kamin mindestens zweimal jährlich kehren zu lassen, wenn Sie Holz verbrennen und einmal pro Jahr, wenn Sie Kohlebriketts nutzen.

KORREKTE BEDIENUNG UND WARTUNG

Der Holzofen sollte gemäß den Herstelleranweisungen verwendet und in keiner Weise verändert werden. Die Schamottsteine im Inneren müssen in gutem Zustand sein. Gelegentlich können sie springen, halten aber noch eine Weile, solange sie fest zusammengedrückt bleiben, bis ein Ersetzen notwendig ist. Ebenso muss die obere Prallplatte korrekt positioniert sein, und der Ofen sollte nicht ohne sie betrieben werden. Die feuerfeste Dichtung oder die Ofendichtschnur rund um die Tür muss regelmäßig überprüft und ersetzt werden, wenn sie stark ausgefranst ist (siehe S. 116). Auch eine gesprungene Türscheibe muss ausgetauscht werden, damit der Feuerraum sicher verschlossen ist.

KAMINGITTER

Die Tür eines brennenden Holzofens offenzulassen, verringert seine Wärmeleistung und ist im deutschsprachigen Raum verboten! In Ländern, wo dies erlaubt ist (z. B. England), brauchen Sie ein Kamingitter und der Ofen darf zu keiner Zeit unbeobachtet bleiben.

VERBRENNUNGEN

Zum Nachlegen vor dem Ofen zu knien, birgt das Risiko, versehentlich am brennheißen Ofen anzukommen. Die unmittelbare Reaktion ist, die Hand auszustrecken, um sich zu retten – jedoch NICHT auf den Ofen, da dies ernsthafte Verbrennungen nach sich ziehen kann. Sollten Sie das Pech haben, sich verbrannt zu haben, ist die einzige Erste-Hilfe-Maßnahme, die verletzte Stelle sofort unter kaltes Wasser zu halten und dort zu lassen. Lassen Sie sich nicht dazu verleiten, diese Notfallbehandlung zu früh zu beenden, da Ihre Haut und Ihr Fleisch starke Hitze erlitten haben und der Kühleffekt eine Weile braucht, sie zu entfernen. Sollte die Verletzung schwer sein, rufen Sie notfallmedizinische Hilfe. Es gibt Cremes und Wundauflagen speziell für kleinere Verbrennungen; es ist ratsam, so etwas im Haus zu haben.

PFLEGE IHRES OFENS

Ihr Holzofen sollte Ihr ganzer Stolz sein und Ihnen Freude bereiten, und es somit wert sein, gepflegt und in Topzustand gehalten zu werden. Das ist nicht belastend, sondern muss bei Bedarf erledigt werden.

DIE VERKLEIDUNG REINIGEN

Die meisten Holzöfen haben gusseiserne Verkleidungen, die frisch geliefert großartig aussehen, durch die Verwendung aber etwas fahl und staubig werden. Es gibt verschiedene Ofenreinigungsmittel, die Sie probieren können. Ich nutze Rostpolitur, eine dickflüssige, graphitbasierte Paste, die aufgerieben und poliert wird, um einen graphitschwarzen Glanz zu erzeugen. Das mache ich ungefähr einmal im Jahr, wenn die Heizsaison vorbei ist, weil ein brennender Ofen die Politur verbrennt, was nicht sehr angenehm riecht.

Mit Schutzhandschuhen ausgestattet, trage ich die Politur mit einem Mulltuch oder Schaumstoffschwamm auf. Ich lasse die außenliegenden Oberflächen und den direkt anschließenden Bereich des Rauchabzugs ein, der die dazu passende schwarze Metallfarbe hat. Dann verwende ich ein anderes Tuch zum Polieren und erhalte einen leichten, graphitartigen Glanz – so gut wie neu!

Ihr Holzofen sollte Ihr ganzer Stolz sein und Ihnen Freude bereiten, und es somit wert sein, gepflegt und in Topzustand gehalten zu werden. Er braucht nur hie und da Pflege.

Oben: *Ein hochwertiger Holzofen ist eine Investition und sollte ordentlich gepflegt ein Leben lang halten. Die jährliche Grundreinigung ist eine gute Gewohnheit, die man sich aneignen sollte.*

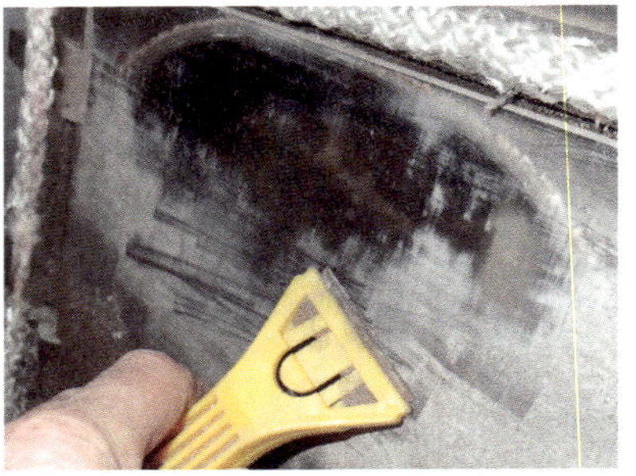

Oben: *Für Emaille- oder Stahlöfen wird oft Backpulver zur Entfernung von Schmutz empfohlen.*

Oben: *Schaber, die dazu gedacht sind, Farbe von Glas zu entfernen, sind ideal für die Reinigung der Glastür Ihres Holzofens.*

GLASREINIGUNG

Der Versuch, das Glas der Holzofentür sauber zu halten, kann zu einer Art Obsession werden – es sieht einfach besser und einladender aus und man bekommt einen viel besseren Eindruck davon, wie der Ofen funktioniert. Die naheliegendste Methode ist die Verwendung von Schabern. Es gibt sie speziell für diesen Zweck, aber man kann auch jene mit Einwegklingen kaufen, die zum Abkratzen von Farbe auf Glas gedacht sind. Nach einer Weile wird dies immer schwieriger, da die Oberfläche des Glases matter wird und das Abkratzen des Rußes kann etwas mühsam werden. Zwei Dinge können helfen: einerseits sollte dies regelmäßig erfolgen, damit sich nicht zu viel Ruß aufbaut, andererseits die korrekte Nutzung des Ofens (siehe S. 104 ff.). Zu guter Letzt gibt es Spezialreiniger für Holzöfen. Manche Menschen greifen lieber nicht auf Chemikalien zurück, aber der Zweck heiligt die Mittel und wenn das Ergebnis besser ist als die anderen Methoden, nur zu!

ENTLEEREN DER ASCHE

Asche ist staubig und schmutzig, haftet innen an der Kante der Ofentür und landet ebenso auf den Leisten außen und am Boden. Es ist wichtig, gröberen Schmutz sofort wegzuputzen, aber man muss nicht jedes Aschekörnchen sofort aufwischen. Wir sind ziemlich stolz auf unser Haus, aber der wöchentliche Staubcheck der Zimmer zeigt, dass sich ein wenig, aber nicht zu viel

TIPP

Die Asche selbst kann als Glasreiniger genutzt werden, tragen Sie aber einen Schutzhandschuh, damit Sie nicht schmutzig werden. Einfach mit etwas Wasser oder Essig mischen und verreiben.

Asche auf den Regalen oder anderen Oberflächen ablagert. Wenn der Ofen ständig sorgfältig abgestaubt würde, würde dies nur zu noch mehr herumfliegender Asche führen, die dort landet, wo sie nicht hinsoll. Ich nehme morgens, wenn der Ofen kalt und sicher ist, einen Handstaubsauger, der die Asche effektiv und mit Leichtigkeit entfernt.

Wenn wir unseren Holzofen an Wochentagen nur abends und wochenends den ganzen Tag und am Abend nutzen, führt das dazu, dass das Aschefach nur einmal zu Beginn des Wochenendes auszuleeren ist. Zuerst sammle ich etwaige Nägel und Ähnliches vom Rost und achte darauf, dass das Aschebett intakt bleibt. Dann führe ich den Aschefachheber in die Passung auf den Einsatz und lege meinen Daumen fest darauf, damit es nicht herunterfällt und sich überall eine Riesenmenge Asche verteilt. Dann mache ich mich vorsichtig auf den Weg zur Hintertür und meide dabei Menschen, herumwehende Vorhänge und Haustiere, bevor ich einen forschen Spaziergang durch unseren Garten mache, um die Asche endgültig zu entsorgen. Das ist bei starkem Wind aus offensichtlichen Gründen nicht ratsam.

TIPP

Wenn Sie die Asche im Garten nutzen wollen, lesen Sie in Gartenbüchern oder online nach oder fragen Sie in Ihrem örtlichen Gartenverein oder im Gartencenter, um sich in dieses recht komplexe Thema einzufinden.

Oben: *Asche mag wie ein schmutziges Abfallprodukt erscheinen, kann aber für Blühpflanzen und Gemüse von großem Nutzen sein. Sie versorgt den Boden mit Pottasche, die den pH-Wert erhöht (und somit Säure reduziert). Dies bedeutet jedoch, dass sie für Pflanzen ungeeignet ist, die einen sauren Boden brauchen, etwa Rhododendren, Rosen und Obstbäume.*

STAUB BESEITIGEN

Wenn einem aus Versehen Asche auf den Boden fällt, müssen zuerst Kinder und Haustiere von einer Invasion in den Ort des Geschehens abgehalten werden. Dann müssen alle losen Gegenstände wie Kissen und Teppiche weggeräumt und gegebenenfalls in Plastiksäcke gesteckt werden, damit man sie nach draußen tragen und den Aschestaub ausschütteln oder ausklopfen kann. Dabei ist es ratsam, eine einfache Staubmaske für den Schutz der Lunge zu tragen. Bedenken Sie, dass die Asche auch an Haaren, Haut und Kleidung haften bleibt.

Sie können den Großteil der Asche mit Handfeger und Kehrblech entfernen, dabei langsam arbeiten, um keinen Staub aufzuwirbeln. Die Asche kann dann direkt in einen Müllsack wandern, der zugebunden und entsorgt wird. Auch wenn wir Asche als Schmutz empfinden, ist sie tatsächlich steril und wirkt wie ein Reinigungsmittel – sie sieht nur nicht gut aus und fühlt sich auch nicht so an. Am besten ist es, einen effizienten Staubsauger mit einem passenden Aufsatz für Hartböden, Teppiche oder Polstermöbel zu verwenden.

Zuletzt müssen alle geraden Flächen von Möbeln, Fußleisten und Dekorationen leicht mit einem feuchten Tuch abgewischt und eventuell poliert werden, um sich aller trockener Körnchen zu entledigen. Ist all dies erledigt, sieht niemand mehr, was passiert ist – schließlich ist es ja nicht so, als hätte man einen Farbeimer verschüttet.

DEN HOLZOFEN AUSEINANDERNEHMEN UND WIEDER ZUSAMMENBAUEN

Es ist keine schlechte Idee, diesen Vorgang einmal im Jahr zu machen, wenn der Winter naht, um sicherzugehen, dass alles in Ordnung ist. Das Auseinandernehmen des Inneren eines Holzofens variiert je nach Modell.

Bei meinem Holzofen lässt sich der Rost anheben, dann rutscht die Prallplatte von oben in den Brennraum. Die Schamottsteine müssen vorsichtig seitlich herausgezogen werden, da sie mit ihrer Verwendung immer zerbrechlicher werden. Da mein Ofen ein Allesbrenner ist, kann der Mittelteil des Rosts herausgenommen werden; daher muss ich ihn vorsichtig von

TIPP

Vor dem Entsorgen der Asche aus dem Holzofen stellen Sie sicher, dass keine Stolperfallen wie ein aufstehender Teppich, Spielsachen oder Schuhe herumliegen und Ihnen auflauern. Vorausgesetzt, das Aschefach ist kalt, kann es sinnvoll sein, es in einen Plastikmüllsack zu wickeln, um zu verhindern, dass die Asche vollends auf dem Boden landet.

Oben: *Das Zerlegen des Ofens kann ein einschüchternder Prozess sein. Das sollte es aber nicht sein, insbesondere nicht, wenn Sie das Handbuch haben, in dem eine Explosionszeichnung der Teile stehen sollte. Sie können mit einer Digitalkamera oder einem Smartphone Fotos der einzelnen Teile in der richtigen Position machen, um sie später wieder in der korrekten Reihenfolge zusammenzubauen.*

der Stange lösen, die das Rütteln des Rostes ermöglicht. Dann hebt sich der Rostunterteil selbst heraus, wodurch die gusseiserne Verkleidung als leere Hülle stehenbleibt.

Die Konstruktion ist recht einfach, funktioniert aber. In diesem nackten Zustand bürste ich vorsichtig die restliche Asche ab und sauge dann den Rest mit dem Staubsauger auf. Solange nichts gesprungen oder gebrochen ist, kann alles wieder zusammengesetzt werden. Wenn Teile beschädigt sind – was aufgrund von Hitzesprüngen gelegentlich vorkommen kann –, sehen Sie in der Teileliste nach und wenden Sie sich an Ihren Lieferanten oder den Hersteller, um Ersatz zu erhalten. Ihr Holzofen sollte nicht ohne alle wesentlichen Komponenten in Betrieb genommen werden.

ERSATZTEILE BESTELLEN

Es zahlt sich aus, Ihr Gerät zu registrieren, wenn es noch neu ist, weil dies nicht nur den Garantiezeitraum verlängert, sondern Ihnen vollen und leichten Zugang zur Website des Herstellers erlaubt, der Ihnen bei Bedarf mit Ersatzteilen oder Rat zur Seite steht. Alternativ können Sie die Ersatzteile

TIPP

Vergessen Sie nicht, auch zu prüfen, ob der Rauchrohranschluss am Eintritt zum Schornstein intakt und ordnungsgemäß abgedichtet ist.

auch durch Ihren örtlichen Händler ordern. Das mag mehr kosten, aber Sie erhalten persönlichen Service. Sie müssen ihm die Artikelnummer und auch den Namen des Ersatzteils sagen können, was Sie der Bedienungsanleitung entnehmen können.

ERSETZEN EINES SCHAMOTTSTEINS

Schamottsteine müssen ersetzt werden, wenn sie gesprungen oder gerissen sind. Das Einsetzen ist nicht schwierig, aber die Prallplatte, die über und zwischen ihnen sitzt, kann das Entfernen erschweren. In der Theorie sollte sie sich nach vorne aus ihrer Vorrichtung ziehen lassen und somit aus dem Weg sein, aber es mag sein, dass Sie sie von der Türöffnung aus nicht entfernen können, weil sie sich verklemmt. Ein Trick ist, die unteren, seitlichen Steine zuerst herauszunehmen, damit die oberen herunterrutschen und dann diese ebenso zu entfernen, während die Prallplatte an ihrem Ort bleibt. Die Erfahrung wird Ihnen zeigen, was am besten mit Ihrem Holzofenmodell funktioniert.

ERSETZEN DER DICHTSCHNUR DER OFENTÜR

Die Dichtschnur der Ofentür ist für zwei Dinge zuständig: Sie stellt sicher, dass die Verbrennungsrate durch die Luftzufuhr und nicht von einer undichten Tür bestimmt wird und sie verhindert, dass unerwünschte und möglicherweise gefährliche Dämpfe die Raumluft verunreinigen. Sie muss ungefähr alle zwei bis drei Jahre ausgetauscht werden, wenn der Ofen regelmäßig genutzt wird. Ersetzen Sie sie, wenn sie ausgefranst und flauschig wird.

Führen Sie einen Schlitzschraubenzieher in den gusseisernen Schlitz, in dem die Schnur sich befindet, um sie herauszuziehen. Schieben Sie den Schrauben-

Oben: *So sehen Schamottsteine aus, die ausgetauscht werden müssen.*

Oben: *Wenn die Dichtschnur Ihrer Ofentür ausgefranst und flauschig aussieht, ist es Zeit für einen Wechsel.*

Oben: *Ein neuer Dichtschnursatz enthält eine Flasche Klebstoff. Außerdem benötigen Sie Klebeband.*

zieher den Schlitz entlang – die Schnur sollte sich recht leicht lösen. Arbeiten Sie sich dann mit dem Schraubenzieher einmal um den leeren Schlitz herum, um die restlichen Spuren der alten Schnur zu entfernen.

Der Ersatz braucht die richtige Größe; das Teilediagramm Ihres Ofens sollte Ihnen diese zeigen. Wenn Sie keine Informationen haben, fragen Sie Ihren Verkäufer oder wählen Sie, was richtig aussieht. Solange Sie die Rechnung behalten und die Verpackung nicht öffnen, können Sie sie wahrscheinlich zurückgeben, wenn es die falsche ist.

Normalerweise ist die Schnur rund, der Schlitz, in den sie hineinsoll, vielleicht aber nicht, weshalb die Schnur beim Schließen der Ofentür flachgedrückt wird; darum sieht die richtige Größe manchmal etwas groß aus, aber einmal an die richtige Stelle gesetzt und in Form gepresst, schließt sie ordentlich. Ein Dichtschnursatz enthält eine Flasche Klebstoff und wird wie folgt eingebaut:

Halten Sie die Schnur einmal rundherum an den Türdichtungsschlitz an. Überprüfen Sie die Länge, wickeln Sie ein Stück Klebeband um die Spitze der Schnur und schneiden Sie sie mit der Schere in leichter Überlänge zu, damit beim Einbau nicht die Gefahr einer Lücke besteht. Tragen Sie den Klebstoff unten in dem Schlitz und rundherum auf und positionieren Sie dann die Schnur; ich empfehle, die Verbindungsstelle an der Angelseite der Tür anzulegen. Drücken Sie nun die Schnur fest in den Schlitz und arbeiten Sie sich rundherum, bis die Enden fest aneinanderstoßen.

Nun brauchen Sie ein langsam abbrennendes Feuer – oder zumindest eines, das nach einer Weile von allein ausgeht. Ziel ist es, den Kleber zu erwärmen, damit er trocknet, ihn aber nicht so stark zu erhitzen, dass er nicht mehr richtig hält. Schließen Sie die Tür, öffnen Sie sie erneut, um sicherzugehen, dass das Seil immer noch im Schlitz liegt, schließen Sie die Tür erneut und lassen Sie das Feuer mit teils geschlossener Luftzufuhr abbrennen, damit der Ofen nicht zu heiß wird. Ihr Holzofen ist nun bereit zur Verwendung und beim nächsten Heizen wird die Schnur ihren Dienst tun.

TIPP

Überprüfen Sie Ihren Ofen regelmäßig wie ein Auto, um sicherzugehen, dass er sicher ist. Wenn er kalt ist, ist es ein Leichtes, ihn innen und außen zu begutachten, um zu prüfen, ob alles richtig funktioniert. Und vergessen Sie auch nicht, Ihren Kohlenmonoxidmelder zu testen!

DEN RAUCHFANG KEHREN

Trotz aller Vorsicht bei der Nutzung Ihres Ofens ist es unvermeidlich, dass sich Ablagerungen im Schornstein ansammeln. Um das Risiko eines Kaminbrandes zu vermeiden, sollte der Schornstein mindestens zweimal jährlich gereinigt werden, wenn Sie Holz verbrennen und einmal im Jahr bei Kohlebriketts. Das Reinigen muss im deutschsprachigen Raum von Schornsteinfegern vorgenommen werden. In Österreich ist jeder Haushalt aufgrund der Kehrordnung verpflichtet, den Schornstein mindestens zweimal jährlich je nach Heizungssystem durch einen Rauchfangkehrer reinigen zu lassen. Sonst muss man den Schornstein stilllegen lassen und darf ihn auf keinen Fall mehr benutzen.

Ein Holzofen muss an einen Schornstein angeschlossen werden. Das Begradigen der Form des Rauchfangs erleichtert ein ordentliches Reinigen des Schornsteins und hält Abgase und Rauch im Schornstein, bis sie über den Schornsteinaufsatz entweichen. Wo ein separater Schornstein mit festen Rohren installiert wurde, dürfte das Reinigen kein Problem darstellen; es müsste aber Zugangsluken geben, wo das Rohr Biegungen aufweist.

Es wird empfohlen, den Kamin mindestens zweimal im Jahr zu reinigen.

Wer möchte, kann sich einen Satz Stäbe und eine Bürste kaufen, um den Kamin selbst zu reinigen. Das ist nicht schwierig, wie ich herausgefunden habe. Es muss rechtzeitig vor dem Winter erledigt werden, damit Sie wissen, dass der Schornstein frei von Glanzrußablagerungen und anderen Hindernissen ist. Es ist nicht so schmutzintensiv wie die Reinigung eines offenen Kamins – das ist ausschließlich eine Arbeit für den Profi, nicht nur wegen des Drecks, sondern auch, weil die unregelmäßige Form richtig gereinigt und Ruß zu entfernen ist. Ruß ist bei einem Holzofen kein Problem, da Glanzruß hier die einzige Ablagerung ist. Sie werden auf Händen und Knien hocken und alte Kleidung tragen, auch wenn es nicht so schmutzig wird, wie Sie vielleicht glauben. Zuerst muss die Prallplatte entfernt werden, um

TIPP

Tragen Sie Kleidung, bei der es egal ist, ob sie schmutzig wird, und legen Sie einen alten Vorhang über den gesamten Ofenbereich, sodass nur noch die Kaminbesen darunter passen. So wird sichergestellt, dass austretender Schmutz im Kamin bleibt.

GLANZRUSSABLAGERUNGEN IM SCHORNSTEIN REINIGEN

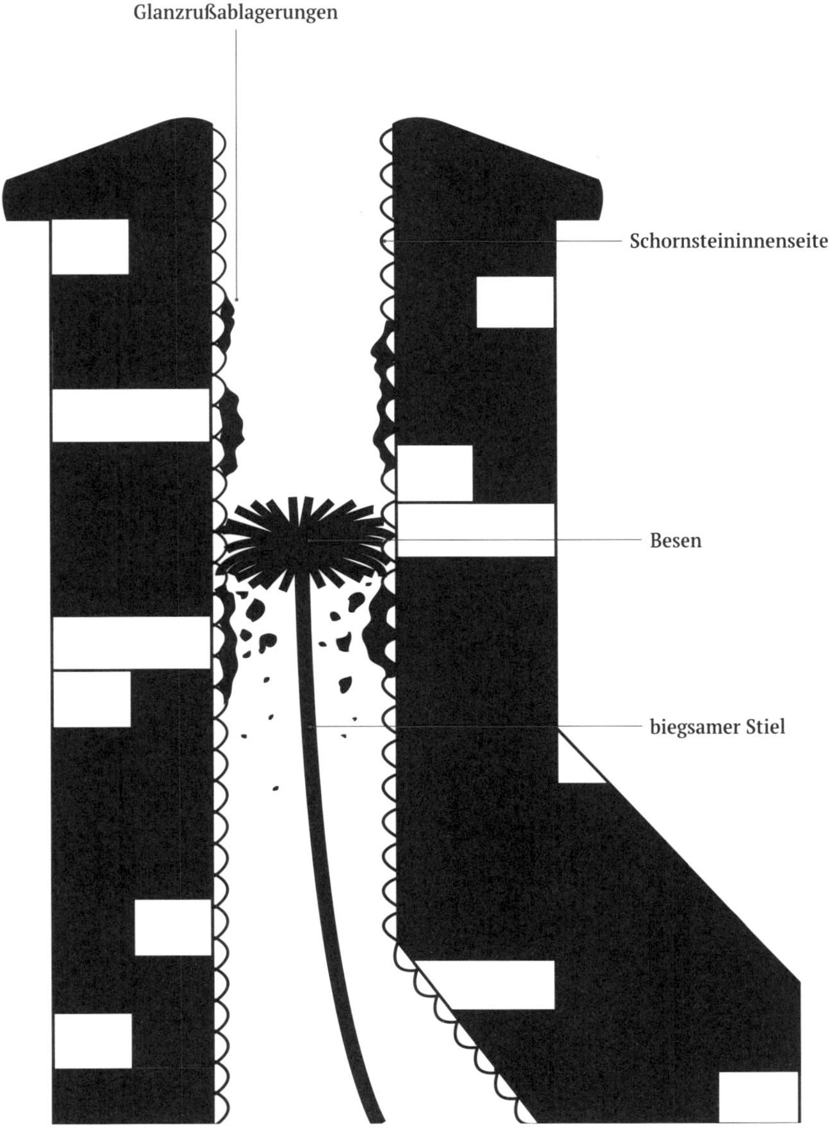

Zugang zum Schornstein zu erhalten. Sie verteilt beim Herausnehmen eine Menge herunterfallenden Unrat.

Danach muss der Kopf des Besens fest unten in den Schornstein gedrückt werden, und wird mit langen Stielen nach oben gestoßen; dabei ist zu bedenken, dass sie sich in einer engen Kurve biegen müssen, um den Brennraum zu überwinden und sich den Schornstein hinaufzubewegen. Sobald die ersten Abschnitte aus dem Blickfeld verschwunden sind, schrauben Sie mehr Stangen an und fahren Sie fort. Eine Vorwärts-Rückwärts-Bewegung löst Ablagerungen, während Sie sich vorarbeiten. Sie fallen den Rauchfang hinunter und in den Ofenbereich, der frei von allem sein sollte, das nichts mit der Schornsteinreinigung zu tun hat. Schließlich sollte der Besen oben am Kaminaufsatz herauskommen und sich lösen (oder in der Abdeckung landen, falls es eine gibt), da er nicht länger in den Rauchfang gepresst ist. Gehen Sie hinaus und prüfen Sie, ob dies der Fall ist, dann ziehen Sie den Besen und die daran befestigten Stangen wieder zurück nach unten; dies entfernt weitere Ablagerungen und hoffentlich sind bis zum Herausziehen aus dem Ofen alle losen Rückstände entfernt und liegen im Ofen oder der Feuerstelle. Nehmen Sie nacheinander die Stangen ab und ziehen Sie den Besen aus dem Ofen. Schließlich fegen Sie mit Kehrrichtschaufel und Handfeger zusammen und vollenden die Arbeit mit dem Staubsauger.

Vorwärts-Rückwärts-Bewegungen lösen Ablagerungen am Weg nach oben. Sie fallen hinunter in den Ofenbereich.

Oben: *Wenn Sie zum ersten Mal einen Schornstein fegen, vergessen Sie nicht auf das Erinnerungsfoto!*

TIPP

Selbst wenn Sie Ihren Schornstein in Eigenregie reinigen, ist es im deutschsprachigen Raum vorgeschrieben, diese Tätigkeiten zusätzlich mindestens zweimal im Jahr von einem professionellen Rauchfangkehrer erledigen zu lassen. Meist können Sie sich die Arbeit damit selbst ersparen.

DAS FEUERHOLZGEDICHT

Ein nützliches Gedicht, um sich die
Verbrennungseigenschaften unterschiedlicher Hölzer zu merken.

Buchenholzfeuer sind hell und klar
Wenn das Holz gelagert ist ein Jahr,
Kastanie taugt nur, so wird's gehegt,
Wenn als Scheit sie weggelegt.
Machst du Feuer aus Holunderholz,
nimmt der Tod dir bald den Stolz;
aber Esche – noch grün oder schon alt
Wärmt die Königin in ihrer güld'nen Gestalt

Birke und Tanne verbrennen in Eile
Helles Feuer, doch leider ohne Weile
Für süßes Brot, hört man die Iren sagen,
muss das Feuer Holz vom Weißdorn nagen
Ulme glimmt wie Grabes Erde
Sogar die Flamme bleibt kühl am Herde
aber Esche – noch grün oder schon braun
kann die Königin mit ihrer goldenen Krone vertrauen.

Pappel sorgt mit bitt'rem Rauch für einen bösen Kniff
lässt Augen tränen und hat den Hals im Würgegriff
Apfel schenkt dir Duft mit Güte,
Birne duftet wie Blumen in der Blüte
Eichenscheite, trocken und alt
halten den Winter draußen, so kalt
Aber Esche – ob nass, ob trocken,
lässt den König in Pantoffeln noch frohlocken.

von Lady Celia Congreve

GLOSSAR

Prallplatte Einsatz im oberen Teil eines Ofens, der die heißen Gase s-förmig leitet.

Bogensäge Kompakte Rahmensäge zum Stutzen von Ästen oder Sägen von Baumstämmen mit kleinem Durchmesser.

Schornsteinkopf/Kaminkopf Sichtbarer Teil des Schornsteins über Dach, meist mit Klinkerziegeln oder Blech außen verkleidet. Darauf kann eine Abdeck- oder Regenhaube oder ein zusätzlicher Aufsatz für besseren Kaminzug aufgebaut werden.

Katalysator Einige Öfen haben einen Katalysator wie ein Auspuff eines Autos. Er reinigt den Rauch, wodurch der Ofen besser für Luftschutzgebiete geeignet ist.

Kettensäge Mit Benzin oder Strom betriebene Maschine mit Kettenschneidwerk und durchgehenden Zähnen, um große Äste und Baumstämme zu sägen. Entsprechende Ausbildung, Lizenzierung und Schutzkleidung sind unerlässlich.

Niederwaldwirtschaft Alte Technik zur Ernte von recht jungem Holz, das für Flechtzäune und Ähnliches verwendet wird; weniger effektiv als Brennholz, da die Zweigabschnitte recht klein sind. Astentfernung über dem Boden, damit neue Äste aus dem Stamm wachsen können.

Klafterholz Holz, das in Bündeln zum Verbrennen zusammengefasst wurde.

Dichtschnur Unerlässliches, asbestfreies Flechtseil, das großer Hitze widersteht und mit Spezialkleber fixiert wird.

Trockenholz Jedes Holz, das nur eine kleine Menge Wasser in Form von Pflanzensaft in den Holzzellen enthält, z. B. Totholz, gefälltes, luftgetrocknetes oder gedarrtes Holz.

Schamottsteine Wärmespeichernde Tonsteine, durch die die Wärme geleitet wird und die den Korpus vor Schaden durch zu große Hitze schützen (nimmt Temperatur in die Poren auf und gibt diese zeitverzögert ab – Speicherfunktion).

Rauchrohr Verbindung zwischen dem Heizgerät und dem Schornstein. Massives Rohr, das den Rauch von einem Ofen in den Kamin leitet.

Schindelmesser Werkzeug zum Holzspalten bestehend aus einer schmalen Klinge im rechten Winkel zum Griff. Durch Schläge auf die Klingenrückseite und Drehen lässt sich das Holz der Länge nach spalten.

Rost Es gibt zwei Grundtypen: für Holzbrennstoff ohne Rüttelfunktion (zum Ascherütteln) oder für Allesbrenner mit Rüttelfunktion, damit die Schlacke in das Aschefach fällt.

Handaxt Obwohl zum Entasten gedacht, ist eine Standardhandaxt auch zum Spalten von Stückholz geeignet.

Anzündholz/Spanholz Fein gespaltenes Holz oder leichte Äste zum Anzünden eines Feuers, damit Flamme und Sauerstoff leicht alle Oberflächen erreichen und die Verbrennung beschleunigen können.

Allesbrennerofen Ofenart für jeden Brennstoff innerhalb seiner vorgesehenen Kapazität, z. B. Scheitholz, Kohle- und Holzbriketts.

Primärluft Luftfluss, der durch den unteren Regler zur Luftzufuhr in den Ofen kommt. Bei der Holzverbrennung behindert ein Aschebett die Luftzirkulation mehr als bei raucharmen Brennstoffen.

Primärverbrennung Verbrennung des Brennstoffs auf dem Ofenrost.

Baumsäge Astsäge. Moderne Versionen haben tödliche Haifischsägeblätter und einen Pistolengriff. Sehr vielfältig beim Säubern von Ästen und Stämmen.

Kaminabdeckplatte Metallplatte, die die Schornsteinunterseite in einem Kamin abdichtet mit Öffnung für den Schornstein. Sorgt für ein sicheres, geschlossenes System und verhindert, dass Asche und Staub in den Raum fallen.

Externe Verbrennungsluftzufuhr Die Luftzufuhr kommt von außerhalb des Raumes, um das Feuer zu unterstützen, ohne dem Raum zu viel Luft zu entziehen (Unterdruck im Raum vor allem bei gut abgedichteten, energieoptimierten Häusern wird vermieden).

Sekundärverbrennung Weitere Verbrennung von Gasen von dem Feuer, während sie sich nach oben um die Prallplatte herum und in den Rauchfang bewegen.

Vorschlaghammer Großer Bauhammer aus Stahl mit Holz- oder Kunststoffgriff. Gibt es in verschiedenen Größen; zur Verwendung mit Spaltkeilen muss er schwerer als die Keile sein.

Luftschutzgebiet/Umweltschutzgebiet Gesetzlich vorgeschriebene Zonen in einigen Städten im Vereinigten Königreich, in den USA und vielen anderen Ländern, die, die Luft in Städten vor Verschmutzung schützen sollen.

Spaltaxt Hat einen breiteren Kopf als die Standardaxt zum Fällen oder Entasten von Bäumen und kann den Kräften des Brennholzmachens widerstehen.

Spalthammer Werkzeug mit langem Griff und kurzem, stumpfem Kopf, meist mit einer Axtseite und einer flachen Seite zum Einschlagen von Spaltkeilen. Kann einen Haken haben, der hilft, teilweise gespaltenes Holz auseinanderzutreiben.

Spaltkeil Langer, schwerer Stahlkeil zum Teilen schwieriger Stämme entlang der Maserung. Wird mit Spalt- oder Vorschlaghammer eingeschlagen, am besten paarweise verwendet, um eine vollständige Spaltung und effektive Rückholung des ersten Keils zu gewährleisten, falls dieser steckenbleibt.

Glanzruß Ein verhärteter Überrest im Schornstein als Resultat unvollständiger Verbrennung. Er kann durch korrekte Einstellung der Luftzufuhr und verringert werden.

Venturi-Effekt Druckreduktion in der Luft (oder einer Flüssigkeit), wenn sie durch einen engen Raum strömt.

Wassertasche bzw. Wärmetauscher An der Ofenrückwand oder darüber, entzieht dem Rauchgas Energie, um Wasser für ein angeschlossenes Radiatorensystem zu erwärmen.

Nasses Holz „Grünes“ Holz, z. B. frischgeschnittenes Holz mit viel Pflanzensaft.

NÜTZLICHE INTERNETSEITEN

Österreichische Bundesforste
www.bundesforste.at

FRED – Feste Regenerative Energieträger Datenbank
www.fred.bayern.de
Online-Datenbank für feste Brennstoffe

Aktuelles Wissen zu Wald, Forstwirtschaft, Naturschutz und Forsttechnik
www.waldwissen.net
Gemeinsame Informationsplattform von vier Forschungsanstalten aus Deutschland, Österreich und der Schweiz

Über den Wald in Österreich
www.waldgeschichten.com
Online-Angebot der Initiative der österreichischen Familienwaldbetriebe & Österreichischer Forstverein

Bundesforschungs- und Ausbildungszentrum für Wald, Naturgefahren und Landschaft
www.bfw.gv.at
Österreichische Forschungs-, Ausbildungs- und Weiterbildungsstelle sowie als Informations-, Koordinations- und Beratungsstelle in den Bereichen Wald, Naturgefahren und Landschaft

Österreichischer Kachelofenverband
www.kachelofenverband.at
Forschung und Aufklärung über technische Belange des Kachelofens

Gesamtverband OfenBau e.V.
www.gvob.de
Interessensvertretung und Information

Bundesministerium für Landwirtschaft, Ernährung und Heimat (BMLEH)
www.bmleh.de
Aktuelle Informationen zu Wald und Holzwirtschaft in Deutschland

Fachverband der Holzindustrie der Österreichischen Wirtschaftskammer
www.holzindustrie.at
Interessenvertretung sowie Information und Beratung

Gesamtverband Deutscher Holzhandel
https://gdholz.de/
Branchenverband des deutschen Holzfachhandels

ÜBER DEN AUTOR

Anthony Bailey hatte eine abwechslungsreiche Karriere, die sich während seines Arbeitslebens ungefähr drittelte. Das erste Drittel verbrachte er als fotografischer Assistent und dann als Studiofotograf in London; das nächste Drittel arbeitete er als Restaurator für Antikmöbel und Planer für maßgeschneiderte Küchen und Tischler. Das aktuelle Drittel verbringt er als Journalist und Redakteur für Holzbearbeitung. Als (technischer) Redakteur verschiedener Holzbearbeitungsmagazine, darunter Woodworking Plans & Projects und als Erstredakteur für Woodworking Crafts fand er auch die Zeit, Bücher zu schreiben, darunter Routing for Beginners, Router Jigs and Templates und Success With Biscuit Joiners.

BILDNACHWEISE

Andrew Perris: 73; Anthony Bailey: 52 (links, rechts), 60 (rechts), 86, 107 (links und rechts), 112 (oben rechts), 115, 116 (unten links, Mitte, unten rechts), 120, 125; iStock/AleksandarNakic (43); Charnwood: 6, 12, 14, 35 (rechts), 41, 49, 98, 112; Jonathan Bailey: 111; Jotul: 30, 35 (links); Morso: 25, 29, 101 (oben links, oben rechts, Mitte links, Mitte rechts, unten links), 106 (oben links); Photocase: Triveo (9, unten), vagner (11, links), birdys (63) rebelxned/Flickr: 93; Shutterstock: unpict (2), melis (9, oben), berna namoglu (11, rechts), viki2win (13), Anatoliy Eramin (20), Paul_ Schwarz (21), the goatman (33), Alexander Tihonov (37), cdrin (39), Virunja (44), fotofred (46), petr73 (51, links), Jo millington (51, rechts), Olesya Kuznetsova (55), carlos castilla (60, links), Anki Hoglund (65), hraska (67), LianeM (68, links), Praewachimi (68, rechts), Ruud Morijn Photographer (69), Jon Bilous (71), Robert Kneschke (75), Rob Bayer (79), Y.P.photo (84, oben), Leonidkos (84, unten), luckylight (85), Noerenberg (89), Robsonphoto (95), Peter Guess (97), unpict (102), VSem (103), ARENA Creative (105), alexkich (106, oben rechts), mady70 (112, oben links), Ami Parikh (113); Thinkstock: iStock/ bartosz_zakrzewski (13), iStock/PetanelaART (53), iStock/leekris (57), Hemera/Nedim Juki (61), iStock/Trevor Buchanan (96).

STICHWORT-VERZEICHNIS

„Hacke dein eigenes Holz und es wärmt dich zweimal." – Henry Ford